CW01302964

The Ascetic Ideal

The Ascetic Ideal

Genealogies of Life-Denial in Religion, Morality, Art, Science, and Philosophy

STEPHEN MULHALL

OXFORD
UNIVERSITY PRESS

OXFORD
UNIVERSITY PRESS

Great Clarendon Street, Oxford, OX2 6DP,
United Kingdom

Oxford University Press is a department of the University of Oxford.
It furthers the University's objective of excellence in research, scholarship,
and education by publishing worldwide. Oxford is a registered trade mark of
Oxford University Press in the UK and in certain other countries

© Stephen Mulhall 2021

The moral rights of the author have been asserted

First Edition published in 2021

Impression: 1

All rights reserved. No part of this publication may be reproduced, stored in
a retrieval system, or transmitted, in any form or by any means, without the
prior permission in writing of Oxford University Press, or as expressly permitted
by law, by licence or under terms agreed with the appropriate reprographics
rights organization. Enquiries concerning reproduction outside the scope of the
above should be sent to the Rights Department, Oxford University Press, at the
address above

You must not circulate this work in any other form
and you must impose this same condition on any acquirer

Published in the United States of America by Oxford University Press
198 Madison Avenue, New York, NY 10016, United States of America

British Library Cataloguing in Publication Data
Data available

Library of Congress Control Number: 2021933148

ISBN 978–0–19–289688–9

DOI: 10.1093/oso/9780192896889.001.0001

Printed and bound by
CPI Group (UK) Ltd, Croydon, CR0 4YY

Links to third party websites are provided by Oxford in good faith and
for information only. Oxford disclaims any responsibility for the materials
contained in any third party website referenced in this work.

Contents

Introduction	1
Essay One: Authority and Revelation	18
1. Authority and Revelation in Religion	18
A. The Adler Case Study	18
B. Qualitative Dialectics	21
C. Dialectic and History	25
D. Losing Concepts	28
2. Authority and Revelation in Ethics	31
A. Moral Individualism	31
B. Fellow Creatures	37
C. Individuality and Testimony	47
D. Border Territory: The Ethico-Religious	59
E. Conclusion: Individuating Responsiveness	69
3. Authority and Revelation in Art	71
A. Stanley Cavell	71
B. William Golding	75
Essay Two: Writing the Life of the Mind	99
1. Autobiography, Biography, and Philosophy	99
2. Genealogy and Truth, Scepticism and Modernism	122
3. Coetzee: Autobiographical Theory	144
4. Coetzee: Autobiographical Practice	150
A. Boyhood	150
B. Youth	155
C. Summertime	172
Essay Three: Knowing, Framing, and Enframing	182
1. The Inner and Outer Worlds of Christopher Nolan	182
A. Scepticism, Plagiarism, and Fanaticism: *Inception*	186
B. Two Become One Flesh: Marriage and Love's Alteration in *Memento*	206
C. Film as Confession: *Following*	212
D. One Flesh, Two Minds: Marriage and Love's Alteration in *The Prestige*	215
E. Losing Your Way: Perfectionism, Education, and Individuality in *Insomnia*	221
F. Asceticism, Morality, and the Will to Truth: The 'Dark Knight' Trilogy	226
G. Pure Cinema, Realism, and Modernism: *Interstellar* and *Dunkirk*	237

2. Physics as Metaphysics: Philosophy, Science, and Technology
   in the Modern Era   251
   A. The Under-labourers of Asceticism   251
   B. The Age of Technology   258
   C. 'Where the World Becomes Picture...'   265
   D. Photography as a Technology of Artistic Modernism   282

References   299
Index   303

Introduction

'The ascetic ideal' is the term Nietzsche uses in *The Genealogy of Morality*[1] for the various ways in which the value-system he labels 'slave morality' evolves, ramifies, and spreads out into the broader reaches of Judaeo-Christian Western culture. The nature and manifestations of that ideal are the explicit topic of the third and final essay in the *Genealogy*; but its work depends upon the two essays which precede it, in which Nietzsche analyses and diagnoses slave morality itself, and in particular its distinctively Christian religious sources. So it might help to provide some initial orientation for this book's investigation of the ascetic ideal if I provide a reminder (however brief and selective) of the central themes of those first two essays.

In the *Genealogy*, Nietzsche presents Christianity primarily as a form of life—one in which a certain set of values orients everything the believer thinks, says, and does; and he is interested not in whether those values are true (a valid representation of the way things are, morally speaking—whatever that might mean), but in their meaning or significance (the value of the evaluation of the world that they embody). For Nietzsche, the truth of Christianity in this sense lies in its veneration of the cross—its demand that believers worship the figure of a humiliated, flagellated, and crucified human being. For the Christian, of course, this figure embodies their commitment to a life of altruistic self-sacrifice, in which the self becomes as nothing for the sake of the well-being of others (particularly the weak and vulnerable). And the divine status of that figure declares that such selflessness is the unquestionable essence of anything deserving the name of morality: it makes a timeless and absolutely authoritative claim upon us as beings responsive to ethical and existential value.

By placing this value-system in its historical context, Nietzsche means to put in question every aspect of this Christian self-understanding. For when Christian morality is presented as a historical phenomenon, we are forcefully reminded that it has a temporal point of origin (which means that the idea of its ceasing to exist at some point becomes thinkable), and that it is not only capable of potentially radical development and alteration thereafter, but might itself have antecedents—prior cultural conditions that helped make possible the value-system whose arrival nevertheless threatened radically to disrupt them. None of these points is

---

[1] Trans. C. Diethe, ed. K. Ansell-Pearson (Cambridge: Cambridge University Press, 1994). References to the *Genealogy* are hereafter to GM followed by essay and section numbers.

intrinsically inimical to Christianity's official self-image (since Christians can acknowledge them—using notions such as a moment of transformative revelation and its unfolding through evolving tradition—without casting doubt on the divine authority of what is thereby revealed and unfolded). But Nietzsche's way of exploiting the undeniable historicality of Christian morality allows him to make more specific claims about its belatedness and mutability—claims designed to implant the suspicion that its underlying significance is very different from its overt self-understanding.

By examining the etymology of key evaluative terms through the lens provided by the broader, lingering cultural traces of the ancient Greek world, Nietzsche devotes his first essay to identifying a pre-Christian value-system he calls 'master morality'—one which contrasts good with bad rather than with evil, and which understands as good precisely that which is condemned as evil by its more familiar alternative. Master morality celebrates those noble souls who can spontaneously and courageously impose their will on the world, achieving their goals and more generally directly translating their desires into effective and satisfying action; and it condemns those who lack the greatness of soul needed to achieve such remakings of the world in their own image—the timid, the feeble, the weak. Christian morality is a mirror image of these valuations: it transposes their positive and negative poles, and its attribution of uncannily substantial reality to the latter reflects its fundamental prioritization of the condemnatory dimension of moral evaluation over its celebratory counterpart.

Nietzsche suggests that this mirroring is not an accident; on the contrary, it embodies a powerfully negative, and resentment-fuelled, reaction against master morality. Christian morality is structured in such a way as to protect and advance the interests of those who suffer most from the hitherto-unquestioned prevalence of master morality—the weak, nature's slaves. Life for them in a society akin to that portrayed in Homer's tales is one in which they are pushed around by nature's masters, and in which their culture celebrates those victimizing them whilst—if it thinks of them at all—condemning them for being victims. By inverting these modes of evaluation, patterns of thought and deed that advantage the weak would be celebrated, and those disadvantaging them (and hence those people who naturally evince them) would be condemned; the lives of the slaves would become worth living, and their inability to assert themselves would be reconceived by all as an achievement that constitutes the pinnacle of human flourishing.

Nietzsche thus reinterprets slave morality's overt advocacy of selflessness as inherently self-interested, and so as hypocritical; altruism not only comes naturally to the weak, but constitutes a vital cultural weapon in the war against those naturally equipped and inclined to disadvantage them. Insofar as slave morality asks us to take pleasure in the systematic punishment of nature's masters simply for giving expression to their greatness of soul, it encourages and rewards an essentially sadistic aspect of our personality; but it also satisfies our masochistic impulses, insofar as it demands that we condemn and repress any manifestation, in deed or thought, of such noble impulses of self-expression and self-imposition as we possess—to scour and scarify our souls as well as our lives. And since such impulses constitute expressions of what Nietzsche sees as the basic principle of life—the drive of all animate beings to impose their will on the world, and to enhance that capacity for mastery—slave morality amounts to a denial of life, a refusal of the vital core of our own existence and of existence as such. In short, Christian morality's endorsement of altruism is in fact an expression of a fundamentally self-interested, sadomasochistic denial of life. It is a whited sepulchre, centred on the entombment of a stigmatized human body—a whole-hearted affirmation of death against life.

In his second essay, Nietzsche presents the phenomenon of punishment, and its associated conceptions of guilt and responsibility, as an exemplary instance of the way in which the forms of our communal life are disrupted from within, in perversely productive ways, by the advent of slave moral thinking. But he doesn't do so in a particularly perspicuous manner: a variety of different aspects and modes of that phenomenon, and a variety of assignments of significance to each aspect or mode, are invoked in his account, at some speed and with no obvious single connecting thread of argument or analysis. So any reader will have to elicit or impose some kind of hermeneutic order on these textual elements; and the following framework might seem particularly tempting to a philosopher.

No form of social life can be maintained without the imposition of disciplinary regimes which prohibit forms of behaviour that damage others, and so implicitly presuppose assignments of responsibility. Again following etymological clues, Nietzsche takes seriously the fact that the term for 'guilt' in German ('Schuld') also means 'debt'; and he accordingly suggests envisaging social discipline as generally involving a view of the wrongdoer as indebted to those to whom he does wrong, and the punishment as his means of discharging that debt. But the focus of such a practice could perfectly well be narrow: a certain kind of public misbehaviour occasions its activation, and undergoing a compensatory form of public suffering is conceived of as its equal and opposite outcome—a way of wiping out the debt, and leaving a clean slate. Such a practice offers a means of satisfying the creditor's sadistic impulses (as well as the debtor's masochistic impulses); but because it is activated solely by the performance of a specific act, it limits the moral significance of the exchange by imputing a strictly limited ambit of moral responsibility.

Since, however, what differentiates action from mere bodily movement is motive or intention, our interest in wrongdoing is naturally extendable into the inner life of our fellow men, and so of ourselves. If, for example, we are concerned to protect society against the damage done by wrongful behaviour, we might conclude that we could more efficiently minimize such wrongdoing by minimizing the emergence of the wrongful intentions that engender them; and this naturally suggests developing practices of critical self-scrutiny, which are designed to extirpate wrongful thoughts as well as deeds. Once again, although such extensions of disciplinary practice into modes of self-discipline extend the domain of moral responsibility, they could remain localized, restricting themselves to combating specific wrongful impulses as and when they emerge, and imposing penances that are precisely responsive to each such motive. But we are soon likely to be struck by the fact that some people seem more prone to a greater variety of such wrongful thoughts, and to their persistent recurrence, than others; and this naturally suggests that something about their character is the underlying source of those thoughts, which now appear as symptomatic of the real moral problem—that of the individual's bad character, the fact that they are vicious rather than virtuous people. And this extends the domain of our responsibility so that it encompasses ourselves as such: it implicitly holds us accountable for being the kind of person we are (condemning the eagle for doing what eagles do, and praising the lamb for doing what lambs do).

Then, however, we might ask ourselves why so many individuals reveal themselves to have such bad characters: why is vice so prevalent, so easy for individuals to fall into, and why is virtue so hard to achieve and sustain? Why is it that human beings seem so inclined to act viciously even when what results has no obvious benefit for them and so many obvious costs? Why is human nature so systematically vulnerable to what one might call the imp of the morally perverse? Then we might be inclined to take seriously the idea that human nature as such (as opposed to the natures of specific individuals) is bad, or vicious—that beyond any individual wrongful deeds, thoughts, and personalities there is something fundamentally awry or misdirected about humanity as a species. And now we find ourselves on the threshold of the Christian doctrine of original sin, according to which we must think of ourselves as incomprehensibly but undeniably responsible for a sinful nature that we acquired simply by virtue of being human—that is, by coming into existence. Little wonder that, in accordance with the creditor–debtor model that initially governed this practice, we find Christians positing the idea that God alone is capable of redeeming such an unconditional or absolute form of guilt (since any human efforts to atone for it will be tainted by that for which atonement is needed). Only someone absolutely or unconditionally good could wipe out such a debt; that is why God gave his only Son to redeem Adam's sin.

On this way of presenting Nietzsche's thinking, the complex nexus of ideas and practices that make up the phenomenon of guilt, punishment, and responsibility appear as something that might have naturally developed over time—it is a rational reconstruction in the form of an envisaged social evolution. Since each stage in the narrative constitutes an intelligible extrapolation of the prior stage, it brings out the interconnections of meaning between them; it shows that the internally complex unity of the currently dominant Christian conception of responsibility is not dismissable as a meaningless aggregation consequent upon a succession of sheer accidents. And since the implicitly teleological overarching narrative is designed to make its audience feel that they are probing ever more deeply and penetratingly into the field of human responsibility, it at once helps us to understand why the Christian interpretation of that field might seem rationally compelling (by virtue of accommodating or improving upon its less extreme or absolute competitors), and also to see more clearly the point at which it might nevertheless be criticized as exorbitant (the dubiously coherent attempt to condemn eagles for being eagles) or even repellent (the self-hating, self-denying doctrine of original sinfulness).

But Nietzsche's critical aims in fact extend far beyond that of indicting Christian accounts of responsibility for going a little too far, or even a great deal too far, down the only available (because logically determined) conceptual road—as if it constituted the singular, full unfolding of the essence of human moral life that was implicit even in its simplest initial forms. He also aims to indict not just the idea that there is only one such road, but also the idea of roads (of logically unfolding sequences of conceptual development) as such; and the basis for that indictment is in fact detectable even in the quasi-evolutionary story I have just narrated—in the fact that it posits various stages or episodes in that evolution, and so implicitly acknowledges the relative distinctness and self-sufficiency of each stage (their ability to make good sense of themselves to those inhabiting them). After all, to acknowledge that each extrapolation from one stage to another can be made to seem not only intelligible but also natural is not to show that it is truly compulsory; on the contrary, we could equally well envisage each (at least analytically separable) stage as informing and informed by a distinct, internally coherent, and sustainable form of life that requires no supplementation or alteration.

If, however, any given stage of my hypothetical development process could constitute a stable cultural form (whatever flaws we may see in its specific shaping of thought and action), there is no compelling reason to expect their actual chronological ordering to reflect my conceptual ordering of them in terms of increasingly extensive and invasive modes of guilt-attribution. The development of an actual culture might equally well move from more to less extensive modes; it may omit intermediary stages (logically speaking) as it does so; or it may find itself accumulating over time more than one way of making sense of its ways of enforcing social discipline. And Nietzsche takes this last possibility very seriously.

On his account, precisely because our current practices of punishment really did emerge from a history centrally involving just these shifting, successive, but relatively autonomous patterns of self-interpretation, they constitute a kind of palimpsest—a cultural node that has attracted and now embodies multiple and conflicting meanings and modes of significance (and so might confuse the naïve cultural historian seeking its single and singular essence, as well as simultaneously offering equal amounts of grist to the mutually hostile hermeneutic mills of utilitarian, Kantian, and Aristotelian moral philosophies, amongst others).

The mode of unity exhibited by cultural-historical phenomena such as punishment is thus not constituted by either purely logical or purely contingent relations between its elements; its integrity over time is secured neither by a timeless essence nor by a sequence of mere accidents. But once it is properly appreciated, the hermeneutic multiplicity that constitutes such unity explains why it mutates over time (since it offers more natural points of purchase for some reinterpretations rather than others); and it also raises the possibility of recovering certain non-Christian modes of interpretation from their current and long-standing domination by the authority of Christian scripture, and turning them in new directions.

So it is not an accident that Nietzsche's treatment of punishment is also the locus of his most explicit discussion of his genealogical method—the only approach he takes to be adequate to the kind of phenomena he aspires to grasp. And a good way into that discussion is to envisage the kind of objection that any well-trained philosopher is likely to raise against an enterprise that seeks to determine the value of a phenomenon by establishing its history: that it commits the genetic fallacy—conflating the question of a value-system's historical origin with that of its intellectual validity. Why, after all, should the fact (if it is a fact) that slave morality is preceded by master morality show that the former embodies a self-interested resentment of the latter? And more generally, why should the purely empirical matter of the precise evolutionary path of slave-morality have any bearing on the evaluative question of whether it embodies the right existential orientation for human beings?

As it happens, Nietzsche himself seems to advance at least one version of this objection; for he famously begins section 12 of his second essay by declaring that 'the origin and the purpose of punishment [are] two problems which are separate—or ought to be: unfortunately people usually throw them together'. So it's difficult to believe that he is going about his business completely oblivious to this kind of worry. But the matter isn't straightforward: for this declaration is actually prompted by Nietzsche's invocation of a stance informed by three more specific, and interrelated, assumptions that he suspects may have a grip on his readers: that a phenomenon such as punishment has a single purpose or meaning, that it is unchanging (hence it has that meaning now), and so that it must have had that same meaning when it first emerged. The canonical instance of such a stance is the belief that an entity's telos is determined from the outset by its functional role (the eye is made to see, the hand to grasp). The position Nietzsche offers as an alternative accordingly does deny that the original purpose or significance of an entity is necessarily determinative of its present nature; but this is not because it affirms an absolute distinction between meaning and history, between the evaluative and the empirical. On the contrary, Nietzsche claims that anything in existence, having somehow come about, is continually interpreted anew, requisitioned anew, transformed and redirected to a new purpose...the whole history of a 'thing', an organ, a tradition can to this extent be a continuous chain of signs, continually revealing new interpretations and adaptations, the causes of which need not be connected even amongst themselves.... the form is fluid, the 'meaning' even more so. (GM, 2.12)

This approach certainly holds open the possibility that the kind of meaning a phenomenon has when it emerges may be occluded or even obliterated by later impositions of other meanings; but it also allows for the possibility that it will be retained, either in a relatively unaltered way, or having been reshaped in more or less radical ways by later layers of interpretation. Nietzsche envisages these contests of interpretation as involving 'more or less profound, more or less mutually independent processes of subjugation'; but he immediately emphasizes that the relevant phenomenon can push back against this subjugation—he mentions 'the resistances encountered every time, the attempted transformations for the purposes of defence and reaction, and the results...of successful countermeasures'. This is precisely the palimpsestic model we uncovered in his conception of punishment: it presents such phenomena as sites of continuous hermeneutic conflict, of power struggles (the power of reinterpretation, and the various other modes of powers whose effects might be achieved by, and might not be achievable otherwise than by, exercising hermeneutic power); and it gives the original meaning of such phenomena a double potential significance—insofar as it remains active over time, and insofar as it shapes the phenomenon's openness to later reinterpretations.

The general problem with the charge of a genetic fallacy from Nietzsche's point of view is that it presupposes what the palimpsestic nature of punishment shows to be mistaken: that a clear distinction can be drawn between what such phenomena are and what has happened to them, between their essence and their history. This is why it assumes that whatever makes slave morality what it is can be grasped independently of the vicissitudes of its history, and more generally of the realm of the cultural, the empirical, the contingent. If, however, the idea of a genetic fallacy assumes a sharp distinction between the ideal and the actual (between the domain of essence, logic, and value, and the domain of the factual), Nietzsche's contrary position is not well understood as simply inverting the evaluative poles of such a vision of phenomena. It is not his view that their essence, nature, or identity should be set aside in favour of, or even entirely dissolved into, the sheer contingency of history—for that too would presuppose the very distinction that he is attempting to put in question. His genealogical model suggests rather that the relationship between the ideal and the actual in the constitution of the identity of a phenomenon is internal, in the way that the identity of a family is constituted by the open-ended interaction of natural history and culture.

A conventional family tree reveals the identity of a family as established by the interplay of biology and society: under the incest taboo, the natural offspring of one set of parents marries the natural offspring of another such set, with their offspring amounting to a culturally-facilitated and -legitimized combination of both, who will then themselves look outside their own families for partners with whom to reiterate this grafting process. Such grafting does not deprive a family of its distinct identity; it is the means by which that identity is maintained through the vicissitudes of human natural history.

Reading the biological as the essential, and the cultural as the historical, the moral of Nietzsche's entitling of his method is thus that the essence and the history of a phenomenon such as slave morality are each informed by the other: its constitutive structure at a given time makes it capable of accepting and absorbing a finite range of contextual factors, and whichever such factor takes that opportunity will reshape its essence in such a way as to reshape which future contexts will invite its application and which aspects of those contexts might then further reshape its nature, and so unendingly on. And the same holds for our concepts of such phenomena—both because their referents are genealogically constituted and because concepts find their primary expression in the words of a language, and so are themselves genealogically constituted (being essentially cultural-historical phenomena themselves).

So when Nietzsche declares that 'only a concept without a history can be defined' (GM, 2.13), he means to invoke a specific notion of what a definition might be—the kind encapsulated in the Fregean ideal of a *merkmal* definition (in terms of necessary and sufficient conditions), the kind that might be appropriate in the atemporal realms of the mathematical, but which when applied to pretty much any other kind of referent simply distorts the phenomena under consideration, and does so in a manner which merits evaluative diagnosis and criticism. A genealogical perspective is thus not a means of depriving a phenomenon or its concept of that identity, but rather the only appropriate way of disclosing that identity without succumbing to the damaging conception of what identity must be with which Western culture has so deeply entangled it.

If the laminated, fissiparous, and internally quarrelsome unity of punishment is anything to go by, we should not expect Nietzsche to arrive at a simple or single evaluative judgement about the value of this, or any other element, of Christian morality. After all, as he freely acknowledges, these various moral phenomena have been subject to—subjugated by—a Christian interpretation of their significance for a very long time; and by Nietzsche's own criteria, this suggests that the Christian world-view exhibits a very high degree of the will to power. Insofar as this will finds expression in deploying and enhancing the capacity to remake the world in our image, then the slave revolt in morality cannot but appear as one of the most successful expressions of the will to power in human history. Human weaklings, lacking the physical and psychological resources to fight nature's masters on their own terms, and oppressed as much by their system of values as by their courage and strength, nevertheless manage so completely to revalue those values that they subject the masters to punitive social critique, to the internalization of those self-critical values, and thereby in effect to enslave them to the purposes and interests of nature's slaves. This looks like more than enough to identify these supposed weaklings as eagles in lamb's clothing.

To be sure, this revolt was led, on Nietzsche's account, by the priests, who are said to constitute one branch of the aristocratic caste—the branch whose members are sufficiently intelligent to see the usefulness of the slaves as a means of achieving power for themselves in and over society, and in particular over their less Machiavellian peers. Unlike the simple, and simply powerful, mode of mastery exemplified by an Achilles, however, the priests systematically interpose thought between desire and action, and in particular find extremely indirect ways by means of which to satisfy their desires for power. In short, they possess a complex interior life of just the kind that it is the natural glory of the Homeric masters, as Nietzsche so often presents them in their immediate translation of self-aggrandizing impulse into effective action, to lack.

At the very least, this suggests a deep division between these two putative categories of nature's nobles; but it also suggests that these priests have a rather dubious claim to being naturally noble at all. For elsewhere in the *Genealogy*, Nietzsche associates the realization of a clear boundary between inner and outer, and the beginning of a genuinely substantial inner life, with the specifically Christian internalization of self-criticism. Within an interpretation of guilt according to which it is possible to commit adultery in one's heart, the focus shifts from redemptions of indebtedness for actions in the public domain to attempts to identify and extirpate the motivational sources of such actions, and so involves turning the sadistic impulses of slave moral evaluation upon oneself (with the practice of confession exemplifying its sacramental significance). As Nietzsche puts it:

> All instincts which are not discharged outwardly turn *inwards*—this is what I call the *internalization* of man; with it there now evolves in man what will later be called his 'soul'. The whole inner world, originally stretched thinly as though between two layers of skin, was expanded and extended itself and gained depth, breadth and height in proportion to the degree that the external discharge of man's instincts was *obstructed*... With it, however, the worst and most insidious illness was introduced, one from which mankind has not yet recovered, man's sickness of *man*, of *himself*: as the result of a forcible breach with his animal past, a simultaneous leap and fall into new situations and conditions of existence, a declaration of war against all the old instincts on which, up till then, his strength, pleasure and formidableness had been based...

> [T]he prospect of an animal soul turning against itself, taking a part against itself, was something so new, so profound, unheard-of, puzzling, contradictory and *momentous* on earth that the whole character of the world changed in an essential way. Since that time, man...arouses interest, tension, hope...as though something were being announced through him, were being prepared, as though man were not an end but just a path, an episode, a bridge, a great promise. (GM, 2.16)

These passages have an uncanny dual-aspect quality to them, with master morality oscillating between being a mythic trace of our wholly animal past (the articulation of a state of nature) and a specific mode of organizing the cultural dimension of any genuinely human life, and slave morality oscillating between being a later such mode and being the mythical means by which the human animal enters into culture in the first place (by dividing himself in two). Either way, however, the priests who lead the revolution are plainly possessed of an inner life of very significant depth and richness, and so must have already been marked by the very self-scrutinizing, life-denying value-system that Nietzsche's account also tells us they create in order to marshal their slave army. But if Nietzsche finds himself affirming the paradoxical conclusion that slave morality makes possible not only its cultural hegemony but also its own existence, that indicates a fundamental tendency on his part to view this life-denying value-system as having always already left its traces on human life—as being what first makes genuinely human life possible, and indeed what first makes human beings and the world in which they live at once interesting, profound, momentous, and promising.

But to appreciate the full extent of that influence, we need to examine the way in which slave morality mutates into 'the ascetic ideal'—a phenomenon to which Nietzsche devotes his third essay in the *Genealogy*.

Although this essay is even more digressive and multifarious than its predecessors, one concept that appears to play a decisive role in facilitating the relevant mutation is 'truthfulness' (and so 'truth'). This is another facet of the pivotal significance within the newly established Christian form of life of the sacrament of confession. It embodies the importance of scrupulous self-examination, demanding that any trace of inner evil detected must be declared—to the priest, and so to God; and the resultant humiliation thereby acquires both an instrumental and an intrinsic value (at once helping to bring us closer to God and declaring our full awareness of our infinite distance from Him). Confession thereby attempts to extirpate all manifestations of what Nietzsche regards as genuine vitality from our inner life, and in such a way as to confirm our own abasement; it both exploits and extends the self's inevitable turning in on itself, but primarily with an eye to its potential for self-denigration.

Truthfulness thereby becomes a core Christian value, understood as essential to establishing an appropriate relationship to God incarnate (who describes himself as 'The Way, the Truth and the Life'). We might call this a vision of flourishing human life as truth-seeking; on Nietzsche's genealogical understanding of such phenomena, once such a vision is articulated and embodied, it becomes capable of relatively autonomous development—by which I mean not only that it is capable of finding new contexts which invite its application, but also that its nature is capable of being decisively modified by those contexts. Nietzsche is particularly interested in four such projections or extensions of this Christian valuation of truth: in secular morality, most obviously, but also in modes of cultural activity that appear to be essentially unrelated to ethical matters—art, science, and philosophy.

The continuity between Judaeo-Christian religion and purportedly post-religious or secular ethics is evident to any eye which—like Nietzsche's—views religion primarily as a form of life or existential orientation. For if an atheist denies the existence of God, but continues to cleave to a value-system which celebrates altruistic self-sacrifice for the sake of the weak and vulnerable, then she continues to embody the life-denying drive of Christianity. And the issue of truth exemplifies that continuity; regard for honesty and truthfulness remain central virtues in putatively post-religious ethics, and they demand potentially significant sacrifices of the direct interests of the truth-teller.

The ascetic qualities of Western art during the pre-modern period, when both patronage and subject matter were deeply informed by the influence of the Church, are fairly evident. But a Nietzschean nose would detect significant continuities between pre-modern and modern art in this respect: there is not only the recrudescence of explicitly Christian content in such world-historical figures as Wagner, but also the broader commitment to truth and truthfulness that is to be found in the system of perspective painting, and in the rise of the novel as a dominant form—with its increasing (and increasingly self-conscious) focus on a realistic depiction of social life, and in particular on a painstaking mapping of the interior life of its individual protagonists with a view to enhancing our compassionate identification with their needs and vulnerabilities. And of course, the artists pursuing truth and truthfulness in these ways persistently understand their choice of career as an essentially self-sacrificial vocation, as if being an artist was a kind of secular martyrdom.

Modern science also develops a conception of the life of the scientist as requiring dedication and self-sacrifice, even to the point of martyrdom for the sake of the truth (Galileo being exemplary here); but the account it delivers of reality begins by dismissing the deliverances of the senses as inherently illusory (as in accounts of secondary qualities as purely subjective phenomena), and then elaborates theories of the truth about matter as lying essentially beyond our unaided bodily grasp, and indeed as graspable at all only by means of mathematics—hence by pure reason and its access to essentially unchanging relations between numbers. Modern science thereby unfolds a picture of the truth that articulates it in terms of what Nietzsche would call Being rather than Becoming—as if the truth about the empirical can only be articulated in terms which transcend the blooming, buzzing incarnate encounter with other bodies (whether inanimate or animate).

Philosophy has, on Nietzsche's view, been committed to valuing Being over Becoming from its origin; and its modern incarnations display a similar commitment, even if in significantly modified terms. Take Kant as an example: his Copernican revolution is intended to validate our assumption that we can attain genuine knowledge of objects in the empirical realm, but in order to do so he has to introduce a distinction between objects as they present themselves to us in experience and objects as they are in themselves, thereby inviting us to consider the latter as the locus of truth properly speaking. But the noumenal realm is by definition beyond the range of possible human cognition; hence, the way things really are with objects and with ourselves is placed essentially beyond our understanding, and within the grasp of reason only insofar as reason affirms both the fundamentality of its own categories (understood as essentially transcendent of the empirical) and their own essential inadequacy to the transcendental realm. This is how Reason's punitive critique of itself imposes on us the humility needed to acknowledge the incomprehensible truth of the world, and of ourselves within it.

Even this brief initial sketch of the ramifications of the ascetic ideal goes beyond the map explicitly outlined in Nietzsche's third essay in various respects. With respect to art, he focuses with undiminished fascination on Wagner and his explicitly Christian late opera *Parsifal*, whilst at the same time expressing the strangely unnuanced belief that in this domain the ascetic ideal means so many different things that 'it is tantamount to nothing!', and vowing to put aside artists thereafter, because 'their position in the world and *against* the world is far from sufficiently independent for their changing valuations as such to merit our attention! Down the ages they have been the valets of a morality or philosophy or religion' (GM, 3.5). No doubt this image of the valet is meant to resonate with his conception of the slave origins of the ascetic ideal; but that hardly justifies Nietzsche's tendency to oscillate here between an unduly impoverished and vulnerable range of examples (in truth, focusing on a single work by one artist whose subject matter is Christian), and a tendency to careless generalization (verging on the tautological).

The same might be said of his treatment of philosophy: Nietzsche focuses primarily on Schopenhauer, whose extremities of moral asceticism are as easy to detect as is the Christian import of *Parsifal*, and so hardly seem to merit the application of a sophisticated hermeneutics of suspicion. My choice of Kant respects Nietzsche's own choice by following Schopenhauer's thinking back to its far more sophisticated source, and by giving the kind of account of Kant that Nietzsche himself provided in *The Birth of Tragedy*; but then one wonders why Nietzsche himself did not choose to confront a more challenging opponent and exemplar in this context. His account of science is more focused and penetrating, and my account follows some of its contours; but it is also frustratingly brief—far shorter than his consideration of Wagner or of Schopenhauer. Instead, he prefers to lavish extensive attention on the figure he calls the ascetic priest. This has the definite advantage of allowing him to elucidate his initial claim that the hegemony of the ascetic ideal reveals that human beings prefer to will nothingness than not to will (GM, 3.1); but on the other hand, such a claim seems to follow directly from conjoining the thought that moral asceticism is life-denying with the thought that life (both human and not) makes manifest the will to power. Giving such a central role in his discussion to the figure of a priest certainly betrays the depth of his conviction that a fundamentally religious physiognomy underlies the mask of the scientist or artist—that what began as a specific form of religious morality has diversified and ramified in ways which ensure that variants of this ascetic ideal in non-religious guises have subjugated Western European culture more generally; but it hardly helps to justify it, and may even seem to his readers simply to beg the question he means to raise.

One aim of this book is, accordingly, to explore the possibility of supplying a more sustained, detailed, and wide-ranging justification of that premise—a necessarily still selective but perhaps more substantial revision or extrapolation of that last and longest essay, but one which takes the form of three essays written in the spirit of their source (which is of course in the first instance the third essay, but since this inevitably involves the two others that make it possible, it is necessarily also the *Genealogy* as whole) whilst taking advantage of the enhanced range of cultural and thematic reference afforded by my historical belatedness. These three essays accordingly share the genealogical form and method of Nietzsche's text, as well as the more specific structural features of its individual essays. They constitute three relatively autonomous but internally related argumentative sequences, each of which takes its bearings from the originary role assigned to the practice of confession in Nietzsche's analysis of the unfolding of the ascetic ideal, by foregrounding differing manifestations of what one might call the human capacity to testify. The first focuses on bearing witness in religion, morality, and art; the second studies the metaphysics, aesthetics, and ethics of selfhood through the lens of autobiographical testimony; and the third examines the conceptions of truth, perception, and embodiment that are inherent in modern metaphysical, scientific, and cinematic attestations of reality.

Despite appearances to the contrary, they follow a single, evolving conceptual thread (in this case, the concepts of authority and revelation); but they also track more local themes and examples across the divisions between the individual essays as their trajectories overlap, branch, and loop back: some are explicitly Nietzschean (truth, becoming, perspectivism), some perhaps not (scepticism, modernism, technology). It has even turned out that my last essay, like Nietzsche's, is also significantly longer than its two predecessors (which are, like Nietzsche's, more closely comparable in length): in part, this is because, whereas my equivalent to Nietzsche's concluding citation of Tertullian in his first essay is a discussion of one William Golding novel, and my analogue to his study of the practice of punishment in essay two is a study of the practice of autobiography, I find myself using Christopher Nolan's entire body of cinematic work as my equivalent of Nietzsche's polemic in essay three about one late Wagner opera.

Of course, I hope that the interest of such a projection of Nietzsche's project will lie not only in its indicating the seriousness with which his claim about the pervasiveness of ascetic values should continue to be taken in our contemporary cultural circumstances, but also in its exposure of the extent to which his initial lines of interpretation and criticism may need to be refined and qualified in order to get a grip on their intended targets, and of the resources that might accordingly be available for those targeted to respond to his concerns and criticisms. But these further aspects of my project depend critically upon appreciating something about Nietzsche's own relation to the phenomenon he analyses which my initial elaboration of his third essay makes all-but-evident—the fact that the genealogical analysis that he employs to criticize the ascetic ideal is itself caught up in the phenomena it analyses.

By this, I don't simply mean to register that the most likely response that his critique will elicit from its target is to accept it as identifying (not the essential nature of slave morality but) a possible, and a particularly painful, way of failing to live up to self-sacrificial ideals to which genuine adherents of slave morality should be sensitive, and whose delineation should accordingly be an occasion for grateful acknowledgement. That would be exactly the kind of self-abasing, masochistic neutralization of his work that Nietzsche should surely expect—one more indication of the apparently limitless extent to which his target can turn expressions of life into fuel for the fire of life-denial. My point, however, although related, is rather different. It concerns the fact that Nietzsche's declared primary concern in the *Genealogy* is to disclose the truth about—more precisely the true value of— morality in general and the will to truth in particular; but that means that his work is a late flowering of that will to truth, more specifically a manifestation of the point at which it turns upon itself, taking its own measure—at once a radical unmasking and a further expression of it. So the subversive purpose of Nietzsche's genealogical method is a further step in the unfolding of the life-denying, sadomasochistic impulse it aims to uproot.

This methodological perversity should not be surprising to anyone sensitive to the perversity implicit in the triumph of the slave revolt, which is the single most successful exercise of the will to power in human history, and so amounts to life finding its most effective expression in a system of values that condemns that which powers it. In this respect, Nietzsche's own expression of the will to power merely reinforces the message implicit in the analysis that results from it—that life, and so the will to power as such, is somehow inherently perverse, is such as to derive its most baroque, sophisticated, and successful elaborations of itself from the energies of its most intimate enemy, its self-posited other. But the methodological expression of such perversity is not, therefore, self-undermining—as if the only conclusion we can draw from its unavoidable indebtedness to its topic and antagonist is that its aspiration to distance us from asceticism must be a fantasy. On the contrary: insofar as it succeeds in taking the full measure of its subject matter and so of itself, it plots its own limits or conditions, and thereby opens up the possibility of reconfiguring or otherwise going beyond them.

After all, if the will to truth (and so the various ramifications of the ascetic ideal that it facilitates and conditions) really must be understood genealogically, then at any given point its various elements or layers of meaning will hold open the possibility of reconfiguring its internal constitution and thereby altering its current modes of informing and deforming our forms of life. One might, in other words, avoid the self-subverting dilemma of either incoherently denying truth or slavishly reinforcing the ascetic will to truth, and instead find non-ascetic ways of keeping faith with it, which will mean reforming that faith in potentially surprising ways—ways in which we might overcome interpretations of truth (not to mention of reality and of the self who seeks it) in which Being has priority over Becoming.

My revision or extrapolation of Nietzsche's essay on the ascetic ideal is accordingly designed to be open to the possibility of such emancipatory perversity. In seeking to substantiate Nietzsche's diagnosis of our culture as dominated by the ascetic ideal, I am also—and by the very same token—identifying sites and resources for the reconfiguration or overcoming of that dominance. For if Nietzsche is right and the ascetic ideal is at once pervasive and perverse, then only its most pure or elaborate expressions can help us to envisage and implement ways of living otherwise.

Acknowledgements

In composing this book, I found myself needing to draw more extensively than usual on previously published writing. In part, this is due to the desire to make its arguments and discussions relatively self-sufficient, and so comprehensible to anyone who reads this book without having any prior acquaintance with my work—particularly with those parts of it originally published in relatively obscure locations. In part, it mirrors Nietzsche's tendency to conjoin applications of his genealogical mode of thinking and writing with repeated returns to and revisions of his own earlier writing (a conjunction between the genealogical and the autobiographical that I attempt to account for in this book, particularly in Essay Two). In part, it reflects the fact that the issues elaborated here are ones that go back to much earlier interests and thoughts, so that my present ways of treating them are inevitably informed by a series of prior elaborations and projections of those early intuitions whose explicit acknowledgement makes it more likely that the current project will be properly grasped. In other words, this book has a strongly palimpsestic structure; but I hope that anyone familiar with any of the earlier writings it incorporates will also appreciate the extent to which they have been revised for the present purposes—by condensation, elaboration, excerption, dismemberment, and other forms of refinement—and the extent to which their relocation to the present context, and the substantial new writing it contains, makes salient aspects of their significance that were hitherto all-but impossible to detect (certainly by me).

Essay One

This essay draws upon:
    Chapter 2 of *The Wounded Animal: J. M. Coetzee and the Difficulty of Reality in Literature and Philosophy* (Princeton: Princeton University Press, 2009);
    'The Work of Saintly Love: The Religious Impulse in Gaita's Writings', in C. Cordner (ed.), *Philosophy, Ethics and Humanity: Essays in Honour of Raimond Gaita* (Oxford: Routledge, 2011), 21–36;
    'A Nice Arrangement of Epigrams: Stanley Cavell on Soren Kierkegaard', in K. Gjesdal (ed.), *Debates in Nineteenth Century European Philosophy: Essential Readings and Contemporary Responses* (Oxford: Routledge, 2016), 248–57;
    'The Well is Not the World: William Golding's Sense of Reality in *Darkness Visible*', in A. Falcato and A. Cardiello (eds.), *Philosophy in the Condition of Modernism* (London: Palgrave, 2018), 325–54.

Essay Two

This essay draws upon:
    'Autobiography and Biography', in R. Eldridge (ed.), *The Oxford Handbook of Philosophy and Literature* (Oxford: Oxford University Press, 2009), 180–98;
    'Quartet: Wallace's Wittgenstein, Moran's Amis', in *The Self and Its Shadows: A Book of Essays on Individuality as Negation in Philosophy and the Arts* (Oxford: Oxford University Press, 2013), 283–319.

Essay Three

This essay draws upon:

'Sharing a Dream of Scepticism', *Harvard Review of Philosophy* 19 (Spring, 2013), 118–36;

'Deep Relationality and the Hinge-Like Structure of History: Michael Fried's Photographs', in M. Abbott (ed.), *Michael Fried and Philosophy: Modernism, Intentionality and Theatricality* (Oxford: Routledge, 2018), 87–103.

Essay One
Authority and Revelation

1. Authority and Revelation in Religion

As part of his first book, Stanley Cavell published an essay entitled 'On Kierkegaard's *On Authority and Revelation*'.[1] He begins it by asking what justifies Kierkegaard in using the very real private and public trials of one man—a minister of the Danish Church named Adolph Adler who claimed to have experienced a revelation and was suspended by his superiors on the ground that his mind was deranged—as the focus of such an unsparing critical analysis. He points out that, for Kierkegaard, it is a case study, analogous to those authoritatively presented by a surgeon to his peers out of an obligation dispassionately to communicate the knowledge that his skilful incisions have revealed. More specifically, this book is about Magister Adler only in a certain sense—the sense in which he is a Phenomenon, a transparence through which the age is caught, in its confusion about the concept of a religious revelation and its occlusion of the concept of religious authority. Since, however, Adler's derangements mirror those of his fellow ministers, Kierkegaard also describes him as an epigram on the Christendom of his age (BA, 305)—by which Cavell takes him to mean that Adler is a terse and ingenious expression of it.

A. The Adler Case Study

On Kierkegaard's account of the matter, the fate of the concept of a revelation and the fate of the concept of authority are internally related, for anyone who presents himself as the recipient of a divine revelation thereby presents himself as divinely authorized to communicate it to others, on pain of offending against God's will; God has, in effect, made him an apostle, someone divinely commissioned to spread this new Good News. And Kierkegaard emphasizes that this authorization is entirely insensitive to the content of the revelation: in his terms, it is the fact of a

---

[1] That being the title under which Lowrie's translation of the Kierkegaard text was published (Princeton: Princeton University Press, 1955), and to which Cavell's essay—collected in *Must We Mean What We Say?* (Cambridge: Cambridge University Press, 1976), 163–79; hereafter MWM—refers. It was most recently retranslated into English by H. V. and E. H. Hong and republished in the Princeton University Press Collected Works under the title *The Book on Adler* (Princeton, 1998); hereafter BA. All quotations will be keyed to this latter edition.

revelation rather than what is revealed that is the decisive factor religiously speaking. How, after all, could a human being coherently claim the authority to set limits in advance to what might constitute the legitimate content of a divine revelation, when the very category of revelation embodies the recognition that human understanding requires divine aid in order to access the truth of things, and so acknowledges that God might at any point utterly reconfigure our best existing understanding of reality in general, and of the divine nature in particular (as, for Christians, he does in God's revelation of himself in Christ)? The fact that Christian doctrine is, anyway, constitutively paradoxical—inherently offensive to our rational capacities—on Kierkegaard's account only underlines this point.

Accordingly, any Christian equipped with a cogent grasp of his religion's concept of a revelation will know that, if they undergo an experience that presents itself to them that way, they must either accept it as being of divine origin (in which case they are absolutely obliged to communicate it, however much its content might offend prevailing religious or ethical understandings) or decide that it is not divinely authored (in which case they accept the risk of offending God). Either way, this person confronts an awful responsibility. If, however, he exercises this responsibility by reflecting on, and critically evaluating, the content of his revelation-experience, then he reveals that he is deeply confused about what it is to undergo a revelation; for he makes his fearful choice a function of his ability to comprehend and articulate what God has to say—the God who, according to Christian teaching, passes all understanding.

Adler's confusion is laid bare in his replies to questions put to him by his ecclesiastical superiors. He accepts that his way of expressing his revelation takes 'an unusual, strange, objectionable, aphoristic and abrupt form' which might reasonably have awoken suspicions as to its authenticity, and defends himself by arguing that 'by working out and calmly developing the relevant ideas over a longer time, I will see my way to have the Christian content unfold in a form more appropriate and more in accord with the specific words of Holy Scripture' (BA, 57, 58-9). Adler thereby focuses on content rather than form or (one might say) origin: he is staking the validity of his claim to have received a divine revelation on his ability to find rhetorically more apt and pleasing ways of giving expression to its content, and more specifically on showing that that content conforms to the existing Christian repository of God's Word. But this amounts to denying that what was revealed to him was also God's Word—that it had just as much divine authority as, say, scripture. This is why Kierkegaard says that Adler's confusion about the concept of revelation leads to the occlusion of the concept of authority; his inability to grasp the grammar of the former concept results in his passing over altogether the pertinence of the latter.

But on Kierkegaard's view, exactly the same confusion and occlusion is manifest in Adler's ecclesiastical superiors; this is shown by the questions that elicit Adler's self-condemning answers. The first asks whether he is willing to acknowledge that he was in a 'confused and excited state of mind' when he underwent his revelation-experience (BA, 55)—quite as if an affirmative answer to that question could determine whether or not he had received a divine revelation. Would his having been in a calm and clear state of mind have supported Adler's claim? One might as well argue that Peter's being a fisherman diminished his claim to be an apostle, or that Paul's fiery temper enhanced his. The second question confirms the confusion: 'Do you perceive that it is fanatical and wrong to expect and to follow such presumably external revelations?' (BA, 60). To imply that the externality of Adler's revelation indicates its invalidity is doubly confused: it fails to see that any contemporary revelation, since it must be new Good News, may go beyond—and perhaps even radically reconfigure—prior revelation as we currently understand it and hence must appear 'external' to it; and it regards the ineluctable originality of any such revelation as necessarily subverting its claim to be of divine origin.

Once again, then, confusion about what a revelation could be leads to the occlusion of the concept of authority on which it depends; and in this case, the Danish Church's own authority is being similarly occluded. For the tenor of these questions is such that they manifest the Church's interest in avoiding its responsibility to pass judgement on whether or not someone can be justified in claiming to have a revelation in nineteenth-century Denmark. All the evidence suggests that they are inclined to conclude that Adler is deranged from the mere fact that he claims to have received a revelation; but since this would undermine their own authority (since this Church claims to be built upon revelation), they base their dismissal of Adler not on an explicit judgement to that effect, nor on a considered judgement that the time of divine revelation is over, that God has hidden himself away (a judgement which risks offending God), but on the grounds that he is no longer in his right mind, and so no longer competent to act as an official of Church or State.

As for Adler himself, after his dismissal he goes on to publish four books which are essentially exercises in biblical exegesis into which the contents of his 'revelation' are interwoven and lyrically elaborated, but with no mention of those doctrines' putatively divine origin. In other words, Adler neither affirms nor revokes his original claim to have received a revelation: he avoids the responsibility his original pronouncement laid upon him. The implication is that these insights are his own—manifestations of his personal daimon, his individual talent; the idea that those insights have a divine origin, and articulate anew a wholly external and unconditional telos or end that confronts all human beings, disappears. In short, Adler conflates the religious category of 'apostle' with the literary or aesthetic category of 'genius'; and this confusion only reinforces his epigrammatic occlusion of the concept of authority, since on Kierkegaard's account, '[a]uthority is the qualitative difference between a genius and an apostle' (BA, 86).

B. Qualitative Dialectics

These are the bare bones of Kierkegaard's dispassionate but not unsympathetic case study. So when Cavell ends his essay by suggesting that 'Kierkegaard is a "case" with the same dimensions, and no less a phenomenon than Adler, if harder to see through' (MWM, 178), the immediate implication is that Cavell understands his own essay as relating to Kierkegaard in the way that Kierkegaard's book relates to Adler. That is, for Cavell, Kierkegaard is a transparence through which certain conceptual confusions and occlusions of his age are caught, and a terse and ingenious expression of certain derangements (ways of letting go of what understanding is understood to be) that he suffers together with his fellows—where the fellows in Kierkegaard's case are not ministers of Danish Christendom (an office he never held) but rather critics of nineteenth-century religious, moral, political, psychological, and economic dispensations and discontents: Marx, Nietzsche, Freud. And the surgical techniques whose skilful application to Adler justify Kierkegaard's apparently callous treatment of him are exactly what Cavell aspires to apply to Kierkegaard himself—techniques that go under the name of 'qualitative dialectics'.

As Cavell summarizes the matter, 'a dialectical examination of a concept will show how the meaning of that concept changes, and how the subject of which it is the concept changes, as the context in which it is used changes: the dialectical meaning is the history or confrontation of these differences' (MWM, 169–70). His essay demonstrates the centrality of such contextual examinations to Kierkegaard's critical practice, and the extent to which the illumination they cast depends not only on bringing out specific differences of meaning when a given expression is used in different contexts, but also on showing how the specific meaning of one expression-in-a-context is a function of its place in a field of other expressions, which have their full, mutually implicating significance only in and for a specific form of human life (as do Christian concepts in a Christian life).

Qualitative dialectic thereby exploits an essential duality in the idea of attending to context: on the one hand, since the smallest shift in local context might alter the meaning of a word, we must learn to distinguish one context of its use from others; but on the other, since each of a word's context-specific meanings themselves exist only by virtue of their location in a broader context of words and action, we must be equally willing to relate the use of different words-in-their-contexts to one another. On this conception of dialectic, sensitivity to local differentiations of meaning and awareness of broader integrations of meaning are not opposing critical strategies, but essentially complementary ways of clarifying significance; for it is a word's holistic relations to other words that partly determines its specific differences in meaning in differing contexts of its use. For example, it is its relatedness to concepts such as 'God' and 'revelation'—as opposed to concepts such as 'shyness' and 'brazenness'—that determines the significance of the concept of silence in a given context as religious rather than psychological.

This instantiates one key dialectical shift that Kierkegaard frequently notes—that from immanent to transcendent contexts; the latter is the domain of our relationship to God. Sometimes Kierkegaard merely asserts, rather brusquely, the reality of that shift, saying that things are quite otherwise in transcendent contexts—quite as if we only need reminding of a distinction we already understand; sometimes he will describe the kind of life which calls for description in Christian categories—as if to say 'in that life, and for that life, the Christian categories have their full, mutually implicating meaning, and apart from it they may have any or none' (MWM, 170). Cavell approves not only of the emphasis on disclosing the meanings of concepts by locating them in a given form of living, but also of Kierkegaard's willingness to suggest that we simply do, or could, know—without such explanation—what it means to say of someone that 'he stands before God' or that 'This night shall thy soul be required of thee'. For he thinks that such remarks exhibit a significant mode of sense-making: he refers to it as knowing what such remarks mean

> in a sense which we may wish to call *heightened*. That we may not know this all the time is no proof against our knowing; this may only indicate what kind of knowledge it is—the kind of knowledge which can go dead, or become inaccessible... [I]t may be characteristic of a particular kind of meaning rather than a situation in which meaning is absent. [It] might even be an explanation for the sense, as I wish to put it, that we are balancing on the edge of a meaning.
> (MWM, 171)

Whatever one thinks of Cavell's willingness to allow for such a possibility of meaning, its delineation exemplifies the kind of flexibility and precision with which Kierkegaard conducts his dialectical critique of the Christendom of his age, and of that age more generally. It allows him to identify contemporary revolutionary impulses and their reactionary counterparts as embodying a confusion of concepts, with 'political and religious ministers madly trying to solve religious problems with political means, the one by "levelling" worldly differences into a horrible parody of what is already a fact, Christianly speaking, and the other by trying to approach by reason what is always and only grasped by faith' (MWM, 165). It also allows him to diagnose those impulses as originating in a kind of human self-alienation—in which people live in relation to their own self as if they were constantly out, never at home—and so to prescribe as its only possible cure our permitting ourselves to be called or fetched home by a higher power, by God.

But Kierkegaard's proposal for curing this malaise brings out the extent to which his diagnosis of it at once relates him to, and differentiates him from, his fellow critics of culture. Marx, Nietzsche, and Freud might each agree that the root phenomenon with which they are concerned could be called 'self-alienation'; they might further agree that an exemplary expression of such alienation is a collective confusion or occlusion of concepts to which a species of dialectical criticism is the only apt response (because such criticism brings a person's words back home to the local contexts and global perspective of their meaningful employment, hence recovers them from a condition in which they mean anything and nothing, and so in which those employing them are alienated from this aspect of their own modes of existence, not at home to themselves). Nevertheless, each critic's use of these key terms must itself be dialectically understood. The meaning of 'alienation', 'conceptual confusion', and 'dialectical criticism' in Marx's mouth will be as different from their meaning in Kierkegaard's as the field of concepts to which Marx relates it in his broader critical thought and practice differs from the field to which Kierkegaard relates it in his; and so will their conceptions of which particular conceptual confusions and occlusions are fundamental to the contemporary scene. Kierkegaard's delineation of the way to overcome that self-alienation makes it clear that his conception of that overcoming and of what is thereby overcome is distinctively religious—expressive of an overarching perspective or form of life that is profoundly different from that in which a Marxist or Nietzschean or Freudian use of the same critical terminology of alienation and its overcoming has its distinctive meaning. Hence, as Cavell says, the key test of the value of Kierkegaard's conception of how to overcome such self-alienation must be to confront it with the competing conceptions advanced by his fellow critics.

This way of presenting Kierkegaard's inward enmity with his dialectically critical others brings out the extent to which dialectical criticism must always be conducted with a certain self-awareness. As Cavell puts it, 'the criticism of religion, like the criticism of politics which Marx invented, is inescapably dialectical..., because everything said on both sides is conditioned by the position...from which it is said' (MWM, 174). The dialectical critic is sensitive to the context-specificity of the concepts that are the object of his criticism because he thinks that meaning is inherently dialectical—that what a word means is a function of the local context of its use taken in relation to the perspective of the one using it. So it follows that his own critical claims must themselves be dialectically understood if they are to be understood at all—that is, they must be grasped as a function of their local context of application in relation to the perspective of the one advancing them.

To overlook this conditionedness is an error into which those who read and respond to such criticism might easily fall. But it is also an error to which the critic himself might succumb—for example, by advancing his criticisms as if they were not themselves as thoroughly conditioned by context and perspective as their objects; and when he does so he opens himself to a particularly intimate and wounding kind of criticism—that of being an undialectical dialectician, accusing others of being not at home to certain aspects of their own lives with concepts in a way which demonstrates that the critic is alienated from his own words of criticism, and so from himself qua critic. Marx would talk of false consciousness, Nietzsche of the man of knowledge's failure to know himself; a Christian might talk instead of offering to remove a mote from one's brother's eye whilst overlooking the beam in one's own.

It is this kind of oversight that is at issue in Cavell's key criticism of Kierkegaard's critique of politics: 'his violence does not see its own position and... the object he attacks is left uncriticized' (MWM, 174). When he excoriates newspapers and gossip and the public, Cavell suspects that Kierkegaard does not consider the possibility that what is wrong with them is itself a function of the age (not the root cause of what is wrong with that age); and as a result he does not see that his undiscriminating condemnation of the public to perdition might itself be a function of a specific feature of his own critical perspective—'a fear of the public [that] is only the other side of a fearful privacy' (MWM, 175).

I take Cavell to be simultaneously invoking two ways of meaning this last phrase. On the one hand, he is offering his own version of the familiar critical charge that Kierkegaard is *theoretically* committed to a concept of privacy as grammatically or logically inviolate, absolutely beyond another's acknowledgement. Cavell understands this putative commitment—as he interprets analogous commitments in other contexts—as fearful, in that it manifests a fear of admitting one's openness to being known, and hence of one's internal relatedness to others. On the other hand, there are Kierkegaard's *practical* self-presentations as essentially known to himself and essentially unknown to others. One comprises his notoriously misleading modes of participation in Copenhagen's social life, which risk treating others as instruments whilst occluding the equally fearful possibility that any aspect of himself as he is behind these social masks might lie beyond his own grasp. But another is to be found in the equally notorious pseudonymity of his writing. Here, Cavell claims, without arguing the case in detail, that Kierkegaard's deployment of pseudonyms too often looks like a strategy he primarily employed for the benefit of others, rather than an indispensable means of clarifying what he himself has it at heart to say (MWM, 178); in other words, its untroubled projection of a picture of others' responses as absolutely transparent and predictable cloaks a denial that genuine knowledge of himself can only be hard-won.

One might, of course, wish to resist both the theoretical and the practical registers of this criticism on Kierkegaard's behalf. They certainly indicate risks inherent in the positions he takes up, and risks that he should—by his own lights—regard as threatening the heart of his project; and perhaps his treatment of Regine shows most clearly how damaging it could be to succumb to it. But it is surely at least possible to reject the idea that one's personal God-relation can be determined by determining that one is a citizen of Denmark without claiming that this relation leaves no determining (or even indicative) marks on one's public mode of existence. And it seems equally possible to use pseudonymous authorship in a way which respects the freedom of others to make their own judgements about the strengths and weaknesses of each existential perspective that is thereby dramatized, so that the actual author's recession behind his pseudonyms indicates not a presumed superiority to his readers but a willingness to respect their privacy. Nevertheless, the seriousness of these charges—what one might call their dialectical intimacy—entails that they must be taken seriously, and either made out or modified from case to case of Kierkegaard's texts and other deeds.

However such concrete investigations may turn out, it is clear that, by using one phrase to activate both registers of significance, Cavell means to imply that each register of his critique dialectically conditions the other in his subject's form of life: and taken together, they characterize that subject as someone whose fantasies of mastery cover fears of subjection to the mastery of others, hence as the embodiment of a sadomasochistic conception of self and other as fixed or fixated objects of cognition rather than sites of unceasing upbuilding and rebuilding. Nietzsche would recognize in this critical portrait another manifestation of slave theology's life-denying prioritization of Being over Becoming.

C. Dialectic and History

There is a further dimension to this Nietzschean diagnosis of Kierkegaard's asceticism; but to see it, we need to explore another reflexive dimension of this textual territory. For since Cavell declares that Kierkegaard's dialectical critical method is both philosophical and philosophically correct (MWM, 169), then—mindful of the parable of the mote and the beam—we might ask ourselves how dialectical Cavell's own criticism of Kierkegaard actually is. Is it a critique that sees its own position—that is, that sees its own conditionedness, and in particular the local context and the holistic perspective within which alone it has such sense and force as it possesses? Answering this question involves recognizing another aspect of the notion of a dialectical-critical method which we have hitherto passed over but which is pre-eminent at its Hegelian point of origin—its sensitivity to specifically historical contexts and conditions.

In the case of Kierkegaard's case study of Adler, the subject and the object of criticism inhabit the same age or period, are one another's contemporaries; indeed, this is part of what makes the former's ability penetratingly and prophetically to discern in the latter the distinctive features and likely fate of their particular era so impressive (at least as impressive as it is in the contemporary case studies that drive the critical work of Marx, Nietzsche, and Freud). The same is not true of Cavell's case study of Kierkegaard; on the contrary, without the passage of time between Kierkegaard's book and Cavell's essay, the latter's perception of Kierkegaardian prophetic criticism as internally related to the projects of those other dialectical thinkers of his age (most of whom came after him) would be inconceivable.

But even if historical distance is a necessary condition for recognizing Kierkegaard's fellowship with these critics, it is surely not sufficient; at the very least, Cavell's perceptions are also profoundly enabled by his allegiances to the later Wittgenstein, although it is important to note that the object of his allegiance is very much not the later Wittgenstein familiar to most philosophers (even most Wittgensteinian philosophers) in the 1960s, when ordinary-language philosophy dominated the Anglo-American scene. At the time at which Cavell's essay was published, he had not yet brought his distinctively deranging reading of the *Philosophical Investigations* (which released him from what an understanding of Wittgenstein was—and still is—understood to involve) to the point of publication *in extenso*: that would come only with the appearance of *The Claim of Reason* in 1979.[2] But its influence pervades all the essays in his first book; and his ability to see Kierkegaard's qualitative dialectic as a *philosophical* method was importantly facilitated by his interpretation of Wittgenstein's method of grammatical investigation as exemplifying a perception of our words and concepts as essentially projective.

Take the word 'feed': we learn to 'feed the cat' and to 'feed the lions', and then, when someone talks of feeding the meter or feeding our pride, we understand them; we accept this projection of it. At the same time, however, such projections are also deeply controlled. We can, for example, feed a lion, but not by placing a bushel of carrots in its cage; and its failure to eat them would not count as a refusal to do so. Such projections of 'feed' and 'refusal' fail because their connection with other words in their normal contexts do not transfer to the new one: one can only refuse something that one might also accept, hence something that one can be offered or invited to accept; and what might count as an offer and an acceptance in the context of a meal is both different from and related to what counts as an offer and acceptance in the context of mating or being guided. These limits are neither arbitrary nor optional; they show how what Cavell calls a word's grammatical schematism determines the respects in which a new context for a word must invite or allow its projection:

> [A]ny form of life and every concept integral to it has an indefinite number of instances and directions of projection; and this variation is not arbitrary. *Both the 'outer' variance and the 'inner' constancy are necessary if a concept is to accomplish its tasks*—of meaning, understanding, communicating etc., and in general, guiding us through the world, and relating thought and action and feeling to the world. (CR, 185)

---

[2] (Oxford: Oxford University Press, 1979); hereafter CR.

This flexible constancy, or essentially non-arbitrary variation, is what Cavell means by the projectibility of language; and it is itself a manifestation of (what Cavell understands as) Wittgenstein's vision of words as governed by criteria:

> [Wittgensteinian] criteria do not relate a name to an object, but, we might say, various concepts to the concept of that object. Here the test of your possession of a concept... would be your ability to use the concept in conjunction with other concepts, your knowledge of which concepts are relevant to the one in question and which are not; your knowledge of how various relevant concepts, used in conjunction with the concepts of different kinds of objects, require different kinds of contexts for their competent employment. (CR, 73)

A word's grammatical schematism is its power to combine with other words—'the word's potency to assume just those valences, and a sense that in each case there will be a point of application of the word, and that the point will be the same from context to context, or that the point will shift in a recognizable pattern or direction' (CR, 77–8). Hence when the acceptability or naturalness of a new projection of a given word is in question, our final judgement will turn upon the speaker's capacity to show that and how the new context into which she has projected it either invites or can be seen to allow that projection by inviting or allowing (at least some modified form of) the projection of those other words to which its criteria relate it, and which are accommodated in familiar contexts of the word's use.

This way of understanding criteria and grammar can certainly accommodate the more familiar Wittgensteinian sense of the importance of distinguishing grammatical connections and differences from their empirical counterparts. And Cavell activates that understanding when he compliments Kierkegaard on his sensitivity to it, and contrasts him with Mill in this respect. As he points out, where Mill expends a great deal of time and effort exploring the question of whether any evidence can suffice to prove a divine revelation (and concludes by allowing that at least nothing prevents one from hoping that such things might happen), Kierkegaard answers with a blunt 'No', on the grounds that 'A revelation cannot be proven by evidence' is a partial articulation of the grammar of the concept of a revelation.

But Cavell's interpretation of Wittgenstein's conception of grammar goes further than this. For it plainly acknowledges the internal relatedness of local differentiations and general integrations of meaning that is central to qualitative dialectic; and it thereby frees Wittgenstein's later philosophical method from any tendency towards what one might call linguistic (and so philosophical) conservatism. For it avoids picturing the recovery of the grammar of ordinary words in the way Wittgenstein's defenders favour as much as his deniers—as a matter of either restricting us to the reiteration of its current ranges of its employment or of establishing entirely new (and so essentially unrelated) applications. Such a picture precisely occludes the essential openness of words to engagement with new contexts, in relation to which further reaches of the significance of those words (further possibilities and impossibilities of our making sense of and with them) disclose themselves. On Cavell's reading of Wittgenstein, to say that words possess a grammatical schematism is to say with full dialectical rigour that the meanings of words are essentially, always already to-be-unfolded; hence, they live and move and have their being in history, with all its complex conditions and vicissitudes. So understood, Wittgenstein's writings reveal themselves as embodying the possibility of a contemporary variant of dialectical criticism of culture (by, for example, criticizing its given forms in the name of its unattained but attainable possibilities of making and enacting sense).

This is why Cavell quietly but plainly implies that Kierkegaard's earlier version of dialectical criticism was not itself as historically inflected or sensitive as it was capable of being. For although Kierkegaard is all too aware that contemporary Christendom was undergoing a crisis to which previous ages had not succumbed, and was to that extent aware of conditions specific to his present age, he appears to have understood that crisis as a falling-away from a prior, ideal (or at least more ideal) state or condition—one in which qualitative differences between aesthetic, ethical, and religious concepts, contexts, and stages or spheres of existence (call them forms of life) were better understood because more faithfully realized in life; and more importantly, he seems to have regarded these differences as ahistorically valid, their availability as standards or ideals essentially unconditioned by time and circumstance—as possibilities that are fixed in number and nature, one might say eternal.

This is another respect in which Nietzsche might detect a distinctively ascetic prioritization of Being over Becoming in Kierkegaard's criticisms of his age, at least on Cavell's interpretation of it; but however that may be, it indicates a certain limitation in Kierkegaard's mode of dialectical criticism. Despite the fact that he registers his age's increasingly pervasive confusion and occlusion of religious concepts, and the intensifying loss of existential integrity and intelligibility (both individual and collective) that this is creating all around him, he never fully confronts the possibility that these registrations clearly portend for Cavell—namely that 'as a given person may never occupy [the religious] stage, so a given age and all future ages, may as a whole not occupy it—that the form will be lost from men's lives altogether' (MWM, 172).

D. Losing Concepts

This idea of losing a form of life together with the conceptual field that articulates it links the Kierkegaardian version of dialectical criticism not only to its nineteenth-century counterparts (including Nietzsche's genealogical method), but also to a more specific, not exclusively Wittgensteinian, and highly influential thread of philosophical projects and debates in the present age of Cavell's essay—the second half of the twentieth century. It is central to Anscombe's 1958 article 'Modern Moral Philosophy', in which she famously claims that the situation in which we currently stand with the notion of 'moral obligation' exemplifies the survival of a concept outside the framework of thought that made it intelligible; Alasdair MacIntyre later transfigures this local observation into the central thesis of his 1981 book *After Virtue,* according to which the language and appearances of morality more generally persist even though its integral substance has largely fragmented and partly been destroyed.[3] Cavell himself had already developed (in writings that would eventually constitute chapter 10 of *The Claim of Reason*) an analogous critique of Stevenson's emotivist analysis of moral discourse, although his view was that Stevenson's portrait of morality was written as if by someone who had lost the very concept of moral thought and discussion—that is, by someone blind to what actually existing moral life is like. Nevertheless, as Cora Diamond points out in her famous 1988 paper 'Losing Your Concepts', if Cavell's critique is right, Stevenson has actually in part lost the capacity to employ moral concepts: for to be able to describe what it is like to use moral concepts is itself a (philosophically reflective) use of those concepts, and to that extent Stevenson's failure is not merely one of perception—it indicates one area of our life with moral concepts that is exactly as MacIntyre takes our moral life to be more generally.[4]

These various diagnoses of situations in which we might be said to suffer from loss of concepts each have to confront a particular worry: if these critics really believe that concepts only have their specific meaning within the relevant framework or context of employment, and if the concept with which they are concerned really does now exist outside that context, then by their own lights it simply cannot any longer be the concept they present it as being. Either it retains its sense in the new historical situation, in which case the lost or fragmented context was not in fact determinative of its intelligibility; or that context really was constitutive of its sense, in which case it must now lack that sense, and so cannot really be said to be the same concept (or indeed, to be an intelligible concept at all).

Cavell's essay reveals that this dilemma is not in fact forced upon those inclined to prosecute any version of the 'loss of concepts' diagnosis. For his projective reading of Wittgensteinian criteria allows him to identify one fate that concepts which suffer the loss of their original enabling context might undergo other than that of loss of sense—that of migration into another context, within which they make a different but related kind of sense. This is, after all, exactly what qualitative

---

[3] Anscombe's essay is reprinted in her *Ethics, Religion and Politics* (Minneapolis: University of Minnesota Press, 1981), 26–42; *After Virtue* was published in London, by Duckworth.

[4] Diamond's essay appeared in *Ethics* 98 (Jan. 1988), 255–77.

dialectics would suggest: for if religious concepts do find a home in what Kierkegaard would call an immanent rather than a transcendental context, then it would be undialectical to imagine that they must either retain exactly the same sense as they had in their original context or take on an entirely unrelated sense. If those concepts are invited by that new context, then something about their original articulation must have prompted, and so should be preserved in, their projection into it; but in order to take up residence in these new sense-constituting circumstances, the field of related concepts with which they are interwoven in their original context will have to be modified in various respects. This means that, if we are to comprehend such projections, we must pay careful attention to the specific balance of constancy and variation through which it is effected in each case; Nietzsche might think of it as requiring of us a genealogical perspective.

The particular case in which Cavell is here interested is that of the two concepts whose loss of religious sense Kierkegaard sees Adler as presaging: the concepts of authority and revelation. And the particular projection that concerns him—more accurately, the projection he thinks we could and should make, or could usefully regard as already, if inchoately, underway—is from a religious context to the then-current immanent context of modern art. But it will help to prepare the ground for that aspect of his interpretation if we first consider a less dramatic or radical mode of projection of those concepts, which takes them in a direction that was at the forefront of Nietzsche's original genealogical concerns—from their transcendental home to the immanent context of ethics. And I propose to begin discharging my own debt to the method of qualitative dialectic or genealogy—the critic's obligation to acknowledge his own position, his enabling context and conditions—by focusing on one way in which those concepts are being projected into the domain of contemporary ethical practice and reflection, rather than Nietzsche's mid-nineteenth century or Cavell's 1960s. (My later discussions of Golding, Coetzee, and Nolan, of contemporary photographic practices and current philosophical accounts of secondary qualities and technology, amount to continuations of this process of acknowledgement.)

I noted in the Introduction how and why Nietzsche would regard the decline of theism as perfectly compatible with a continued and even intensified commitment to the self-denying and life-denying altruistic values bequeathed to us from (Judaeo-)Christianity. But I also suggested there that, like any other historical phenomenon, the ascetic ideal must itself be understood genealogically—as possessed of a historically evolving essence whose multiple layers are as likely to come apart, or come into conflict with each other, as to maintain a stable and robust internal coherence. And since the same is necessarily true of cultural expressions of resistance to that ideal (including movements such as Nietzsche's genealogical project), we should not be surprised if post-Nietzschean developments in moral life throw up phenomena that are best understood as complex and tension-laden amalgamations of ascetic and counter-ascetic elements. I want to suggest that the debate in contemporary moral philosophy between the movement known as 'moral individualism' and its Wittgenstein-inspired critics is one such phenomenon. This conflict (once it is understood as structured around competing conceptions of authority and revelation) shows itself to be an exemplary instance of the way in which hostility to ascetic value-systems can take on self-undermining forms, and in which ascetic impulses can draw strength from genealogical insights. But in order to establish this hermeneutic claim, I will have to recapitulate the critical evaluation of moral individualism that I developed in an early chapter of my book *The Wounded Animal*,[5] and then assess the cogency of the responses offered to that critique by the defenders of that movement.

2. Authority and Revelation in Ethics

A. Moral Individualism

In that chapter, I organized my discussion around Jeff McMahan's recent, much-praised, and influential book entitled *The Ethics of Killing*, and critically evaluated it in terms of three main issues: McMahan's use of thought-experiments; his conception of what genuinely rational moral argument and judgement must be; and his aversion to the use of literature in attempting to clarify and further our moral thinking. Taken together, they suggest a deep-rooted investment in various forms of intellectual abstraction.

In his book, McMahan puts the technique of thought-experimentation to highly systematic use; and its deployment culminates with his presentation of the following imaginary situation.[6] Suppose that a woman, without family or friends, dies giving birth to a healthy infant. At the same hospital there are three 5-year-old children, who will die if they do not receive organ transplants, and the newborn has exactly the right tissue type. If McMahan's moral theory is right, it is morally permissible to 'sacrifice' the orphaned infant in order to save the other three children. McMahan recognizes that he seems to be confronting a *reductio ad absurdum* of his position, and confesses that 'I cannot embrace [this implication] without significant misgivings and considerable unease' (EK, 360); and yet, he continues to draw on the theory that has this implication throughout his extensive ensuing examination of abortion and euthanasia.

McMahan's tale of the 'Sacrificial Newborn' is a paradigm case of the work done by thought-experiments in moral philosophy. Its sole rationale is to present us with a lightly clothed (in this particular instance, consequentialist) calculation, designed to bring out an implication of adopting a particular moral principle or

---

[5] (Princeton: Princeton University Press, 2009), ch. 2.
[6] *The Ethics of Killing* (Oxford: Oxford University Press, 2002); hereafter EK.

value. The constructive process might be characterized as follows: first eliminate anyone with whom the newborn might have a human relationship (since their distress might complicate the sums), then stipulate enough older children to outnumber our orphan (thereby reminding us that three is at least three times greater than one). It's a deliberately arithmetical tale, morality by numbers—and the simpler the texture, the clearer the point.

But what if our concern were not clarity but understanding, or an engagement of our moral imagination with something resembling the texture and complexity of human reality? Not only is medical unlikelihood bypassed for McMahan's purposes (no tissue-typing problems); we hear nothing of the family and friends of the three 5-year-olds. This is presumably because their obvious joy at the redemption of their children would simply shift the balance of calculation even further in the same direction. But what if the mother of one of these children discovers the source of her daughter's new organs? Would her joy be untainted by this knowledge? Is it obvious that she, or any of the parents involved, would regard it as legitimate for this healthy orphan to be thus abused? Is it obvious that any of them, or indeed any of the hospital staff, would not feel an obligation to the memory of the newborn's dead mother that might make them hesitate over its 'sacrifice'?

Such questions might seem unfair; McMahan's purpose is not to produce a gritty exercise in literary realism, but rather to make a theoretical point—indeed, to acknowledge a point against his own theory that my carping response simply underlines. Certain possible complications in the telling of the tale are excised simply because they are irrelevant to the issue at hand, which is the relative strength of the moral claims made on us by human infants and young children. His case is deliberately constructed so as to clear the scene of any other, potentially polluting concerns to which our moral intuitions might be responsive. We couldn't be further from the role and significance of the cases studied by Kierkegaard and Cavell (and Nietzsche).

Such thought-experiments in ethics presuppose that we can get clearer about what we think concerning a single, specific moral issue by abstracting it from the complex web of interrelated matters of fact and of valuation within which we usually encounter and respond to it. But what if the issue means what it does to us, has the moral significance it has for us, precisely because of its place in that complex web? If so, one would not have to be a qualitative dialectician to think that abstracting it from that context amounts to asking us to think about something other than the issue that interested us in the first place; it is, in effect, to change the subject.

This drive towards abstraction pervades McMahan's book (and here we shift from the theme of thought-experiments to that of rational method in moral thinking). For his treatment of the specific issues of abortion, infanticide, euthanasia, and suicide applies conclusions reached by his prior discussion of the nature of death and killing, which are in turn guided by conclusions reached in his opening account of the nature of persons. The reason for this structure is evident enough. Only if we understand the nature of persons can we understand what it is (and why it is bad) for them to die; only then can we understand what is bad about causing them to die by killing them; and only then can we understand what, if anything, is bad about the specific forms of killing known as abortion and euthanasia.

Such a pattern of reasoning sharply distinguishes ethics from metaphysics, and grounds the former on the latter. For McMahan, the relevant rational foundations of ethics are not themselves ethical; establishing the essential nature of a certain kind of entity will have consequences for our moral thinking, and may be why we engage in it, but that metaphysical issue is in itself ethically neutral. This certainly sounds sensible; for it seems to amount to the truism that we should settle the more general issue before moving to the more particular, or rather, get the rational foundations of our moral thinking in place before we engage in specific moral disputes. Appearances, however, can be misleading.

McMahan's account of personhood builds upon that of Derek Parfit, who claims that, in normal circumstances, personal identity (what makes me one and the same person across time) is a matter of the holding of certain relations of psychological continuity and connectedness—relations of memory, desire and its satisfaction, intentions and their fulfilment, and so on.[7] McMahan revises this account so that psychological continuity is treated more broadly, and as a matter of degree; but he also argues that identity is preserved only if the relevant psychological continuity is grounded in the physical and functional continuity of enough of those areas of the person's brain in which consciousness is realized. Hence, according to this 'Embodied Mind' account, a person in the early stages of Alzheimer's has reason to be egoistically concerned about what may happen to his body even in the final phases in which the mental life associated with his body will no longer be even weakly psychologically connected from day to day.

Despite its title, McMahan's account risks substituting a brain–body dualism for the religious or Cartesian mind–body dualism he so detests (transplant the right part of a person's brain into a new body, and you preserve his identity). And when the embodiedness of his favoured brain-parts is really thrust upon his attention, he misses its true significance. Consider another of his 'cases', that of dicephalus. This is his version of a rare but real medical condition, which occurs when a human zygote divides incompletely, and results in twins conjoined below the neck. Referring to the specific, real-life case of Abigail and Brittany Hensel, McMahan flatly asserts that 'no one doubts that they are separate and distinct little girls' (EK, 35). Each, he tells us, would have her own private mental life and her

---

[7] Cf. *Reasons and Persons* (Oxford: Oxford University Press, 1984).

own character; there are 'of course' two personal or biographical lives, although their shared set of organs sustains a single biological life.

But McMahan makes no effort to imagine the meaning of his claims to the girls themselves. Will Abigail feel that she has an utterly distinct personal or biographical life from her sister, or her sister from her? Neither can ever play on her own with other children, have a joyful or furious private conversation with her mother, retreat to her room to rage or sulk or think in solitude, or go out alone with a boyfriend. Suppose they were to have a child; as McMahan notes in passing, it would be the child of both, a child with three parents. What significance might their motherhood have for each of them ('biographically'), given its rootedness in their common flesh? Would it confirm, modify, or undermine their sense of separateness and union? And what significance will their private mental life have to them when it exists only in the context of such enforced, embodied intimacy with one another?

McMahan's treatment of this 'case' fails to acknowledge that the nature of their embodied lives simply cannot be broken down and distributed between biological union and psychological distinctness in any straightforward way. If a sense of the separateness of persons is part of our concept of personhood, and that sense would be radically disrupted in the case of dicephalic twins, then so would our concept of personhood. Our ordinary concept of a person has the sense and the significance it has because it is embedded in the normal circumstances of our ordinary embodied lives with others; alter those circumstances, and our ordinary concept will not simply carry over, hence its structure cannot be straightforwardly illuminated by their study.

It is quite as if McMahan thinks that we first develop a concept of a person (say, as a psychologically continuous entity), and then relate to those we identify as persons in ways we judge appropriate to their metaphysical genus, so that those relations might be evaluated for their consistency with our independently given nature. But our concept of a person is in fact constituted by, finds its life and sense in the context of, the normal forms of our lives with other persons—with embodied, flesh-and-blood creatures inhabiting structures of language and culture. And since those lives have an evaluative dimension, since their commonality and variety cannot adequately be characterized except in terms which invite ethical questions (as Abigail's relations to her sister, her parents, and her children plainly do), the same is true of our concept of a person. Personhood is not the metaphysical foundation of an interpersonal ethics; it is itself an ethical notion. To attempt to analyse it whilst remaining morally neutral is bound to produce exactly the air of mad conceptual science with which McMahan's description of his dicephalus case is imbued. And such ways of viewing human animals will inevitably hang together with certain ways of viewing non-human animals.

Recognizing that human interpersonal relations typically exhibit a requirement of mutual respect, McMahan locates its rational and metaphysical basis in the mature human being's possession of certain psychological capacities—a rationally guided will, or sophisticated forms of self-consciousness. He then points out that some human beings lack these capacities, and concludes that they must fall below the threshold of respect. Their moral claims on us should be assessed not in terms of inviolable rights but in terms of their interest in continuing to live, and this interest can be compared with, and sometimes traded off against, competing such interests (hence the 'Sacrificial Newborn' case). By the same token, certain higher non-human mammals, being possessed of at least analogous versions of the psychological continuity that grounds the human interest in continuing to live, should be seen as having analogous second-tier moral status to that of human foetuses, infants, and the severely disabled.

For McMahan, then, the moral status of human beings is not univocal, and moral status of the second-tier variety at least is not restricted to members of the human species. To deny this second claim is to exhibit speciesism; it is to load moral significance onto a purely biological category. This follows from his commitment to the characteristic principle of the position known as 'moral individualism'—according to which 'how an individual may be treated is to be determined, not by considering his group memberships, but by considering his own particular characteristics'.[8] To bring out the force of that principle, McMahan asks us to imagine administering genetic therapy to a canine foetus which confers human levels of self-consciousness, rationality, and autonomy upon it as it develops. It follows, he claims, that it would then have become a person in the morally relevant sense of that term; and that means that, amongst other things, we would have no more reason to administer such a therapy to a severely cognitively impaired human adult than to a normal, healthy dog.

Trying to convince us of this, he says 'Let us assume, for the sake of the argument, that a dog with human intelligence could have a life that would be well worth living even in a society in which it would be a freak, would have no acceptable mate, and so on. In short, let us put those contingent problems aside' (EK, 319). Easy for us to do, one might think; not so easy for the dog. Would a human being, deprived of any acceptable mate and regarded as a freak by his fellows, be faced with merely contingent problems that would leave his capacity to conceive of himself as a person essentially unaffected? What interpersonal relations (of friendship, family, gossip, common hobbies and interests) would be conceivable for our Superdog; and in their absence, what would the sense be of calling it a person nonetheless? I don't say that there could be no sense in doing so. I say only that the sense it would have is not the sense it has when human beings acknowledge one another as persons. The forms of embodied common life open to distinctively human creatures provide the context within which our notion of

---

[8] James Rachels, *Created from Animals* (Oxford: Oxford University Press, 1990), 73.

personhood has the sense it has. These forms are not the practical enactment of a logically prior or analytically separable intellectual hypothesis about capacity-possession that might turn out to be metaphysically ungrounded.

In other words, our concept of a person is an outgrowth or aspect of our concept of a human being; and that concept is not merely biological but rather a crystallization of everything we have made of our distinctive species nature. To see another as a human being is to see her as a fellow creature—another being whose embodiment embeds her in a distinctive form of common life with language and culture, and whose existence constitutes a particular kind of claim upon us. We do not strive (when we do strive) to treat human infants and children, the senile and the severely disabled as fully human because we mistakenly attribute capacities to them that they lack, or because we are blind to the merely biological significance of a species boundary. We do it (when we do) because they are fellow human beings, embodied creatures who will come to share, or have already shared, in our common life, or whose inability to do so is a result of the kinds of shocks and ills to which all human flesh and blood is heir—because there but for the grace of God go I.

This supposedly speciesist conception of humans as fellow creatures in fact provides a far more satisfying and powerful way of reconceiving our relations with non-human animals than anything McMahan's argument provides. For non-human animals, too, can be seen as our fellow creatures in a different but related sense of that term. Their embodied existence, and hence their form of life, is different; but in certain cases, the human and the non-human forms of creaturely existence can overlap, interact, even offer companionship to one another, and in many ways, some non-human animals can be seen as sharing a common fate with us. They too are needy, dependent, subject to birth, sexuality, and death, vulnerable to pain and fear—in short, they are fellow sons and daughters of life. Seen in this light, the excesses of modern-day factory farming stand out clearly enough without further metaphysical analysis.

As the appearance of a phrase from Walter de la Mare suggests, it is not surprising to find clear and sustained articulations of such a conception in literary works of outstanding quality; for the ethical significance of mortality is an artistic as well as a philosophical perennial. However, McMahan's discussion of the treatment of mortality by the greatest writers of Western culture is the one point in his enormous book when his scrupulous equanimity deserts him, to inadvertently comic effect. For what he finds in this tradition is 'a dreary record of evasion and sophistry' (EK, 95–8). Socrates 'prates' about obtaining a great good in the other world whilst drinking his hemlock (no chance of irony here, just hypocrisy); Schopenhauer's attempt to reconcile us to our place in the unending cycle of life is 'wringing a meagre drop of consolation from the rags of bad argument'; and Tolstoy's 'The Death of Ivan Ilyich', despite being 'of course' a masterpiece, is also a 'conspicuous piece of evasion'. Ivan's deathbed vision is a *deus ex machina* which irritatingly leaves us to guess at what his reassuring illumination actually is. Even when one of Tolstoy's biographers tells McMahan that it is the acceptance of his own mortality that brings Ivan peace, he is profoundly unsatisfied. 'Not only is there no textual support for this conjecture, but insofar as Ivan Ilyich accepts mortality, this is not an explanation of his finding peace but is itself precisely what requires explanation.'

McMahan certainly won't find a sentence in the story in which Ivan says 'I must accept my mortality!'; nevertheless, every word in Tolstoy's text works to articulate just such a vision. It does so by presenting Ivan's gradual acceptance of himself as an utterly unexceptional human being, as confronting a fate common to all human creatures. That acceptance begins when he is himself accepted as a fellow creature by his servant, Gerasim ('we shall all of us die, so why should I grudge a little trouble?', Gerasim remarks, as he massages his master's aching legs), and so begins to accept Gerasim as his fellow. And it is furthered when his young son, his eyelids bruised by self-doubt and self-hatred, creeps in tears to his sickbed to gaze in pity on his sufferings. But because that text contains no premises, independently established, allowing us to advance further hypotheses, perhaps even to draw novel and ingenious conclusions in the fullness of time, McMahan can identify no power of rational conviction in it. If, however, we stop laying down such requirements in advance, then we might have some hope of seeing that, in nothing less than the text taken as a whole, Tolstoy is inviting us to appreciate a particular way of seeing human life—a way of seeing ourselves as mortal creatures subject to a common and uncanny fate, but capable nevertheless of living well, of doing the right thing. Is it simply accidental that a gifted philosopher so much at home in the genre of the thought-experiment should be incapable of recognizing the rather different way in which that of the short story might provide it?

B. Fellow Creatures

In an article published before *The Wounded Animal* appeared, McMahan defended himself, and moral individualism more generally, against the criticisms I advanced in that book; he took as his target my earlier review of his own book, upon which I drew in composing the relevant passages of *The Wounded Animal*, but since the main substance of my criticisms remained unchanged, his article amounted to an advance rebuttal of that portion of my book.[9] I took no account of that rebuttal because I hadn't yet come across it; but since it will prove relevant to

---

[9] McMahan's article is '"Our Fellow Creatures"' (*Journal of Ethics* 9 (2005), 353–80); hereafter OFC. My original review, entitled 'Fearful Thoughts', appeared in the *London Review of Books* 24 (22 Aug. 2002), 16.

my current concerns, it is worth taking some time here to atone for my oversight by responding to McMahan's reply.

McMahan's interpretation of my position is shaped from the outset by two assumptions. He quotes a long passage from my review, which reappears on pp. 33–34 of this essay (it begins '[t]he forms of embodied common life' and ends 'there but for the grace of God go I'); and he interprets it as claiming or implying two things. First, 'that certain moral concepts derive their substance from the form of life in which they have evolved' (OFC, 362); and second, that 'the considerations to which [Mulhall] appeal[s] are essentially relational' (OFC, 363). However, neither claim in fact shapes either the passage he quotes or my treatment of these issues more generally.

The first claim is McMahan's way of stating a rather different claim that I do make in the relevant passage: namely, that our forms of life provide the context within which certain of our moral concepts have the sense they do. McMahan's report of my claim sharply distinguishes concept from form of life, and makes the sense of the former dependent upon the presence and/or nature of the latter; my claim presents concept and form of life as internally related and partly constitutive of each other, hence it precisely denies the existence of an asymmetrical dependence-relation between two essentially distinct phenomena. McMahan takes my horizontal, holistic vision of the relation between the two to be a vertical and hierarchical one, and takes the notion of 'form of life' as providing an independent and prior basis or foundation for the sense of our concepts. This is, of course, exactly what one would expect from someone whose whole vision of moral philosophy depends upon assuming that rational ethical stances must be grounded in independently establishable metaphysical doctrines. And it is precisely the methodological assumption that my original critique goes to some trouble to isolate and criticize at the outset. Whether that criticism is successful may be an open question; but it is surprising to find McMahan writing as if I actually share the assumption I am attacking.

The second mistaken interpretative assumption needs a little more explanation. At the beginning of his article, whilst broadly agreeing that his work shares the moral individualist orientation of James Rachels (whose memory McMahan's article is intended to honour), McMahan points out that he may differ from Rachels in one respect. When the moral individualist advocates that our treatment of a given creature be determined by its individual characteristics, should those characteristics only include its intrinsic properties, or can relational properties also be included? McMahan is unsure of Rachels's view; but on his own view, relational properties should be included.

> If it excludes *all* relational properties—such as this child's being *my* child—as morally significant, then the moral individualism that he defended is stronger than that to which I am committed. For I accept that *some* special relations

between or among individuals are morally significant and are a source of moral reasons, though only of 'agent-relative' reasons—that is, reasons that do not apply to people generally but only to those who are participants in the relations.
(OFC, 354)

So when McMahan reads a passage in which I claim that 'to see another as a human being is to see her as a fellow-creature—another being whose embodiment embeds her in a distinctive form of common life with language and culture, and whose existence constitutes a particular claim on us', he interprets it as invoking a relational property as a candidate basis for treating human beings in a certain way.

Because the radically cognitively impaired share in *our* common life and are therefore *our* fellow creatures, they make a claim on *us*. The claims they would make on moral agents from Mars would be no different from the claims of comparably endowed animals, apart from any additional claims they have by virtue of their relations with other human beings. (OFC, 363)

The fact that neither this passage, nor any other portion of my remarks, deploys either the distinction between intrinsic and relational properties or that between agent-neutral and agent-relative reasons might have given McMahan pause. So might the fact that he has introduced the idea of relational properties as part of a wider moral individualist project of identifying a rational metaphysical ground for attributions of ethical significance, when just two sentences before the sentence on which he focuses, I reiterate my wholesale rejection of that model (by saying that the forms of embodied common life are not the practical consequence of a logically prior metaphysical hypothesis about property-instantiation). But the clinching piece of evidence that something has gone hermeneutically awry is McMahan's blithe invocation of 'moral agents from Mars'.

In order to give some substance to his idea that creaturely fellowship is a relational property, and so generates only an agent-relative reason for action, McMahan needs to be able to draw a contrast between those agents relative to whom a given creature makes a claim by virtue of possessing that property, and other agents upon whom that creature makes no such claim. But since the present candidate for an agent-relative moral reason is the relational property of being human, and since any and every moral agent hitherto encountered is a human being, the distinction between agent-relative and agent-neutral reasons threatens to break down, or at least to become hard to draw, just when it is most needed. The problem is solved by inventing a broader category of non-human moral agent: to be sure, that category has so far remained empty or null, but since there is surely nothing incoherent about the very idea of such a being, its mere possibility will suffice to secure the crucial distinction.

The problem is that key elements of my original discussion effectively amount to a rejection of the coherence of such an idea. For a Martian moral agent belongs with Dicephalus and Superdog in McMahan's conceptual bestiary: it is a product of multiple abstraction, each aspect of which I subjected to criticism. McMahan's Martian moral agents would presumably have a very different mode of animate being to our own: a (potentially radically different) body, means of expression, and mode of interaction with their Martian fellows, which on my account would entail a (potentially radically different) context for concepts such as agency or personhood, whose sense would shift accordingly (if their projection into such contexts turns out to be possible at all). But on McMahan's account their status as moral agents is utterly unaffected by such things, because that status is secured in other ways—by their possession of the appropriate intrinsic and relational properties which ground their postulated capacity to respond to moral reasons for judgement and action. The casualness with which he invokes the idea of Martian moral agency makes sense only if he thinks that we can set aside any practical problems involved in identifying the presence of such grounding properties and grounded capacities in an alien creature. But to think in these terms is precisely to distinguish personhood from being-Martian in exactly the way that McMahan wishes to distinguish personhood from being-human—as if our mode of animality were a mere vessel for that personhood, as opposed to being a constitutive mode of its manifestation. In my original discussion, I objected to the former and at least sketched out a version of the latter; so it is disheartening to find that McMahan is so quick to assume that my basic position in fact requires rejecting the latter and embracing the former.

A broader abstractive impulse lurks behind, and in part depends upon, these more local ones. For by invoking Martian moral agents, McMahan in effect constructs a conception of the domain of morality more generally that is only contingently connected to that of human beings. The issue here is not just that McMahan means to allow for the possibility that not all human beings are persons, and not all non-human animals lack moral standing; those are arguments about who or what falls within the field of vision of the genuinely moral agent. The deeper point is that whenever any kind of being adopts an authentically moral point of view, they are taking up a perspective that essentially transcends that of human beings (or indeed, any other kind of animate or animal life). It is the perspective of pure reason, the point of view of the universe or at least of nowhere in particular within it: and this vision meshes perfectly with McMahan's sensitivity to traces of 'speciesism', and with his preference for grounding ethics on an evaluatively neutral metaphysics (since the language of the latter at least appears to have a better chance of constituting the lingua franca of a genuinely universal basis for rational moral exchange and improvement).

In this way, moral individualism's concern to free ethical thought from what it sees as an arbitrary restriction to human beings ultimately delivers a vision according to which the moral significance of the embodiedness and the animality of human and non-human forms of life is passed over, and the ways in which moral thought is non-accidentally informed by the human condition is denied. This putative mode of affirming the value of life in general thus turns out to amount to a kind of life-denial: its obsessive interest in detaching rationality from its imaginative, affective, and animal context deprives it of the resources needed to be properly sensitive to differences in life's manifestations, and of the ability to acknowledge its own rootedness in the animate human realm—a realm of Becoming rather than pure rational Being.

The range of assumptions about objectivity, rationality, value, and reality required to articulate such an ascetic conception of ideal moral thought is broad and complex; perhaps they can be defended, but to draw upon them as though no such defence was necessary, and as if any minimally rational philosopher must accept them, is dispiriting. And although I don't make this point explicitly in my discussion, Cora Diamond (who is also under investigation in McMahan's article) emphasizes throughout her work the availability of an alternative to this conception—one according to which the meaning (both the sense and the significance) of moral thought as such (regardless of whether or not its content is such as to expel some human beings from full moral standing or to assign that standing to some non-human beings) can only be grasped if it is grasped as a dimension or articulation of the distinctively human mode of life. That alternative may itself require further defence, but its availability in the writings of those he criticizes should at least have led McMahan to realize that he cannot simply assume the legitimacy of his own.

At one point, McMahan comes close to recognizing the presence of this alternative—when he speculates that I might hold that the radically cognitively impaired share in our common life simply because it is a feature of that life that we recognize them as our fellow creatures: that 'this recognition permeates the shared meanings and values that are constitutive of the common life' (OFC, 367). McMahan quickly asserts that this cannot be right: 'It would make whatever we collectively do automatically self-justifying' (OFC, 367). He then goes on to acknowledge that I claim that non-human animals are also our fellow creatures, although in a different way; and he takes this to show that a further assumption is at work in my thinking:

> Presumably on this view the strength of the moral claims that our fellow-creatures make on us varies, other things, being equal, with the degree of an individual's fellow-creatureliness; otherwise the claims of animals would be equal in strength to those of our fellow human beings. But this view has troubling implications, if we also recognize that there can be variations in the degree to which different human beings are our fellow creatures.   (OFC, 368)

McMahan cites a hypothetical African tribe whose forms of life are utterly alien to us as an example of those with a lesser degree of human fellowship: and he then goes on to argue that the radically cognitively impaired are in a similar boat, and that some non-human animals will have a claim on us that is just as strong as that made by these human beings.

Once again, however, my actual position is being run through a highly distorting filter. After all, if this interpretation of it makes it immediately self-contradictory, one might wonder whether this casts some doubt on the rectitude of the interpretation. And since I explicitly deny that the radically cognitively impaired are less our fellows than those who do not suffer that impairment, surely the logical conclusion is that I must not think that human fellowship is a matter of degree. That assumption looks obvious only to someone who thinks that human fellowship 'is a function of various different and overlapping forms of commonality and common life' (OFC, 367). But I don't think any such thing: although I do offer various reminders of the extent to which human and non-human animal forms of life overlap and interact, I don't present the fact that they too are 'needy, dependent, subject to birth and death, vulnerable to pain and fear' as independently given properties of certain creatures whose presence justifies the attribution of morally relevant fellowship. Such a mode of presentation might well justify the thought that fellowship is a matter of degree, but it's the pattern of reasoning of a moral individualist. To be sure, I happily admit that if the relevant features of that context were to change radically, then the sense of that conception of shared creatureliness would also change: but acknowledging such shifts is entirely consistent with my taking a horizontal rather than hierarchical, and an internal rather than external, view of the meaning-relations between context and concept.

My remarks are meant to be reminders of the broader context within which the conception of non-human animals as our fellow creatures has the sense it has; and they are deliberately (and, I assumed, self-evidently) couched in terms which make it clear that their significance is itself being disclosed from the point of view of that evaluatively charged conception. This is why I help myself to Shakespearean talk of 'the shocks and ills to which all flesh and blood is heir' (Does that sound like a relational property? Perhaps it does, if you think that Tolstoy's writing is a tissue of conspicuous evasion). When Cora Diamond talks in like vein of 'the sense of mystery surrounding our lives, the feeling of solidarity in mysterious origin and uncertain fate', she too is presenting the creaturely conditions of birth and death in what Rai Gaita might call the accents of pity and wonder; but of course, McMahan can make nothing of this. Having cited Diamond's remark, he asks:

> Is there a mysterious origin that all human beings...have in common that no animal shares? We all, it is true, have our origin in being born of human parents, and that is something that no animal shares. But it is neither very mysterious nor of any obvious moral significance. (OFC, 371)

Here we hit a problem of intelligibility that in my view goes very deep. On the one hand, there is a long tradition of artistic and philosophical reflection on human mortality and commonality within which complex tapestries of sense-making have been woven around the 'fact' that each of us is flesh of our mother's flesh, that our parents shape our identity in profound ways before we ever come into that identity, and can become compelling objects of attention and exploration, as well as embodiments of undismissable claims upon us, throughout our lives. Within this tradition, one might say that we keep on making and remaking our sense of their significance precisely because we know that it is inexhaustible and ultimately beyond our grasp—that our coming into being in just these circumstances as a child of just these people, each of whom provokes and resists understanding in the way any human being does, is itself something that provokes and resists understanding. And on the other hand, there is the equally recognizable mood or posture from which nothing could seem more banal or straightforward than the biological and sociological facts of human reproduction.

Cora Diamond would call this 'a difficulty of reality'.[10] By that, she means that our origins are recurrently experienced, by some people (perhaps by most people, at least some of the time) as an aspect of reality that is resistant to thought—perhaps painful, perhaps awesome and astonishing, in its inexplicability—and that its significance is tied to that resistance; but for others (perhaps the very same people at other times), the same phenomenon simply does not present such a difficulty—it does not at once provoke and resist our everyday modes of sense-making. For the latter, the very idea of a 'difficulty of reality' will remain opaque, whereas for the former it will be an indispensable way of acknowledging the most fundamental aspects of the human condition. In short, the impulse to invoke the concept of 'a difficulty of reality' is as much a difficulty of reality as any of its putative instances—one of the ways in which people can constitute an enigma to others, and to themselves. How, then, are we to establish lines of communication between these two groups of people, or between these mutually unintelligible moods or postures within a given individual? A start might be made by at least acknowledging that there is a genuine problem here.

However that may be, it's worth emphasizing that my broader discussion has the same flat and holistic methodological shape as my specific remarks about non-human animals. It aims to outline a conception of what it is to be human that is indeed to be found in the shared meanings and values that constitute our common life: but it is not the only such conception, it is not immune to change, and it is not automatically self-justifying. There are certainly other conceptions available—if there were not, we would hardly need reminding of the attractions of this one; and all of them are the possible subjects of (potentially radical) change and criticism.

---

[10] 'The Difficulty of Reality and the Difficulty of Philosophy', in A. Crary and S. Shieh (eds.), *Reading Cavell* (London: Routledge, 2006), 98–118.

To be fair to McMahan, even philosophers much more sympathetic to Diamond and Wittgensteinian moral philosophy more generally than he is have made this mistake. For example, as I point out elsewhere in *The Wounded Animal*, in a largely celebratory essay on her work (as well as that of Stanley Cavell), John McDowell seems to make an analogous error when he offers what he admittedly describes as 'a brief, and necessarily oversimplified' sketch of Diamond's attitude towards eating what she calls our fellow creatures.[11] According to McDowell, just as anyone who thought it might be alright to eat other human beings merely shows that her use of the phrase 'human being' does not express everything many of us mean by it, so 'for Diamond it is not a matter for debate whether it might be all right to eat our fellow creatures...Those who make meat eating into a philosophical topic of the usual kind just reveal that they do not mean what Diamond means by "fellow creature"' (WML, 300). In particular, it is part of what Diamond means by that term that no form of rearing non-human animals for human consumption could possibly be right.

> It should not seem to change the situation if we imagine animal husbandry being as it is depicted in a certain genre of children's stories, in which the relations between farmers and their animals are like the relations between people and domestic pets. Such stories necessarily leave unmentioned how the animals' lives end, and if one views animals as Diamond does, one would have to see sending them to be turned into food, however friendly one's previous relations with them were, as a betrayal. Factory farming...amplifies the evil of meat eating, but it is not the essential thing. (WML, 300-1)

This account of Diamond's views seems simply to accept the validity of McMahan's charge that she advances fixed or fixated and automatically self-justifying collective positions. But the account is insufficiently nuanced.

First, there is no necessary connection between being a vegetarian and believing that all ways of rearing non-human animals for food are impermissible; some vegetarians may abstain from eating meat precisely because of the particular farming methods presently used to produce it, and would rescind that abstention should those methods change. On the basis of Diamond's various discussions of the ethics of eating meat, it is far from obvious which version of vegetarianism she personally endorses; the fact that—for example—she finds philosophical illumination in J. M. Coetzee's presentation of Costello's radical hostility to eating meat

---

[11] 'Comment on Stanley Cavell's "Companionable Thinking"', in A. Crary (ed.), *Wittgenstein and the Moral Life: Essays in Honour of Cora Diamond* (Cambridge, MA: MIT Press, 2007), 299–304, at 300; hereafter WML. Both Cavell's and McDowell's essays respond to Diamond's discussion of J. M. Coetzee's character Elizabeth Costello, as presented in his *Elizabeth Costello: Eight Lessons* (London: Secker and Warburg, 2003). Chapter 5 of *The Wounded Animal* presents a version of the critique of McDowell that I here reiterate.

provides no decisive evidence either way. But suppose that McDowell is right in assuming that there are no circumstances in which Diamond would think it permissible to eat meat. Must she therefore (as McDowell appears to suggest) believe that anyone who thinks that there might be such circumstances, and wishes to discuss what they may be, either cannot regard animals as her fellow creatures, or cannot mean what Diamond herself means by that phrase?

Much in Diamond's own writing suggests that this is something like the reverse of her own view. To begin with, she illustrates what she means by regarding non-human animals as fellow creatures by quoting a de la Mare poem about a bird, without giving any indication of thinking that the meaning of the vision embodied in the poem is determinable only by establishing its author's views on eating meat. Furthermore, she elsewhere cites a poem by Jane Legge whose author deploys the genre of the nursery rhyme to bring out the implicit tension between differing aspects of our ways of relating children to animals.[12] It reminds us of our systematic use of animals in children's stories in ways which invite their recipients to identify with and value them, and juxtaposes this with our equally systematic practice of feeding the children with the flesh of those same animals. We might respond to this poem by denying the reality or extent of that tension; or we might choose to resolve it, in which case we need to determine which of the two practices should be altered, and how. But either way, the poem's value as a contribution to moral thinking presupposes the possibility of reconfiguring our existing practices, and the constellations of value they crystallize.

Another of Diamond's literary reference points—Laura Ingalls Wilder's 'Little House on the Prairie' books—offers a powerful vision of a rural American world in which human beings who treat the non-human animals surrounding them (both domesticated and wild) with compassion, dignity, respect, and even awe, in ways that naturally suggest a perception of them as 'fellow creatures'. But these people would be utterly bewildered at the suggestion that eating some of these animals would essentially betray that perception. The question of how the animals they rear for food should be treated is not only intelligible to them, but morally central to their relationship with those animals—as we see when they condemn those amongst them who treat their livestock with neglect or cruelty, or despise those who hunt for wild game in certain ways. In such a context, the difference between farming and factory farming would be essential, not amplificatory. And they certainly regard some animals as vermin, and so as treatable in ways that cows and sheep, or wolves and cougars, are not. In fact, it is precisely insofar as they relate to their animals in ways which embody such distinctions that they manifest their conception of them as fellow creatures—as each living out different

---

[12] Cited in 'Eating Meat and Eating People', in Diamond, *The Realistic Spirit* (Cambridge, MA: MIT Press, 1991), 319–34.

forms of mortal existence, and so as each relating differently to one another and to their human fellows.

To be sure, other human communities might embody different understandings of how to treat non-human creatures as our fellows; and those who are profoundly impressed by the moral claims non-human animals make upon us might find this older, rural American vision of that fellowship to be flawed or internally contradictory in certain ways. But that is precisely my, and I think Diamond's, point. The notion of non-human animals as our 'fellow creatures' is neither the repository of a single, unified sense to which anyone who grasps the notion must conform, nor a fundamentally equivocal concept which must mean something essentially different to everyone who applies it at all differently; it is rather a relatively stable locus of historically extended, thoughtful contestation (a genealogical node).

The idea of animals as our fellow creatures is certainly shared by or at least familiar to many, and has been long embedded in our thinking; but its precise range of application and its particular inflections of moral significance have been and are the subject of historical and cultural variation, and of reasonable but real disagreement. For the idea can be employed in various intelligible ways, and each such pattern of use can be comprehensibly extended (and each such extension comprehensibly contested) in various ways—extensions and contestations that differently exploit the way any such pattern of use, as embodied in a human form of life, ties together (or conflicts) with our existing and envisageable ways of employing a range of related ideas (such as 'wild animals' or 'vermin'). There is no reason to assume that any given human community's many and varied ways of thinking about and treating non-human animals across the full range of its encounters with them—even one for which the idea of 'fellow creatures' has real purchase and resonance—will interweave so tightly and coherently as to form an impregnable, monolithic whole (and no reason to view the attainment of such an airless, self-confirming, and profoundly monotonous state of affairs, entirely immune to alteration or unexpected renewals of interest, as desirable or even conceivable). Accordingly, we should expect to discover a variety of gaps, points of friction, and even of flat-out contradiction that might be utilized in order to reorient our moral imagination in a number of different ways.

This is the vision of words as imaginatively projective that emerged a little earlier in my discussion. It is utterly central to Diamond's (and to Cavell's) conception of language; and yet much of what McDowell says about Diamond's views about eating meat seems to presuppose a contrary vision—when, for example, he claims that anyone who suggests that some non-human animals might be eaten, or that some ways of treating non-human animals are worse than others, is seen thereby to reveal that they do not mean what Diamond means by 'fellow creature' (WML, 300). This seems to imply that different ways of understanding what treating non-human animals as 'fellow creatures' might or should amount to in a given context indicates that the phrase differs sharply and decisively in its meaning when employed by these two speakers—quite as if each is playing a different language-game with the same term (so that 'fellow creature' is ambiguous in the way 'bank' is ambiguous between 'money bank' and 'riverbank'). McDowell thereby risks returning Diamond into the hands of McMahan's vision of Wittgensteinian moral philosophers as necessarily presupposing a shared linguistic and moral community, and as rendered utterly impotent by the possibility of linguistic and moral disagreement.

For if McDowell's account were correct, invoking the notion of non-human animals as 'fellow creatures' would not allow Diamond and her interlocutor even to clarify the nature and extent of their moral disagreement, let alone to find a way of alleviating or overcoming it. Unless they already agree on the meaning and the essential implications of the idea of non-human animals as fellow creatures, its invocation could only underline their disagreement, showing each to be armed with a way of meaning the idea that merely reflects her own initial judgement and insulates it and her from that of her interlocutor. (In similar vein, McDowell tells us that it is only because most of us still use the phrase 'human being' in a certain way that the idea of cannibalism is not up for debate (WML, 300); so what happens if we stop using the phrase that way, or if some of us start using it differently?)

By contrast, Diamond thinks that, insofar as the idea of non-human animals as our fellow creatures makes sense to her and her interlocutor, pointing them both towards a multifarious but familiar (if often overlooked) range of thoughts, feelings, and ways of engaging with animals, it indicates a horizon within which each can make sense to the other, each can account for her own way of understanding that notion and of living out that understanding, and one might even succeed in bringing the other to see that her present way of regarding animals might bear refinement. Such an outcome is not guaranteed; but the traumatic reality of moral disagreement about such matters is difficult enough without characterizing it in terms of a vision of language which appears to remove the very possibility of enhanced understanding of one's differences, let alone that of alleviating or overcoming the disagreement.

C. Individuality and Testimony

The moral I draw from my critical evaluation of McMahan's riposte to my original discussion of his work is not that I won the argument between us: what seems much more striking to me is that we haven't so far really succeeded in having an argument at all, because as far as I can see, McMahan has not yet succeeded in properly grasping the position that I (along with other moral philosophers influenced by Wittgenstein) are defending. No doubt McMahan may also think that I haven't yet properly grasped his position: but that simply reinforces my perception that there is a systematic failure of mutual intelligibility in this domain.[13] So what I'd like to do in the remainder of this discussion of moral philosophy is attempt to find a perspective from which the nature of that failure of understanding might at least become clearer, even if it may not increase our optimism about the prospects of overcoming it. The pivotal concepts in this attempt turn out to be those of authority and revelation.

I want to begin by recalling the extent to which proponents of what McMahan calls the Wittgensteinian tradition in moral philosophy rely upon the power of examples to drive their reflections.

In Alice Crary's recent book *Inside Ethics*,[14] she offers a range of examples designed to show the moral pertinence of simply being human; and I will focus on two. One is fictional: Crary cites a novel by Daniel Keyes entitled *Flowers for Algernon*,[15] whose protagonist (Charlie Gordon) begins life with serious intellectual disabilities, undergoes a form of surgery which enhances his cognitive capacities, and then finds that these effects are merely temporary, and so suffers a rapid intellectual decline which takes him below his original mental level and results in his premature death. The novel describes one occasion before the surgery, in the bakery in which Charlie works, when he fell asleep standing up and a co-worker kicked his legs out from under him; when criticized for doing so, the co-worker dismisses it by saying that Charlie was incapable of understanding this as a form of abuse. The second is not fictional: it concerns the work of disability theorist and moral philosopher Eva Feder Kittay, who—in a range of papers—talks about her own daughter Sesha, who has cerebral palsy. In one paper she describes how Sesha was being wheeled from the bathroom back to her room in a small home where she lives, clad only in a towel, through a public corridor where young male residents and staff could encounter her; her aim is to convey to us how such an arrangement constituted a slight to Sesha's dignity without regard to whether she was in a position to experience it as such.[16] Kittay also describes an encounter with Peter Singer and Jeff McMahan, both fully aware of her daughter's condition, in which she reports the latter as repeatedly voicing his contention that it would be less bad to kill her than to kill 'one of us', and the former comparing people in similar conditions of impairment to dogs, pigs, and chimpanzees, inviting Kittay to identify the specific respects in which her

---

[13] Mark Hopwood has recently developed his own way of characterizing and attempting to overcome this impasse, which uses the concept of beauty in ways that run helpfully parallel to my own efforts, in 'Terrible Purity: Peter Singer, Harriet McBryde Johnson and the Moral Significance of the Particular', *Journal of the American Philosophical Association* 2/4 (Winter 2016), 637–55.
[14] (Cambridge, MA: Harvard University Press, 2016); hereafter IE.
[15] (New York: Harcourt Brace, 1966).
[16] 'Equality, Dignity and Disability', in Mary Ann Lyons and Fionnuala Waldron (eds.), *Perspectives on Equality* (Dublin: Liffey Press, 2005), 93–119.

daughter differed from those animals, and so merited the assignment of superior moral status.[17]

These examples are bound to remind anyone familiar with Wittgensteinian material on such questions of two examples used in various places in his work by Rai Gaita, although both have a role in his book *A Common Humanity*.[18] The first concerns a relationship Gaita describes in his earlier memoir, *Romulus, My Father*:[19] in that book he tells us how Romulus and his close friend Pantelimon Hora befriended a man named Vacek Vilkovikas, another immigrant labourer on a large construction project in Australia. A few years after arriving, Vacek—as Gaita puts it—lost his mind; he lived for a time in the hills near the Gaita home, between two boulders which he covered with branches and sheets of tin for shelter, talked constantly to himself, and sometimes cooked in his urine. Gaita declares that Vacek never seemed strange to him when he was a boy, and when reflecting on this fact later, he concludes that this was because his father and Hora had never condescended to Vacek:

> Had they condescended to him—had it shown in their tone of voice or demeanour, in their body language as we say—the cruel sensitivity children often possess would have made me conclude that Vacek was not entirely 'one of us'. As it was, the contrary was true. Their treatment of Vacek enabled me to see him, his strange behaviour notwithstanding, as living yet another form of human life. Though I learned to be wary of his offerings of food and to make other small adaptations, I accepted that it took 'his sort to make all sorts' (to borrow the fine words of D. H. Lawrence).   (CH, 2–3)

As this last phrase suggests, Gaita freely acknowledges that Vacek was recognizably leading one kind of human life: he did not bear the marks of the incurably afflicted, nor was he constantly and visibly in torment. Matters were otherwise when Gaita worked for a time in a psychiatric hospital. The patients there were judged to be incurable, and appeared to have lost everything which gives meaning to a human life; they rarely had visitors and were often treated brutishly by the staff. Some psychiatrists were different: they worked devotedly to improve their patients' conditions, and spoke resolutely of their inalienable dignity; and Gaita admired them enormously for it. Then:

> One day a nun came to the ward. In her middle years, only her vivacity made an impression on me until she talked to the patients. Then everything in her demeanour towards them—the way she spoke to them, her facial expressions,

---

[17] 'The Personal is Philosophical is Political', *Metaphilosophy* 40/3–4 (July 2009), 606–27; hereafter PPP.
[18] (London: Routledge, 2000); hereafter CH.   [19] (London: Review, 1998).

the inflexions of her body—contrasted with and showed up the behaviour of those noble psychiatrists. She showed that they were, despite their best efforts, condescending, as I too had been. She thereby revealed that even such patients were, as the psychiatrists and I had sincerely and generously professed, the equals of those who wanted to help them; but she also revealed that in our hearts we did not believe this...

I admired the psychiatrists for their many virtues—for their wisdom, their compassion, their courage, their capacity for self-sacrificing hard work and sometimes for more besides. In the nun's case, her behaviour was striking not for the virtues it expressed, or even for the good it achieved, but for its power to reveal the full humanity of those whose affliction had made their humanity invisible. Love is the name we give to such behaviour. (CH, 18–20)

The tenor of these four examples is, I hope, clear: they are intended to help us see that, with respect to those suffering profound cognitive impairment, it is not that their lack of certain attributes reduces their claim to the moral standing of fully human beings, but rather that we should respond morally to that lack in the light of their full humanity. But it is surely equally clear what the response of moral individualists is likely to be: these examples merely activate a set of powerful emotional responses that are built around our extant moral convictions, without providing any rational considerations that might justify either those convictions or the affective states they facilitate. In other words, this set of exchanges between moral individualists and their critics threatens to devolve into a face-off between mutually uncomprehending positions, a dialogue of the deaf.

In my view, appreciating why this disagreement is so hard to move beyond will ultimately depend on paying attention to the form of the examples that these critics of moral individualism are drawn to: in particular, to the form in which they are presented to us. But I want to begin by looking more closely at their content, for certain details in these examples not only help us to see more clearly exactly what the idea of 'full humanity' invoked by the critics of moral individualism might amount to, but will also prove important when I broach issues of form a little further down the line. In doing so, I will look most closely at Gaita's work, since it offers a more extensive and systematic elaboration of the idea of 'full humanity' than does that of Crary (or indeed, Diamond); but I do not thereby mean to suggest that Diamond or Crary explicitly endorses every aspect of Gaita's particular stance.

The specific issue that is most clearly highlighted in all four examples is the suggestion that severely cognitively impaired people can suffer serious harm when their full humanity is not respected by other human beings, even if they are not in a position to appreciate that this harm has been done. In other words, regarding them in the light of their full humanity is partly constituted by regarding them as fully capable not just of being wronged by others, but also of being wronged in ways that strike just as deeply as they would if directed at those who lack such impairments. Crary goes further: she thinks that, in the case of Charlie Gordon, 'far from being mitigated by [his] intellectual disability, the injury... inflict[ed] on him is exacerbated by the fact that Charlie doesn't register that he is being hurt and so isn't in a position to defend himself' (IE, 138).

Gaita makes an analogous point, and develops it in a way which activates a broader range of issues concerning good and evil in human life. What he variously calls the full humanity, the inalienable preciousness or dignity of every human being, the unconditional respect that is owed to them regardless of their physical, mental, social, or moral state, or of the obstacle they may constitute to our pursuit even of morally worthy ends—this is something that he thinks we may well only come to appreciate fully in the light of a soberly remorseful contemplation of what we have done if and when we fail so to respect them. But Gaita points out that the unconditional nature of the moral standing possessed by the victims of evil-doing simply in virtue of their humanity must also be possessed by those who inflicted this evil. This is what grounds his perception that justice is owed even to the most radically evil, that (as Gaita almost puts it) not even those who have destroyed others in the spirit of ridding the world of vermin should themselves be destroyed in that spirit; and this perception is in part made manifest in the conviction that even *they* are not beyond the reach of a sober remorse—not essentially incapable of coming to realize the evil that they did by confronting the reality of the individuals they wronged.

In this sense, the standing possibility of remorse reveals in an exceptionally powerful way the peculiarly precious individuality of both victim and victimizer— that of the former being manifest in her vulnerability to evil as well as in her capacity to haunt her victimizer, the latter manifest in her ability not only to do evil but also to be haunted by those to whom that evil was done. This angle of approach reveals an understanding of human beings as individuals precisely insofar as they can (and so they must not) have evil done to them, and must not (although they can) do evil to others. For only beings who can suffer, beyond any particular harm done to them, from its being done by a fellow human being in the spirit of denigration or contempt, and who can suffer from the fact that, beyond any particular harm they inflicted on a fellow human being, they did so in a spirit of denigration or contempt, are beings whose individuality manifests moral depth or texture of the kind with which Gaita is concerned—the kind which can claim our unconditional respect.

The second detail I want to pick up is most evident in Eva Kittay's paper; and it comes out when she questions whether Singer and McMahan know what they mean when they speak of a group they call 'the severely mentally retarded' or 'the radically cognitively impaired'. Her point here does not have to do with the potentially offensive tenor of some of these labels; it concerns their assumption that the members of that group can unproblematically be regarded as effectively in the same condition. Kittay knows from personal experience with members of such groups that 'each human with a severe impairment is impaired after [his or her] own fashion' (PPP, 615). So, since she knows from experience that her daughter has a strong love of music, she knows that McMahan is just wrong to claim that the severely cognitively impaired are incapable of aesthetic pleasure. More importantly for my purposes, she also knows from experience that she does not know the full extent of Sesha's limitations.

> I am often surprised to find out that Sesha has understood something or is capable of something I did not expect. These surprises keep coming when she and her friends are treated in a manner based not on the limitations we know they have but on our understanding that *our* knowledge is limited. If my daughter's housemates had not been told of their father's death on the premise that they cannot possibly understand the concept of death, we never would have known that they could have a grief as full and as profound as any I have seen or experienced. (PPP, 619)

This passage brings out what one might call (adapting Kant) the reflective as opposed to the determinant dimension of properly sensitive moral evaluation: rather than subsuming particular cases under prior principles and categories, we have to be willing to allow what is disclosed by careful attention to the particular person and situation in front of us to inform (hence to revise and refine) such general understanding as we can claim to possess. And part of this willingness to prioritize the particular is a willingness to acknowledge that other people are inherently capable of surprising us.

In Sesha's case, this is essentially a capacity to reveal unsuspected reaches and depths in her engagement with the world, and so to reveal unsuspected limitations and opacities even in those who have engaged with her in a genuinely loving spirit; but there is an analogous feature in the case of Gaita's nun. For her presence in the hospital, and the spirit in which she engages with its patients, radically revises Gaita's existing moral understanding of the place. Prior to her arrival, he had recognized the brutish inadequacy of the attitudes of the hospital staff, in part by contrast with the stance of the small group of devoted psychiatrists; these were the only two moral possibilities, and it was clear which was to be preferred. Suddenly, however, this genuinely attractive moral stance comes to seem profoundly limited, and is shown to be so by the revelation of another such stance that neighbours it, previously unimagined and apparently unimaginable but now undeniably attainable because beyond all question already attained by another. And this disclosure also discloses the extent to which Gaita's previous grasp of a range of morally pertinent terms—goodness, love, life—was shallow and impoverished; it induces the signature Socratic realization that he had hitherto understood so little of what those terms might mean, and so of the reality they aspire to disclose.

One direction leading off from this feature of the story of the nun would take us towards what Stanley Cavell calls moral perfectionism, conceived of as a dimension of the moral life without any elitist presuppositions, and without which moral theories—whether consequentialist, deontological, or Aristotelian—would suffer profound damage.[20] I will return to this theme in the other essays that make up this book. But in the present context I want to go in another, not entirely unrelated, direction, and connect it with Gaita's Wittgensteinian background— more specifically, with an apparently rather different issue in Wittgenstein scholarship concerning how best to envisage what is involved in being the kind of creature whose form of life is linguistic.

On one very familiar reading of Wittgenstein's later writings, our actual, everyday uses of words are not simply to be compared with (and hence recognized as essentially distinct from) the uses of words in deliberately simplified, imaginatively constructed language-games, but are rather to be understood as themselves language-games, or at least as sets or arrays of language-games. On this account, ordinary language for Wittgenstein is actually composed of, and so analytically separable into, a very large number of language-games with words: they comprise the basic units or building blocks of language, and hence of linguistic competence—not a philosopher's artefact, but rather the *heimat* of our words, our haven from metaphysics. On another reading, however—one primarily associated with Rush Rhees—such a picture of language would actually undermine Wittgenstein's conception of what it is to be a speaker. For speakers are potential conversers, possible participants in conversations; but if understanding the meanings of words really were exhausted by grasping rules for their use, if words were equivalent to pieces in board-games, then they could not form the medium of conversational exchanges.[21]

Understanding how to converse—how to follow the development of a conversation, how to make a pertinent or telling contribution to it, how to redirect its focus, how to acknowledge the relevance of another's contribution without agreeing with it, how to recognize when it has reached a dead end or when a little further persistence will bring it to an illuminating resting-place—understanding all this is not something that can be reduced to the application of a body of rules, or fruitfully compared with learning how to make moves in a game. According to Rhees, this kind of understanding is essentially responsive both to the subject matter of the conversation and to the individual contributions of those participating in it; but moves in chess do not have a subject matter, and do not give any individual player the logical room to give expression to what they bring to a game from their experience outside it. If being able to speak involves being able to

---

[20] Cf. his *Cities of Words* (Cambridge, MA: Harvard University Press, 2004).
[21] Cf. his *Wittgenstein and the Possibility of Discourse*, ed. D. Z. Phillips (Cambridge: Cambridge University Press, 1998).

converse, then it cannot just be a matter of applying words in accordance with criteria, of making linguistic moves, or of doing things with words.

Putting Rhees's suggestion otherwise, we might say that conversations display both unity and diversity. What makes a conversation a single or continuous thing (both synchronically and diachronically) is the participants' common and sustained orientation towards a particular topic or subject matter (or a set or interlinked chain of such topics); what makes it a conversation as opposed to a collective monologue is the distinctive perspective that each participant brings to bear upon its subject matter. For the contribution that each speaker makes to the conversation will reflect not only the particularity of her own experience of the world, but also the distinctive array of knowledge (as well as the distinctive modes of its acquisition) that she has thereby acquired or mastered. Think, for instance, of the ways in which an employee of a logistics business, a Greenpeace member, and an internet entrepreneur might contribute to a conversation about government efforts to shift the distribution of goods from road to rail.

Consequently, the capacity to converse hangs together with the possibility of growth in one's understanding, both of the specific subject-matter and of reality more generally: one might learn not only pertinent facts of which one was previously unaware, but also come to appreciate how the various dimensions or aspects of a topic relate to one another, and thereby attain a deeper understanding of how that topic relates to other topics, and how and why one person might see those internal and external relations differently from another. Such an enhanced understanding would manifest itself, amongst other ways, in an enhanced ability to converse with others, since it would partly be constituted by a deeper grasp of how different individuals might bring their experience and competences to a particular conversation, and how one might best engage with what they have to say with a view to understanding it better and perhaps convincing them to see things otherwise. For a speaker to be a potential conversation partner is thus for them to have something to say (something genuinely responsive both to the reality of the subject matter and to the particular perspectives and concerns of one's conversation partners) and something of their own to say (something each is prepared to stand behind, to own rather than to disown—something through which each stakes and declares herself).

This is already enough to suggest that, on this way of inheriting Wittgenstein's (and so perhaps Austin's) vision of the nature of speech, the methods of ordinary-language philosophy have an ineliminably moral or spiritual dimension—inviting and requiring us to confront the cares and commitments of our standing as fellow speakers. But in the present context, I want to emphasize the relevance of this conception of speakers as conversers to the case of Gaita's nun; for it seems fair to say that Gaita and the nun are in effect conversing silently with one another about the hospital patients. It is not just that, in the light of the nun's example, the patients reveal hitherto-unsuspected depths of moral significance to this young hospital helper; what makes it possible for them to do so is the nun's capacity to bring the whole of her experience and individuality to bear on her relations with the patients and her fellow helpers, in such a way as to make undeniable—to show—a hitherto-unrealized perspective on what they are doing and with whom they are doing it. To put it another way: Gaita is surprised—more accurately, stunned—not just by the revelation of the full humanity of the patients (as intelligible beneficiaries of someone's clear-sighted love, just as Sesha is so revealed in the light of her mother's clear-sighted love), but also by the revelatory capacities of human interaction and interlocution as exemplified by the nun.

There is thus an internal relation between acknowledging the full individuality of our fellow human beings and viewing them as potential participants in a conversation. To think of another as a fellow speaker is in crucial part to think of her as capable of bringing her individuality to bear in her contributions to our attempts to grow in our understanding of the world around us (including the people with whom we share it), and so as someone capable of revealing our current understanding of that world to be shallow and impoverished. To have the capacity to surprise one's interlocutors in such ways, ways which depend upon the authoritative marshalling in speech and action of one's individuating responsiveness to the world is thus at the heart of the conception of full humanity, as Gaita and others conceive of it. To be human is to be part of a community that contains fellow human beings who are capable of such revelatory disclosures of self, other, and world; it is to participate in what Gaita calls the realm of meaning—the realm in which the question of the meaning of life, and of one's own life, arises or is avoided; in which some have a deep or rich inner life and others lack it; in which we can betray our past or make a mockery of it, or strive not to do so.

The relevance of conversation as 'a centre of variation' (that is, a specific phenomenon around which other related phenomena can be illuminatingly grouped or organized, an object of comparison or a lens through which certain otherwise-neglected aspects of the relevant phenomena come into clear focus, even if others may thereby go out of focus, here and now) is proved as much by the incidence of conversations that go nowhere, break down, or never find a mutually intelligible starting-point, as it is by those which fulfil the highest hopes of their participants. For it is only potential conversation partners that can become embroiled in conversations that go nowhere or break down or never get started; only those essentially capable of successful interlocution are capable of failing to do so on any particular occasion, in any of a multitude of ways. The critical point is that dialogical intercourse is a standing possibility, and as clearly revealed as such in its failures as in its successes—one might call it the horizon within which our lives with language are lived.

One might think—McMahan plainly would think—that such a strong or substantial conception of what it is to be fully human only supports the view of the moral individualists, since it seems merely to widen and deepen the gap between those of us at least capable of relating to our lives in such terms and those essentially incapable of so doing. That would amount to treating 'the capacity to be a conversation partner' as a candidate criterion for a morally relevant individual characteristic. Since, however, applying that criterion would only restrict the community of human beings with fully-fledged moral standing even further than it is by the criteria moral individualists standardly employ, the idea that this is the spirit in which Gaita's claims are meant to be taken is patently absurd; it would require us to assume that he is incapable of grasping an immediate, central (and self-undermining) implication of his own view.

There is an analogy here with the debate between Richard Hare and Iris Murdoch over the question of whether one should view morality through the lens of choice or of vision—as a matter of each individual's freedom to choose which principles to live by, or as a matter of our struggles to see more clearly the way things really are in the world and with other people. When Murdoch advocates her morality of vision, it is always open to Hare to say that he can fully accommodate her view within his morality of choice, by treating it as one view that anyone is free to choose; but in so doing, he patently and absurdly fails to appreciate that any such treatment amounts to failing to take that view seriously (since part of its content is a rejection of the primacy of choice).

In the case of Gaita, there is a further problem with such an individualist reinterpretation of his stance—one which overlaps with the second issue I touched on earlier when highlighting McMahan's willingness to reach for the notion of Martian moral agents. For Gaita's idea of dialogical intercourse is not just a horizon inhabited solely by those with the capacity to be fully-fledged conversation partners; it is also the horizon *within which* such people respond to those who lack that capacity, and respond to them as no less our human fellows simply because they have suffered impairments that might equally easily have befallen us. In other words, appreciating that our fellowship with the severely cognitively impaired is not itself impaired by their condition is one of the revelations that the unimpaired (and the impaired—remember Sasha's grief) can and do effect within that horizon. It is precisely the exercise of capacities that some of us lack (exercises often prompted by encounters with those who lack that capacity) that reveals the moral irrelevance of that lack. And here we find ourselves confronting the formal feature of my chosen examples that I earlier promised would prove pivotal.

Without exactly acknowledging the fact, our discussion has shifted from the significance of Sesha's capacity to surprise her mother to the significance of the nun's capacity to surprise Gaita; otherwise put, I have been exploring and exploiting a parallel between what the nun reveals about the hospital patients and how she reveals it—between the stunning disclosure of the patients' full humanity, and the equally stunning capacity of one human being to effect such disclosures on another. In effect, then, our analysis has already shifted from the level of content to that of form—from investigating what the anti-individualists' vision of full humanity consists in to identifying the way in which they present themselves as having gained access to that vision, and the way in which they grant us access to it.

The crucial point to notice in this respect is that all four examples share a triangular structure: in every case, the philosophical critic's relation to the person or persons whose moral standing is at issue is mediated by a third person. In Crary's examples, she encounters Charlie through the words of Daniel Keyes, and Sesha through the words of Eva Feder Kittay; for Gaita, his relation to Vacek is mediated through his father (and Hora), and his relation to the psychiatric patients through the nun. In each instance, the moral status of a profoundly cognitively impaired person is disclosed, not directly, but by another person's individuating responsiveness to them, which the philosopher regards as morally authoritative; the text through which that responsiveness is evoked is thus a declaration on the part of the philosopher that he or she does so regard that other person—it is, in short, an act of testifying or bearing witness to that authority. And Gaita makes this point explicit:

> [A]s someone who was witness to the nun's love and is claimed in fidelity to it, I have no understanding of what it revealed independently of the quality of her love. If I am asked what I mean when I say that even such people... are fully our equals, I can only say that the quality of her love proved that they are rightly the objects of our non-condescending treatment, that we should do all in our power to respond in that way. But if someone were now to ask me what informs my sense that they are *rightly* the objects of such treatment, I can appeal only to the purity of her love. For me, the purity of the love proved the reality of what it revealed. I have to say 'for me', because one must speak personally about such matters. That after all is the nature of witness. (CH, 21–2)

In other words, it is the nun's incarnation of her moral vision that not only reveals a new dimension of moral significance in human life but also authorizes it. The rightness of her vision is justified by the purity of her love; or more precisely, Gaita's conviction of its purity rules out for him any speculation about whether it was justified. That is why he talks of being claimed in fidelity to her love: he has to speak personally because that is the nature of witness, and the only pertinent mode of authority or authorization here is that which attends an encounter with a particular other, the kind to which one can testify.

And of course, the notion of testimony or witness has a further, reflexive application in this context. For if Gaita is testifying to the nun's authority, then the testimony he gives invites, or rather compels, those to whom it is given either to testify to it in turn or to decline to do so. Each of his readers must judge whether Gaita's recounting of his encounter with this vision of goodness beyond virtue in the person of the nun is itself authoritative for him or her—something that claims us in fidelity to it, hence to him and to the nun. This places us in a very distinctive (although perfectly familiar) evaluative relation to the author we are reading: we must evaluate his authority, just as he evaluated the authority of the nun, and we must each do it for ourselves. This leaves us very exposed: there are no impersonally available standards or principles—no canons of argument, no algorithms, no objectively established list of criteria—onto which we can slough our responsibility. And it likewise places enormous pressure on the witness's own speech, his or her mastery of language: in order to testify authoritatively to the nun's authoritative witness to the full humanity of the patients, Gaita must find and deploy a language through which her vision and its (and her) authority might be compellingly disclosed to his readers.

The centrality of this obligation helps to explain why this group of philosophical critics tend to invoke literary or fictional examples as readily as real ones, and why Eva Kittay at one point declares that—in order to convey her perception of what it is to be human—'you need a *very good writer*' (PPP, 621); for literary texts live or die on the authority that its authors are able to claim in relation to their readers, so such authors confront this challenge in everything they do, and the successful ones will constitute a ready source of authoritative human speech (and an essential one if you doubt your own capacity to find authoritative words for your perception).

But Gaita faces a particular difficulty in fulfilling this obligation in the case of the nun; for her perception of the patients as fully her equals at once draws on and revivifies the inherited resource of a religious language of love for all God's children, and Gaita did not and does not share the nun's faith. So he has to find a non-religious language in terms of which to articulate her theologically informed perception, one which acknowledges its religious roots but which can be honestly deployed by the non-religious without sacrificing the specificity of her vision (and so running the risk of breaking faith with what it disclosed). And given our genealogical interest in the ascetic ideal, it might be worth exploring further whether what Gaita wants to say really can be said with the necessary authority without invoking the specifically religious forms of the language of love—whether it is simply an accident of history and culture that, when attempting to capture the preciousness of human individuals, ' "sacred" is so much better', so much less precious, a word than 'precious'.[22] This will help us to evaluate more concretely Nietzsche's suspicion of the genealogical dependence of putatively non-religious moral stances upon their religious predecessors, and so his critique of secular defenders of the ascetic ideal in morality.

---

[22] Gaita, *Good and Evil: An Absolute Conception* (rev. edn., London: Routledge, 2004), p. xxvi; this revised edition of his first book contains a new preface which reflects on the original edition's strengths and weaknesses. All page references to this work will be to GE.

D. Border Territory: The Ethico-Religious

In the 2004 Preface to *Good and Evil*, Gaita offers this comment on the strengths and weakness of the word 'sacred' for his purposes:

> 'Sacred' is a word whose elaboration points in two directions—to theological and metaphysical doctrine, and to the language of love. Philosophers, especially bioethicists, have tended to focus on the doctrine. As a result there is little philosophical writing that is inward with the kind of experiences that incline someone to be sympathetic to talk of the sanctity of human life, even if they feel they cannot speak that way themselves... If one is not to distort the significance of the fact that the language is richly anthropomorphic, one must listen to it with patient sympathy. (GE, pp. xxvi–xxvii)

Gaita is here drawing attention to what he elsewhere calls the age-old distinction between the God of the philosophers and the God of religion.

> The God of the philosophers is a metaphysical entity whose properties, if not His existence, are given to reason... idealized as operating perfectly when it is free of the disturbances of practical and affective human living. The God of religion, on the other hand, is defined by the requirement that belief in him must deepen our ordinary human understanding of what matters in life... religious claims are always made fully in the realm of meaning. Metaphysical claims... are most clear-sightedly made when one sees the world as from no place within it. Or so their proponents believe.[23]

Gaita plainly, and rightly, believes that anyone who thinks that the nun's way of employing and living out her conception of her patients as children of God either supports, or is itself in need of support from, a set of metaphysical doctrines concerning the God of the philosophers will necessarily fail to grasp the real religious meaning of her words and deeds. Call this the moral individualist conception of how rational religious belief must be structured. If we reject it, however, what response can and should Gaita offer to those, such as Stanley Hauerwas, who grant that one can testify to the rightness of the nun's demeanour without thinking that it had to be underwritten metaphysically, but who nevertheless asks whether her behaviour would have been possible were it not for the history of religious practice in which her vocation takes its place?

Hauerwas is trying to raise the question of whether the living reality of secular versions of the language of love is even now dependent on the continued vivacity

---

[23] *The Philosopher's Dog* (Melbourne, Australia: Text Publishing, 2002), 135.

of religious versions of that language. Gaita freely admits that its secular variants are historically dependent on their religious originals; but if the forms of life that presently sustain religious practices of the relevant kind were to disappear permanently, how, if at all, would secular variants of its conceptions survive? This line of thought is what drives the recent work of philosophers such as Charles Taylor, who queries the adequacy of secular moral sources for the task of maintaining our present (and from a naturalistic point of view, exorbitant) moral commitments to those in need, and who also doubts whether the historical shift from religious to secular forms of moral thinking was based on a compelling critical evaluation of the stance from which it departed.[24] Here, Taylor's conception of practical reasoning as a reasoning in transitions is relevant: for it reminds us that what, from one point of view appears as a successful separation of the viable essence of a form of moral thinking from its unacceptable excesses, will appear from the other as the excision of utterly vital articulations of that essence.[25]

The point can be put in terms that might be more congenial to Gaita himself. *Good and Evil* is basically in conversation with other secular points of view on moral matters, and aspires to show the continuing attractions of its absolute conception of good and evil in the light of objections and difficulties raised from secular perspectives in general, let alone specifically Nietzschean ones. This is hardly a small or insignificant task, and it might well reflect a realistic assessment of where the centre of gravity of our present culture's moral thinking is located. But as a consequence, the book barely begins to converse with the religious variants of the secular perspective from out of which it speaks, despite the fact that its perspective grew out of that religious tradition or traditions, and draws in various ways upon its language and literature. Hauerwas might be seen as extending an invitation to begin that conversation; but Gaita's actual response seems to suggest a certain unwillingness to accept it.

> That history [of religious practice] is a mixture of doctrine and practice expressed in the language of love—a complex history of the relations between the God of the philosophers and the God of religion. But now, abstract the God of the philosophers from the God of religion. What do we have? Oversimplifying a little, but not I think at the expense of the point, we have God's gratuitous love for his creatures. It now looks as though to say that we are sacred because God loves us provides no reason for believing that the kind of compassion the nun showed... is rationally intelligible. External to human life and activity the love of God may be, but unless the way it is external provides such a reason, it seems not to do what is needed for someone who believes the rightness of the

---

[24] See his *Sources of the Self* (Cambridge, MA: Harvard University Press, 1989).
[25] See 'Explanation and Practical Reason', in his *Philosophical Arguments* (Cambridge, MA: Harvard University Press, 1995), 34–60.

nun's behaviour is insufficiently accounted for unless there is reference to God or to the metaphysical properties of the patients... Nothing that can be said about human beings—about their natural or their metaphysical properties—could ground it, in the sense of providing rational foundation for it. It cannot even make it less offensive to reason. How is God's gratuitous love for his creatures different? (GE, p. xxviii)

This response is bewildering, because it seems to pass over or repress the fact that Hauerwas's question is predicated on *accepting* Gaita's point that the God of the philosophers is not needed to underwrite the God of religion. Gaita's answer to that question appears to assume that invocations of God's love would be worth making only if they provided an external rational foundation for viewing human beings as sacred. But to interpret the religious language of love in such terms (as necessarily aspiring to locate a natural or metaphysical property of human beings, or the world they inhabit or the creator of that world) is precisely to take it as invoking the God of the philosophers rather than the God of religion—the very dimension or aspect of the history of religious practice from which Gaita begins by claiming to have abstracted. After all, if the God of religion fully inhabits the realm of meaning, then His invocation in the nun's discourse is surely best understood as an attempt to elaborate further upon the full significance of her talk of human beings as sacred—that is, as a clarificatory move within the realm of meaning rather than an attempt to invoke something independent of it that might ground any particular stance within that realm.

The same is surely true of what Gaita refers to as the dimension of doctrine in the history of religious practice. For whilst certain theological accounts of religious belief are couched in what both Gaita and I would regard as damagingly metaphysical terms, and so amount to reconstructions of the God of religion as the God of the philosophers, others are better understood as more systematic elaborations of the practice-based religious language whose distinctive forms (and forms of obscurity) initially prompts them—that is, as further moves in the realm of meaning, within which both Gaita and Nietzsche locate religion. Religious and theological talk of God's love as gratuitous, and even as external, may be given a metaphysical turn; but if those invocations of gratuitousness and externality can be elaborated and clarified in ways that can claim to grow out of and to transform our ordinary human understanding of what matters in life in ways whose exemplary instantiations claim us with authority, then even the doctrinal dimension of talk of 'sacredness' is better thought of as essentially a further range or reach of the religious language of love.

These seem to me to be significant limitations in the patient sympathy with which Gaita tries to attend to religious forms of the language of love, notwithstanding the many other ways in which he succeeds in making human sense of its work. But one might take his reference to the 'richly anthropomorphic' quality of that language as carrying a different, if more implicit, message: namely, that such sense as can presently be made of religious forms of the language of love (whether practical or theological) can be captured without significant remainder in its secular variants. So taken, the following question inevitably arises: what, if anything, might a religious believer take Gaita's conception of the inalienable preciousness of every human being to lack or miss in comparison with a conception of human beings as sacred? What is the difference between love and God's love?

As we have seen, Gaita identifies three interrelated features as distinguishing the transfiguration wrought upon the non-reductively naturalistic conception of individuality by the work of saintly love. These were: the revelation that such individuality was not forfeited by the afflicted or the radically evil; the radical singularity of victim and victimizer as revealed by remorse or guilt; and a qualitatively distinct conception of evil beyond vice.

So the first thing a religious believer like the nun might say is that, at the very least, her tradition provides the resources for a uniquely thoroughgoing acknowledgement of all three features. The parable of the Good Samaritan, the conception of all human beings as our neighbours that it embodies and that was put into practice in Christ's ministry amongst the despised and the outcast, provides an endlessly demanding and essentially non-excluding conception of who counts as our fellow human beings. The tale of Abraham and Isaac presses its vision of the radical singularity of the individual in his relation to God to an extreme, with Isaac's individuality presented as embodying the irreplaceable future of God's people as a whole, and Abraham finding himself placed beyond the reach of morality, reason, and language by the claim God's words exercise over him. And the distinctively Christian doctrine of original sinfulness helps to constitute and reveal a conception of the human capacity for evil that outstrips any of its secular counterparts in critical force.

Our religious believer might further say that Christianity faces up to an aspect of these features with which Gaita seems uncomfortable—namely their mysteriousness (what Diamond would view as their embodiment of a difficulty of reality). By this, I do not simply mean that the conception which embodies them neither has nor needs any rational or metaphysical foundation; nor that it goes beyond anything necessitated by the features of human life from which it grows; nor even that it is unnatural, in the sense that its claims on us run counter to aspects of our character and inclinations as rational animals that appear both obvious and fundamental even from the perspective of a non-reductive naturalism. These are points that Gaita repeatedly makes about the works of saintly love, even in its secular variants, both in the first edition of his book and in his 2004 Preface to it. But in that Preface, he expresses an anxiety about his previous willingness to use the term 'mystery' in these contexts, and he explains his reasons for it in a very helpful way:

I now regret using the expression 'ethical other-worldliness'. It sounds either too religious or too theoretically formidable. For the same reason I regret talking of mystery, even though I distinguish between things that are contingently and things that are necessarily mysterious. The latter are not mysterious to us because our epistemic or other cognitive powers are limited. But mystery is a word with much baggage, most of which I prefer not to carry. I should have been content to characterize the wondrousness of saintly love—to mark its conceptual features, to locate it in a sympathetic conceptual space and to leave it at that. Because I went further, some readers may feel that I did so in order to establish a further thesis— that there are deep mysteries for deep people to marvel at. (GE, pp. xxx–xxxi)

The religious believer may well feel, by contrast, that Gaita's initial willingness to employ the term was well grounded, precisely because if he had refrained from characterizing the wondrousness of genuinely saintly love as necessarily rather than contingently mysterious, he would not have properly or fully marked its conceptual features. Take evil as expressed in the doctrine of original sinfulness, for example: rather than viewing that doctrine as an attempt to provide a deep metaphysical explanation for deep people, we might rather view it as marking the presence of a capacity for evil-doing that runs so deeply in our nature as to defy comprehension, and that makes the bare possibility of an absolute goodness that can acknowledge such evil without responding to it in ways simply that further that evil equally resistant to our understanding. To talk of these aspects of human life in terms of God's love and our refusal of it is precisely not to attempt to account for them, but rather to characterize them as essentially beyond any such accounting.

It will appear as no accident to the religious believer that Gaita addresses the notion of mystery in close proximity to that of ethical other-worldliness; for part of what ties together the three mysterious features of the transfigured conception of human individuality in Christian thought is Christ's exemplary act of self-renunciation on the cross. Gaita makes it clear in *Good and Evil* that what helps to distinguish Socrates' conception of good and evil even from its Aristotelian rival, and to ally it with the works of saintly love, is the ethic of renunciation that lies at its heart, and that finds expression in Socrates' three famous, interrelated claims: that the good man cannot be harmed, that evil is always done out of ignorance, and that it is always better to suffer evil than to do it. As it happens, Gaita expresses some reservations about the Socratic position: whilst recognizing the attractions of the position it stakes out beyond any non-reductive naturalism, and perceiving that it depends upon acknowledging that what counts as a significant harm (and in particular, what kind of harm one does to oneself in doing evil) depends critically upon the conception of good and evil one espouses, he ultimately rejects the thought that every temptation to do what one knows to be wrong will, upon a proper understanding of its nature, be rendered not only deliberatively but also motivationally impotent. For such a view posits a vision of the soul's capacity to unify itself that is, he thinks, conceptually rather than psychologically awry:

> What 'counts for nothing' deliberatively will always 'count for nothing' motivationally only if our attachments to one another do not threaten 'the requirements of virtue' when they conflict with it.
>
> The sufferings which lead us into temptation are often connected with our deepest loves, and these determine our self-understanding, not merely as 'human all-too-human', but just as human. They are connected with the sense our lives make for us and they condition the unique kind of individuality that I have argued is fundamental to what is disclosed in remorse. The question then is not whether knowledge can overcome weakness... but whether there are not deep and irreconcilable tensions between the requirements of morality and what conditions those requirements. Those who have felt the full force of this question have either tied themselves to the mast or spoken of detachment from the world.
> (GE, 238–9)

That wonderful final sentence carries the faint implication that invocations of 'detachment from the world' risk being empty, mere talk, and that the only serious moral option here is a sober, realistic acknowledgement of the limits of one's nature as a rational animal—a resort to earplugs and rope. But this would seem to imply that the other-worldly ethic of renunciation that distinguishes Socrates from Aristotle, and so marks the boundary at which saintly love begins to do its transfigurative work, cannot ultimately be taken as fully, humanly serious—that it is erected on a conceptual confusion concerning the extent to which moral claims can disavow the conditions of their own possibility, the natural roots from which they grow. By contrast, the religious believer will say that her religious language of love creates the conceptual space in which one can not only talk of detachment from the world but also mean it, stand behind it, precisely insofar as it conceptualizes the capacity for such radical self-renunciation as an effect of God's grace, as a miraculous transfiguration of originally sinful human nature; and of course, that moment of renunciation is always already matched and countered by a return of the world on transfigured terms, as Abraham receives his only son back again. Here is a way of inviting us to move from Odysseus' condition to that of Kierkegaard's knight of infinite resignation, and then to that of his knight of faith, who alone can fully see the sublime in the pedestrian.

Thus far, I have focused on identifying ways in which the religious language of love might be thought of as deploying articulations and elaborations that intensify, extend, and so deepen the emphases it shares with its secular variants. But there is another way of attempting to grasp the difference between talk of love and talk of God's love—a way that Kierkegaard's discussion of Adler gestures towards, and that Cora Diamond has recently developed in attempting to comprehend Wittgenstein's obscure remarks about the indispensability of a picture or pictures in the life of a religious believer.[26]

Diamond's suggestion is that we can see one and the same particular mode of life and thought in two different ways: either as one in which a picture is used, but not essentially, or as one in which the use of the picture is essential. Her primary example is of the centrality of the belief that God has a name to a certain tradition of Judaic thought. Diamond connects this belief to the particular significance we attach to the individuality of those human beings we love or care for, our sense that their significance is unique and irreplaceable, and so not capturable in any general or conceptual terms (say, by reference to their distinguishing characteristics). This conception might include a recognition of the ways in which an encounter with a particular person might transform our concepts—as George Eliot, whom Henry James described as that magnificently ugly woman, might give a totally transformed meaning to the term 'beauty'. She shows the concept up, moving us to use it almost as a new word, certainly as a renewed one.

Diamond suggests that part of the importance of the idea of God as having a name lies in the sense that his revelation of himself to us in his doings reorients our concept of 'divinity' in a parallel way. This God, through his actions, converts or gives a transformed content to the word 'God', so that it now functions as a proper name (rather than, say, as a general term for the property of divinity); but he also provides more generally the converted terms without which those who encounter God's self-revelation could not understand the kind of conduct or responsiveness demanded of them. In other words, the use by the believer of that language involves trust in the God who provided it for him; all that authorizes, say, characterizing the scattering of the people of Israel as God's action is the fact of God's having said that it is (via his prophets). And of course, such an account is plainly circular, in that it explains how we can use such anthropomorphic language in speaking of God in terms of how he chooses to make himself available to us.

In other words, the picture-language is used in describing the picture-language; and from the point of view of the believer, unless it is so used, our description of his anthropomorphic picture-language will not adequately capture its essential nature (as a transfiguration of our ordinary uses of such language revealed to us by the very object it allows us to encounter). In this sense, one might say that the picture lies at the very base of all his thinking, in that the picture is inescapably involved in any description which he can acknowledge as describing his use of words, his life with those words. And if we respond by asking what, in his religious uses of language, counts as God's having spoken or revealed himself in such ways,

---

[26] See her 'Wittgenstein on Religious Belief: The Gulfs Between Us', in D. Z. Phillips and M. von der Ruhr (eds.), *Religion and Wittgenstein's Legacy* (London: Ashgate, 2005), 99–138.

the believer might respond to this as a way of delivering God's speech acts and activities into our hands, thereby attempting to constrain his actions by reference to our linguistic conventions—when the very point of his belief in God as having revealed himself to us is rather to remain open to the possibility that in doing so he will transfigure all the concepts in terms of which we can acknowledge and respond to his claims upon us.

We don't, of course, have to accept the religious believer's conception of what is essential to his language; we might rather view the pictures that he sees as indispensable to it as essentially dispensable, for example as merely local variations on a recognizably general set of religious forms of speech whose basic lineaments could be captured without using those pictures. But we must then accept that we have not captured the essence of his life with those words as he understands it.

The pertinence of these reflections to Gaita's relation to religious forms of the language of love is, I hope, clear. For where Gaita's patient, sympathetic attention to the richly anthropomorphic language of religious faith appears to see certain limits on the extent to which that language can transfigure the terms of ordinary human understanding of the meaning of life—by, for example, finding the ethical substance of the notion of God's children in our understanding of a parent's love for her child—Diamond finds that the religious conception of God as bearer of a name draws on one familiar aspect of our notion of human individuality (a person's capacity to transfigure our understanding of a concept) in order to capture a more drastic and wide-ranging sense in which familiar anthropomorphic terms undergo a conversion of meaning in religious contexts. Diamond's vision is thus very close to Gaita, insofar as her notion of the conversion of concepts in the shock of a personal encounter exploits one way in which Gaita himself attempts to illustrate the alterity of other individuals (their capacity to surprise us, to turn our understanding of them, of ourselves and of the world around us, upside down); and yet it is also radically distant from it, insofar as she finds in the revelatory religions of the Book a conception of God as instantiating that kind of radical alterity, and so of our encounters with God as capable of turning (or renewing or making new) the language we use to characterize Him in such a way as to turn our conception of Him, of us and of the world around us, upside down.

From such a perspective on religious belief, even Gaita's patient sympathy might seem like a way of missing the essence of religious forms of the language of love; and it will be correspondingly hard to take seriously the suggestion that the secular variants of that language, from the perspective of which anthropomorphic religious picture-language is essentially dispensable to its central moral vision, can be regarded as their exemplary equivalents. To be sure, it is one thing to raise the possibility that many of the everyday concepts employed by the faithful undergo radical conversion or transfiguration, and quite another to trace in detail what those conversions amount to from case to case, in the lives of believers and in the more or less systematic reflections on those transfigured uses that partly constitute the religious traditions that bear them. But if that possibility is a real one, then the nature of Gaita's project would seem to demand that he pays more systematic attention to doctrinal and theological, as well as liturgical and practical, elaborations of the meaning of religious belief if he is to render truly compelling the thought that the work of genuinely saintly love can be done by those in whose lives the concept of a saint has no living, full-blooded place.

Taking these two lines of critical response to Gaita together, the question of how far his absolute conception of good and evil embodies an ascetic vision of the world becomes usefully complicated.

To begin with, if we take seriously Diamond's claim that the excision of religious pictures from religious language brings about their radical transformation, then we might want Nietzsche to be more impressed—dialectically speaking—than he is by excisions of God's name from secular successors to Christian forms of slave value-systems; one might even wonder whether the presence of such essential pictures marks a potential limit to the diagnostic and critical reach of his genealogical method. For if it is essential to the self-understanding of those employing a religious picture-language to use that picture-language in characterizing it, then genealogical descendants of that form of life which employ words that no longer do so would have effected what the religious believer would regard as a decisive discontinuity with their predecessors, even if that predecessor's way of talking remains as one laminate in the palimpsest of our evaluative practices.

Such a response does not amount to a rationally compelling subversion of the conceptions of identity and difference embodied in Nietzsche's genealogical method; but it does indicate that those conceptions may themselves be shaped by evaluative commitments that limit or condition their ability to speak to the lives of their primary interlocutors in ways they can acknowledge as comprehending them from within. Then again, Nietzsche might claim to detect in such an insistence on religion's absolute segregation from its successors exactly the sado-masochist self-denial (at once punishing its offspring for failing to conform to their progenitor's essence and punishing itself for failing to subjugate the wider culture) that he would expect from it.

Suppose, however, we conclude that Gaita can succeed in fully animating his conception in relative autonomy from full-blooded religious commitments: its evaluative orientation would seem to remain vitally congruent with those historical sources—for example, in its willingness to impose unconditional prohibitions and requirements on us that are insensitive to significant natural differences between human beings, that extract significant sacrifices from those least afflicted by the shocks and ills of human mortality, and that resist modification in the light of evolving social, cultural, and technological circumstances. Excising any mention of God's name might strike Diamond as a potentially fateful move in the realm of meaning; but it would not impress Nietzsche as the basis of a claim to have transcended an ascetic evaluative orientation to life.

But our comparison of Gaita's position with that of moral individualism brings out other points that would, or should, have a greater capacity to complicate Nietzsche's responses; for it suggests that it is Gaita's version of ascetic moral thinking that best acknowledges a range of distinctively Nietzschean emphases. Not only does he treat morality as a phenomenon of the realm of meaning (as an existential orientation, a mode of sense-making), and so as something deeply rooted in specifically human forms of life; he also takes seriously our creatureliness—not just our distinctive bodiliness, but our embeddedness in the broader cultural and natural environment (we might call it a full acknowledgement of the naturalness of acculturated human modes of being, of the depth of our participation in nature's flux). Gaita's vision of human individuality also gives pride of place to exemplary human others, and in particular their capacity to show up our existing conceptions of the world as impoverished: the realm of meaning as he understands it is sensitive to reality's capacity to transcend our existing ways of making sense of it—to the inherently unpredictable although retrospectively intelligible ways in which our modes of sense-making are open not only to mutation but also to radical revision.

Compare these ways of acknowledging the life of the body and the inherently genealogical nature of sense-making with the moral individualist conception of pure rational foundationalism—a conception that reduces bodily life (whether human or not) to a distracting accompaniment to what truly grounds a creature's moral status, that divorces rationality from the historical and cultural specificity of human forms of life, and that occludes its ineliminable dimension of imaginative creativity, its openness to an unpredictable future, its being-in-transition. Which of these ways of making sense of our moral status, and which way of making sense of such sense-making exercises, is more deeply aligned with Nietzsche's attempts to overcome our settled tendencies to denigrate our bodies and to prioritize Being over Becoming?

If, however, the anti-moral individualist view of the unconditional value of individual human beings really does attribute ineliminable and essential value to Becoming (by emphasizing our imbrication in the fluctuations of nature, and our capacity for generating radical revelations of moral significance, and so unending processes of self-overcoming self-interpretation, whose genealogical ancestor lies in the role of revelation in Judaeo-Christian religious life), is this asceticism, or its opposite? Perhaps it exemplifies asceticism's tendency to overcome itself, and thereby at once to fulfil itself and to transcend itself (just as the ascetic valuation of truth engenders Nietzsche's genealogical overcoming of it). At the very least, it embodies a highly complex, multivalent rearticulation of the historically accrued layers of thought, word, and deed that make up the contemporary palimpsest of European moral life.

E. Conclusion: Individuating Responsiveness

However, that may be, it's time to draw some tentative lessons from my extended discussion of moral individualism and its critics. First, the content and the form of the moral vision advanced by the critics of moral individualism that I have been examining are internally related; for the essential role of the morally authoritative Other in the mode of presentation of that vision amounts to an exemplary instance of the distinctive characteristics that that vision attributes to human beings. An individuating responsiveness in word and deed to the reality of others and the world, a capacity to speak for oneself in such a way as to claim authority by displaying it, an ability to reveal hitherto-inconceivable truths about reality as undeniable and thereby to disclose serious limitations in our previous understanding of that reality: these are ways in which these others exemplify the richly individual moral texture of human life in bearing witness to its real presence in and pertinence to even the most impaired, evil, or otherwise afflicted of our fellow human beings.

Once we appreciate this internal relation, we can see more clearly that the writings through which these anti-individualist philosophers present their positions constitute a very specific kind of speech act, and so demand a very specific mode of evaluation—exactly the mode of evaluation appropriate to the individuals who disclosed the real moral significance of our full humanity to them in the first place. Since they present their own conviction in this vision of our full humanity as effected by and so reflective of the moral authority of the individual whose words and deeds embodied and disclosed it, we must judge whether the testimony they offer to that individual's authority is itself authorized by their own words—whether their texts claim us in fidelity to that individual and her vision, which means whether their texts claim us in fidelity to their authors. This is not a matter of identifying true premises and interrelating them in such a way as to derive true conclusions; it is a matter of saying what one means and meaning what one says—of speaking authoritatively: which means avoiding banality, sentimentality, and kitsch, striving for honesty, attending to the full particularity of one's own experience and bringing it to words in all its richness and limitations.

It follows that, unless we recognize these anti-individualist authors as themselves aspiring to exercise the individuating responsiveness that they attribute to human beings, and more particularly as bearing witness to what others have helped them to see by virtue of such responsiveness, then we will simply fail to get to grips with the work that their words are intended to do. If we look for essentially impersonal arguments, exercises of what I earlier called determinant judgement, we will find nothing and we will risk concluding that these writings amount to an egregious failure of moral reasoning rather than a different mode of ethical reflection altogether.

And it is worth pointing out that correctly identifying the nature of the speech acts they are performing hardly renders them immune to critical evaluation; on the contrary, it exposes them to terms of criticism that one might think are far more painful and penetrating—far more personal—than the resources of the predicate calculus can muster. Would you rather be told that your major premise is false, or that your writing has succumbed to sentimentality or self-pity? Would you rather be accused of misunderstanding a topic, or told that your appreciation of human life is shallow and banal? Gaita's agonizing over the aptness of the vocabulary with which he strives to convey his moral vision is itself indicative of his sense of dangers of this kind as threatening the success of his enterprise.

On the other hand, insofar as the moral individualists fail to take seriously the specific conversational mode in which the work of their critics is intended to address its readers—insofar as they fail to attend to the particular details of the examples that work presents, and the specific similarities and differences in each work's mode of their presentation, and instead comb each text with a predetermined conception of what a pertinent contribution to the conversation must be like—then their approach will necessarily fall victim to a kind of failing that is very different in its nature from a simple misunderstanding; for they will have failed to manifest any trace of individuating responsiveness to the particularity of their would-be interlocutors.

Recall, for example, the way Singer and McMahan invite the mother of a woman with cerebral palsy to compare her daughter to pigs or monkeys with a view to specifying the differences between them. Now, really think about what it means not just to oblige her even to contemplate the comparison (to hold her daughter imaginatively in that context), but to imply that this is no more than a request that she undertake the bare minimum that is required of any rational being, and in addition to claim that the form in which the request is issued reflects a sustained effort of what McMahan calls 'voluntary self-censorship' on his and Singer's parts (hence amounts to an achievement of moral tact). On the one hand, it is plain that McMahan at least registers a sense of dissonance between his conception of the truth of his view and his awareness that he can't simply say it to someone deeply involved in the realities of the situation he is judging; in Gaita's terms, he shows signs of appreciating the potential offensiveness of issuing such an invitation to a fellow inhabitant of the realm of meaning. But he resolves that dissonance not by questioning the content of his views, but by interpreting his inability to offer it as a further manifestation of his moral sensitivity (his dislike of making other people miserable). This is a particularly salient instance of the avoidance of genuine individuating responsiveness; it conjoins the appearance of morality with the absence of its spirit in the way that marks a truly moralistic moral philosophy.

3. Authority and Revelation in Art

A. Stanley Cavell

Before diverting into the domain of ethics, I noted that the primary moral Cavell draws from Kierkegaard's qualitative dialectical analysis of authority and revelation—the projection of those concepts that he thinks we could and should make, or could usefully regard as already, if inchoately, underway—is from their religious context to the then-current immanent context of modern art (in the 1960s). And in returning to this issue after my diversion (and its disclosure of the deeper complexities inherent in the apparently simpler modulation of asceticism from religion to ethics), it may be easier to appreciate the precision with which Cavell characterizes the dialectical shifting of sense from a religious to an aesthetic context. He specifically does *not* say that it indicates that for us art has become religion—'([that] may or may not describe the situation, [but] as it stands describes phenomena other than those I have in mind)'—but rather that 'the activity of modern art, both in production and reception, is to be understood in categories which are, or were, religious', that 'our serious art is produced under conditions which Kierkegaard announces as those of apostleship, not those of genius' (MWM, 175).

If concepts are inherently projective, then when concepts originally employed in a religious context come to be employed in an artistic context, it cannot be right to say either that they retain their religious meaning in their new artistic context (i.e. to say that art has become religion) or that their meaning in that new context is wholly and solely artistic rather than religious. For if the new artistic context invites and allows the projection of those originally religious concepts, then it discloses a further range or dimension of significance of those original concepts. One might say that it unfolds an internal relation between what we have understood religion to be and what we have come to understand art to be. It thereby discloses an artistic register of significance in religion and a religious register of significance in art, or more precisely a sense in which the place of serious art in the late twentieth century is comprehensible only as a genealogical descendent of serious religious thought and practice in the nineteenth century. But of course, to understand that relation in a properly dialectical way one needs to understand *three* historical contexts: not only that of serious mid-nineteenth-century religion and serious mid-to-late twentieth-century art, but also that of serious mid-nineteenth-century art (since one could not understand serious twentieth-century art's capacity to invite the projection of religious concepts independently of understanding that capacity's indebtedness to its own historical conditions).

What Cavell means by the serious art of his age is anyway patently internally related to serious art in the mid-nineteenth century. For what he takes to be artistically serious in his then-contemporary circumstances—the work of figures such as Stella, Newman, and Caro—is familiarly known to us as modernism; and he understands such artworks as persistently and necessarily confronting the possibility that they are not so much deficient aesthetically in this or that respect, but rather fail to count as a work of art at all—a possibility that is a function of the artist's inability simply to rely on his inheritance of any range of artistic conventions as guaranteeing the status of his work as art, so that he confronts his relation to the history of his enterprise as an undismissable problem, something he can neither take for granted nor simply reject as irrelevant, in every work he makes. And for Cavell, this kind of condition 'does not arise as a problem until some point in the 19th century' (MWM, 176).

We will examine the history, nature, and significance of the modernist moment in art in more detail in later essays; but we can already see that, in making this point about its emergence, Cavell is placing it dialectically, disclosing its internal relatedness not only to Kierkegaard's critique of religion but also to the analogous critiques of analogous spheres of society (themselves understood as internally related to one another) by Marx, Nietzsche, and Freud. This implies that the condition of modernism in the arts is one further expression of the experience of self-alienation and the attempts at its overcoming that these dialectical critics were concerned to expose and espouse: modernist artists understand themselves to be inhabiting a foreign aesthetic land—to be not-at-home with themselves as painters or musicians or sculptors, to be at once unable to find their feet with their aesthetic inheritance and unable to discard the desire to re-establish that footing. And precisely because they cannot do so by relying on inherited conventions, their condition foregrounds questions of authority and revelation: the authority of such an artist's expressions is absolutely in question (not only as expressive of good art but as art at all), and its reality or lack of it is revealed in every individual work he produces (or defers producing—perhaps because he is awaiting inspiration or its proper means of articulation, perhaps because he is lacking in courage).

What, however, of the more specific claim Cavell makes—namely that Kierkegaard's 'description of the apostle's position characterizes in detail the position I take the genuine artist to find himself in' (MWM, 177)? We know that this does not mean that the modernist artist simply *is* an apostle; this would be as undialectical—as ungrammatical a remark—as saying that he simply is not. What, however, are the detailed points of comparison and contrast, as the grammar of a religious concept is rearticulated in a modernist aesthetic context?

[The modernist artist] is pulled out of the ranks by a message which he must, on pain of loss of self, communicate; he is silent for a long period, until he finds his way to saying what it is he has to say (...for he knows that there are no techniques at anyone's disposal for saying what he has to say); he has no proof of his authority, or genuineness, other than his own work (...this is expressed by the absence of conventions within which to compose); he makes his work repulsive...because mere attraction is not what he wants (...this has to do with the various ways in which art has today withdrawn from, or is required to defeat, its audience); he must deny his personal or worldly authority in accomplishing what he has to do (...he cannot rely on his past achievements as securing the relevance of his new impulse; each work requires, spiritually speaking, a new step); art is no longer a profession to which, for example, a man can become apprenticed (...it is 'a call', but there is no recognized calling in which it can be exercised); finally, the burden of being called to produce it is matched by the risk of accepting it (...in accepting or rejecting it, the heart is revealed).

(MWM, 177)

It is not just the condition of modernism that shapes or informs this transfiguration of the concept of an apostle; the projection is also prepared for by two internal features of Kierkegaard's mode of presenting that concept in its religious home. The first is that, as we noted earlier, he chooses to sharpen our perception of its distinctness by contrasting the apostle with the genius, defining the latter in terms of immanence (as opposed to apostolic inhabitation of the transcendent). By this, Kierkegaard means to emphasize that the genius is born rather than called: he may need time to develop his power, but it is wholly immanent to him. He also means that the genius has no essential orientation towards an audience, hence towards the delivery of a message of any kind: that to which he gives expression in his work is himself, and it is expressed primarily for himself—as a way of realizing himself and his view of life. Insofar as what he has to say makes a genuinely original contribution to a wider human endeavour, it will be by forging a new set of artistically productive conventions which others can inherit; so his novelty is always gradually assimilable into everyday human practices.

This Romantic, Kantian conception of genius was plainly central to the grammar of contemporary artistic activity as Kierkegaard understood it; but since that centrality is historically mutable, it doesn't constitute an a priori reason for denying the possibility of future congruence between a suitably reconfigured domain of art and certain religious concepts. Indeed, since Kierkegaard's emphasis on difference here is clearly a therapeutic response to what he sees as a real temptation to conflate the demands of apostleship with the demands of genius (one to which Adler succumbs), he is implicitly acknowledging that the boundary between art and religion is capable of being transgressed, that transactions across that boundary can be invited and entered into. And this implicit admission is reinforced by the second internal feature of Kierkegaard's presentation of Adler: the fact that he introduces him by drawing a distinction between a premise-author and a genuine author.

The premise-author is someone who possesses the premises but does not arrive at any conclusion: he has acquired and intellectually endorsed the premises for judging, acting, and living in a certain way, but he never really puts those premises into action—never realizes or takes up the concrete existential stance or life-view that they delineate. Such a person has, in effect, failed to author their own existence—failed to enact any particular conception of how to live a meaningful or significant life. In this sense, any and every human being confronts the risk of becoming a premise-author; but for those who choose authorship as their vocation, any such personal irresolution will inevitably be reflected in their relation to that calling—in any specifically aesthetic literary tasks they take up in such an existentially inauthentic condition.

As Yi-Ping Ong has pointed out, Kierkegaard's critique of Adler here makes contact with his earlier critical review of a novel by Hans Christian Andersen.[27] In the latter, Kierkegaard argues that any novelist who lacks a properly realized life-view will produce novels that evince the same lack, and so will have deprived himself a necessary condition for artistic success in that genre. For it is the work's incarnation of a particular concrete view of life that confers internal cohesion and decisive purposiveness on its fictional world, and thereby allows the reader to be convinced of its independent reality, as well as making it possible for the fictional characters who inhabit it to do so in a way which resembles our inhabitation of the real world—as situated agents, centres of ineluctably but impersonally conditioned freedom, and so as individuals with whose struggles the reader can identify and become absorbed. And the very thing that facilitates that absorption—the fictional world's coherent boundedness as a self-sufficient aesthetic whole—is also what permits the author to recede from view, to absent himself from that world.

If, by contrast, an author lacks existential integrity, the fictional worlds he attempts to create will lack aesthetic integrity. Such an author will intrude upon the reader as the advocate of a particular message or the annotator of experiences and associations of purely private interest; his looming presence will theatricalize his world, depriving it of coherence and significance, reducing it to an arbitrary mélange, a psychobiographical effusion or a mere instrument for realizing the author's coercive designs on the reader. And in being reduced to authorial puppets or mere assemblages of impulse and activity, his characters will thereby lose their own integrity as exemplars of situated agency, as sharers of the human condition whose apt representation is precisely what facilitates readerly absorption, since it presents them as beings for whom the position of the reader (like the position of the author) is invisible or non-existent, essentially absent from their world.

Of course, Adler is not a would-be novelist; so the particular terms in which Kierkegaard criticizes Andersen's aesthetic failure (terms to which we will recur in

---

[27] 'From the Papers of One Still Living', in Kierkegaard, *Early Polemical Writings*, ed. and trans. Julia Watkin (Princeton: Princeton University Press, 1990), 61–103. Ong's reading of this essay is in her *The Art of Being* (Cambridge, MA: Harvard University Press, 2018), ch. 1.

a different context in later essays) will not apply to him. Nevertheless, Adler is, on Kierkegaard's view, an exemplary instance of a premise-author who also takes up the calling of writing: what distinguishes him, existentially and aesthetically, is that his premise is a revelation-fact. Like anyone else possessed of a religious premise or life-view, he confronts the existential challenge of living it: but since his premise is the reception of a divine revelation, he confronts the challenge peculiar to the apostle, that of being the bearer of good news: hence, to enact his religious identity existentially just is to enact it aesthetically—to communicate, to articulate, to speak and write.

More specifically, he has been called to communicate the revelation, and only the revelation, to all, on pain of offending God; he is required to communicate whilst absenting himself qua communicator entirely from the scene, absolutely to foreground the message over the messenger, and thereby to facilitate a direct relation between each reader and her God. But Adler's existential inability to grasp the distinctive nature of his premise turns him away from the self-abnegating communicative mission of an apostle and towards a writing project which he embarks on solely as a means of attaining personal self-understanding, and in which he is guided by purely aesthetic criteria (the kind appropriate to the calling of a genius rather than an apostle). His authorship is thus triply inauthentic: he is a premise-author as a Christian, as an apostle, and as a writer.

So, although the failure of authorship to which Kierkegaard is primarily referring in his analysis of the Adler case is ethical or existential—a failure to be the author of a real human life, a failure to realize one's intellectual investments in action and thereby to live a life that is genuinely one's own—the range of concepts he utilizes in order to articulate his diagnosis of Adler, and of Andersen, strongly suggest that literature is not merely one field in which such failures can be detected, but that such literary failures are somehow exemplary or representative of this kind of existential failure more generally—perhaps particularly when religious premises are at issue. Even in the middle of the nineteenth century, then, Kierkegaard's work demonstrates the availability of an understanding of the artist as capable of confronting spiritual demands, and so a conception of art, ethics, and religion as internally related matters (however different the form of the individual lives of those who incarnate primarily aesthetic, ethical, or religious world-views). Once again, then, Kierkegaard's emphatic attempts to distinguish religion from art can be seen to subvert themselves, and to prepare the way for genealogical perceptions of the kind Cavell ends his own essay by delineating.

B. William Golding

William Golding's *Darkness Visible* appeared fifteen years after *The Spire* (and twelve years after the three interlinked novellas published under the title *The*

Pyramid)—by far the longest period of silence in his career.[28] Whatever the personal reasons for this (and John Carey's recent biography[29] identifies a long struggle with writer's block, the damaging effect of a negative review of *The Spire*, an accident at sea in which Golding and his family were very nearly killed, a developing drink problem), it also suggests a phase of artistic reflection—taking stock, considering what had been achieved and what new achievements might be possible or at least worth attempting. *The Pyramid* had already declared Golding's willingness to contest the restrictive allocation of his work to the genres of myth and fable; its narrative unfolds in roughly contemporary social circumstances (that of a small English town named Stilbourne). In *Darkness Visible*, he takes on the larger task of assessing the condition (not of Britain but) of England—of finding his own terms for expressing and evaluating the sense of social, cultural, and political decline or decay by which so many people in England seemed gripped in that decade (as the radical energies of the sixties dissipated and the spirit of Thatcherism crystallized).

The English town at the heart of *Darkness Visible* is called Greenfield, and it contains an ironmonger's of character named Frankley's. Early in the nineteenth century, it moved into rickety buildings next to the towpath of the newly cut canal; it thrives until the convulsions of the First World War, after which decline sets in and accelerates inexorably, despite various attempts to avert it by diversifying the goods it sells and its ways of selling them, until in the late seventies the business closes and the building is demolished. Frankley's is thus 'an image in little of society at large', by virtue of its 'complex disorder of ancient and modern' (DV, 42): the shop gradually buried itself under the accumulating sediment or remainder of each new generation of overstocking; and each internal rearrangement of departments remodelled a building that was already an architectural palimpsest when Frankley's first came to occupy it.

> The buildings were indeterminate in date, some walls of brick, some tile-hung, some lath and plaster, and some of a curious wooden construction. It is not impossible that parts of these wooden areas were in fact medieval windows filled as was the custom with wooden slats and now thought to be no more than chinky walls. Certainly there was not a beam in the place that did not have here and there notches cut, grooves and an occasional hole that indicated building and rebuilding, division, reclamation and substitution, carried on throughout a quite preposterous length of time. (DV, 38)

One innovation marks the point at which Frankley's tips from vigour to decline. After the First World War 'the place grew a spider's web of wires along which

---

[28] *Darkness Visible* (London: Faber, 1979); hereafter DV.
[29] *William Golding: The Man Who Wrote* Lord of the Flies (London: Faber, 2009).

money trundled in small, wooden jars' (DV, 39): each shop assistant would propel the money and receipt for a transaction to a central cashier, who would return the change by the same means, with bells marking each stop on the jar's travels. Hence the decreasing levels of trade are marked by increasing periods of silence, which—combined with the muffling effect of the building's construction—ensure that every so often 'a jar would hiss over [a] customer's head like a bird of prey, turn a corner and vanish in some quite unexpected direction' (DV, 39). When a new Mr Frankley abolishes the overhead railway, seeing it as a slur on the elderly, august shop assistants, and reintroduces separate tills, it becomes clear that the spider's web had done two things.

> First, it had accustomed the staff to moderate stillness and tranquillity; and second, it had so habituated them to the overhead method of money sending and getting that when one of these ancient gentlemen was offered a banknote he immediately gestured upwards with it as if to examine the watermark. But this, in the evolution or perhaps devolution of the place, would be followed by continuing silence and a lost look while the assistant tried to remember what came next.
> (DV, 39–40)

Consider the overhead railway as an image in little of the spiritual life of the larger society within which Frankley's conducts its business. Then we might conclude that that spiritual life blossoms in response to the moral convulsion of a world war; that affairs of the spirit take on a more predatory aspect the less often we traffic in them; and that their elimination on the grounds of respect for individual dignity in fact engenders disorientation, hollowing out a previously meaningful (even joyful) gesture language.

Now consider Frankley's as an image in little of the text that contains it. Then we should expect that text to be fundamentally concerned with spirituality as called forth by the extremities of war, liable to misinterpretation in malignant terms, and requiring expression in a language of gestures but crippled or deformed in the drive towards that expression by the disorientation of those to whom that language now belongs. Indeed, since the inheritors of this language—both characters and author—are also inhabitants of the society for which Frankley's goes proxy, the means of expression for which they are groping will have the same palimpsestic quality as that of their preposterously ancient society—the same layers of overlapping sedimentation, the same overstocking, the same subjection to unceasing 'rebuilding, division, reclamation and substitution' (DV, 38) that Nietzsche detects in his exemplary instance of moral phenomena (the practice of punishment). In that sense, the key obstacle confronting anyone seeking a viable contemporary spiritual language may be the sheer multiplicity of available terms or modes of discourse rather than their absence: the problem is not the absence of spiritual concepts but how to recover a meaningful personal and collective means of spiritual expression from a bewildering, historically diverse and ineliminably hybrid profusion of such concepts.

It is in this condition that one of the novel's central characters—Matty—finds himself; and its first part is devoted to recounting his attempts to make sense of his spiritual vocation, to himself and to post-war English (and, briefly, Australian) society. But the author of this recounting is himself in a condition analogous to Matty's: for to recount Matty's struggle to articulate both his understanding of himself as a prophet, and the prophetic visions to which he is subjected, is itself to attempt to articulate a prophetic vision of the condition of England; and the nature of this task, as well as the responsibilities taken on by anyone claiming the authority to engage in it, is conditioned by exactly the circumstances Matty confronts.

There is, of course, an apparent difference between the two tasks: for where Matty directly claims spiritual authority for his visions (Kierkegaard would call them revelations), and so for the actions they authorize, Golding claims (need only, and perhaps can only, claim) artistic authority for his vision of Matty's spiritual life. *Darkness Visible* is not a sacred text, but rather a literary text about the sacred (both textual and extra-textual). Hence the novel's epigraph: 'Sit mihi fas audita loqui'. With these words, Virgil seeks permission from the gods to relate his vision of the Underworld into which Aeneas travels, in the company of the Sibyl and under the protection of a golden bough of mistletoe. If Matty is Golding's Aeneas, then Golding is Virgil: his authority is poetic.

But in registering that distinction, Golding also problematizes it. For these words of Virgil call on the gods to allow him to articulate a vision of hell: in other words, this Roman poet presents his literary enterprise not only as having a spiritual subject matter but also as subject to spiritual authorization—quite as if the poetic and the sacred are inextricably woven into one another, internally related. It thereby appears to be an essential part of Golding's vision that our disorientation in relation to religious concepts includes or entails a disorientation with respect to the inherent otherness of the religious and the poetic—one which leaves us no longer open to the claim of each to be the other's particular or intimate other. After all, Roman texts were (perhaps until yesterday) as much a part of the cultivated English mind as the texts of ancient Greece and Christianity—as indeed was much of what eventuated in Western culture from their interaction. So if Virgil's *Aeneid* is part of the palimpsest that constitutes contemporary English culture, so too is the idea of the spiritual and the poetic as interpenetrative. But the only way to validate that assumption is to attempt to activate that cultural resource. So the success of Golding's enterprise will turn on whether or not that attempt finds acknowledgement in his readers—on whether or not we can see what he means by invoking such reference points, and so see what he claims to see by their means.

The opening sequence of *Darkness Visible* is rightly regarded as one of its most powerful. It describes a group of firemen who watch incredulously as a small boy walks out of an inferno of blazing buildings during the London Blitz. Since the fire is of such intensity that it melts lead and distorts iron, it seems impossible that any human being could have survived it, but—although Matty is badly burned on the left side (so that even extensive plastic surgery leaves one side of his head bald and his left ear a purple stump)—he survives, and is eventually despatched from the hospital to Foundlings School in Greenfield.

This sequence insistently raises a question about what kind of being this boy is: he appears to 'condense out of the shuddering backdrop of the glare, and at the moment of his appearance he seemed to one of the watching firemen 'to be perhaps not entirely there—to be in a state of, as it were, indecision as to whether he was a human shape or merely a bit of flickering brightness. Was it the Apocalypse? Nothing could be more apocalyptic than a world so ferociously consumed' (DV, 15). This fireman is a bookseller, and one described as suffering 'from a romantic view of the classical world' (DV, 11); so this conceptual lens from the New Testament is no more and no less natural to him than that of Pompeii, or of seeking a piece of wood to placate Pan when he first glimpses Matty (DV, 12). And the hybridity of his interpretative framework is emphatically continuous with that of his narrator (as well as with the nature of the preposterously old country's capital):

> There was an area east of the Isle of Dogs in London which was an unusual mixture even for those surroundings. Among the walled-off rectangles of water, the warehouses, railway lines and travelling cranes, were two streets of mean houses with two pubs and two shops among them. The bulks of tramp steamers hung over the houses where there had been as many languages spoken as families that lived there. But just now not much was being said, for the whole area had been evacuated officially and even a ship that was hit and set on fire had few spectators near it. There was a kind of tent in the sky over London, which was composed of the faint white beams of searchlights, with barrage balloons dotted here and there. The barrage balloons were all that the searchlights discovered in the sky, and the bombs came down, it seemed, mysteriously out of emptiness. They fell in or round the great fire...
>
> Under the tent of searchlights a structure had built itself up in the air. It was less sharply defined than the beams of light but it was far brighter. It was a glare, a burning bush through or beyond which the thin beams were sketched more faintly...
>
> The drone of bombers was dying away. The five-mile high tent of chalky lights had disappeared, been struck all at once, but the light of the great fire was bright as ever, brighter perhaps. Now the pink aura of it had spread. Saffron and ochre

turned to blood-colour. The shivering of the white heart of the fire had quickened beyond the capacity of the eye to analyse it into an outrageous glare. High above the glare and visible now for the first time between two pillars of lighted smoke was the steely and untouched round of the full moon—the lover's, hunter's, poet's moon; and now—an ancient and severe goddess credited with a new function and a new title—the bomber's moon. She was Artemis of the bombers, more pitiless than ever before.   (DV, 9, 13)

Most obviously, these passages elicit conviction by their precision at the purely descriptive level: they allow us to see in a literal sense, to see what the firemen standing on the edge of what was no longer part of the habitable world would have seen. But the fourth sentence of the passage (and of the book) subverts this literality, or perhaps it subverts our sense of what it is for words and sentences to be literally employed. It asserts that there was a tent in the sky over London—not that the searchlight beams and barrage balloons looked like a kind of tent, but simply that there was one (the kind composed of beams and balloons). But Golding does not just prefer metaphor to simile, a literal falsehood to a truthful comparison; he goes on to write as if the falsehood were simply, literally true, as if its metaphorical validity immediately authorized its availability for purely descriptive purposes—proceeding, for example, to describe the extinguishing of the searchlights as the striking of a tent. And no sooner has talk of a tent become the new benchmark for literal truth than it engenders a new dimension of metaphorical significance. The fire is presented as having built itself up under the tent, as if expanding into the accommodation provided for it; and no sooner does it fill that structure than it is redescribed (not as like but *as*) a burning bush—quite as if the idea of the tent as living quarters for a desert people immediately engenders a vision of it as providing shelter for the Ark of the Covenant, which in turn discloses the fire as the self-sustaining manifestation of God's appearance to Moses. From now on the fire simply *is* a burning bush; and the literal truth of that characterization in turn licenses the later metaphorical characterization of its attendant smoke as 'two pillars', those marks of divine protection afforded the Israelites in their desert journey out of Egypt.

In this way, the most outrageously imaginative characterizations of the real become bare denotations of its actuality: the literal truth about things answers to the most extravagant of metaphors. Poetry is truth-telling, a means of entering more deeply into reality rather than of wandering away from it; and more specifically, ancient poetic forms of truth-telling are not only not made redundant by modernity: by disclosing their utterly contemporary usefulness, they also disclose hitherto unsuspected ranges of their meaning. The moon of the bombers still merits the name 'Artemis', but reveals a degree of pitilessness in that divinity (and in reality) that earlier moon-worshippers might not have imagined.

From the outset, then, this novel deploys concepts from different layers in the spiritual palimpsest of English culture; but in the case of the tent and the burning bush, those elements also serve a reflexive purpose. For one can think of the strict geometry of the tent as the narrative structure of the novel in which it is presented, and the burning bush as the vision of spiritual reality (of reality as spiritual) it is designed to invoke and accommodate, even if it is fated to be first melted and ultimately dismantled or struck by that vision—the poetic equivalent of the string that is frayed and broken by divine music, as Matty's spiritual elders put it in one of his own visions (cf. DV, 238). Just as God's fiery self-manifestation to Moses requires a bush in or on which to burn, so any vision of divine fire needs a linguistic and literary medium; but unlike the Creator, the artistic creator cannot prevent his creation from consuming that which conjures and contains it.

During his time in hospital, Matty's relationship to language is presented as being as unusual as language's relation to him. First there is his name, or rather the curious business of his acquisition of a name, its assignment being the responsibility of an office that, working through the alphabet in rotation, had just made use of the letter 'v'.

> The young wit who was given the job of using 'w' suggested 'Windup', her chief having displayed less than perfect courage in an air raid. She had found she could get married and still keep her job and she was feeling secure and superior. Her chief winced at the name and drew his pen through it, foreseeing a coven of children all shouting 'Windup!', 'Windup!' He made his own substitution, though when he looked at what he had written it seemed not quite right and he altered it. There was no obvious reason for doing so. The name had first jumped into his mind with the curious effect of having come out of empty air and of being temporary, a thing to be noticed because you were lucky to be in the place where it had landed. It was as if you had sat silently in the bushes and— My!—there settled in front of you the rarest of butterflies or birds which had stayed long enough to be seen and had then gone off with an air of going for ever, sideways, it might be. (DV, 17)

As its final, syntactically strained sentence makes clear, this passage operates within the assumption that the relation between name and bearer is non-arbitrary. Philosophers and other theorists of language may tell us that names are not sentences, a fortiori neither apt or inept characterizations of the object or person they denote; but the depth of our resistance to such assertions is already evident in the ease with which we see the malicious joke in the young wit's coining of the name 'Windup' in honour of her chief: if we didn't intuitively regard names as fitting their bearers, why would we so unquestioningly accept the idea that a person's name might woundingly declare an unflattering aspect of his character? But it is not just that the chief experiences his eventual choice of name for Matty as somehow right for him: it is that the way in which the final sentence articulates that experience (thereby hovering undecidably between his way of experiencing it and the narrator's way of imagining that experience) involves treating Matty's rightful name as if it were a thing, and indeed the very thing it names.

According to this baptismal narrative, there is a moment of (non-original, alphabetically guided) invention, then a substitution, then an alteration, before Matty's name is settled on; and it is no sooner settled on than it is subjected to slippage in other's mouths throughout the novel (into 'Wandgrave', 'Wheelwright', 'Windgraff', 'Windrave', and so on), until his full name is finally bestowed upon him only as the final moments of his life are described (DV, 247). That name is Matthew Septimus Windrove—so even the chief's initial substitution is not ex nihilo, since the 'Wind' element is retained throughout, and we might well suspect that the intermediate version was 'Windgrove'. One could say, then, that Matty's name—taken as a linguistic element in the baptismal passage, and in the novel as a whole—literally is unceasingly mutating, on the move, possessed of an air of moving on for ever sideways. But the final sentence portrays his name as in truth unchanging and everlasting; what is temporary is rather its availability, which is a function of its willingness to grace us with its presence and our willingness to be receptive to that presence. The right name arrives, and then departs, but it never mutates; the office's preliminary revisions are rather increasingly successful attempts to reshape our language to accommodate it, to receive an apt impression of its own beautiful, independent life. In fact, Matty's rightful name is portrayed as if it *were* that which it names, as if it were its bearer; after all it is Matty himself whom we have already been invited to think of as the rarest kind of human creature (if he is even human at all), someone whose inhabitation of this world is momentary, his presence a fortunate but temporary phase in an endless journey that passes orthogonally through our locale. According to the final sentence, then, Matty's name is Matty, and Matty *is* his name: this act of naming penetrates to the essence of the being named, just as Adam in the Book of Genesis is authorized by God to give each creature its rightful name.

But whilst the passage operates within this Adamic assumption of fusion between name and bearer, its author simultaneously exploits the difference between the two. He tells us that Matty's rightful name is rare, beautiful, even partaking of eternal life, but he doesn't tell us what that name is until the novel's climax; he earns initial credit for his claim by virtue of the rare beauty of the passage in which the claim is made, but he builds upon that beginning by exploiting the long period of non-disclosure in two ways. First, he depicts Matty's nature and life in such a way that it can claim to manifest the rare beauty that results from participation in eternity; but the continuing mystery of his real name simultaneously leads the reader to feel that a crucial piece of the puzzle about Matty's nature and life is always missing. As a result, when his rightful name is revealed, its claim to the rare beauty of eternal life can now draw on the sustained achievement of that long and complex portrayal of its bearer, and at the same time it appears as the culminating element in that portrait—the nominative detail that goes proxy for the whole (appearing just as Matty's life reaches its apotheosis). Name and bearer thereby become mutually implicating, inextricably interwoven: what Matty's name means to us is indistinguishable from what Matty has come to mean to us, both part of that meaning and the whole of it. Matty is Matthew Septimus Windrove (the seventh chapter of Matthew's Gospel, and in particular its seventh verse, that exemplary articulation of the mighty wind of the Holy Spirit, which drives him to rove restlessly between places and countries, and perhaps also leaves him riven, both body and soul). Matty is his name.

So much for language's relation to Matty; what of Matty's relation to language?

> As the various aids to recovery were removed from him and he began to speak more, it was observed that his relationship to language was unusual. He mouthed. Not only did he clench his fists with the effort of speaking, he squinted. It seemed that a word was an object, a material object, round and smooth sometimes, a golf ball of a thing that he could just about manage to get through his mouth, though it deformed his face in the passage. Some words were jagged and these became awful passages of pain and struggle that made the other children laugh. After his turban came off in the period between the primary work and what cosmetic work was possible, the ruin of his half-raw skull and blasted ear was most unappealing. Patience and silence seemed the greater part of his nature. Bit by bit he learnt to control the anguish of speaking until the golfballs and jagged stones, the toads and jewels passed through his mouth with not much more than the normal effort. (DV, 17–18)

Coming immediately after the baptismal narrative, this passage continues to envision words as material objects, whilst leaving it unclear how far that vision is the narrator's and how far it is merely the narrator's way of capturing Matty's experience of language (which means leaving the distance between Golding and his protagonist as ours to determine). But no sooner has the narrator translated his own metaphorical equivalence between words and golf balls or jagged stones into a tool for literal description than he offers a new metaphorical equivalence on that basis: golf balls and jagged stones are aligned with toads and jewels. Did these toads and jewels just leap into Golding's mind out of thin air, no more than a glancing and temporary alternative means of expression; or are we here privileged to observe an exotic form of words establishing a further staging post in its unending journey through English language and culture? In defence of the latter possibility, I adduce three sources for these toads and jewels—three layers of the English cultural palimpsest as embodied in one cultivated poetic mind.

First, there is the ancient folk-myth about toads—that their ugly exterior hides something of great value. Golding's passage (by interrupting Matty's increasing mastery of words with a reminder of his physical condition) certainly invites us to apply the myth to Matty himself—that risibly ugly creature who contains a jewel of great worth, the divine fire out of which he originally condensed. But the passage directly applies this image not to Matty but to the words coming out of his mouth, all of which are presented as if emerging through a communicating passage from his interior, and so as all expressive of his interior jewel. This relates his divine fire to language, the Word to words; but it simultaneously discriminates within the field of language by identifying as jewels only those words which cause him pain and anguish to pronounce or exteriorize—the jagged stones (for the paratactic juxtaposition of the two metaphorical pairs offers the toads as equivalents of the golf balls). So speaking the Word, communicating it to others by externalizing its jewel-like nature will necessarily demand awful passages of pain and struggle from the speaker—indeed, deforming physical contortions.

The second source is *As You Like It*, and an early speech by Duke Senior:

> Now, my co-mates and brothers in exile,
> Hath not old custom made this life more sweet
> Than that of painted pomp? Are not these woods
> More free from peril than the envious court?
> Here feel we not the penalty of Adam,
> The seasons' difference, as the icy fang
> And churlish chiding of the winter's wind,
> Which when it bites and blows upon my body
> Even till I shrink with cold, I smile and say,
> 'This is no flattery: these are counsellors
> That feelingly persuade me what I am.'
> Sweet are the uses of adversity,
> Which like the toad, ugly and venomous,
> Wears yet a precious jewel in his head;
> And this our life, exempt from public haunt,
> Find tongues in trees, books in the running brooks,
> Sermons in stones, and good in every thing.
>
> (II.i.1–17)

Shakespeare's character here invokes the ancient myth for new purposes. Most immediately, he presents adversity as something whose venomous ugliness brings about a sweet consequence—just as Matty's subjection to adversity will ultimately bring forth goodness. But the nature of that adversity is highly specific: the reverse the Duke suffers is banishment from court to the Forest of Arden, hence from urban civilization to the rural heartland of England—an early example of the Shakespearean green world that provides perspective on ordinary life and the means to transform it. Matty's obdurate resistance to contemporary social conventions is thereby presented as a potentially transfigurative attachment to the truly fundamental dimension of life—the basic bodily rhythms of the human animal's life form.

The particular sweetness the Duke prophesies also resonates with Golding's portrayal of Matty: for he associates inhabitation of the green world with access to the true language of nature, and so to true language—for the native tongue of the natural world is presumably the most truly apt expression of the nature of things, thus the one language in which words make manifest the essence of every thing of which they speak, and indeed make it manifest as good. The Duke's way of claiming that there is such a language even takes on the lineaments of that of which it longingly speaks: for each synonym it deploys for that language alliteratively bonds itself to each exemplary instance of the nature which speaks it—trees have tongues, but brooks have books, and stones sermons. Each of his words for language mirrors and so points us towards the respect in which each of our existing words for each natural thing already incarnates its nature. What the green world gives us is thus not a new language, but a proper appreciation of our old language as always already penetrating to the essence of things. This finding of the language of nature is in fact a refinding of our natural language (specifically of English, since these alliterative alignments involve the material properties of English words). In Matty's terms, the jewels of his spiritual language make manifest the divine fire out of which all creation is forged (although it will not be until the séance in part three that his words, and so words as such, will reveal their divinity—DV 232-3).

But the Shakespearean context problematizes any attempt to derive from the Duke's speech a straightforward endorsement of the Adamic myth of language by which *Darkness Visible* appears to be orienting itself. This is because that speech is an exercise in the familiar literary genre of pastoral, bequeathed to the Renaissance by classical antiquity, according to which Nature stands opposed to art, and is to be praised for its very artlessness (its refusal of painted pomp, its embrace of the reality of the seasons and the body). But this genre suffers from what A. D. Nuttall has called a 'central psychosis': the fact that it is in art that the artless is celebrated.[30] The pastoral is a product of urban life, as the Duke is the product of the court; its generic identity is a poetic articulation of the very mode of existence it condemns. The paradox is evident in the Duke's attempt to dispraise language by praising the language of nature; as one of his courtiers immediately points out, he has translated 'the stubbornness of fortune into so quiet and sweet a style' that it constitutes an exemplary instance of that against which he claims to be taking a stand. It does not follow that the Duke, or any other pastoral poet, does

---

[30] A. D. Nuttall, *Shakespeare the Thinker* (New Haven: Yale University Press, 2007), 231.

not genuinely love the simple green world; but the very success of his loving depiction of it only confirms his exile from it.

Is the same true of the play in which the Duke makes this speech? Shakespeare plainly attempts to avoid the trap, since *As You Like It* not only contains a critique of the Duke's pastoralizing, but also offers a counter-version of it, by making its green world real in a way that the Duke's speech does not: for it contains genuine rustics, of the earth earthy—such as Audrey, Corin, and William, the rawness of whose imagery and existence mounts a counter-attack by nature against pastoral's defeat of nature by style. When Corin tells us 'that the property of rain is to wet and fire to burn; that good pasture makes fat sheep; and that a great cause of the night is the lack of the sun' (III.ii.23–8), his wisdom approaches tautology, but precisely because of that it conveys a strange strength and fullness of meaning; it is no less a deployment of words than the Duke's speech, but perhaps it approaches more nearly the linguistic condition to which the Duke's polished alliterative allusions to the tongue of the trees or the stone's sermons self-subvertingly advert.

So by alluding to this play, does Golding's talk of toads and jewels align him more with the Duke, or with the Duke's creator? How far does *Darkness Visible*'s Greenfield collude with the classical models and modes it draws upon (including that of pastoral), and how far does it disrupt or displace them, in order to find or reactivate the reality to which they aspired? Is Matty an artful representation of spiritual artlessness, or the real thing, in all its raw harshness? Like Shakespeare's generation of a genuinely English pastoral out of a critique of its prior forms, Golding's regeneration of raw spirituality (we might call it an English spiritual) out of a collage of inherited spiritual forms cannot avoid a version of Nuttall's pastoral psychosis: for both inevitably create a new artistic form, one which engenders a realistic effect rather than reality itself. It does not follow that either artist does not love what each aspires to depict; but it does mean that both confront the apparent paradox that their success in depicting it only confirms their exile from it. The real question is: can any artist, and indeed any human being, hope for anything other than exile—whether from pastoral or from spiritual reality—in our present cultural condition, or indeed in any cultural conditions we can recognize as pertinent to art?

The third source invoked by Golding's toads and jewels is one of Hans Christian Andersen's fairy tales or fables, 'The Toad' (1866). The youngest, smallest, and ugliest member of a family of toads who have tumbled into a well is frustrated by the restrictions of their admittedly safe environment; having imbibed her mother's tale of the precious jewel that one family member carries in her head, she declares that she certainly doesn't possess it, before climbing out of the well to explore the larger green world surrounding it. She meets a variety of more or less threatening inhabitants of that world—a disgusted farmer, some welcoming frogs, a hubristic caterpillar, a poet and a naturalist (the former saving her from the latter's specimen jar)—until the head of a family of storks take her to their rooftop nest, a final voyage that she thinks indicates their willingness to have her join their coming migration to Egypt but which is in fact a result of their need for food.

> 'I must go to Egypt' said she. 'All the longing and all the pleasure that I feel is much better than having a jewel in one's head'.
> And it was just she who had the jewel. That jewel was the continual striving and desire to go upward—ever upward. It gleamed in her head, gleamed in joy, beamed brightly in her longing
> The Stork's beak pinched her, and the wind whistled; it was not exactly agreeable, but she was going upward—upward towards Egypt—and she knew it; and that was why her eyes gleamed, and a spark seemed to fly out of them.
> 'Quunk!—ah!' The body was dead—the Toad was killed! But the spark that had shot forth from her eyes; what became of that? The sunbeam took it up; the sunbeam carried the jewel from the head of the toad. Whither?
> Ask not the naturalist; rather ask the poet. He will tell it thee under the guise of a fairy tale...
> But the jewel in the head of the toad?
> Seek it in the sun; see it there if you can.
> The brightness is too dazzling there. We have not yet such eyes as can see into the glories which God has created, but we shall receive them by-and-by; and that will be the most beautiful story of all, and we shall all have our share in it.[31]

Andersen's adaptation of the ancient myth transfigures the jewel from an object to a drive—the continual striving and desire to go upwards; it is what one might think of as a perfectionist intimation that the well is not the world, that another, better state of the world always lies just beyond the limits of the world one currently inhabits. There is no final, complete, or attained state of that world and so of the self or soul that inhabits it; rather, there is either a lethal willingness to accept one's currently attained world, or a refusal ever to regard any attained world as final or complete. The little toad's vitality lies in her striving, not in anything she already possesses or might come to possess; otherwise put, it is the impossible desire to become one with the incomprehensibly transcendent sun, which is at once beyond the gaze or reach of mortal beings and yet always already one with those beings insofar as they yearn for it.

But Andersen also tells us that the incomprehensible nature of jewel and sun can nevertheless be comprehended—if not by the naturalist then by the poet, and in the form of a fairy tale (*this* fairy tale). What grants this genre its power is, however, its willingness to acknowledge that its own grasp of this dazzling

---

[31] Quoted from the translation at http://hca.gilead.org.il/the_toad.html.

brightness takes the form of acknowledging its own utter inadequacy in comparison with another mode of storytelling, that of God's narrative for creation and for human beings within it. And just as we shall all have our share in that most beautiful of stories, so the fairy tale's portrayal of the jewel's participation in the sun is successful only by declaring its own willing dependence upon, and so its ultimate participation in, the Christian story of the Son (, the Father, and the Holy Spirit). By declaring its own nothingness in relation to that divine narrative (and doing so in terms provided by the sacred texts which convey it, such as 'Now we see through a glass darkly; presently we shall behold Him face to face'), it identifies the mode of its participation in that narrative—namely, that of withdrawing any claims to authority of its own by crediting such authority as it may presently have to another Author. Since its nothingness is manifest only in relation to that unattained but attainable narrative perspective, any proper declaration of that nothingness relates it and its readers to that other perspective, and so makes of itself a way into that divine story—a spark thrown off its dazzling sun.

It becomes increasingly clear as part one of *Darkness Visible* develops that Matty can only become himself precisely by such an act of directed or dialectical self-abnegation—by declaring himself as nothing in relation to the God of the Old (and New) Testaments, and thereby aspiring wholly to identify his life with the Christian form of life, to become an individual in whom that impossibly perfected story condenses or crystallizes. But the author of *Darkness Visible* makes no such vow: Christian concepts and traditions remain prominent throughout the text, but they are frequently interwoven with (and sometimes put into conflict with) resources deriving from other layers of the cultural sedimentation that helps constitute the English society out of which it was written.

This is evident in the very phrase whose palimpsestic significance we are currently delineating: Golding's toads and jewels inherit and revivify ancient folk-myth, the pastorals of classical antiquity and Shakespearean revaluation, and European fairy tale. He thereby acknowledges his indebtedness to the genres of myth and fable, whilst presenting them not as limits upon his present project but as elements in a broader field of its poetic resources—more specifically as conventions that his project aspires to reconstruct in order better to realize their orienting aspiration to represent the reality of things. But this heterogeneity of genres also shows that, unlike Andersen, Golding resists the subordination of poetry to any particular religious authority, the absolute subsumption of his literary authority within that of Christianity; he is not Aeneas but Virgil, not a religious visionary but rather the artistic envisioner of Matty's religious visions. And yet: when Golding reaches the point of envisioning the hell that Matty seeks to avert but which is as integral to his religious sensibility as heaven—when in parts two and three he follows Sophy, the metaphysical twin of twentieth-century terrorism, from her initial nihilistic intuitions to her whole-hearted creative imagining of their realization in the world—the question of his authority to relate what he has seen unavoidably recurs. Virgil asks divine permission to say what he has seen of the Underworld; when that request reappears as the epigraph to Golding's novel, to whom does he imagine that it is directed, and in what spirit?

By the end of his stay in Australia, Matty's agonizing struggle to find a way of meaning Christian words and deeds—to find himself in those religious resources—comes to a climax. After the apparently castrating crucifarce or crucifiction he undergoes at the hands (or feet) of an Aborigine named Harry Bummer, he performs his own version of the Old Testament prophetic practices of Elijah and Ezekiel in downtown Darwin, to disruptive effect; and before returning to England, he searches for somewhere low down, a place at once hot, fetid, and supplied with water, in which he can undertake a ritual (at once final and initial or initiatory). Watched only by uncomprehending frogs and lizards, he strides into and through a deep, isolated pool at night-time, dressed only in a chain fastened around his waist from which heavy steel wheels are slung, and holding a lit, antique lamp over his head; at the midpoint, his head is wholly submerged, with only the hand and arm grasping the lamp remaining above the surface of the water. Once he reaches the other side, he heaves the lamp four times at each point of the compass; then he goes on his way (DV, 72–6).

Matty remains silent throughout, but his actions speak for themselves: more precisely, they *say* themselves, as Wittgenstein puts it when characterizing what he calls a gesture language, or the gestural dimension of language.[32] The medium and the message are one; what it signifies and its mode of signification are inextricable. One might say that Matty's actions are perfectly adapted to their purpose: their meaning would be altered or diminished if any element of the ritual were other than it is (intuitively, the shape and raw material of the steel wheels matters as much as their weight, as does the old-fashioned design of the lamp). On the other hand, the significance of those actions in that place is importantly dependent on the wider context within which the ritual is performed; in particular, our sense of its meaning is inseparable from our knowledge that Matty is performing it, and so from everything we know about Matty's life up to this moment (which means pretty much everything in *Darkness Visible* up to this point). These are not contradictory responses, any more than saying of the expression in someone's eyes both that it is unique and that it expresses what it expresses only in the context of her face.

When Wittgenstein discusses Sir James Frazer's account (in *The Golden Bough*) of the annual ritual in which the priest-king of Nemi is slain by his successor, he offers the following response:

---

[32] For more on this, cf. my *Inheritance and Originality* (Oxford: Oxford University Press, 2001), pt. 1, sects. 45–6.

Put that account of the King of the Wood at Nemi together with the phrase 'the majesty of death', and you see that they are one.

The life of the priest-king shows what is meant by that phrase.

If someone is gripped by the majesty of death, then through such a life he can give expression to it.—Of course this is not an explanation: it puts one symbol in place of another. Or one ceremony in place of another.[33]

One way of giving expression to our understanding of Matty's ritual would be to put it together with the following passage: 'and the light shineth in darkness and the darkness comprehendeth it not'; another would be to put it together with the phrase 'you have been baptized with water; you shall be baptized with the Holy Spirit'. Either phrase might crystallize what is compelling about Matty's ritual, and so about his life; or they might leave us cold, dissatisfied; or we might oscillate between these responses as our mood or circumstances shift—balancing on the edge of a heightened meaning, to use the terms through which Cavell characterizes Kierkegaard's brusque grammatical reminders about words used in transcendent rather than immanent contexts. But even if such phrases do satisfy us, they do not do so by finding a non-ritualized or unceremonial equivalent for the meaning of the ritual; they rather amount to the substitution of one ritual symbol or ceremonial gesture for another. Insofar as they capture the impression the ritual makes, they do not so much represent its meaning as re-enact it: one might equally well say that the ritual gives expression to what grips us about the words. Each is the other's explanation; the meaning of both is equally ceremonial or gestural.

If we acknowledge this ritual and these phrases (both from the beginning of John's Gospel) as one, then we acknowledge an internal relation between the meaning of the ritual and the meaning of Christianity; but this ritual is not a Christian rite, not a rite of passage into or within the Christian church—it is Matty's remaking of Christian elements into a language that articulates what he (prophetically) feels, something that he has just distinguished from what he (prophetically) sees (DV, 71). The same holds of his culminating spiritual insight, during his employment as a caretaker at Wandicott House, an exclusive private school outside Greenfield. Having just had his sexual potency restored by a dream in which Sophy appears as the woman in the Apocalypse (to which he responds by dancing to the sound of Beethoven's Seventh, the symphony Wagner ceremonially characterized as 'the apotheosis of dance'), he has a vision in which his fellowship with his two spiritual elders is revealed, and all three throw down their crowns at the feet of a great spirit in white, who will stand behind the schoolchild Matty has been asked to guard, and whom he will save from a terrorist kidnap attempt. Surely here, one might think, the intense colours of his spiritual passion have

---

[33] *Remarks on Frazer's* Golden Bough, ed. R. Rhees, trans. A. C. Miles (Doncaster: Brynmill Press, 1979), 3e.

finally come neatly and evenly to fill in the outlines provided by the Christian story (cf. DV, 22); but even here, those outlines are broken—the specificities and exclusivities of doctrine bypassed, the orthodoxies of liturgy and rite dispensed with. Christianity remains Matty's sole spiritual language until the end; but he works only with those elements that work for him, and is more than willing to fuse or stitch them together with any extra-Christian elements that also seem to work.

How does Golding make his depiction of Matty's immersion ritual so powerfully impressive—conveying its ceremonial meaning without lapsing into attempts to explain or summarize that meaning non-ceremonially? His description of Matty's actions is both like and unlike the book's opening description of his entry into the world. They are alike, in that this scene comes vividly to life primarily by an absolutely receptive transcription of its external physical details, so that the reader seems to be standing at the edge of the pool observing everything that happens; every element of deed and context exhibits itself before our eyes in such a way that we are simultaneously convinced that the man's purpose is utterly inscrutable (because hidden away inside his head, a point of view from which Golding scrupulously excludes us) and utterly transparent (wholly manifest in what the man does). But unlike the opening account of the Blitz, this radically external description reduces its metaphorical content to the barest minimum—no tents or bushes, no goddess of the outback, nothing figurative that is no sooner invoked than deployed as if literally true. Any reasonable natural scientist or anthropologist could accept the descriptive resources employed here; but the result is that the basic constituents of the natural world disclose themselves as capable of being (even perhaps as always already) irradiated with spiritual meaning.

Crucially, however, before this vivid transcription of the ritual, Golding writes a kind of prologue to it—two long paragraphs cast in predominantly subjunctive or counterfactual form, in which the narrator imagines someone walking into this hidden environment, and reports on what every available sense would have supplied such a person:

> Human feet would have felt the soft and glutinous texture, half water half mud, that would rise swiftly to the ankles and farther... The nose would have taken all the evidence of vegetable and animal decay, while the mouth and skin... would have tasted an air so warm and heavy with water it would have seemed as if there was doubt as to whether the whole body stood or swam or floated. The ears would be filled with the thunder of the frogs and anguish of nightbirds...
>
> Then, accustomed to the darkness by a long enough stay and willing—it would have to be by sacrifice of life and limb—to trade everything for the sight, eyes would find what evidence there was for them too. It might be a faint phosphorescence round the fungi on the trunks of trees... or a swift flight of sparks flashing between tree trunks...

By then, feet that had stayed that long would have sunk deep, the mud moving to this side and that, the warm mud; and the leeches would have attached themselves down there in an even darker darkness, a more secret secrecy and with unconscious ingenuity, without allowing their presence to be felt would have begun to feed through the vulnerable skin.

But there was no man in that place; and it seemed impossible to one who had inspected it from far off and in daylight that there ever had been a man in the place since men began. (DV, 73)

Suppose we were to put this passage together with the following sentence from the Book of Genesis: 'And the earth was without form, and void; and darkness was upon the face of the deep': we would, I think, see that they are one. But it is not just that the distinct natural elements of the scene blur and blend into one another (liquid earth, watery air, animal decay), to the point that natural form as such dissolves; a similar effect simultaneously occurs at the level of narrative form. For what begins as an act of imagining what someone else—no one in particular—might experience quickly dissolves into an act of imagining what such experience would have been like for the narrator, and one so intensely detailed and penetrating that it quickly takes on the aspect of a report from someone who really did walk into the pool in the encroaching dark, even someone who is currently standing—all senses alert—in that softly glutinous water. In this way, distinct imaginative acts blur into one another, and acts of imagination blur into transcriptions of experience.

The uncanniness of all this compels the narrator to think of his imaginary person in the pool—that is, himself—as risking life and limb for the experience, and to associate his imaginative residence in the water with suffering leeches to feed silently on him. Here, the blurring or blending goes into reverse: the realities conjured up by the narrator's imaginative capacity to penetrate the experiences of others now begin to penetrate him, disclosing the porousness of his own identity and beginning to leech his lifeblood. Why this sudden sense of lethal vulnerability? Because the narrator's act of imagination places him in the very position that Matty will occupy later that night: it is a kind of trial effort, a preliminary attempt at taking on Matty's perspective or view on the world, becoming that incarnation of 'the Spirit of God moving upon the face of these waters' for which the previously cited verses of Genesis directly prepare the way. This (un)holy essay is something from which the narrator withdraws as a seeming impossibility, but an impossibility encountered specifically from the point of view of someone who had inspected it in daylight—from Matty's perspective.

In short, Golding tries to imagine the context and core experience of the ritual from Matty's point of view, and the experience so disturbs him that he denies its very possibility and retreats to the perspective of an observer for the ritual itself. He experiences his own character, when driven by deep spiritual feeling to inscrutable but exquisitely apt ritual gestures, as threatening to drain away his creator's vitality; he fears the uncanny porousness of his imagination to its own creations, and in particular the secret ingenuity with which this imaginative creation threatens to destabilize every boundary or limit within and between authorial self and authored world—to dissolve the structure of reality altogether.

What lesson should Golding's readers draw from this ceremonial double gesture of immersion-and-withdrawal about the porousness of the barrier between themselves and the world of *Darkness Visible*—about the risks of allowing its creator to draw us into that world? For remember: the protagonist of this ritual scene is Matty—the good man, the prophet, the saint. What might happen when we are invited to imagine Matty's opposite, his dark twin?

At the end of part three, Sophy's plot to kidnap a child from Wandicott House School is falling apart: her terrorist sister has hijacked the plan (together with Sophy's boyfriend) for her own purposes, the arrival of unlooked-for visitors means that the stable room in which she grew up cannot be used to incarcerate the kidnapped child, and Matty has anyway forced her key accomplice to abort the kidnap itself. Having been ejected from the stables, but before discovering that the kidnap attempt has failed, in the depths of the countryside outside Greenfield, her attention is caught:

> There was a loud thumping noise in the hedge and it stopped her dead. Something was bouncing and flailing about and then it squeaked and she could make out that it was a rabbit in a snare, down there by the ditch that lay between the towpath and the woods. It was flailing about, not knowing what had caught it and not caring to know but killing itself in an effort just to be free, or it may be, just to be dead. Its passion defiled the night with grotesque and obscene caricature of process, of logical advance through time from one moment to the next where the trap was waiting. (DV, 249)

Still before receiving the bad news from her accomplice, but ecstatic at the sight of the conflagration at Wandicott House painting the sky red, 'she saw what the last outrage was and knew herself capable of it. She shut her eyes as the image swept round her' (DV, 251). Within that image is the kidnapped boy, now incarcerated in the stinking toilet of an abandoned, rotting barge she had previously explored on the towpath outside Greenfield. The child's arms are bound behind his back, as are his feet and knees; more ropes hold him on either side to the boat's walls, and a huge pad of sticky stuff covers his mouth and cheeks. His violent struggles against those bonds 'sound like a rabbit thumping' (DV, 251), and are redoubled when he hears her voice; but somehow, as she enters the confined space, inhales its disgusting smell of ancient and fresh urine, and removes the child's jersey and shirt, her boyfriend's commando knife is in her hand.

She swept her hand over his naked tum and belly button, the navel my dear if you must refer to it at all and she felt paper-thin ribs and a beat, beat, thump, thump at left centre. So she got his trousers undone and held his tiny wet cock in her hand as he struggled and hummed through his nose. She laid the point of the knife on his skin and finding it to be the right place, pushed it a bit so that it pricked. The boy convulsed and flailed in the confinement and she was or someone was, frightened a bit, far off and anxious. So she thrust more still and felt it touch the leaping thing or be touched by it again and again while the body exploded with convulsions and a high humming came out of the nose. She thrust with all the power there was, deliriously; and the leaping thing inside seized the knife so that the haft beat in her hand, and there was a black sun. There was liquid everywhere and strong convulsions and she pulled the knife away to give them free play but they stopped. The boy just sat there in his bonds, the white patch of elastoplast divided down the middle by the dark liquid from his nose.

(DV, 252)

Few commentators fail to note this passage, although only in passing, and those who do go into more detail typically misdescribe what actually goes on: they report Sophy as castrating the boy, or as stabbing him through his genitals.[34] These critical lapses are striking, and deeply significant. Specifically, they occlude the fact that Sophy stabs the child through the heart, which the passage repeatedly describes as leaping and thumping, thereby presenting it as going proxy for the boy's whole body (as it thumps and leaps in its confinement), and so characterizing both heart and body in terms first applied to the trapped rabbit in the ditch—a creature already identified with Sophy herself, the human animal whose obscene passion defiles the night as she flails hysterically in her desire to be free, or to be dead. These commentators thereby fail to note that Golding equates her murder of the child with self-murder, understanding it as an attempt to annihilate not just that frightened anxious, far-off part of her self that retains some connection with goodness, but her existence as such, which she conceives of as nothing more than a grotesque and obscene caricature of process or narrative.

This specific failure of vision is also, however, a way of averting one's critical gaze from the scene as a whole; it is a way of covering it up and so of ushering it offstage even whilst appearing to do the reverse. Just like those who can hardly bring themselves to mention the scene at all, such critics deny its true reality, and so participate in the general critical reluctance to admit that we have indeed read every word of it, and so that Golding has compelled us to read every word of it. He has here exercised his unequalled imaginative powers in such a way that Sophie's

---

[34] Cf V. Tiger, *William Golding: The Unmoved Target* (London: Marion Boyars, 2003), 195, and M. Kinkead-Weekes and I. Gregor, *William Golding: A Critical Study of the Novels* (London: Faber, 2002), 252, respectively.

imagining of the final outrage appears to us as the narrative of an actual event, and our reading of it is as a kind of participation in that event. The boundary between imaginative representation and reality dissolves within the world of the novel, together with the boundary between that imagined world and its readers; and we experience both dissolutions as the result of that world's creator's willingness to dissolve the boundary between himself and his creation—to immerse himself in the reality of Sophy's evil, which means devoting his imagination to making that evil real in a way which seriously problematizes the distinction between reality and a literarily engendered sense of reality.

Put this account of child-murder together with the phrase 'darkness visible', and you see that they are one. But if this scene really epitomizes the meaning of the novel's title, and so of the novel itself, why has no critic of the novel ventured to quote extensively from it, let alone to cite it in its entirety? If to do so is to experience once again what it depicts, and so to inflict it on those who read that criticism, one can hardly blame them. Such a refusal is, after all, the most direct way of registering the perception (at once critical and moral) that this scene is obscene, something whose outrageous content ought really to remain offstage (as the etymology of the term requires) because, staged in this way, to borrow the words of one of J. M. Coetzee's characters, 'it made an impress on me the way a branding iron does. Certain pages burn with the fires of hell'.[35]

If we will not quote this passage—this exemplary element of the palimpsest that is *Darkness Visible*—we seem to imply that Golding should not have created it, and so should not have created the whole fictional world for which it goes proxy (however much praise we lavish on every other aspect of that world); but if we do quote it, we seem to risk violating basic tenets of literary criticism and morality alike (by failing to keep what is, precisely insofar as it is poetically successful, beyond the pale of rightful representation). Some might prefer to think of such citation as the critical equivalent of the creative strategy at work in Golding's depiction of the pool ritual—that is, as one of immersion-and-withdrawal. For if a critical immersion in Sophy's vision reveals the artistic means by which Golding creates in us the sense that this evil is no literary artefact but the thing itself, it necessarily reveals that impression to be a literary creation or effect, and thereby allows us to withdraw from any identity-threatening participation in it. Others might rather stay true to their initial sense that these pages really do burn with the fires of hell, and conclude that this text genuinely disables criticism. Golding himself vowed never to talk about *Darkness Visible*, and he was true to his word. Many readers will take this as a ceremonial gesture intended to encourage a similar act of self-abnegation by those whose passionate interest in the text is precisely what tempts them to talk about it critically; but I think there are ways of

---

[35] *Elizabeth Costello*, 171.

acknowledging that gesture without so taking it—for example, by finding ways of talking critically about the novel which bring out the fact that, and the ways in which, it says itself.

However that may be, in the context of our present concerns, Golding's work might also be viewed as pertinent to a number of questions: whether contemporary life can still provide a context which can invite or even compel the continued application of the religious concepts of authority and revelation; whether that question is internally related to the continued applicability of the ethical and the artistic inflections of those same concepts; and whether such a context would thereby nourish a life-denying asceticism, or constitute a bulwark against the nihilistic evisceration of any conception of life as genuinely meaningful.

The novel gives us two reasons to take Matty as an authoritative and revelatory incarnation of the continued vitality of the concepts whose vicissitudes we have been tracking throughout this essay. The first is offered when he leads a spiritual séance with two elderly characters who have observed the main character's in the novel's narrative throughout their conflict-at-a-distance: the bookseller Sim Goodchild and the teacher Edwin Bell. When Sim offers his hand to Matty in greeting:

> [He] looked down at the hand as if it were an object to be examined and not shaken. Then he took the hand, turned it over and peered into the palm. Sim... looked into his own palm, pale, crinkled, the volume, as it were, most delicately bound in this rarest or at least most expensive of all binding material—and then he fell through into an awareness of his own hand that stopped time in its revolution. The palm was exquisitely beautiful, it was made of light. It was precious and preciously inscribed with a sureness and delicacy beyond art and grounded somewhere else in absolute health.
>
> In a convulsion unlike anything he had every known, Sim stared into the gigantic world of his own palm and saw that it was holy. (DV, 231)

A little later, as all three hold hands around a table, Sim has another uncanny experience:

> Edwin spoke above his head. Or, not Edwin and not speech. Music. Song. It was a single note, golden, radiant, like no singer that ever was. There was, surely, no mere human breath that could sustain the note that spread as Sim's palm had spread before him, widened, became, or was, precious range after range beyond experience, turning itself into pain and beyond pain, taking pain and pleasure and destroying them, being, becoming. It stopped for a while with promise of what was to come. It began, continued, ceased. It had been a word. That beginning, that change of state explosive and vital had been a consonant, and the realm of gold that grew from it a vowel lasting for an aeon; and the

semi-vowel of the close was not an end, since there was, there could be no end but only a readjustment so that the world of spirit could hide itself again, reluctant as a lover to go and with the ineffable promise that it would love always and if asked would always come again. (DV, 232–3)

According to these spiritual visions, Matty's authority reveals an absolute affirmation of the literal and the figurative body of distinctively human existence—both flesh and language. Disclosed in the utterance of a single, exemplary word (what else could it be but 'love'?) is a vision which fully acknowledges and thereby transcends both pain and pleasure, and both Being and Becoming. In short, it takes the fundamental terms of analysis required in order to prosecute the Nietzschean charge of sadomaoschistic asceticism and transforms them into the raw material of a future promise.

In the lives of Sim and Edwin, these momentary visions may fail to take root in practical activity: neither man is more than lukewarm, spiritually speaking, as is evidenced in Sim's continuing expressions of hatred for Sebastian Pedigree—the man who taught Matty, and whose pederastic impulses led to the loss of his job and his social standing in Greenfield. But Matty's long struggle to save his old teacher does not cease after his death by fire when rescuing the kidnap victim. The novel ends with Mr Pedigree sitting on a park bench clutching the ball that he uses to lure unsuspecting children: he has a vision of Matty approaching him through an ocean of gold that partakes of the nature of both light and air, sun and wind; and within that vision Pedigree converses with him, expressing his own interpretation of his nature:

'There've been such people in this neighbourhood, such monsters, that girl and her men, Stanhope, Goodchild, Bell even, and his ghastly wife—I'm not like them, bad but not as bad, I never hurt anybody—*they* thought I hurt children but I didn't, I hurt myself. And you know about the last thing the thing I shall be scared into doing if I live long enough—just to keep a child quiet, keep it from telling—that's hell Matty, that'll be hell—help me!' (DV, 264)

The moment he is asked, Matty responds:

[T]he golden immediacy of the wind altered at its heart and began first to drift upwards, then swirl upwards then rush upwards around Matty. The gold grew fierce and burned. Sebastian watched in terror as the man before him was consumed, melted, vanished like a guy in a bonfire; and the face was no longer two-tone but gold as the fire and stern and everywhere there was a sense of the peacock eyes of great feathers and the smile round the lips was loving and terrible. This being drew Sebastian towards him so that the terror of the golden lips jerked a cry out of him—

'Why? Why?'
The face looming over him seemed to speak or sing but not in human speech. Freedom.
Then Sebastian, feeling the many-coloured ball that he held against his chest, and knowing what was to happen, cried out in agony.
'No! No! No!'
He clutched the ball closer, drew it in to avoid the great hands that were reaching towards him. He drew the ball closer than the gold on the skin, he could feel how it beat between his hands with terror and he clutched it and screamed again and again. But the hands came in through his. They took the ball as it beat and drew it away so that the strings that bound it to him tore as he screamed. Then it was gone. (DV, 2645)

Beneath the surface of this passage lie a number of other passages from Golding's earlier novels—most notably Christopher's final submission to what he perceives as the destructive claws of his Creator (in *Pincher Martin*), and Sammy Mountjoy's transfigurative vision effected by torture in a Nazi prison camp (in *Free Fall*). But this palimpsestic effect risks occluding the specific complexities of that surface within its immediate textual context. For the passage literalizes the figurative significance of the ball, identifying it with the impulse it serves, and thereby with the heart and so the nature of the man defined and deformed by that impulse; and it conflates this figurative heart of Pedigree's with his literal heart. At the same time it contrasts Matthew Septimus Windrove's desire for that heart with Sophy's desire for the heart of her fantasized victim: where she envisions murder, he envisions freedom—more specifically Pedigree's freedom from himself, and from the hell that that self will otherwise create for him.

Can we think of Pedigree as someone whose preciousness entails that he should not be treated as if he were vermin? Can we think that of Sophy? Would the creation (or re-creation) of a world in which we could do so amount to progress or regression in our collective self-perfecting? What authority are we willing or able to acknowledge in Golding's creation of such a world?

Essay Two
Writing the Life of the Mind

1. Autobiography, Biography, and Philosophy

Of the two central, interrelated literary genres of the life story, autobiography has been more central to the interests and the development of philosophy in the West than biography. It might even be argued that one could write an instructive (if not exactly exhaustive) history of Western European philosophy by concentrating solely on examples of philosophical autobiography; at the very least, such texts as Augustine's *Confessions*, Descartes's *Meditations*, Rousseau's *Confessions*, and Nietzsche's *Ecce Homo* would be pivotal to any attempt to narrate the story of the life of the mind in the West. So the question arises: why should this be the case? Why should such a highly specific mode of writing play such a deeply influential role in Western philosophy's unfolding and contested conception of itself? And if that philosophy can find clarity about itself through a philosopher's attempts to attain clarity about himself, is that in part because any individual's pursuit of self-understanding—at least within the framework of Western culture's self-understanding—will find itself drifting or drawn towards philosophical modes of reflection? If philosophical autobiographies are as central to the history and development of their genre as the illustriousness of my examples suggests, that may be because the impulse to take up certain specifically philosophical problems lies at the heart of autobiographical (and hence, biographical) writing as such.

Since what we call philosophy seems capable of taking an interest in, even presuming to adjudicate upon, any and every aspect of human life, it is no surprise that philosophers should take autobiography to be just as much capable of generating philosophical questions as any other piece of human business, and hence as capable of supporting what one might call 'the philosophy of autobiography'—within which one might expect to find a critical investigation of the assumptions and concepts presupposed by any particular autobiographical exercise. But why should these assumptions and concepts—as opposed to those deployed by historians and scientists, or those informing our concerns with the mind and morality—be of any particular, even of an obsessional, interest to philosophers? And why should philosophy repeatedly feel the need to express and to revolutionize itself through essentially autobiographical modes of writing?

The peculiar kind of authority that philosophy assigns to its pronouncements is pertinent here. Unlike history, philology, or molecular biology, philosophy doesn't have a distinctive subject matter; its peculiar kinds of questions are essentially parasitic upon the existence of other disciplines and domains of human life, they can arise with respect to any of those phenomena, and there is no body of distinctively philosophical knowledge or technique or method which must be mastered by anyone who wishes to try to answer those questions (or at least nothing that is not itself essentially subject to philosophical contestation and questioning). And yet philosophers continue to claim sweeping authority for their pronouncements; they variously think of the results of their thinking as giving us access to the a priori, as speaking with necessity and universality, as deliverances of pure reason. How is this to be understood?

If we imagine the philosopher, at once gripped by her sense that her insights truly penetrate to a realm of impersonal necessity and yet unable to deny that those insights are unsupported by any impersonally authoritative expertise, I think that we will naturally conjure up a picture of an exposed self, one whose claims to the agreement of others necessarily place her individual existence on the line. In other words, philosophy demands an exemplary self-reliance, a mode of the self's relation to itself in which the individual self is deemed representative of selfhood as such. This does not abandon the philosophical claim to universality: it merely follows Aristotle in thinking that the universal can only be attained through and made manifest in the particular. Without some such picture of oneself as both particular and representative (even if representative only by virtue of one's particularity, which then at least exemplifies the human capacity for individuality—for differentiating oneself from every other human being), why would anyone write an autobiography? And one might then ask whether having such a picture of oneself is inherent to selfhood as such—a condition of being oriented as a subject in (and of) human life.

A picture of philosophical authority as essentially but impersonally self-revelatory or autobiographical is detectable throughout the history of the subject in the West, from Socrates onwards. Even if we restrict ourselves to the modern period in Europe, we encounter Descartes's presentation of himself as subjecting himself to the threat of madness in a search for epistemological purity whose results he invites us to prove by enacting their production ourselves; we find Locke, Berkeley, and Hume acting on the conviction that one individual's discovery of something about his own mind (the absence or presence of an idea) is authoritative for all; and in more recent times, we find Austin and Wittgenstein speaking of what we say when, and thereby establishing how things are in the world, on the basis of their own individual sense of the fitness of words to their contexts of application. Each such inflection of the autobiographical impulse in philosophy obviously invites the charge of arrogance; its inherent humility may be less obvious, but it is no less real. For since the representativeness claimed for the philosopher's individuality is such that any individual can also claim it, it can always be contested or denied. Hence, such self-reliance actually constitutes an important counter-example to the often rather less humble and self-aware modes in which philosophers have claimed authority over others.

If philosophy's peculiar combination of arrogance and humility can in this way be grounded in its conception of the self's relation to itself, then philosophy has a particular reason to preoccupy itself with the assumptions and resources of autobiographical writing; for this will achieve not only a clearer understanding of the self, but also thereby a clearer self-understanding. It then becomes a matter of doubled or reflexive significance for philosophy to ask what it betokens about the self that it is capable of an autobiographical relation to itself. And since the idea of a biography is one factor in the meaning of the idea of the autobiographical, this question also involves addressing the question of what it betokens about the self that other selves are capable of establishing a biographical relation to it.

We might begin to investigate these tangled relations by asking whether others could regard a creature who is essentially incapable of relating to itself as the possible object of an autobiography as the possible object of a biography. Is it internal to our conception of what it is for someone to have or to live a life of which there might be a biography that she be capable of taking an autobiographical stance towards herself? Otherwise put: Is our concept of the self such that its distinctive mode of existence must be writable, articulable in thought or speech, from both the first-person and the third-person perspectives?

Various sceptical lines of thought—some concerning the nature of the self, others concerning the representational powers of language, and both often claiming a Nietzschean ancestry—would reject this idea from the outset. To tell a story about oneself is, according to such suggestions, necessarily to falsify oneself; it is to impose a form and structure upon that which, like any aspect of the real, essentially transcends such constraints. The basic line of argument with respect to language is laid out in Nietzsche's early essay 'On Truth and Lying in an Extra-Moral Sense'.[1] He there claims, amongst other things, that any application of language to reality—being an attempt to confine the particular within necessarily general terms—falsifies any specific thing to which that term applies by positing it as identical to all the other instances to which it applies: subsuming every individual leaf in the forest under that concept elides their particularities of colour, decay, or size, and our attempts to subsume those differentiating properties under concepts simply posits a new but equally spurious identity between different things (e.g. 'red leaves'), omitting ever more granular particularities for us to try and fail to capture in ineluctably general categories. The moral is general; but it has the particular implication that any application of words to the human self necessarily misses its target, even when it is the self itself that applies them to itself,

---

[1] In In *The Birth of Tragedy and Other Writings*, ed. and trans. Raymond Geuss and Ronald Speirs (Cambridge: Cambridge University Press, 1999).

even when it simply tries to name itself. As Beckett's narrator in *The Unnamable* puts it: 'I, say I. Unbelieving...I seem to speak, it is not I, about me, it is not about me.'[2]

A. S. Byatt's novel, *The Biographer's Tale*, pivots around these kinds of anxiety.[3] Its protagonist, Phineas Nanson, is driven to take a biographical interest in the biographical work of Scholes Destry-Scholes as a reaction to the ways in which Literary Theory (in his view) reduces individual texts to mere instances of general structures; 'I must have *things*,' he wails. 'Facts,' his supervisor proclaims: 'The richness, the surprise, the shining *solidity* of a world full of facts. Every established fact—taking its place in a constellation of glittering facts like planets in an empty heaven, declaring *here* is matter, and *there* is vacancy—every established fact illuminates the world' (BT, 4). But even Destry-Scholes is discovered to have recoiled from, or rather to have reoriented, his biographical work in the direction of fictive accounts of the lives of Carl Linnaeus, Francis Galton, and Henrik Ibsen—a taxonomist, a statistician, and a playwright who famously invokes the image of the self as a centreless onion: three debunkers of the inspiring conception of genuinely individual elements of reality, and hence of human individuality. And even here, in these fragmentary, hybrid literary exercises, Destry-Scholes's own self remains absent, withdrawing from the biographer's grasp.

Peter Conradi, invoking a passage from one of Iris Murdoch's novels which expresses an analogous suspicion, draws a moral for his own biographical work on Murdoch:

> In *Under the Net*, Hugo teaches Jake that 'all stories are lies' because truth is *local and particular*. This was the truth I sought. The biographer must **construct** a story. I decided to tell a *succession* of short stories that might be mutually contradictory, but were each internally coherent, and (I felt) individually truthful.[4]

But of course, if all stories are lies, then even a succession of internally coherent but mutually contradictory short stories could not (even in principle) be individually truthful. If Hugo is right, then the biographer and the autobiographer alike simply cannot achieve truth, and so cannot coherently seek it; but then we might ask whether Hugo's sense of the inherent particularity of truth really justifies the conclusion that its articulation in language, and particularly in the language of story, must fail.

---

[2] S. Beckett, *Molloy; Malone Dies; The Unnamable* (London: Picador, 1979), 267; hereafter U.
[3] (London: Chatto and Windus, 2000); hereafter BT.
[4] 'Writing *Iris Murdoch: A Life*—Freud versus Multiplicity', *Iris Murdoch Newsletter* 16 (Winter 2002/Spring 2003), 6.

To revert to Nietzsche's example: to say that something is a leaf (when it is) is not to capture every particular property it possesses, some of which differentiate it from other leaves, even from other instances of the same kind of leaf; but it is not to say something false about it either. It is to give the beginnings of a true account of it, to represent it as it really is (by representing it as having features that other particular leaves also have, by virtue of which they count as 'leaves'); and that account can be expanded, its particularity or granularity enhanced, as far as our particular purposes of description and understanding require us to go, by putting in the hard work needed to attend to and capture the relevant further features of that particular leaf. Why, then, should the truth about a particular human being be lost the moment a story is constructed in which to capture it? Surely its fate rather depends (as Conradi's avowed moral and his biographical practice both suggest) on how one constructs the story—with what degree of particularity, from which perspectives, and with what degree of awareness of its specific conditions (both enabling and disabling).

Whatever the merits of Nietzsche's early expressions of general disenchantment with language's powers of representation, what is generally taken to be his mature scepticism about selfhood is equally in play in contemporary manifestations of scepticism about (auto)biographical narratives. But here it is important to appreciate that Nietzsche's doubts in this domain are directed at certain conceptions of selfhood rather than at selfhood itself.[5] When he criticizes the idea of the subject as an indifferent substratum, something behind the strong person which has the freedom to manifest strength or not, he is targeting an absolutized notion of responsibility—one which says not merely that a person may choose whether or not to exercise a particular power of theirs, but that a person's characteristic array of powers, dispositions, and capacities taken as a whole is one (relatively superficial) thing and the person herself another thing altogether. This posits the person as a transcendent and utterly unconstrained point of view upon her entire character, and so facilitates holding individuals unconditionally responsible for every specific expression of any aspect of that character (as if eagles could be held responsible for their species nature: as if human beings created themselves and so their lives ex nihilo). And when he criticizes metaphysical accounts of the self which posit its essence as 'something I know not what' that grounds its ever-changing interweaving stream of consciousness, he does so because it renders the self essentially untouchable by any psychological changes it might undergo, and so by any worldly vicissitudes that might effect such changes. It thereby discounts and devalues our capacity for (and vulnerability to) profound change; in short, it amounts to a life-denying privileging of Being over Becoming.

---

[5] GM, 1.13 is the crucial reference point here.

One can reject either way of absolutizing our responsibilities and our identity without denying that we have any responsibility, or any continuity over time; we need only acknowledge that what those responsibilities and continuities amount to will vary, and will be differently subject to evaluation, from case to case. And in like manner, we can acknowledge that any story about the life of a self must be told by someone, and so from a particular point of view and in a particular context, without denying that any such story can be truthful, or that one such story may be closer to the truth than another. Nietzsche's late emphasis on the necessary perspectivalism of such accounts, and of knowledge-claims more generally, is often taken to express yet another form of scepticism; but then one needs to ask what an absolutely non-perspectival account of a given phenomenon might amount to—what it could possibly mean to give an account that is utterly unconditioned, given by no one in particular from no particular point of view, and capable of conveying an absolutely total representation of its subject matter. This is not a possibility of which our finite condition as knowers deprives us: it is a fantasy—the fantasy of a God's-eye view on reality, deployed to denigrate what knowing really is and could conceivably be for embodied creatures inhabiting an independently existing world.

Nietzsche's perspectivism is thus a tool for diagnosing yet another way in which we continue to live under God's shadow; and it is a metaphorically coded invitation to improve our understanding of a given phenomenon by becoming aware of what is conditioning our current understanding, and enriching it by constructing additional accounts derived from other perspectives on that same phenomenon (the more perspectives, the fuller the picture, and the easier to identify and correct for what limits and empowers each). And in the particular case of accounts of the self, Nietzsche's metaphor tells us that we are obliged to confront, rather than simply to shirk, the hard work needed to establish from case to case the extent to which any particular constructed story of an actual life may be truthful, or may falsify, or may require specific supplementation.

However we understand our Nietzschean inheritance, on the more analytic or Anglo-American side of post-Kantian philosophy the idea of the inherent narrativity of selfhood has proven persistently attractive. For example, Alasdair MacIntyre has famously argued that the possibility of giving a narrative account of the self is internal to what it is for the self to be a self.[6] He claims that selves are agents, and that human actions are necessarily such that they are comprehensible in narrative terms. Actions are not just pieces of behaviour, exhaustively describable in terms of physical movements; they are intentional, and hence can be comprehended only by relating them to the intentions, beliefs, and goals of the person performing them; and those intentions can be understood only in terms of

---

[6] In *After Virtue*; hereafter AV.

the settings or contexts in which they are embedded. I am presently writing a piece of philosophical prose; I might also be said to be furthering my career, following a line of thought from earlier writing and teaching, avoiding domestic commitments, and so on. It is therefore pertinent to ask what I am doing—in other words, to expect me to be able to specify under which of these various descriptions I primarily take myself to be doing what I am doing; and the answer I give will locate my action in a specific setting, which will in turn form part of a larger setting or context. I thereby render it comprehensible—that is, recountable as an episode in a set of nested stories—not only to myself but to others; and in the absence of such embedding, there is nothing that might count as an action to be understood either by myself or others, and so nothing of agency in what I do—only matter in motion. As MacIntyre summarizes the matter:

> I am presenting... human actions in general as enacted narratives. Narrative is not the work of poets, dramatists and novelists reflecting upon events which had no narrative order before one was imposed by the singer or the writer; narrative form is neither disguise nor decoration... It is because we all live out narratives in our lives and because we understand our own lives in terms of the narratives that we live out that the form of narrative is appropriate for understanding the actions of others. Stories are lived before they are told—except in the case of fiction. (AV, 197)

On this understanding of agency, the identity or unity of a self is the unity of a narrative, a unity of exactly the kind to which autobiographical and biographical stories typically give expression; and since the form such stories give to human lives corresponds to the form that such lives actually have, it must in principle be possible for such stories to capture the truth of a human life (even if practical difficulties of all kinds might prevent its attainment in any given case).

Such an understanding can allow for the possibility that calling a given event or action a beginning or an end confers significance of a kind upon it, and hence is debatable, since it claims only that the nature of the debate takes for granted the constraints of a narrative tale. It can also acknowledge that individuals are not entirely free to live out whatever story they please—that they are only co-authors of the narrative in which they are their own heroes, insofar as we enter upon a stage that is not of our own design, into ongoing, interlocking narratives that are not of our own making, playing subordinate parts in the dramas of others as well as the central part in our own. It can even allow for the possibility of the most thoroughgoing rejection of the terms in which one's inherited settings inform the narrative options one confronts in living out one's life; for such rejection is simply one extreme way in which one lives out the drama of one's own existence in relation to the other dramatic narratives within which it is embedded. Most centrally, however, it rebuts the charge that to give a narrative account of a human life is necessarily to falsify it—to impose on it an order or form (a structure of beginnings, unfoldings, reversals, achievements, triumphs, disasters, and endings) appropriate to fiction but essentially lacking in reality.

On this kind of approach, then, autobiography and biography are motivated by the requirements of truthfulness because human life as such is possessed of narrative form and structure, and the distinctively human form of individual existence is constituted by the exercise of our capacity to tell our own stories. The specific modes of that narrativity may be historically and culturally specific, just as certain forms of self-interpretation (such as those of the Homeric King or warrior) may recede beyond our social grasp only to be replaced by others (say, those of President or spy); but the fact that such modes or genres of narrative self-interpretation reach back to the ancient Greek roots of Western Judaeo-Christian culture suggests that their deployment is in effect constitutive of distinctively human life within its horizon (as well as potentially congenial to Nietzsche's ambivalent affirmations of Homeric characters).

MacIntyre's Aristotelian approach thus brings the techniques of certain kinds of fiction and those of biography and autobiography into close and philosophically stimulating proximity; but it is not clear how well he handles his consequent obligation to show how the two genres might be distinguished (given that they are not to be distinguished by reference to the narrative forms they assume or impose). MacIntyre claims that, whereas with respect to real people, stories are lived before they are told, with respect to fictional people it is otherwise; presumably, he does not mean by this that fictional lives are told before they are lived, but rather that they are not lived before they are told—even, perhaps, that the living of them and the telling of them are in some sense one and the same thing. And later, he remarks that '[t]he difference between imaginary characters and real ones is not in the narrative form of what they do; it is in the degree of their authorship of that form and of their own deeds' (AV, 200). Both remarks, however, blur the distinction between author and character in fictional narratives.

David Copperfield and Sherlock Holmes have exactly the same degree of authorial control over their own actions, exactly the same need to accept the constraints of the settings of their actions, and exactly the same responsibility for what they do within those constraints, as did Charles Dickens and Sir Arthur Conan Doyle, or indeed any real human beings; if they did not, their authors would not have produced a satisfying fictional depiction of human individuals. David Copperfield certainly lived the events of his life that he is recounting before the event in his life that is his recounting of them; he is remembering his childhood and youth. To be sure, Dickens and Doyle invented Copperfield and Holmes, and hence might be said to be in this sense entirely in control of their creations (although fiction writers are prone to articulate their experience of their characters in precisely opposite terms—as beings who reveal their nature and destiny to their authors, and as alive only insofar as their authors suffer this revelation of their autonomy); but Dickens and Doyle are not characters or forces of any kind in the world in which Copperfield and Holmes live out their lives, the world of the novels in which they are characters.

This point—which I touched on in Essay One when outlining Kierkegaard's critique of Andersen, whose disruptive presence in his fictional world derealizes his characters in the eyes of his readers—reveals a deep confusion in the attempt to illuminate the nature of the real human self's relation to itself by this kind of reference to an author's relation to the characters in a story he has written. For if we say that a human being's relation to itself is that of (part-)author of a tale in which she is the hero, then she must be regarded both as a character in the story told by the author and as the author of that story; but these two kinds of relation to the fictional character are not only radically different, but not obviously combinable. An author of a fictional narrative is (at least according to the model we are considering) at liberty to choose who to write about, the nature of the world she inhabits, and the events that will make up her life; but as MacIntyre acknowledges, human individuals have no such absolute freedom in relation to the narratives of their own lives. Whereas a character in a fictional narrative of the realistic kind (that is, a fictional narrative of the real world) relates to the settings and circumstances in which she finds herself, and to herself, in exactly the way a real human being does; hence her position reiterates that of the real person, rather than contrasting illuminatingly with it.

None of this necessarily undermines MacIntyre's core claim that real human lives necessarily have a narrative structure; indeed, insofar as this line of thought depends upon seeing a correspondence between the narrative unity of fictional and real characters as essential to the former's ability to elicit our suspensions of disbelief, it reinforces it. What we need to get more accurately into focus is not any spurious set of differences between a fictional character's relations to her existence and that of a real person, but rather a real and important set of differences between a real person's relationship to another person, and her relationship to a fictional character. For example, the techniques of realistic fiction can give its readers modes of access to the inmost thoughts and feelings, the most subtle and fine-grained details, of a fictional character's consciousness that are simply unavailable when one is trying to grasp the significance of a real person's thoughts, sayings, and doings. The point here is not that another's most complex thoughts and feelings are beyond expression by that other, and so beyond acknowledgement by her others; if an author can articulate them in a fictional case, there is no reason in principle why a real person cannot convey such things. The point is rather that, with respect to another real person, the sincerity of her self-expressions may be open to question at any given point; whereas when certain fictional techniques are used to convey to us a fictional character's stream of consciousness, we cannot coherently question whether what is thereby conveyed is true.

This point needs careful handling, however, if we are not to succumb too completely to the will to truth. My claim is not that everything we learn in a work of fiction about a character's inner life—even when it is the character that informs us of it—is trustworthy. The narrator of Agatha Christie's *The Mystery of Roger Ackroyd* does not tell us everything he could, and he certainly does not tell us everything he is thinking; but he never lies, and if he did, his narrative would be unreadable; a completely unreliable narrator—as opposed to one who gives himself away—would not be a narrator at all. Furthermore, the shadow of unreliability in a fictional character's autobiographical narrations is not exactly equivalent to that which hangs over real journals and memoirs. Any biographer must certainly be sensitive to the possible inaccuracies, deceptions, and self-deceptions embedded in her subject's autobiographical writings; but these are controlled or constrained for the reader of a fictional autobiography in ways that the real biographer simply cannot take for granted.

It would be essentially pointless, even incoherent, for an author to write a work of fiction taking the form of an autobiography that was largely fabricated by its fictional author, but whose status as a fabrication was undetectable to its readers; whereas a real person's autobiography might well be written with the perfectly intelligible intention of meeting both conditions, and could even succeed. And the deployment of other fictional techniques similarly excludes certain possibilities of fabrication or deception; for example, when Jane Austen reports Elizabeth Bennet's interior responses to Darcy's letter, there is simply no room for her readers intelligibly to raise the question of whether those responses are what they are reported to be.

Of course, even characters presented to us in such ways might exhibit certain species of self-deception.[7] For example, one of Kingsley Amis's protagonists, John Lewis, is a married librarian in the Welsh town of Aberdarcy, who becomes involved in an affair with the wife of the one of Aberdarcy's more influential town councillors—an affair much complicated by differences of temperament, class, and wealth, not to mention very different levels of guilt and anxiety about its possible consequences. At the beginning of their relationship, after visiting a nightclub together and kissing for the first time, John returns home to his wife and two young children and reports the following train of thought:

> Feeling a tremendous rakehell, and not liking myself much for it, and feeling rather a good chap for not liking myself much, and not liking myself at all for

---

[7] The case I'm about to introduce is one I have analysed in much more detail in the final chapter of my *The Self and Its Shadows: A Book of Essays on Individuality as Negation in Philosophy and the Arts* (Oxford: Oxford University Press, 2013).

feeling rather a good chap, I got indoors, vigorously rubbing lipstick off my mouth with my handkerchief.[8]

Is John a good chap or not? The difficulty is that he seems to exemplify what one might call a paradox of self-censure; the course of his reflections appears both self-undermining and morally dubious. There is nothing wrong in itself in someone's reflecting on one of his beliefs about himself (in this case, the belief that he is a good chap) as a further psychological fact about him, hence as something from which certain conclusions about himself may be drawn (after all, it is). But his initial sense of shame can only be the basis for his belief that he is rather a good chap if it does actually manifest what he takes to be true of himself, if it expresses his conviction about himself (as having behaved shamefully, as being a disgrace); but to commit himself to the belief that he is a good chap is precisely to decide that he is not a disgrace, and so must require the withdrawal of his initial judgement about himself. However, since it is only his commitment to the initial judgement that gives him any reason to endorse the second-order judgement, its withdrawal would entail that he must withdraw that second-order judgement.

Looked at more broadly, John's dislike of himself is rooted not (or not only) in a sense of shame about his adulterous activities, but also in a sense of shame about his tendency to romanticize their nature (as manifest in describing himself as a 'rakehell'). But as his choice of self-description implies, he no sooner romanticizes himself than he is aware that he has done so: the ironic excess of the description inserts a gap or distance between his interpretation of what he is up to and what he is really up to, and because that description comes from him—because the novel is a first-person narrative—its inordinateness registers his unwillingness or inability simply to identify himself with his own initial self-interpretation. In this respect, John's description of himself as a tremendous rakehell exemplifies something absolutely fundamental to his character—his incessant attempts at (or at least, his incessant inability to avoid) establishing ironic distance from any and every description of himself that might be thought to capture his identity.

He is a librarian—but in the way Sartre's waiter is a waiter: it is a pure performance, a perfect following-out of the script that role thrusts upon him, usually to great comic effect. He really believes that he loves his wife and children, but he struggles to realize or enact that belief in his dealings with them. He regards himself as a savage critic of bourgeois pretensions in those who claim superior social status in Aberdarcy; but he cannot carry out this role without extreme self-consciousness, he is infuriated by his tendency to recognize admirable human qualities in those he should be criticizing, and he eventually finds himself conducting

---

[8] Kingsley Amis, *That Uncertain Feeling* (London: Panther, 1955), 81; hereafter UF.

a deeply unsatisfactory affair with one of the most shamelessly self-serving, egotistical, and unkind members of that group.

The structure of ironic self-distancing that generates the process of recursive reversals of judgement exemplified in the passage I quoted is thus not only already at work in the very phrasing upon which the recursive process operates; it is at work, implicitly or explicitly, in a variety of ways throughout the language of the novel. It is, one might say, the signature of its narrative voice—the interior monologue of a subject who no sooner feels something than he questions its sincerity or justice, who oscillates unpredictably between performing pitch-perfect parodies of what others expect him to say or do and really saying what he thinks (typically in tones of savage sarcasm), who no sooner resolves to do something than he eagerly does the opposite. This is someone who is not so much governed by an uncertain feeling as he is constituted by feeling uncertain, someone who truly is not what he is and is what he is not—the Existentialist individual as Angry Young Man.

So we find ourselves once more confronting the fact that Amis's self-censurer has not only a name and a highly specific character, but also a particular status: he is both a highly specific character in a fiction and the narrator of that fiction. It is only because it is John himself who describes himself as a tremendous rakehell that we can be confident that ironic self-distancing does not merely come in at a relatively late or isolated stage in his thinking (and so opens itself to interpretation as instantiating a very specific form of moral weakness), but goes all the way down into the most basic or immediate forms of his experience—call it his orientation to the world. And to be reminded that our access to John's story is always through his consciousness is to be reminded that we are only in a position to be confronted by the paradox of his self-censure because we have already been given access to his interior life; we are reading the novel in which he appears, and more specifically reading his account of the events it narrates. Access to his interior life is thus not something we have to achieve—it is not something of which he might even in principle deprive us altogether, since his mode of fictional being is such that it is automatically bestowed on anyone who makes his literary acquaintance.

Our evaluation of John Lewis accordingly has to take into account his relationship with those who are reading about him, and so the significance of the possibility that the themes of sincerity and irony that dominate the world of the fiction might also have a bearing upon the relationship between that world's author, its inhabitants, and its readers. For John has no choice to make about whether or not he discloses himself to us: insofar as his existence is that of a fictional narrator of a fiction about himself, disclosure is a consequence of his mode of being, or rather of his existing as opposed to not existing as a fictional character. As his readers, accordingly, we are automatically given the necessary access to the grounds for judging him to be a good chap that he cannot in good conscience provide to anyone inhabiting his fictional world (because it would risk the charge that he is transparently attempting to gain credit with them for his self-criticism—call this the paradox of self-exposure). We cannot relate to him at all except as someone to whom moral credit is owed (insofar as it is owed)— someone who deserves our approbation to at least this extent, and who does not risk that credit by creating the conditions under which we can recognize its reality.

If, however, we truly take seriously his status as fictional, then we also need to consider the full implications of the fact that he is a fictional creation, and ask ourselves how these considerations affect the moral credit of his creator; in other words, we need to consider not just the character–reader relationship but the author(–character)–reader relationship. For suppose, as most literary critical readers (and no doubt many readers simpliciter) have certainly done, that *That Uncertain Feeling* has a strong autobiographical element—putting it crudely (but not in terms of any simple identity-relation), that John Lewis is a powerful synthesis of some of the characteristic thoughts, feelings, and situations of Kingsley Amis with those of his closest friend Philip Larkin in the mid-1950s (not to mention the succeeding decades). What, then, are we as readers to make of the fact that someone whose incessant self-ironizing has very likely incorporated the paradox of self-censure, and who has accordingly encountered the problem of self-condemning self-exposure, should decide to write a novel in which the central character undergoes the paradox but (by virtue of his status as narrator of the fiction) automatically escapes the problem of self-exposure?

John Lewis thereby gets all the moral credit owing to him for being a (relatively) good chap; but since the only people in a position to credit him with it do not inhabit his world, it hardly improves his standing within it. But if those same readers are inclined to see an internal relation between John Lewis and his creator, then they will similarly be inclined to give Kingsley Amis the credit that he shows to be due to his creation—and Amis inhabits one and the same world as his readers (doesn't he?), hence a world in which those lines of credit can be established and maintained (perhaps over a whole career). Would such a way of gaining credit be to Amis's credit?

We shall return to such issues of self-deception a little later. But they exemplify the kinds of specific comparison and contrast that will truly clarify the differences between our relations to real people and our relations to fictional characters, and the different ways in which these differences emerge in biographical and autobiographical genres. MacIntyre doesn't attend with sufficient patience to these complexities; and as a result, his portrait of the essentially narrative unity of the self can appear to be not only inaccurate but also symptomatic—as if designed to repress something central to the issues with which he is concerned. For his doomed attempt to cross or graft a picture of absolute authorial freedom onto the more familiar, constrained kind encountered both in reality and in realistic fiction strongly suggests that he is tempted to overlook or repress some limit or condition inherent in the way in which human individuals relate to their own existence (and to occlude thereby some limit or condition inherent in attempts by others to narrate that existence from without—to write a biography of the kind of existence that necessarily possesses that kind of relation to itself).

Some suggestions as to what this limit might be can be gleaned from Heidegger's conception of the nature of distinctively human being—what in *Being and Time* he calls Dasein.[9] Heidegger's portrait of human existence is in tune with many aspects of MacIntyre's account. For him, Dasein treats its own being as an issue—that is, every moment of its existence confronts it with the question of how to go on with its life, of which amongst a given range of possibilities it should realize; it thereby projects itself into the future, and does so from a present position which is the result of past such projections, and thereby partly constituted by individual and social factors that either never were or at the very least are no longer within its control—a position into which it has been thrown.

This vision of human existence as thrown projection suggests not only that Dasein's mode of being is temporal (more specifically historical), but also that its every element is comprehensible only as a situated transition—a movement within a nest of interlinked narratable structures, an episode in the story of a life. Heidegger reinforces this image by recounting Dasein's temporality in terms of fate and destiny; an individual relates authentically to its life—relates to it as its own, as expressive of its individuality, rather than disowning it—when it recovers from its past a heritage of certain possibilities that it can project into the future as fateful for it, thereby helping to realize (by co-authoring with other Dasein) the destiny of a people.

On the other hand, Heidegger's conception of human historicality also implicitly subverts Macintyre's emphasis on the necessarily narrative unity of the self. The troublesome term here is 'unity'. For whilst Heidegger's talk of Dasein as thrown projection can be understood as emphasizing that Dasein's existence has a necessarily temporal or historical dimension, and hence that its unity is a matter of being a whole articulated in time (as opposed, say, to a Cartesian conception of the self as having the essentially punctual unity of an immaterial substance existing outside time), Dasein's temporality at the same time resists any idea of human existence as unified or whole.

Take, for example, the projective aspect of Dasein's being—what Heidegger calls its being-ahead-of-itself. This means that, for as long as Dasein exists, it necessarily relates itself to existential possibilities; whenever one is actualized, it is actualized as a situation within which (better, *as* which) Dasein relates to some other, unactualized range of possibilities. Hence, Dasein always already relates itself to what is not yet; it stands out into the future, and so there is always

---

[9] Trans. J. Macquarrie and E. Robinson (Oxford: Blackwell, 1962).

something outstanding, something essentially incomplete, in its mode of being. And yet, of course, Dasein does have an end; there is necessarily a point at which every individual life comes to an end—the point of one's death. But when that point of completion is reached, Dasein is not thereby made complete; for it is no longer there. Dasein's death is not an event in its life, even the last; the point at which it can no longer be said to relate itself to what is not yet actual, and thus to be essentially incomplete, is also the point at which it no longer exists.

MacIntyre seems to think that human mortality straightforwardly confirms his conception of the narrative structure of the self. For when confronted with a critic who claims that life has no endings, and that final partings occur only in stories, he says: 'one is tempted to reply 'But have you never heard of death?' (AV, 197). But on Heidegger's analysis, the human subjection to death in fact introduces an obstacle to narrative understandings of human life. For if my death is necessarily not an event in my life, I cannot grasp it as an episode—even as the final episode—in the story of my life; I may be the hero, as well as the part-author, of the story of my dying, but I am necessarily not the chief, or even the sole, protagonist in my death. Hence, Heidegger concludes, I cannot relate to my own death as simply one more possibility of my being, one more possible way of existing that is bound to be actualized sooner or later; for its actualization is my absence, and hence not a possibility of mine, although the life that is mine is marked at every moment by my relation to that impossible possibility. My mortality is not a matter of my life's necessarily having one and only one ending; it is a matter of every moment of my existence possibly being the last such moment, and of my being unable to grasp what that might mean—at least, in the sense in which I can grasp (can understand or imaginatively inhabit) the realization of any other existential possibility or narrative event in my life (such as getting married, or winning the Booker Prize, or mowing the lawn). I cannot grasp it from the inside, as it were (as something that will happen to me), and yet it (what?) looms over and constitutively defines the character of every moment of the life that I do inhabit from the inside, the life that is mine to own or to disown.

How is the self to capture this impossible but necessary knowledge of itself, to articulate autobiographically the way in which its relation to itself in every moment of its existence is marked by its relationship to its own mortality? On Heidegger's view, it is only through an acknowledgement of this relationship that any human being can establish and maintain what he calls an authentic relationship to her life. Grasping the fact that death threatens my existence as a whole, that it cannot be outrun and that no one else can die my death for me is what will allow me to grasp that my life forms a whole (each choice forming and formed by the overall narrative arc of my existence), that I am ultimately responsible for it, and that I can either take on that responsibility or live in flight from it. Without understanding whether, and if so how, a given person has succeeded or failed in living a genuinely individual life, how can we claim to have understood that person's life, and so that person? But on Heidegger's account, the person herself cannot properly be said to have access to a perspective from which her own mortality can make narrative sense to her. So, in struggling for authenticity she confronts a constitutive resistance to self-knowledge, a limit to the story of her life—to the idea of her life as a story—beyond which her own understanding of herself cannot reach; but it is only in relation to this disruption or dislocation of its narrative structure that her life can attain (and be seen to attain) its individual narrative shape.

And if the self's mortality threatens to subvert the possibility of autobiographical understanding, then how might another self articulate a biographical understanding of that individual? The biographer has the apparent advantage of being able to grasp her subject's death as an event in life—one greeted by mourning, funeral rites, the reading of the will and the unfolding of its legacies (financial, emotional and cultural). But this is to grasp her subject's death as an event or episode in the lives of others, in the world that the subject no longer inhabits; it is not to grasp her death as hers—in its mineness, as Heidegger would say. Further narrative contexts and consequences come into view from this third-person perspective, and provide ways of understanding unavailable to the subject that might expand or subvert certain aspects of her self-conception; but the pervasive opacity—the internal relation to nothingness—that the first person encounters as constitutive of its own mortal identity remains untouched, and to that degree so does the person.[10]

Similar damage is done to the idea of the self as a narrative unity—or rather, the same damaging difficulty appears from another angle—if one shifts emphasis from Heidegger's sense of the self as projective, as being ahead-of-itself, to his sense of the self as thrown, or being-already (being-always-already). This aspect of his analysis of Dasein is in fact made rather more prominent in Sartre's rereading of *Being and Time* in conjunction with his rereading of Descartes, as presented in *Being and Nothingness*.[11] Sartre's starting point is to contest Alain's Cartesian declaration that to know is to know that one knows. This is one aspect of Descartes's conception of the self as essentially transparent to itself; the Cartesian mind cannot be in a particular state—for example, that of doubting—without simultaneously knowing that it is in such a state, and hence knowing that it is (i.e. that it exists as doubting). To be thinking and to be aware of oneself as thinking are two aspects of one and the same state of the self; hence each such state provides the basis for a cogito argument—for the self's certainty of itself, in every punctual moment of its existence, as existing and as existing in a particular state,

---

[10] Hermione Lee's essay 'How to End it All' (in her *Body Parts: Essays on Life-Writing* (London: Chatto and Windus, 2005)) is sensitive to the exemplary particularity of the difficulties and temptations encountered by biographers when writing of the death of their subjects.

[11] Trans. Sarah Richmond (London: Routledge, 2018); hereafter BN.

and ultimately for the self's knowledge of itself as a self-identical immaterial thinking substance.

But Sartre argues that Descartes conflates the self's necessary potential for self-awareness with its actualization, and does so because he occludes the temporality of the self. Sartre stresses that all mental states are intentional—they are directed at something other than themselves; to desire is to desire something in particular, to perceive is to perceive something, and so on. Typically, the self is absorbed in the object of its given state of consciousness: for example, when someone in wartime (subjected to strict rationing) counts the number of cigarettes in his case, he is entirely absorbed in the question of the case and its contents, and entirely unaware of being so absorbed. He can, however, become aware of his absorption; if someone sits down at his café table and asks what he is doing, he can activate the capacity inherent in any genuine self to take any of its own conscious states as the object of its conscious awareness. But in so doing, he actualizes a new state of himself—one whose intentional object is no longer the cigarettes but rather his state of absorption in the cigarettes; and in actualizing that self-conscious state, he is necessarily no longer occupying that state of unselfconscious absorption. To take oneself as one's intentional object is to take up another state of oneself, and to relegate the state that is now one's intentional object to one's past. And if one now takes one's self-consciousness of that prior absorbed state as one's new intentional object, one will necessarily no longer exist in that self-conscious state, but in a new state (whose intentional object is one's previous awareness of oneself as having been absorbed in the cigarettes).

In short, one can be conscious of oneself only as one was, not as one is; the self's necessary capacity to direct its attention to itself as well as to that which lies beyond it is realized, and is only realizable, in time, and hence is essentially incapable of bringing the whole of itself (including its present state) into self-consciousness. In effect, then, the phenomenon of self-consciousness does not (as Descartes believed) show that the self is essentially transparent to itself and identical with itself; it rather condemns the self to non-self-identity, to a necessary inability to coincide with itself, to gather itself up as a whole in its own awareness. Heidegger talks of this as an aspect of the self's Being-guilty—its inability to have power over its own being from the ground up. Sartre sees it as exemplifying the for-itself's nature as being what it is not, and not being what it is.

Once again, this conception of the self is in part congenial to a MacIntyrean analysis of selfhood as a narrative unity. After all, Sartre's conception of self-consciousness precisely allows the self to take up a perspective on its immediate past states, and so on its past as a whole, without which the idea of understanding itself as the hero of an unfolding narrative would not be possible. And further, on Sartre's view, if the self really did coincide with itself, if what it previously was entirely exhausted or determined what it is, then the self would lack freedom; it would lack the ability to be part-author of its own narrative as it extends into the future.

Nevertheless, there is a fundamental conflict between MacIntyre's position and that of Heidegger and Sartre. For part of their point is that the self necessarily transcends any narrative it might be in a position to tell about itself, since any such narrative will always fail to include the moment of its own narrating, and the inclusion of that moment will necessarily fail to include the moment in or through which it is included, and so endlessly on. The narrative of *David Copperfield* does not include David's act of writing that narrative as an episode within it; and if it did, what of his act of writing about that act of writing? This may be what the film director John Boorman is trying to get at when he remarks at the conclusion of his recent autobiography that 'I suppose the only completely satisfactory ending to an autobiography would be a suicide note'.[12] In fact, however, such a note could not be completely satisfying, since it would remain promissory; to write a suicide note and to commit suicide are two rather different things. William Golding's novel *The Paper Men*,[13] in which an English novelist tells the story of his resistance to an American academic's attempts to write his biography, may actually get closer to Boorman's ideal, although it too fails to attain it; for it ends not so much in mid-word but in mid-phoneme, as the scribbling novelist notices that his would-be biographer, frustrated and enraged to the point of violence, is lurking in the woods outside his home: 'How the devil did Rick L.Tucker manage to get hold of a gu' (PM, 191).

Herbert McCabe makes it clear, in his book *The Good Life*, that this is not simply a point about the complications of being immersed in time; it is another way of approaching my earlier point about the difference between authors of narratives and the characters or personas in them, this time in an explicitly autobiographical context.[14]

> These problems have to do with the fact that 'I' cannot function as a proper name. 'I tell you' is not part of a story in which 'I' is a character; it *is* the telling of a story. It is a sign of authority, of authorship as such (it is, as Aquinas would say, formal not material to the story). My life-story is not the story of 'I' but the story of Herbert McCabe, who has become a persona, a persona distinct from I, the author. As Herbert McCabe in the story I have been made flesh and dwell among the other characters. How, then, do we get beyond any story to meet the ultimate author, the ultimate authority?   (GL, 75)

Certainly not by telling any further story about the author, since that merely presents us with another author-as-character, beyond which again lies the author-as-author, the formal condition for there being a story at all.

---

[12] Cf. *Adventures of a Suburban Boy* (London: Faber & Faber, 2004).
[13] (London: Faber, 1984); hereafter PM.
[14] *The Good Life* (London: Continuum, 2005); hereafter GL.

Consequently, even autobiography does not and cannot take us to the author it is ostensibly about in the way that an ordinary story takes us to the character in the story; even if the autobiographer's last chapter concerns his writing of this very autobiography, it cannot bridge the unbridgeable gap between author-as-author and author-as-character. But this does not mean that we cannot meet the author; it means that we meet him not in reading about him qua character, but just in the form and the fact of the story itself, in the tale and the telling of it—in short, in its authority (the authority it claims, and the authority we cede it).

McCabe illustrates this point by reference to the Bible, understood as the autobiography of God. On the one hand, no one has ever seen or grasped God, and no one ever could; put otherwise, there can be no life story of the eternal God as such, since 'eternal life' means 'non-narrative life', which is a contradiction in terms. On the other hand, we are told that the Word has become flesh: God has become incarnate in a narrative, in the character of the Son, over against those of the Father and the Spirit. The Bible (the whole of the Bible, from Genesis to Apocalypse) is the story of the Son; the historical life of Jesus is the Trinitarian life of God played out as history. Hence, encountering God and participating in divine life is possible, but not by directly encountering the author of this narrative as author; it rather involves understanding the narrative as God's story—that is, regarding the historical narrative of the Son as authorized and so authored by God, reading it as in form and fact the authoritative revealed image of the unseen and unseeable Author of all things. It means, in other words, belonging to the community of readers (the Christian community) who acknowledge the Bible as God's Word.

Heidegger and Sartre might baulk at the theological inflection of this example, but they would not reject the fundamental point it registers about the ineliminable difference between formal and material conditions of autobiographical authorship. In their less Thomist terms, it might be thought of as the way in which one's understanding of one's life from the inside involves a sense that one always necessarily comes to understand it belatedly; the self's life is lived before it is understood, and hence, even if it is then understood in narrative terms, the self must also acknowledge that the reach of its story about itself encounters a constitutive limit—a point from which its story as a whole, and each episode within it, must simply be accepted as having begun, beyond any complete recounting (even one which invokes the ongoing, conditioning narratives of other selves or institutional contexts).

In one sense, MacIntyre actually makes this Sartrean point when he explicitly claims that human lives are lived before they are told. But he does not seem to see that this very point determines an internal limit to the cogency of his claim that lives are enacted narratives, or at least to the thought that this fact about them confers a certain kind of unity on those lives. For Sartre and for Heidegger, to exist in time is not only a condition for the possibility of there being a narratable self, an individual possessed of a life of which she can render an intelligible account; it is also an ineliminable obstacle to the completeness or totality of that account.

If the self's autobiography will necessarily fail to include the whole story about that self in this sense, could any biographer of the self do better? They would not be caught up in their subject's structural inability to catch up with herself; indeed, after the death of the subject, every episode in her life will be available for investigation, as will the nest of other narratives (of other selves, of institutions and cultures) that interlocked with the subject's life, and thereby—so one might think—a far more encompassing conception of her life as a narrative whole. But that way of telling the story of the subject's life avails itself of a perspective essentially unavailable to the subject, and entirely occludes the perspective on that life which the subject of it necessarily occupies; so such a biography would to that extent be false to her subject's relation to her life, and hence false to an essential aspect of her subject's life. One might say: presenting her life as such a narrative whole does not, and could not, tell the whole story of that life.

Suppose one accepts that offering more and more information of the kind available to the biographer (and typically, even necessarily, unavailable to the biographical subject)—contextualizing the life ever more intensively and extensively, in the manner of so many contemporary biographies—can never fill a gap engendered by the constitutive difference between the first- and third-person perspectives on a life. It would not improve matters to imagine that one should instead attempt ever more systematically and penetratingly to adopt the first-person perspective upon that life—to dedicate one's account to the task of imaginatively inhabiting the subject's relation to her own life. For this would be to assume that the subject possesses an understanding of these aspects of her relation to her own life that others lack; whereas the true point of Heidegger's and Sartre's investigations is to show that the first-person perspective also encounters a constitutive opacity here (another of Diamond's difficulties of reality).

We need not, however, conclude that the very idea of giving a narrative account of the self, or even the idea that the self has a narrative unity, must be given up. The true moral of these analyses is rather that we must reject a particular idea of what it is to conceive of the self as having a narrative unity, and hence of what it might be to articulate that unity in discourse, whether in autobiographical or biographical form. In McCabe's terms, we need to reconceive the way in which we think such narratives acquire and manifest authority; for Heidegger and Sartre it is a matter of how they, and so we, achieve authenticity.

This is not essentially a matter of authenticating the deliverances of one's memory or the provenance of a document, or of claiming the authority that might flow either from being the central character in a certain sequence of events or from synthesizing the accounts of all involved in it—the familiar (and hardly unimportant) ways of acknowledging any individual's privileged and yet contestable capacity to determine the narrative of her life, and so the most obvious means of securing autobiographical and biographical trustworthiness. What these philosophers are rather trying to argue is that any truly authentic or authoritative exercise in these genres will reflect a conception of the self as simultaneously demanding and resisting subsumption in a unified narrative.

Heidegger's conception of Dasein's relation to its own end and its own beginning as embodying an enigmatic resistance to comprehension precisely assumes (rather than denying) that Dasein's existence must be understood in terms of its relation to beginnings and endings, and hence as having narratable (that is, that distinctively human mode of temporal and historical) structure. What he wants to avoid is any conception of that narrative structure as inappropriately transparent, self-sufficient, and total—as if the kind of identity across time possessed by human selves could be modelled on that possessed by physical objects or substances, with a capacity for self-understanding in narrative terms simply added on. To exist as self-conscious beings in time is indeed to be committed to understanding ourselves in narrative terms; but it is also to be committed to understanding that our existence simultaneously resists being understood in such terms. The very terms that allow us to make sense of ourselves—terms like beginnings and endings—also disclose dimensions of ourselves as beyond or before such ways of making sense; and it is in this disclosure of their own limits that they disclose a fundamental aspect of our own existence as limited or conditioned, as natal and mortal—in other words, as finite.

A conception of the interrelated genres of biography and of autobiography that acknowledged human finitude in such a way would therefore be one which acknowledged that the individual human life which it was concerned to elucidate was necessarily not such as to be wholly elucidatable, or elucidatable as a whole. It would find ways of bringing its readers up against the enigma residing in any human life, taken in all its individuality. Wittgenstein once remarked: 'We say of some people that they are transparent to us. It is, however, important as regards this observation that one human being can be a complete enigma to another... We cannot find our feet with them'.[15] Heidegger aims to convince us that no human being can be completely transparent, either to others or to itself; his analysis of Dasein begins from the perception that there lies a priori an enigma in the human mode of being, and hence insists that we can never—in philosophy, biography, or autobiography—entirely find our feet with one another, or with ourselves.

If Heidegger and Sartre aspire to acknowledge the enigma of human individuality, they are addressing what many would regard as the primary motivation for our interest in both autobiography and biography—what Dinah Birch has described as a 'simultaneous hunger for the singularity of a life that has separated

---

[15] Wittgenstein, *Philosophical Investigations*, 4th ed. (Oxford: Blackwell, 2009), II, xi, p. 223; hereafter PI.

itself from the crowd, and an eagerness to identify the values that make that life recognizably human'.[16] After all, if individuation is our name for the process whereby one human being distinguishes herself from others, then the capacity for individuation is what connects her to all other human beings. It is to this capacity, and the obligations and opportunities it imposes, that Carlyle may be referring when he claims that '[e]very mortal has a Problem of Existence set before him... to a certain extent original, unlike every other; and yet, at the same time, so *like* every other; like our own, therefore; instructive, moreover, since we also are indentured to *live*'.[17]

The Sartrean perspective brings to prominence another aspect of the interwoven genres of autobiography and biography with which philosophy can and should be interested—the degree to which the writer's relation to her subject is not only epistemological (concerning how one might come to know, or fail to know, the other) and metaphysical (concerning the nature of the kind of being to be known), but ethical. Sartre is notorious for arguing in *Being and Nothingness* that Being-for-others—relating oneself, understood as a for-itself, to other creatures in one's world possessed of the same kind of Being—enacts a power struggle: a struggle for power over another, against another's power over oneself, and against one's desire to have power over others and oneself. Imagining himself seated in a public park, he further imagines seeing another human being pass by. What is it to see him as another person?

> The Other is in the first instance the permanent flight of things towards a term that I apprehend at the same time as an object at a specific distance from me, and which escapes me inasmuch as it unfolds its own distances around it... [There] is a regrouping at which I am present but which escapes me, of all the objects that populate my universe... This green [lawn] turns towards the Other a face that escapes me. I grasp the relation of the green to the Other as an objective relation, but I am unable to grasp the green as it appears to the Other. Thus, all of a sudden, an object has appeared that has stolen the world from me... The Other's appearing in the world corresponds, therefore, to a frozen sliding away of the universe in its entirety, to a decentring of the world that undermines the centralization I simultaneously impose... [T]he world... seems as if it has been pierced, in the middle of its being, by a drainage hole and... is constantly flowing out through that hole. (BN, 350–1)

For Sartre, then, part of the problem of existence set for all individuals is to find a way of acknowledging the otherness of other individuals. He sees us as prone to adopt a variety of strategies to ensure that we deny that otherness, since its

---

[16] *TLS*, 19 Sept. 2003, 7.   [17] Cited in Dinah Birch's review, *TLS*, 19 Sept. 2003.

acknowledgement entails denying that we are at the centre of the universe, which we equate with a denial of our own individual reality in the world. And of course, our otherness sets the same ethical problem for others. But since biographical writing is one form of the way in which we encounter others in their individuality, it must confront versions of exactly the same ethical problem, and display versions of the same ways of failing to solve or resolve or dissolve it—as two ideas of self-denial cross. Feeling able to ventriloquize one's subject's thoughts at vital moments of her life, feeling compelled to accumulate heaping piles of factual information about the subject's life and circumstance without discrimination, feeling entirely unable to make, or entirely unable to stop making, judgements about the other's actions and thoughts—these would all appear through Sartrean eyes to be not so much technical or generic errors, but rather signs of metaphysical and ethical difficulties—forms of the general failure to find a way of accommodating the individuality of others without seeming to sacrifice one's own.

It is a matter of some controversy whether Sartre allows for the possibility of ever overcoming these spiritual challenges, or whether he defines the human condition as one of suffering the inevitable failure of such acknowledgement. As Ray Monk has emphasized, Sartre's own biographical practice—understood as driven by, even perhaps driven by the need to validate, his theory of the self—plainly counts as a failure in these terms; whereas Raimond Gaita's biography of his father (a biography that is also, necessarily, an autobiography) exemplifies one way in which these spiritual challenges can be met, with real philosophical profit.[18]

The same difficulties emerge in the course of a fictional attempt to address these problems, and thereby to contribute to what one might call the ethics of biography (which once again appears impossible to separate from an ethics of autobiography). It comes from Byatt's *The Biographer's Tale*, when Phineas Nanson is reflecting on his biographical pursuit of the biographer's biographer, Scholes Destry-Scholes:

> I think I was so taken by Destry-Scholes' biography of Elmer Bole precisely because the over-determinism of Literary Theory, the meta-language of it, threw into brilliant relief Destry-Scholes' real achievement in describing a whole individual, a multi-faceted single man, one life from birth to death. I appeared to have failed to find Destry-Scholes himself. I have to respect him for his scrupulous *absence* from my tale, my work. It will be clear that I too have wished to be *absent*. I have resisted and evaded the idea that because of Destry-Scholes' *absence* my narrative must become an account of my own presence, *id est*, an autobiography, that most evasive and self-indulgent of forms. I have tried both to use my own history, unselfconsciously, as a temporal thread to string my story

---

[18] Ray Monk, 'Philosophical Biography: The Very Idea', in J. Klagge (ed.), *Wittgenstein: Biography and Philosophy* (Cambridge: Cambridge University Press, 2001).

(my writing) on, *and* to avoid unnecessary dwelling on my own feelings, or my own needs, or my own—oh dear—*character*. It will be clear to almost any attentive reader, I think, that as I have gone along in this writing...I have become more and more involved in the act of writing itself, more and more inclined to shift my attention from Destry-Scholes' absence to my own style, and thus, my own *presence*. I now wonder whether *all* writing has a tendency to flow like a river towards the writer's body and the writer's own experience?

(BT, 214)

Can the flow of that river be reversed, without flowing into the abyss of the other's existence beyond the writer's grasp? The key to these difficulties seems to lie in acknowledging the distinctive way in which the human subject's presence takes the form of a certain kind of absence: to grasp the reality of selfhood, one must grasp that it is beyond the grasp of any narrative account that might be given of it, whether by itself or by another. But if autobiographical and biographical exercises can be genuinely authoritative or authentic only insofar as they make present the self's absence, and so enact a kind of self-abnegation (with the narrating self absenting itself from its account of the narrated self's beyondness to itself) then biography, autobiography, and fiction must be forms of spiritual exercise, and engaging in such exercises must be inherent to becoming, that is being, what we think of as a person.

2. Genealogy and Truth, Scepticism and Modernism

The previous section of this essay drew on ideas derived from Aristotle, Heidegger, and Sartre to emphasize three main points: that the narrative unity of the self presents itself to contemporary philosophy as at once a necessary and a limiting idea (an indispensable orienting framework that inevitably overcomes itself); that biographical and autobiographical modes of life-writing are internally related possibilities of such a self; and that the history of philosophy—with its recurrent exemplary turns towards the autobiographical (in Augustine, Descartes, Rousseau, Nietzsche...) and its modes of address (aspiring to universal necessity whilst ultimately reliant upon the personal)—imply an internal relation between philosophy and autobiography.

Even taken on its own terms, one pattern of thinking driving the dialectic that delivers these conclusions would be likely to trigger Nietzschean alarm bells. For deep in the background lies the theological structure referred to by McCabe, in which the relation of the Creator to his Creation combines his necessary absence (qua author, or Father) with his indispensable presence (qua character, or Son)—an inherently enigmatic mode of non-self-identity revealed to us by the (Spirit-inspired) divine autobiographical narrative that is the Bible.

Our phenomenological models of self-deconstructing self-narrativity may present themselves as distinct from this Thomist pattern; but by retaining (by diurnalizing or secularizing) the idea of the self as needing to articulate itself whilst always exceeding the grasp of any such mode of making sense of itself, these accounts of unceasingly becoming and overcoming the stories we tell about ourselves risk remaining firmly within the shadow of God's wing.

Moreover, as we just saw, this model sets us a spiritual task: that of capturing what can be truthfully said about ourselves, including the truth that the full or complete truth about ourselves exceeds our grasp (whether the grasp is ours alone or that of another self). But this amounts to an inflection of what, in the Introduction, I identified as a central manifestation of the ascetic ideal—an existential and aesthetic descendant of the confessional matrix of the will to truth. And if we are willing to count literary realism (even in its modernist forms) as another branch of that truth-seeking impulse, then we have reason to view philosophy, autobiography, and J. M. Coetzee's body of writing as internally related phenomena. Specifically, it becomes easier to appreciate why philosophy has an affinity with the autobiographical (which is itself a genealogical descendant of the confessional impulse), why philosophers seem to find Coetzee's texts so uncannily attractive (think of the granitic nature of their truth-seeking impulse, their lack of concern for detailed transcriptions of the blooming, buzzing world of social particularity as they drive towards deeper disclosures of the reality of the world, language, and the embodied human mind and soul, and so inevitably desire to disclose the truth of their own linguistic and literary condition), and why Coetzee's own work takes such a sustained turn towards the autobiographical.[19]

This essay will shortly follow that turn in Coetzee's writing practice in much more detail, with a view to using it as a lens through which to enhance our understanding of philosophy and autobiography. Since, however, the will to truth to which I propose to relate all three modes or bodies of thought and work is itself rooted in the hypocritical, sadomasochistic, life-denying value system of slave morality, to disclose this affinity is surely to raise very serious questions about their value. In particular, given my present concerns, the genealogical affinity of the autobiographical with the confessional places the persistence of our desire to produce and to reflect on such texts, and the modes of self-relation that they presuppose and reinforce, in a far from flattering light.

We must, however, remember that the genealogical analysis that Nietzsche employs to force these questions upon us is itself implicated in the phenomena it analyses. For his work is a late flowering of that will to truth, more specifically a

---

[19] He has published three volumes that are usually characterized as autobiographical (*Boyhood* (1997), *Youth* (2002), and *Summertime* (2007)): revised versions of all three texts were recently republished in an omnibus volume entitled *Scenes from Provincial Life* (London: Harvill & Secker, 2011); hereafter SPL.

manifestation of the point at which it turns upon itself, taking its own measure, which means plotting its own limits and thereby helping to open up the possibility of reconfiguring or otherwise going beyond them. And this emancipatory perversity is plainly analogous to the reflexive turn taken within artistic realism by the advent of modernism, which seems to me to be best understood not as suspending or breaking with the truth-seeking impulse of realism but as following it through, as fulfilling it by turning it upon itself (seeking the truth about this mode of artistic truth-seeking). On the one hand, it only enhances the punitive dimension of the artistic vocation, by locating the artist as an avant-garde antagonist to the current conformity of his audience, a prophet who suffers the contempt of his own generation in the hope of attaining redemption in the eyes of their descendants. On the other hand, its critique of the nature and validity of its own conventions might also hold open the possibility of configuring them differently, thereby taking artistic realism beyond its ascetic origins and inherited forms.

It would therefore not be surprising if a modernist realist such as Coetzee should turn out to stand in a relation to the will to truth that is structurally analogous to Nietzsche's—at once indebted to it and critical of it, attempting to turn it against itself to potentially emancipatory effect without denying that this possibility is one of the will to truth's most significant bequests to us. After all, if the will to truth really must be understood genealogically, then at any given point its various elements or layers of meaning will hold open the possibility of reconfiguring its internal constitution and thereby altering its current modes of informing and deforming our forms of life. One might, in other words, avoid the self-subverting fate of merely denying truth, and instead find non-ascetic ways of keeping faith with it, which will mean reforming that faith in potentially surprising ways—ways in which, as Nietzsche might have it, we overcome interpretations of truth, and so of reality and of the self who seeks it, in which Being has priority over Becoming. We might in particular consider the possibility that becoming is the self's distinctive mode of being, and conceive of the self as Nietzsche does: as path, as episode, as bridge, as great promise—as transitional.

The mode of this overcoming will, of course, be inflected by the mode of modernism one understands Coetzee to be furthering. The interpretation of 'modernism' I have applied to Coetzee in my previous work was derived from the work of Stanley Cavell in philosophy and of Michael Fried in art history, theory, and criticism.[20] So my interpretation of Coetzee's strategies for overcoming asceticism is bound to be shaped by Fried's and Cavell's sense of what modernist art more generally seeks to achieve; and that sense is itself shaped by their sense of what modernism seeks to avoid, and thereby defines as its uncannily

---

[20] See esp. chs. 9 and 10 of my *The Wounded Animal: J. M. Coetzee and the Difficulty of Reality in Literature and Philosophy* (Princeton: Princeton University Press, 2009).

intimate antithesis. I touched upon this nexus of issues briefly in Essay One: here I need to explore that context in more detail.

Cavell and Fried were colleagues at Harvard during the 1960s, and were deeply invested in the high modernist project in painting and sculpture that dominated the Anglo-American art world at that time. Although both men wrote numerous essays on the nature of that project, each of which further articulated a shared field of organizing concepts, the single most influential piece of writing that emerged from their mutually enabling conversations was Fried's essay 'Art and Objecthood', which advanced a ferocious critique of minimalist (or literalist) work of the kind produced by Donald Judd, Robert Morris, and Tony Smith, presenting it as at once the logical conclusion of a Greenbergian misreading of modernism and the systematic negation of modernism's true concerns and value.[21] Fried summarizes his critique in three concluding theses:

1. The success, even the survival, of the arts has come increasingly to depend on their ability to defeat theatre.

2. Art degenerates as it approaches the condition of theatre.

3. The concepts of quality and value—and to the extent that these are central to art, the concept of art itself—are meaningful, or wholly meaningful, only within the individual arts. What lies *between* the arts is theatre. (AO, 163–4)

To appreciate Fried's reasons for advancing these theses, we need to grasp his conception of theatre and the theatrical, which emerges more clearly if we appreciate the distinction he claimed to perceive between the kinds of relationship between work and beholder that modernist and minimalist works each sought to bring about. And to appreciate that, it helps to understand the sense in which he thinks that the minimalists misread the modernist project.

Fried and Cavell both accept the basic Greenbergian insight that modernist artists such as Stella and Caro were producing works of art which were devoted to interrogating their own conditions of possibility rather than operating within an inherited understanding of their nature and significance. Each such work critically evaluates in some way the features hitherto taken for granted as essential to something's being a painting or a sculpture, with a view to testing whether they do or can continue to maintain that significance, or whether something that undeniably presented itself to us as a sculpture or a painting could be made by radically modifying or even eliminating those features; and such critical questioning

---

[21] Cavell's essays are to be found in MWM. Other relevant material appears in his *The World Viewed* (Cambridge, MA: Harvard University Press, 1971); hereafter WV. Fried's essay, together with a wealth of supporting material from the same era of his thought, appears in his *Art and Objecthood* (Chicago: Chicago University Press, 1998); hereafter AO.

naturally led these artists to confront both the conventional and the material bases of their media.

For example: one might think that, although a piece of sculpture may or may not be coloured, it must be sculpted (that is, worked in some way—carved or chipped or polished), it must have the coherence or spatial integrity of a natural object, and it must have a base (on which to stand, from which to rise). Then we encounter a work by Caro:[22] it rests on the ground, it consists of an open and discontinuous juxtaposition of unworked pieces of metal, and those pieces are not so much coloured rods and beams and sheets as rods and beams and sheets of colour (as though the colour helps to dematerialize its supporting object). And yet, Cavell testifies, he is convinced, is in fact simply stuck with the knowledge, that this is a sculpture: so now he no longer knows what a sculpture is, what it is for anything—even the most traditional and exemplary instances of that art—to be a sculpture. For how can objects made this way elicit the experience and responses that he (and we) had thought confined to objects made so differently?

Or again: one might think that we can always in principle draw a clear and stable distinction between literal and depicted shape with respect to a painting—between the shape of the support and the shape(s) of its pictorial elements. Then we encounter Frank Stella's *Moultonboro III* (1966).[23] It represents a yellow triangle (whose outer boundary is marked by a continuous band of lighter yellow) partly wedging itself into the upper-right-hand quadrant of a red square, with a Z-shaped blue band marking their line of contact and linking the embedded apex of the triangle to the painting's upper horizontal boundary. We might be tempted to say that this work certainly allows (and might even invite) us to experience the seven-sided literal shape of the canvas as the irregular external boundary of that pictorial superimposition, and so to grasp the painting as acknowledging its material basis in this way; but Fried's testimony declares otherwise.

First, does the literal boundary result from the superimposition, or does it generate it? Is this pictorial arrangement the painter's way of making sense of the literal irregularity of the support, or does the support have that shape because it makes possible this pictorial arrangement? Which is dependent on which? Second, although the canvas certainly *has* a single, continuous literal shape, its pictorial shape actually works to deny its availability to our experience; for the relationship of the two depicted shapes of which it *is* the boundary compels us to segment it according to which of the two shapes the relevant stretch of that boundary belongs to—to experience it as segmented portions. And when we so segment it, we are further prevented from regarding those segments as simply or straightforwardly either literal or pictorial. Take the segment of the canvas's literal shape that corresponds to the triangle's base: because it is swept out by

---

[22] As discussed by Cavell in 'A Matter of Meaning It', in MWM, 213–37.
[23] As discussed by Fried in 'Shape As Form', repr. in AO, 77–99.

the light-yellow band that runs around the entire triangle, it is swept up by that band and drawn directly into the larger pictorial structure. And insofar as the Z-shaped band links the line of contact between triangle and square to the work's upper horizontal boundary, it discloses that boundary-segment as no more literal (i.e. as a segment of the shape of the canvas support) than it is pictorial (i.e. the top side of the red square). The boundary it marks is both, and so neither.

It is in these ways that Stella's painting means to destabilize and ultimately dissolve the taken-for-granted distinction between literal shape and depicted shape; more specifically, he demonstrates that the applicability of that distinction is not in fact a condition for something's being a work of painterly art. It amounts for Fried to an unprecedented reconception and realization of this register of a painting's conventionality and materiality—one in which neither kind of shape can be said to depend on the other, because each is rendered radically continuous with the other, to the point at which the distinction between them is rendered nugatory, null and void. And yet it is a painting, and a particularly powerful one.

Two points about Fried's and Cavell's ways of characterizing their encounters with these modernist works are pertinent to my concerns. The first is that these objects not only actively seek their audience's engagement, but also actively resist their initial assumptions about their nature and significance: their attempts to interrogate their own conditions are also attempts to interrogate the assumptions and expectations of those for whom they are made. And they can take such an active and questioning role in their relationship with their audience because they have a robust inner complexity as works of art: that complexity poses a challenging task of apprehension, and one that is inseparable from attempting to work out why the work's maker placed its various elements in these specific relations to one another—what they might have meant by so doing. And although that inner complexity may very well have a material aspect, it must have an aesthetic aspect—an ineliminable dimension of meaning or significance, something of its own to communicate or convey.

After all, modernist questioning of aesthetic convention is done by aesthetic means and amounts to an aesthetic achievement. Stella's painterly critique of the distinction between pictorial and literal shape shows that a painting lacking in pictorial shape could still be aesthetically significant, but it certainly does not show that any canvas or surface (let alone any object) with a literal shape is ipso facto a candidate picture; on the contrary, it establishes the viability of shape *as such* as a new aesthetic form or medium. And Caro's creation of non-sculpted sculptures does not show that any unworked object is a viable sculpture; it demonstrates that some unworked objects might elicit and merit an attribution of sculptural significance if their not being worked is compensated for by something else about them that is capable of bearing aesthetic meaning (their juxtaposition, or their mode of bearing colour). In this sense, modernist works have something to communicate, even if that is primarily something to do with the nature, significance, and viability of our current means of artistic communication; so they must employ some means of communicating meaning, of saying something—they must employ a medium, even if it is one they forge and reforge from work to work.

I will return to that last point, but first I want to summarize where we are. On Fried's account, the central point of a Caro sculpture or a Stella painting is to foreground relationships amongst elements within the work, so that the beholder's experience of it primarily provided insight into the overall structure of intentions that made the work the complex and autonomous aesthetic entity that it was, and so challenged the beholder correctly to identify the significance it independently possessed. One might say that they place or situate their beholders: to reveal their meaningful structure just is to reveal our own concrete location—to grasp what conditions our perspective on them (what assumptions or expectations we bring to them), and so to put them in question. By contrast, a Tony Smith sculpture deliberately minimized such internal relationships in favour of foregrounding the relationship between the work and the viewer (more precisely between the work, the gallery space, and the embodied, ambulatory viewer whose experience of the overall scene amounted to the ongoing, present-tense registration of every shift in those elements). Minimalist works thus tended to be single, simple, holistic objects; and they engendered an inherent indeterminacy in the beholder's experience of these objects. Since those works deliberately play to the gallery, in the sense that what mattered to their makers was the beholder's ongoing perception of her negotiation of the total gallery situation, each person's experience was at once equivalent to, and incommensurable with, every other; in a sense, each person's experience *was* the work, and so evaluating such experiences as right or wrong, closer to a correct apprehension of the work or further away, made little sense.[24]

Fried's reason for calling this kind of object–beholder relationship 'theatrical' is obviously not a wholesale prejudice against theatre as an art form; but neither does it simply activate the prejudicial connotations of that everyday term. It rather resonates with the use to which the concept was put by Denis Diderot and Stanley Cavell.

Diderot's highly influential critical writings of the second half of the eighteenth century (viewed by Fried as part of the prehistory of painterly modernism) used his experiences of theatre and painting to illuminate one another. On the one hand, he called for a new stage dramaturgy that would find in painting the inspiration for a more convincing representation of action; on the other, he called for a new kind of painting, whose various elements were related to one another not by a merely intellectual rationale but by an inherently dramatic unity.[25] Such pictorial unity was far more easily achieved in the genre of history painting than,

---

[24] Cf. ch. 1 of Fried, *Four Honest Outlaws* (New Haven: Yale University Press, 2011).
[25] Cf. ch. 2 of Fried's *Absorption and Theatricality* (Chicago: University of Chicago Press, 1980).

say, still life or landscape, since the former involved the actions and passions of human subjects, and so made possible the creation of a *tableau*—an instantly apprehensible perception of the causal necessities binding people together at a moment of crisis. Their complete absorption in the drama in which they participated at once held together the depicted world and—since they were oblivious to anything beyond it, including those beholding the depicted scene—convinced those beholders of that scene's reality.

It was this kind of convincingly unified representation of action that Diderot advocated in theatre, which he perceived as currently corrupted by modes of actorly performance that addressed themselves directly to the audience rather than inhabiting the dramatic relationships between the characters in the world of the play. Such blatant 'playing to the gallery' succeeded only in making the audience aware of themselves as attending a performance, and so prevented them from becoming absorbed in the drama; in short, such theatricality defeated theatre, just as an analogous neglect of genuinely dramatic pictorial unity defeated painting. And in both artistic media, theatricality could itself be defeated and the audience's conviction in the work recovered and maintained, only by foregrounding the relationships between the characters in the depicted world.

Stanley Cavell's reading of *King Lear* specifies how one such defeat of theatricality by theatre might be achieved.[26] He argues that its events are driven by Lear's inability to acknowledge the love of his youngest daughter: since he cannot respond lovingly to it but refuses to acknowledge this, he cannot acknowledge her as his loving daughter (because that would require him to acknowledge himself as her unloving father). But by denying the reality of his relation to Cordelia, he denies (that aspect of) her reality, and so deprives her of it: he converts her into a fictitious creature, a character in the abdication scene he conceives and directs. In short, he theatricalizes her. And Cavell further argues that, insofar as we fail to recognize in Lear's and Cordelia's situation an utterly familiar working-out of family dynamics—arguing instead that the play's beginning is a fairy tale or a brute beginning that simply must be accepted—we find ourselves in Lear's position. We disclose ourselves as failing to acknowledge Lear and Cordelia, as denying their specific reality and location in the complex web of the play's human world, thereby converting them into mere characters; we theatricalize them.

However, because Shakespeare's play is constructed so as to allow us to discover ourselves exhibiting the very blindness Lear displays (by catching ourselves having overlooked what is continuously placed in front of our eyes and ears), it gives us the chance to stop: to stop denying the reality of the Cordelias in our lives, by learning how to stop denying the reality of the characters in the tragic drama we

[26] See 'The Avoidance of Love', in MWM, 267–356.

are watching. In a theatre, we cannot go up to Lear and Cordelia (if we approached the stage the characters would vanish, leaving only bewildered actors): the conventions of theatrical performance make it impossible either to declare our presence to the characters or to hide it, as we must with others outside the theatre. But, says Cavell, 'we can put ourselves in their *present*. It is in making their present ours, their moments as they occur, that we complete our acknowledgement of them. But this requires making their present *theirs*' (MWM, 337).

These characters live through a sequence of moments each of which constitutes the present for them as it does for us, and which they accordingly relate to as shaped (but not determined) by past moments and shaping (but not determining) future moments. Hence if I am to confront them (even those in a tragic drama), I must not import my knowledge of the play's ending into my judgement of their current situation, or regard their current behaviour as necessitated by past events: I must not deny their conditioned freedom. I must also acknowledge that my knowledge of them has limits, and that my perception of them might be repudiated altogether (for example, by a more responsive beholder); I must, in other words, acknowledge their separateness from me, the fact—embodied in the theatrical convention that audience members are silent, hidden, and isolated—that there is a point at which I am helpless before the acting and suffering of others. However, to identify that point correctly I must acknowledge the fact and the cause of their suffering; as Cavell puts it, 'It is only in this perception of them as separate from me that I make them present. That I make them *other*, and face them. And the point of my presence at these events is to join [with every audience member] in confirming this separateness' (MWM, 338).

This Cavellian emphasis upon the reiterated achievement or avoidance of presentness is echoed by Fried when he contrasts our experience of a minimalist work as one of endless duration (each shift in it being as [im]pertinent as any other) with our experience of a modernist work as one in which that work is wholly manifest at every moment. 'It is this continuous and entire *presentness*... that one experiences as a kind of *instantaneousness*, as though if only one were infinitely more acute, a single infinitely brief instant would be long enough... to experience the work in all its depth and fullness, to be forever convinced by it' (AO, 167). But why does he claim that such presentness is essentially unavailable to any work that falls between the individual arts, that is, between artistic media? The answer lies in Fried's and Cavell's conception of what an artistic medium is.

This conception is thoroughgoingly historicist and essentially opposed to the assumption that the aesthetic possibilities of a medium are determined by independently given features of its material basis.[27] Musical works of art are not the result of applications of a medium that is defined by its independently given

---

[27] For a detailed version of Cavell's argument, see chs. 5, 11, and 14 of WV.

possibilities; for it is only through the artist's successful production of something we are prepared to call a musical work of art that the artistic possibilities of that physical material are discovered and explored. Such possibilities of sound, without which it would not count as an artistic medium, are themselves musical media—ways in which various sources of sound have been applied to create specific artistic achievements, e.g. the fugue, the aria, the sonata. They are the strains of convention through which composers have been able to create, performers to practise, and audiences to acknowledge, specific works of art.

Art attains the condition of modernism when it can no longer take a given set of such conventions for granted: then artists make the business of interrogating those conventions internal to the meaning of their work, so that each work works to determine whether and how any given convention might (in however revised a form) continue to make possible the creation of work whose significance might match that of the best work of the past, or whether the work itself might form the source of new conventions. Minimalist work misinterprets this modernist need to test the continued artistic viability of the distinctive material conditions of e.g. the medium of painting (say, the shape of the support) as revealing that artistic sincerity in fact requires the total hypostatization of those conditions. Accordingly, for evolving and self-questioning but meaningful artistic deployments of such material they substitute the production of objects that offer only their material properties to their beholders—works that strive to exemplify bare or mere objecthood entirely apart from convention.

Hence minimalist works necessarily aspire to occupy the space between artistic media (those necessarily normative phenomena): but to Fried, that amounts to imagining a meaningful object whose significance floats absolutely free of the kinds of convention or norms through which human beings are alone capable of making meaning. It is the artistic equivalent of trying to say something whilst denying any responsibility for speech's necessary conditions: reliance on convention, inheritance of history, and the taking-up of specific relations to concrete others for which one can be held accountable. Nietzsche would see in this a deeply ascetic discounting of Becoming in favour of Being: all of the blooming, buzzing complexity of the forms of life of the human animal present themselves as modes of constraint or imprisonment—limitations on our ability to make our mark on the world, artistically and otherwise. It is also a version of what Cavell means by 'scepticism'—although in his hands, that familiar philosophical phenomenon takes on a different aspect.

On Cavell's reading of Wittgenstein, scepticism about the existence of the external world cannot be refuted; but neither can it be accepted, at least not in the terms in which it presents itself for our acceptance. For the philosophical sceptic undertakes to reveal to us that we cannot claim to know that the external world exists, thereby presuming that we think of ourselves as knowing or being certain that it exists, and proposing that we should instead think of ourselves as doubtful or uncertain of it; and his opponent traditionally undertakes to demonstrate that we can and should claim to possess the certainty that the sceptic claims we lack, by refuting his grounds for doubt. According to Cavell, the real difficulty is one in which both parties to this dispute are equally implicated, and to which they are equally blind—namely, the deeper presumption that the human relation to the world is fundamentally one of knowing (or of failing to know), that is, that it is an essentially cognitive relation; for on Wittgenstein's perception of the matter, that relation cannot intelligibly be characterized in such terms as knowledge, doubt, certainty, or belief.

That particular things in the world are thus-and-so—that the pen is in the drawer, or that the bird in the tree is a goldfinch—is something of which we might be doubtful, or that we might believe as opposed to knowing with certainty; but it makes no more sense to claim to know that the world as a whole or as such (the worldly horizon or context within which we relate cognitively to particular objects and states of affairs) exists than to claim that there are grounds for doubting that it does. For the world is not an object, not even an enormously large one, the largest. And our relation to the world is not (as our relation to objects might often reasonably aspire to be) one of knowing—such a way of conceptualizing it makes that relation more distant, less intimate than it really is; it is rather one of acceptance (or rejection), accepting (and accepting responsibility for) that in the absence of which any claim to know that something is thus-and-so would be empty, unintelligible.

On Wittgenstein's view of that matter, what one thereby takes responsibility for (or fails to)—what aligns speakers with their world—is grammar: the criteria in terms of which one identifies an object as the kind of object it is, and that constitute a speech act (say, one of claiming to know or to doubt) as the kind of act it is. The sceptic is thus wrong to claim that our relation to the world is cognitively deficient, because he is wrong to conceive of it as cognitive in the first place; but then any opponent of scepticism who takes it as his task to refute the sceptic, by recovering certainty or knowledge in the face of such doubt, thereby retains the sceptic's fundamental assumption and so his critique of scepticism merely gives it further expression.

The sceptic manages at once to acknowledge and to occlude the critical difference between objects and the world by attempting to imagine a context in which the fate of a particular claim to know an object might appear intelligibly to figure the fate of our capacity to word the world as such. This would be a best case of knowledge—the kind that leads us to say 'If I don't know this, I don't know anything'; and a best case of knowledge necessarily involves what Cavell calls a generic rather than a specific object (or better, an object conceived of generically rather than specifically). A specific object would be a Louis XVI chair (as opposed to one designed by William Morris) or a goldfinch (as opposed to a sparrow). The claim to know that this chair is a Louis XVI or that this bird is a goldfinch can be questioned and settled by the citation of criteria: in particular, a concrete ground for doubting the truth of a concretely entered claim can be countered by citing a ground for rejecting the (ground for) doubt: 'True, sparrows also have those eye-markings but not that distinctive wing shape.' A generic object would be a tomato or a chair—not one genus of tomato as opposed to another, but a tomato taken simply as exemplary of objects in general (of objecthood or externality as such), and taken as presenting itself to us in cognitively exemplary circumstances (with no specific ground for doubting our capacity to know of its real presence, no respect in which we are less well placed than we could be for the making of that judgement). Hence, we are willing to say that 'If there is legitimate ground for doubting that that thing is really there, here and now, then the cognitive accessibility of the world as such is uncertain'.

If there were some deficiency in our expertise or our position with respect to this tomato, then a doubt about its identity or its reality might be made to stick; but by the same token, that doubt would not generalize—would not indict human cognitive capacities as such. It is only in the absence of such local deficiencies that the fate of knowledge as a whole, and so the reality of the world as a whole, can appear to be at stake; but then the difficulty for the sceptic is to enter or invoke a ground for doubt that we are willing (even compelled) to take seriously, to regard as intelligible, despite floating free of any specific feature of the subject, object, and context under interrogation. Such a willingness would force us to regard ourselves as being in a position to enter an intelligible claim to know that object, in the absence of any concrete other to whom those words might intelligibly convey information, knowledge that we could imagine him lacking. And for Cavell, that problem is insuperable, because resolving it would require the criteria in terms of which we articulate our basic grasp of objects to function as criteria of existence, made to settle the sheer reality of things, when they are in fact and could only be criteria of identity—criteria for something's being *so* (this as opposed to that) rather than for something's *being* so (being real, really there as opposed to illusory or otherwise unreal).

This means, first, that we cannot use criteria to rebut doubts about the sheer existence or reality of things: there are no criteria satisfied by a real chair or tomato that could not be satisfied by a chair or tomato encountered in a dream or a hallucination (as Kant puts it, existence is not a predicate, not a matter of a thing's possession or lack of a specific feature or features). And second, it means that the criterial alignment of speakers with the world is something that can indeed suffer failure: the failure is one of will as opposed to cognition (call it the willingness or capacity to make sense, to consent to continue employing criteria, taking responsibility for their application, accepting the world they disclose), but failure it nonetheless is, and equally catastrophic in its way (since such a failure or withdrawal of consent amounts to a loss of intelligibility, the onset of disorientation in the world and within oneself as an inhabitant and articulator of that world).

Against this background, we can see that the minimalist ideal of mere or bare objecthood is an outcropping in art of what Cavell calls generic objecthood in the context of epistemology. The epistemological sceptic needs simultaneously to relate to his object both specifically and generically, but oscillates unendingly between those antithetical states. But in the field of aesthetics after modernism, those modes of objecthood and subjecthood are separated and opposed: the modernist artwork aspires to maximize its specificity and thereby intensifies the specificity of its beholder (addressing, and so facilitating each beholder's acknowledgement of, the real particularity of her perspective and situation), whereas the minimalist artwork aspires to generic objecthood, and thereby attenuates or derealizes the beholder's sense of her situatedness (theatricalizing their relationship, and fictionalizing her).

In other words, insofar as minimalism aspires to avoid presentness, it constitutes an expression of scepticism; and like any form of scepticism, it is a sheer fantasy—although, as Fried's argument also makes clear, a fantasy of the kind that we can find ourselves inhabiting, attempting to live out (insofar as we attempt to occlude our responsibilities for meaning what we say and do, which includes our responsibility for acknowledging the conditions which make that possible). The 'space' between artistic media that minimalism apparently aspires to inhabit is mere appearance, and what inevitably results from trying to occupy it is the antithesis of art.

This is not to say that modernism and what is currently called 'intermediality' are antithetical. For that term could be taken to refer not to a fantasized 'space between media', but to specific modes of crossing borders between particular media—for example, medial transposition (e.g. film adaptations of novels), media combination (e.g. multimedia installations), intermedial reference (e.g. references to theatre in a film), and even (accepting Fried's analogy between artistic media and natural languages) translations of literary texts. His modernist understanding of art and its media is perfectly consistent with such genealogically-structured critical categories, since works which fit them need not deny the historical specificity, conventionality, or intentionality of the media that undergo such crossing or result from it. As long as the relevant media are not treated as predefined by their material basis, and as long as none of these specific categories of cross-mediality is illegitimately inflated or absolutized (e.g. by identifying 'opera' as a mode of media combination, or by claiming that all media are mixed media), nothing in Fried's and Cavell's conception of modernism contests them; indeed, such modes of artistic exploration would be the likely outcome of testing the continuing artistic efficacy of existing structures of convention.

One apparently small detail of Cavell's canonical treatment of scepticism (in *The Claim of Reason*) in fact confirms this intuition of a complementarity between literary modernism, intermediality, and philosophical scepticism, and so will allow us to take one further hermeneutic step, whilst drawing together

GENEALOGY AND TRUTH, SCEPTICISM AND MODERNISM 135

the various threads of this section of my essay. For, towards the end of his extended articulation of his interpretation of scepticism as an attempt to make a claim to knowledge in a non-claim context, Cavell refers back to the generic object used (that is, the object used generically) by H. H. Price:

> All of existence is squeezed into the philosopher's tomato when he rolls it towards his overwhelming question. The experience is one I might now describe as one of looking at the world as though it were another *object*, on a par with particular envelopes, tomatoes, pieces of wax, bells, tables, etc. If this is craven, it is a craving not for generality (if that means for *generalization*) but for *totality*. It is an expression of what I meant when I said that we want to know the world as we imagine God knows it. And that will be as easy to rid us of as it is to rid us of the prideful craving to be God—I mean to *rid* us of it, not to replace it with a despair at our finitude…
>
> Perhaps I go too far; or not far enough. I do not know whether I have communicated the experience I am trying to get before us. Let me try another way. (CR, 236–7)

What interests me here is that the first sentence of this paragraph is a virtual transcription of two lines from T. S. Eliot's 'The Love Song of J. Alfred Prufrock':

> And would it have been worth it, after all,
> After the cups, the marmalade, the tea,
> Among the porcelain, among some talk of you and me,
> Would it have been worth while,
> To have bitten off the matter with a smile,
> To have squeezed the universe into a ball
> To roll it towards some overwhelming question,
> To say: 'I am Lazarus, come from the dead,
> Come back to tell you all, I shall tell you all'—
> If one, settling a pillow by her head,
>   Should say: 'That is not what I meant at all.
>   That is not it, at all.'
>
> (ll. 87–98)

And those two lines themselves transcribe lines from Andrew Marvell's *To His Coy Mistress*:

> Now therefore, while the youthful hew
> Sits on thy skin like morning dew,
> And while thy willing soul transpires
> At every pore with instant fires,

> Now let us sport us while we may;
> And now, like am'rous birds of prey,
> Rather at once our time devour,
> Than languish in his slow-chapt pow'r.
> Let us roll all our Strength, and all
> Our sweetness, up into one Ball:
> And tear our pleasures with rough strife,
> Through the iron gates of life.
> Thus, though we cannot make our sun
> Stand still, yet we will make him run.
>
> (ll. 33–46)

Is this nested, interdisciplinary exercise in intertextuality just a grace note in Cavell's rhetorical performance—a glancing and entirely dispensable reference that might give pleasure to those who happen to notice it? Or are Eliot's Prufrock and Cavell's Price related to one another in ways that bring out deeper-running connections of thought and feeling?

The latter possibility would help, to begin with, to account for the fact that the first occurrence of Prufrock's 'overwhelming question'—in its opening lines—gives it what one might call a distinctly philosophical inflection:

> Let us go, through certain half-deserted streets,
> The muttering retreats
> Of restless nights in one-night cheap hotels
> And sawdust restaurants with oyster-shells:
> Streets that follow like a tedious argument
> Of insidious intent
> To lead you to an overwhelming question…
>
> (ll. 4–10)

Philosophical scepticism is very often characterized as at once tedious, insidious, and overwhelming (in this respect, it may be thought to exemplify the distinctive character of all philosophical arguments, insofar as they press upon assumptions that appear beyond question, but then crumble to reveal the groundlessness of our existence). However, within Cavell's map of the sceptical territory, the most obvious implication of picturing Price as Prufrock is that it figures an internal relation between a philosophical interrogation of a human being's ability to grasp the reality of the world and a literary portrayal of a question about one human being's ability to grasp the reality of another human being. For the critical consensus (reinforced by Eliot's ironic allusion to Marvell's very different protagonist) is that Prufrock is a man who wishes to pose an erotic or amorous question to a woman, but ultimately lets 'I dare not' wait upon 'I would'; so Cavell's transposition of Price's question into Prufrock's is first of all an early, implicit adumbration of a theme that comes to dominate the fourth and strangest part of *The Claim of Reason*.

In the modern era, philosophical scepticism comes in two main variants: as well as scepticism about the external world, there is scepticism about other minds; and Cavell sees a complex relation between these two expressions of the sceptical impulse—one which begins to unfold if we ask whether there can be a best case of knowledge of another mind. On the one hand, even though the recognition of others possessed of minds like our own involves the application of a distinction within our world (rather than casting doubt on that world as such), generating a concrete ground for doubting that another humanoid creature is minded (as opposed to being an artefact, or a zombie) will still face the double bind of aspiring to generalize doubt on the basis of a concrete ground: either the ground is specific, and so won't generalize, or it will lack specificity, and to precisely that extent will lack any content.

On the other hand, if we recollect Cavell's conviction that our relation to the world is one of acceptance rather than certainty, then we should expect there to be an analogous contrast available in the other-minds case—that, say, the reality of other minds should be seen as a matter not of knowledge but of what Cavell calls acknowledgement or its absence. To acknowledge another, however, requires acknowledging that other's relation to me (I cannot acknowledge this woman as my daughter without acknowledging myself as her father); acknowledgement thus singles out both knower and known. So our question about a best case of knowledge amounts to asking: is there a case in which a given other embodies my view of psychic reality as such, an other who is (not generically or unexceptionably other but) exemplary of all others, of humanity as a whole? Is there a particular other upon whom I stake my capacity for acknowledgement (which means my capacity for acknowledging the existence of others and for revealing my own existence to those others) altogether?

There is no general a priori answer to the question, so formulated: whether there is a best case of knowledge of other minds is for each person to answer for himself or herself, whereas with external-world scepticism, if there is a best case at all, it is available in principle to all, impersonally. If, however, we were to acknowledge the existence of such an exemplary other, then the very singularity of the relationship *would* allow scepticism to generalize (rather than disallowing it): for if I cannot credit what *this* other shows and says to me, then the remainder of the world and my capacities in it will become irrelevant—matters not beyond my knowledge but past my caring. I am not removed from the world; it is dead for me. All for me is but toys; there is for me no new tomorrow; my chaos is come (again?).

In other words, scepticism about other minds begins to disclose itself in the terms of Shakespearean tragedy: what philosophy encounters as an intellectual difficulty is dramatized in the relationships between Lear and Cordelia, or Othello and Desdemona, as a matter of psychic life and death. These couples live their scepticism, with the women bearing the brunt of the men's jealousy, vengefulness, and narcissism, their inability to acknowledge the woman's separateness or independence.

But Cavell is not content to utilize Shakespeare simply to compare and contrast other-minds scepticism with external-world scepticism; he is equally concerned to elaborate the idea that the former is allegorical of the latter. One ground for this lies in another aspect of the grammar of the concepts of belief and doubt: since their primary use is to characterize one's relation to the claims of others (we believe or doubt others' testimony, and thereby what they tell us), the sceptic's willingness to employ them to characterize one's relation to the external world places that world in the position of a speaker, someone lodging a claim on us (so that the grammar of belief discloses the idea of the generic object as a displacement or inflection of the exemplary other, as bearing witness to its independent reality). This is a vision of the world as not only animate but articulate, claiming a relationship of exclusive intimacy; and it recasts external-world scepticism as having an affective as well as a cognitive significance—quite as if a loss of conviction in the reality of that world would place it past our caring as well as beyond our knowledge (so that our ways of picturing our relation to it betray an emotional dimension analogous to that disclosed in other-minds scepticism—acting as covers for, and so as expressions, of love, jealousy, hatred, and despair concerning the reality of its independence from us). One might say that, just as the concept of acknowledgement incorporates that of knowledge by tying it to a requirement for a response, so with the concept of acceptance: this idea of the world as requiring an acknowledgement of its independent reality, and so an acknowledgement of ourselves as transient inhabitants of that world, hence finite or conditioned, is what ties scepticism on Cavell's view of the matter to Romanticism.

Prufrock fits surprisingly neatly into this context; for his unconsummated relation with the object of his desire amounts to a particularly painful version of the self-thwarted impulse to make a claim in a non-claim context. He cries that it is 'impossible to say just what I mean!' (l. 104), and asks 'how should I begin | To spit out all the butt-ends of my days and ways?' (ll. 59–60).[28] He imagines the woman as entirely certain of her own meaning ('That is not what I meant, at all'— l. 110), but without being at all certain that this speculation captures her real state

---

[28] It is this Prufrockian mood to which Cavell is adverting when he ends the paragraph we're examining by saying: 'Perhaps I go too far; or not far enough. I do not know whether I have communicated the experience I am trying to get before us. Let me try another way' (CR, 237). The sceptic with whom Cavell is contending is himself, in certain moods: or at least, he can only be successfully contested insofar as Cavell is willing and able to inhabit the mood or experience from within which the sceptic is speaking.

of mind (since that certainty is only ever imagined by him, never actually expressed, precisely because he fails to elicit any expression from her). But where she appears as unknown, he imagines himself as vulnerable to the knowledge of others, and to her knowledge in particular: he winces at the idea of 'a magic lantern [throwing his] nerves in patterns on a screen' (l. 105), making his thoughts visible to all; and he pictures the eyes of others 'fix[ing] you in a formulated phrase' which leaves him 'sprawling on a pin...pinned and wriggling on the wall' (ll. 56–8). It is quite as if he maintains her unknownness in order to avoid self-exposure: where Marvell's protagonist articulates the intensity of his desire and aspires to encourage his mistress' responses by emphasizing how swiftly time passes, Prufrock repeatedly defers that moment of mutually disclosive expression by claiming that there will be time for it, but not yet (ll. 23–48). But his restriction of his potential mistress to the realm of his imagination, his denial of her independent reality, in fact ensures that he fails to live his own life, and thereby to realize a self that might be capable of exposure to others. He lives his scepticism.

Against this general Shakespearean background, Prufrock's invocation of *Hamlet* takes on a new salience:

> No! I am not Prince Hamlet, nor was meant to be;
> Am an attendant lord, one that will do
> To swell a progress, start a scene or two,
> Advise the prince; no doubt, an easy tool,
> Deferential, glad to be of use,
> Politic, cautious, and meticulous;
> Full of high sentence, but a bit obtuse;
> At times, indeed, almost ridiculous—
> Almost, at times, the Fool.
>
> (ll. 111–19)

Prufrock is suspiciously eager to compare himself to Polonius (whose name is never uttered, but l. 116 contains all of its constituent letters in the right order[29]), and one does not have to be Freud to wonder whether such a fervent denial of any comparison between himself and Polonius' Prince amounts to an acknowledgement of its pertinence; but the general problem of transforming intention into action is certainly faced by both, and Hamlet's particular version of that problem is the subject of an essay by Cavell in which he relates that play's protagonist to his understanding of the way Descartes at once conjures and aspires to overcome the sceptical impulse. Descartes famously argues that the only redoubt of certainty which might withstand the threat that I may be dreaming or under siege by an evil

---

[29] As Christopher Ricks has pointed out in 'Shakespeare and the Anagram', *Proceedings of the British Academy* 121 (2002), 111–46.

demon is the self's inability to doubt its own existence, here and now—as is shown by its inability to say, or rather to mean, the words 'I do not exist'.[30] Cavell (re-)interprets this canonical Cartesian meditation as follows:

> [I]n Descartes's *Cogito* argument... to exist the human being has the burden of proving that he or she exists, and... this burden is discharged in *thinking* your existence, which comes in Descartes... to finding how to say 'I am, I exist'; not of course to say it just once, but at every instant of your existence; to preserve your existence, originate it. To exist is to take your existence upon you, to enact it, as if the basis of human existence is theatre, even melodrama. To refuse this burden is to condemn yourself to scepticism—to a denial of the existence, hence of the value, of the world. (DK, 187)

For Cavell, Hamlet is the ghost of the play that bears his and his father's name: his refusal of participation in the world amounts to his haunting of it, and what debars him from genuine existence is revenge. More specifically, it is his father's posthumous attempt to compel his son to take his place, to make his life come out even for him, to set it right so that he (the father) can rest in peace. It is this bequest that deprives his son of his identity—by depriving him of the ability to mourn his father (as a dependent sexual being incapable of sustaining his wife's desire), and by prohibiting him from accepting his mother as an independent sexual being whose life of desire survives the birth of a son and the death of a husband.

In other words, Hamlet's failure to achieve genuine existence is in effect a failure fully to acknowledge the fact of his birth, and thereby his full participation in the human condition: it is an effect of his inability to acknowledge the dependence of his own existence on the existence of two others, and thereby to achieve independence from (which means acknowledging the independence of) both. Even if his parents are not his primary concern, Prufrock is surely an equally powerful, if distinctively modern, incarnation of the human ability to haunt one's own existence, to find reasons to defer its enactment in the face of the possibility (in his case) of revealing himself as a dependent sexual being incapable of provoking another's desire.

A further connection between Eliot and Cavell emerges if we attend more closely to the immediate argumentative context of the paragraph in which Prufrock is conjured. For in the pages leading up to it, Cavell confronts a particular version of the sceptical impulse—one which pictures our vulnerability to doubt in terms of the possibility that future experience (of an object) might lead

---

[30] 'Hamlet's Burden of Proof', in *Disowning Knowledge in Seven Plays of Shakespeare* (Cambridge: Cambridge University Press, 2003), 179–92; hereafter DK. The relevant interpretation of Descartes is laid out in 'Being Odd, Getting Even', in *In Quest of the Ordinary* (Chicago: University of Chicago Press, 1988), 105–49.

us to withdraw our initial claim to know its real presence before us. This version thereby invokes the idea of 'the totality of experience' as an ideal standard for definitive verification of any knowledge claim; and in attempting to counter such scepticism, its opponents are tempted to reach for propositions whose status as verified might meet that ideal standard—claiming, for example, that we have absolutely conclusive evidence that houses do not turn into flowers, or that the words in books do not undergo spontaneous changes.

But for Cavell, these responses share the hysteria against which they are struggling: if these were facts, we should be able to imagine what it would be like if houses and flowers did turn into one another. But what would the difference then be between stones and seeds? Where would we live and what would we grow in our gardens? What would 'grow' mean? What would 'house' and 'flower' mean? Both the sceptic and the anti-sceptic assume that we relate to statements of this kind as if the evidence in their favour were constantly growing, or diminishing, or precariously maintaining a given level of credibility as human experiences increase in number; it's as if they think that looking again and again at houses and flowers were seeing again and again the one *not* turning into the other.

In short, the notion of 'absolutely conclusive evidence' is being used outside its ordinary context; and although such projections are not objectionable in principle, employing them in such contexts has consequences for how we might mean them in such uses. And in the paragraph preceding the one we are primarily examining, Cavell offers the following summary of those consequences:

> I asked ... whether it is *merely* in fact the case that houses do not turn into flowers (or that printed words do not undergo spontaneous changes, or, more generally, one could add, that there are separate enduring objects in the world). Let us now ask: What are we imagining when we think of this as merely 'in fact' the case about *our* world, in the way it is merely in fact the case that the flowers in this garden have not been sufficiently watered, or that there are six white houses with rose gardens on this street? It is my feeling that such things could present themselves to us as just more facts about the world were we to (when we) look upon the whole world as one object, or as one complete set of objects: that is another way of characterizing that experience I have called 'seeing ourselves as outside the world as a whole', looking in at it, as we now look at some objects from a position among others. This experience I have found to be fundamental in classical epistemology (and indeed moral philosophy). It sometimes presents itself to me as a sense of powerlessness to know the world, or to act upon it; I think it is also working in the existentialist's ... sense of the precariousness and arbitrariness of existence, the utter contingency in the fact that things are as they are. (Wittgenstein shares this knowledge of the depth of contingency. His distinction in this matter is to describe it better, to live its details better. I would like to say: to remove its theatricality.) (CR, 236)

When this paragraph is read in conjunction with its successor, three themes take centre stage. The first is the idea of a 'totality of experience', and the pressure Cavell is trying to place on our assumption that we understand what we mean when we invoke it. Prufrock may also be labouring under the misapprehension that we can make sense of such an idea: after all, would he so quickly despair of the task of beginning to 'spit out all the butt-ends of my days and ways' (l. 60) if he were not imagining that any such expectoration—being finite—must necessarily fail to capture absolutely everything his days and ways contained? More generally, however, the idea of a totality of experience is a central notion in the thought of the philosopher whose thought is widely acknowledged to inform Eliot's own philosophical and aesthetic vision—F. H. Bradley. For Bradley's metaphysics takes our perception of reality as containing a multiplicity of objects and relations (including ourselves and our mental states) to be mistaken: as it is in itself, Reality is undifferentiated and it is ideal—it is, in short, a single and all-inclusive experience which embraces every partial diversity in one comprehensive and harmonious whole (and thus differs in its essence from any experience with which we are familiar). In other words, Bradley's Absolute Idealism depends upon the idea of a totality of experience, whilst simultaneously acknowledging our inability to make sense of what such a thing might be. So Cavell's invocation of Prufrock places Bradleyian Idealism as much in the sceptical dock as Price's rather more empiricist sense-datum theory of perception.

The second theme implicit in this passage is more explicit in the paragraph that follows it: for the notion of a totality of experience hangs together with the idea of looking in at the world as a whole, which is plainly one version of the idea of occupying God's position in relation to the world. As Cavell understands it, insofar as this verificationist version of scepticism expresses a craving for totality (rather than generality), it expresses a desire to know as God knows, and so expresses the desire to be God. And he characterizes his own project as attempting to rid us of this prideful or hubristic denial of our finitude without simply replacing it with a despairing acceptance of it: it is, in short, an attempt to acknowledge our finitude. In both respects, Cavell's position reveals a Nietzschean resonance.

Prufrock delineates a comparable sense that his overwhelming question has a religious dimension. For, having squeezed the universe into a ball and rolled it towards that question, he imagines himself saying: 'I am Lazarus, come from the dead | Come back to tell you all, I shall tell you all' (ll. 94–5). There are two Lazaruses in the Christian Bible. Lazarus the beggar is paired with the rich man Dives in one of Jesus' parables: when Dives dies and goes to hell he begs God to send Lazarus from heaven to warn Dives' five brothers of the fate that awaits them, but God asks why they would believe Lazarus if they haven't heeded Moses or the prophets. Lazarus the brother of Martha and Mary falls ill and dies, and Jesus brings him back to life. Both biblical characters have a claim to participate in Prufrock's characterizations of himself.

Had the first Lazarus been sent by God, he would have been burdened with a redemptive message, one which reveals the ultimate truth and value of life, and which is not meant only for Dives' relatives but for everybody (and so would have come back to tell all to all); and the woman's rejection of Prufrock's testimony plainly matches the response God foresees from Dives' brothers (as her sophisticated social circumstances match theirs). By contrast, the second Lazarus is notoriously mute after being returned to life; but his raising from the dead is prefaced by something being rolled (the stone sealing his tomb has to be moved away), and there is a sense in which it nevertheless tells all to all: for this event both precipitates and previsions the universally redemptive passion narrative of the one who brings it about. It is the news that Jesus is capable not just of miraculously curing the sick but also of removing death's sting that prompts the Jewish high priest to initiate their proceedings against him; and those proceedings culminate in Jesus' own death and burial in a tomb, whose stone is later discovered to have been rolled away to reveal only the neatly folded grave-clothes (whose presence on the revived Lazarus is so heavily emphasized in the Gospel narrative—'he that was dead came forth, bound hand and foot with graveclothes, and his face was bound about with a napkin. Jesus said unto them, "Loose him and let him go"' (John 11:44)). It isn't hard to see Prufrock's woman's imagined rejection as equally fit to embody the world's reaction to Christ's incarnation of redemption.

On one level, of course, Prufrock's instinct to identify with messengers of redemption is ironized throughout the poem: he repeatedly expresses that instinct only to disavow it ('Though I have seen my head (grown slightly bald) brought in upon a platter | I am no prophet', ll. 82–3) and thereby to instantiate modernity's inability to imagine how such matters of life and death might be realized in our spiritually threadbare, obsessively self-deprecating and self-sabotaging cultural circumstances. On the other hand, each disavowal requires, and so makes legitimate, another expression of the instinct: and in Prufrock's case, that instinct takes the form of envisioning his relation to the woman of the poem in terms provided by his relation to God. Here is how Cavell pictures the matter later in *The Claim of Reason*:

> As long as God exists, I am not alone. And couldn't the other suffer the fate of God? It strikes me that it was out of the terror of this possibility that Luther promoted the individual voice in the religious life. I wish to understand how the other now bears the weight of God, shows that I am not alone in the universe. This requires understanding the philosophical problem of the other as the trace or scar of the departure of God. This descent, or ascent, of the problem of the other is the key way I can grasp the alternative process of secularization called romanticism. And it may explain why the process of humanization can become a monstrous undertaking, placing infinite demands upon finite resources. It is an image of what living our scepticism comes to. (CR, 470)

The third theme that takes centre stage when we read Cavell's allusion to Prufrock in its full local context is, of course, that of theatre. For he associates Wittgenstein's way of acknowledging the contingency of reality and the precariousness of human existence as one of removing its theatricality—not the theatricality of reality and existence, but rather the theatricality of previous philosophical attempts (whether verificationist or existentialist) to acknowledge reality and existence, to acknowledge our finitude. But as we have seen, his invocation of Prufrock, and so of Prufrock's motivated disavowals of Hamlet, also engendered an idea of theatricality: Cavell's thought here was that human existence must be understood as theatrical insofar as we acknowledge that we must take our existence upon ourselves, we must enact it (or fail to). Putting these two invocations of theatre together, we reach the suggestion that the theatricalization of human existence can, and can only, be overcome by means of theatre. And we thereby return to the basic line of thought underlying Cavell's and Fried's work on artistic modernism in painting and drama.

For present purposes, the moral I want to draw from this aspect of Fried's and Cavell's work is that the modernist artistic ideal they define in opposition to the theatricality of minimalism (and various other forms of what they call modernizing or postmodern art) is the achievement of presentness. Eliot's portrayal of Prufrock both confirms the centrality of this counter-term and gives it further specificity insofar as Prufrock's tragicomic struggle might be characterized as an unsuccessful but unceasing attempt to achieve presentness to another, to the world they jointly inhabit, and to himself. Heidegger would call it concern and solicitude, understood as aspects of Dasein's being as care; Cavell prefers acceptance and acknowledgement, understood as aspects of self-enactment or self-realization. In the remainder of this discussion, I want to essay a reading of Coetzee's engagement with autobiography as a site at which he stages a genuinely radical critique of his own asceticism—one that goes to the root of the matter precisely because it grows from it—which amounts to an analogous search for genuine presentness.

3. Coetzee: Autobiographical Theory

I said earlier that Coetzee's turn towards the autobiographical began with the composition of *Boyhood* in 1997; but it might equally be said to have begun with the publication of *Doubling the Point* in 1992.[31] This volume of essays and interviews collects a representative sample of Coetzee's critical writings between 1970 and 1990, with each subset of essays preceded by the transcript of an interview

---

[31] Ed. D. Attwell (Cambridge, MA: Harvard University Press, 1992); hereafter DP.

between Coetzee and David Attwell that aspires to set the biographical, cultural, and intellectual scene for that set (including the relations, if any, between these critical writings and Coetzee's fictions), and a similar dialogical exchange framing the collection as a whole. That framing exchange makes it absolutely explicit that interviewer and interviewee are both happy to think of what they are doing as facilitating an intellectual autobiography of a certain kind, although one which both articulates and enacts a certain problematization of the very concept of an 'autobiography'.

For when Attwell begins the interviews by raising the issue of the autobiographical, Coetzee accepts its pertinence, but immediately claims that all writing is autobiography: 'everything you write, including criticism and fiction, writes you as you write it' (DP, 17). The thought here is that all writing reveals to the writer what he wants to say, even constructs it, and what it reveals may be quite different from what the writer initially thought or half believed that he wanted to say. And Coetzee goes on:

> I don't see that 'straight' autobiographical writing is any different in kind from what I have been describing. Truth is something that comes in the process of writing, or comes from the process of writing...
>
> I am tempted to try out the following definition of autobiography: that it is a kind of self-writing in which you are constrained to respect the facts of your history. But which facts? All the facts? No. All the facts are too many facts. You choose the facts insofar as they fall in with your evolving purpose. What is that purpose in the present case? Tentatively I propose: to understand the desire that drove me to write what I wrote from 1970 to 1990—not the novels, which are well enough equipped to perform their own interrogations, but everything else, the critical essays, the reviews, and so forth—pieces whose genre does not usually give them room to reflect on themselves. (DP, 18)

So Coetzee accepts the suggestion that this book is autobiographical, but only on a certain understanding of what that might mean; and various aspects of that understanding are worth emphasizing. First, 'writing' here is a synecdoche for any kind of articulation or actualization of the self; producing texts is one exemplary way in which attempting to give expression to one's thoughts and desires (in what one says or does) serves as much to create as to report them. Second, Coetzee appears to risk running together the idea of writing the self and writing about the self: he justifies the claim that all writing is autobiography by presenting an argument to the effect that all writing contributes to the construction of the self-who-writes. But the self who is thereby constructed is not necessarily the object of the writing that constructs him, which is surely what one might think distinguishes specifically autobiographical writing from other kinds. On Coetzee's account, however, it is the fact that all writing is self-writing that makes it so much as possible for the self to write about itself, since there would be no self (possessed of a realized individual array of thoughts and desires and projects) without it; and that same fact is what entails that the act of writing about itself will reconstruct the self who engages in it.

For if autobiographical writing, insofar as it is writing, reconstructs the self who produces it, it must reconfigure its own subject. The self-who-writes-an-autobiography may thereby attempt to subject itself to the constraints of a set of facts about its own history; but it inevitably selects which facts will constrain it, and does so in a way which reflects its current purposes, which are themselves the product of prior self-writing (including that produced by the subject of this self's storytelling), and which will themselves be reconfigured by the present writing. Hence, the autobiographical subject will always be the subject of another subject's story; and that act of storytelling will necessarily distance the teller of the tale from himself. So any autobiographical story will involve three subjects: the subject of the story, the recounter of that story, and the subject that the recounter becomes by virtue of his act of recounting. The truth about the first will always be the truth as it discloses itself to the second through his writing, which will also reconstitute the truth about the second, thereby ensuring that any autobiographical story about the second will reveal the truth about him only as it discloses itself to a third; and so endlessly on. This does not amount to a denial that autobiographical writing can disclose truth; it rather amounts to a specification of what such truths about beings capable of expressing and so constituting themselves are, and how they can and must be disclosed. And this specification contains no image of an unchanging essence of the subject lurking beneath the vicissitudes of its experience; it rather amounts to a concrete working-out of selfhood as (in part, autobiographical) becoming.

Suppose we apply this general framework to the text which begins by outlining it—to *Doubling the Point*. Then we might profitably distinguish between the self of the interviewee who begins this act of textual production with a necessarily tentative and provisional grasp of its own autobiographical purpose in doing so, and the self who is produced by that act of writing (about) itself. This self would be the one from whose perspective the final text of the volume is produced, the interview transcript entitled 'Retrospect'. And that self has the following to say for itself:

> In these dialogues you have asked what I, in my blind way, have seen as I look back over the past twenty years of writing; and now you ask what I see when I look back over the dialogues themselves.
>
> I must reply that more and more I see the essay on Tolstoy, Rousseau and Dostoevsky emerging as pivotal... for two reasons. One, that there I see myself confronting in a different genre... the very question that you have faced me with in these dialogues: how to tell the truth in autobiography. Two, that I find the

story I tell about myself has certain definiteness of outline up to the time of that essay: after that, it becomes hazier, lays itself open to harder questioning from the future...

Standing on the hillock or island created by our present dialogue, let me tell you, in the retrospect it provides, what the story of the past twenty years looks like when I make [it] pivot on the essay on confession, written in 1982–3.

(DP, 391–2)

The remaining three or four pages of text then provide a condensed third-person present-tense narrative of Coetzee's life up to the point at which he moves to Texas in the mid-1960s and commences the fifteen-year programme of formalistic, linguistically based criticism whose fruits are collected in the volume at hand. It is at this point that, in 1991, '*he* now begins to feel closer to *I*: *autre*biography shades back into autobiography' (DP, 394).

In other words, this narrative covers the chronological ground that will be covered more extensively, in the same third-person present-tense form, in the first two volumes of 'autobiography' that Coetzee will soon go on to publish (in 1997 and 2002); indeed, it picks out as particularly significant for understanding the depth and intensity of the protagonist's sense of being alien (not alienated) the period of his childhood between 1948 and 1951 spent in rural Worcester—the period with which *Boyhood* is almost exclusively concerned. Since both *Boyhood* and *Youth* were written later than 1991, the interviewee in *Doubling the Point* would likely characterize them as even more definitely *autre*biographical than autobiographical. Moreover, given that *Doubling the Point* covers the intellectual and critical life of the same protagonist from 1970 to 1991, it would appear in retrospect to have as much claim to be a continuation of Coetzee's autobiographical project as *Summertime*, which also claims to cover a period in the 1970s when he returned to South Africa, but in fact appears to condense two very different time periods in its subject's life, and adopts a radically different form (being structured as a series of transcripts of interviews conducted after Coetzee's death between a biographer and five people who knew Coetzee in the relevant period, and book-ended by passages from this Coetzee's notebooks).[32] Or perhaps I should say that Coetzee began his autobiographical project with the present volume, and so by attending to a relatively late period of his life, and that the later volumes barely succeed in catching up with that initial attempt (which, from the perspective afforded by *Summertime*, now looks like a first version of the formal fictional strategies that third volume deploys in an even more complex manner— we might call it their autobiographical source).

---

[32] For more on this condensation, cf. ch. 10 of D. Attwell, *J. M. Coetzee and the Life of Writing* (Oxford: Oxford University Press, 2015).

However that may be, why does the essay on confession look to be pivotal from the perspective of *Doubling the Point*? The interviewee offers us two reasons, stating them separately, but inviting us to see them as internally related: he points out that an essay in which he first confronts the question of how to tell the truth in autobiography is also the point at which his own autobiographical outline loses its definiteness, laying itself open to harder questioning from the future. The suggestion appears to be that the essay marks the moment at which he shifts from being a writer merely reacting to the situation in which he finds himself (as a white South African in the second half of the twentieth century; disabled, disqualified, alien; being and writing without authority) to one in which he engages with that situation at a philosophical level (cf. DP, 392). On this way of thinking, the advent of philosophy within the life of this man-who-writes introduces a haziness in his autobiographical relation to himself, in the story he tells about himself; but that haziness only becomes evident to him because this advent of philosophy has prompted him to confront the autobiographical dimension of his existence in the first place (a confrontation that produces the volume from whose autobiographical perspective the advent of that haziness becomes perceptible). In short, philosophy at once activates and problematizes one's capacity to write oneself by writing about oneself: the philosophical can no more be disentangled from the autobiographicality of the human than that autobiographicality can be disentangled from the philosophical.

What, however, does this philosophical exploration of the autobiographical—as incarnated in the pivotal essay of the collection—disclose? The essay is focused on the confession understood as an autobiographical genre to be distinguished from both memoir and apologia, on the basis of an underlying motive to tell an essential truth about the self. More specifically, Coetzee tells us that he 'will follow the fortunes of a number of secular confessions, fictional and autobiographical, as their authors confront or evade the problem of how to know the truth about the self without being self-deceived, and of how to bring the confession to an end in the spirit of whatever they take to be the secular equivalent of absolution' (DP, 252). The religious source of this secular variant is explicitly acknowledged here, and it is reinforced by the choice of authors examined: after a brief appearance by Augustine, Tolstoy and Dostoevsky predominate, with Rousseau providing only a brief interlude in which the Russian masters' obsessive concern with the relation between the religious and the secular is downplayed.

Against the background provided by this selection of writers, Nietzsche would not be surprised to see that Coetzee associates the genre of the confession as such with the desire to tell an essential truth about the self, or that he perceives the secular confession as confronting a structural problem to which its religious counterpart had a decisive solution: since acts of confession are always subject to the threat of self-deception, and any apparent success in the task of unmasking oneself as deceptive might itself be a further self-deception, how is any confessor to bring this cycle of self-doubt to an end once it is set in motion?

For the religious believer absolution, and hence the work of grace (mediated by the priest, but originating in God), effects this closure; but how might non-believers achieve it? On the one hand, any confessing narrator who never raises a question about his own motives will appear naïve, and so lacking in authority; but on the other, once he raises the possibility of self-deception, he embarks on a process whose inability decisively to overcome scepticism will engender impatience, disillusionment, and boredom on the part of his audience (thereby losing his authority in another way). Otherwise put: if the autobiographical impulse is to maintain its credibility as seeking for the truth, it must find a way of bringing the threat of self-deception to heel, which will mean finding a secular way of ending its confession which possesses the kind of authority that resists a recurrence of such scepticism about its author's motives.

In 'Retrospect' (I mean the concluding section of *Doubling the Point*), Coetzee describes this essay as the site of a debate or submerged dialogue between two people: the person he then was and may still be, and the person he desired to be and was feeling his way towards. The first of these persons he entitles the Cynic, who believes that

> there is no ultimate truth about oneself, there is no point in trying to reach it, what we call the truth is only a shifting self-appraisal whose function is to make one feel good, or as good as possible under the circumstances, given that the genre doesn't allow one to create free-floating fictions. Autobiography is dominated by self-interest... one may be aware of that self-interest, but ultimately one cannot bring it into full focus. (DP, 392)

The other person is not given an equivalently articulate identifying discourse: he is simply associated with Grace: 'a condition in which the truth can be told clearly, without blindness... [In] Dostoevsky, the interlocutors are called Stavrogin and Tikhon' (DP, 392). The internal representative of grace is, in other words, a monk, or at least the reincarnation of monkish virtues: but Coetzee never claims to have become this person, either in the essay (which is here recharacterized as a dialogue between two persons or two of his personas) or in his current reflections on it. On the other hand, having described himself as feeling his way towards Grace in the essay, he invites us to consider whether the perspective he now adopts on it—one which sees it as already giving expression to grace as well as to the cynical person he actually then was—shows that he has gone beyond being a site of debate between those two personae and has now at least felt his way closer to a secular variant of grace (and so to a mode of autobiographical writing that at least attempts a solution to the problem of attaining authority over sceptical doubts about what it reveals). It might therefore be profitable to examine more closely the volumes of autobiographical writing which appeared after *Doubling the Point*, with a view to evaluating their ways of confronting and overcoming that problem.

4. Coetzee: Autobiographical Practice

A. Boyhood

Boyhood begins Coetzee's autobiographical project by emphatically aligning it with Tolstoy, and so with the religious and ascetic context that the essay on confession itself insisted upon. For Tolstoy's first published writing was entitled *Childhood*, was soon followed by two further volumes (entitled *Boyhood* and *Youth*), and for a long time all three texts were considered to be essentially autobiographical in nature. This view met with considerable hostility from their author from the first moment he encountered it, in his editor's response to his first volume (encapsulated in his unauthorized decision to entitle it *The Story of My Childhood*). The editor of the current Penguin Classics edition has no difficulty in constructing an extensive list of the differences between Tolstoy's childhood and that of the story's protagonist, Nikolenka; and as the author's preferred title indicates, his aim was rather to examine an idea, that of a certain representative or universal period of growth of the self—an archetype rather than an individual.[33]

Such a Platonic aspiration, as well as the assumption that a fictional rendering of it might be more successful than a factual autobiography, would be likely to appeal to the person Coetzee wanted to be, as would the sheer difficulty Tolstoy encountered in getting his readers to believe that his writing was not autobiographically intended (since acknowledging the difficulty would mean confronting the question of what created it—not just our readiness to read an author's life into his fiction, but our unwillingness to acknowledge the ineliminable contribution made by the fictional to any autobiographical project). On the other hand, Coetzee both invites and problematizes any direct correlation of Tolstoy's project to his own by producing a text which appropriates the title of Tolstoy's second volume for a narrative with a protagonist (call him 'John') whose age directly maps onto the protagonist of Tolstoy's first volume, and whose story resonates with that of Nikolenka in a number of significant respects.

Both inhabit (or at least had access to) a rural paradise whose attractions include the possibility of hunting, and from which they are exiled; both have an irresponsible father and a deeply beloved mother; both experience the loss of a parent—in Nikolenka's case, the death of his mother: in John's case, his father's

---

[33] Cf. Judson's Rosengrant's editorial introduction to his translation of Leo Tolstoy, *Childhood, Boyhood, Youth* (London: Penguin, 2012); hereafter CBY.

catastrophically shameful, self-annihilating retreat to his bedroom (which John initially interprets as, and wants to be, a deathbed, a scene of self-murder); both narratives make a point of interrogating the significance of shifting pronouns—Nikolenka when navigating the social complexities of his family's life in the city, John more pervasively (as a protagonist presented to us in the third person); and both supplement the climactic parental catastrophe with a story about the death of a more distant intimate of the family—Nikolenka's servant Natalya Savishna, John's Aunt Annie.

It is therefore hard to avoid the conclusion that Coetzee's text is intended to test its own ability to find a secular equivalent to Tolstoy's religious mode of authoritative access to a solution to the problem of self-deception, hence to his attachment to truth-seeking in confession. That problem, as we saw, is in a sense a formal one: it is a matter of how to find a way of ending the revelatory confession that is neither aesthetically nor ethically inept, which also means finding an authoritative way of beginning the confession (since only the clear envisioning of how a confession ends can permit an equally authoritative beginning, and indeed only the right kind of beginning could make possible the right kind of end). Suppose, then, that we look more closely at how Coetzee's *Boyhood* begins and ends.

The first chapter opens with a portrait of John's mother's imprisonment in their house in Worcester—in a poorly built new house on a lifeless, dusty estate outside town, with nothing but housekeeping to keep her occupied and no means of travel. The narrator tells us that John's mother resists this imprisonment by acquiring a bike and learning to ride it; but her husband and neighbours mock her incessantly for this unwomanly practice, and eventually she stops riding and the bicycle disappears, and with it her ability to escape from her present life towards her own desire. John knows this, but sides with his father and against her. But the chapter recounts an episode that precedes the mother's escape attempt, one concerning a problem she confronts with the hens that the family keep in the yard to provide eggs, when they acquire a disease that causes them to cease to lay.

> His mother consults her sister in Stellenbosch, who says they will return to laying only after the horny shells under their tongues have been cut out. So one after another his mother takes the hens between her knees, presses on their jowls till they open their beaks, and with the point of a paring-knife picks at their tongues. The hens shriek and struggle, their eyes bulging. He shudders and turns away. He thinks of his mother slapping stewing steak down on the kitchen counter and cutting it into cubes; he thinks of her bloody fingers. (SPL, 3)

On one level, the hens suffer his mother's condition—encountering the world's mysterious but irresistible impulse to amputate their mouths, to pick at their tongues, to render them voiceless, they articulate their pain inarticulately, in shrieks and struggles; it is as if John's mother's pain finds expression in the mouths of her hens.[34] And yet in this situation she takes up the position of the victimizer rather than the victim: so should we think of her as taking out on those less powerful than herself the pain that those more powerful than her have inflicted, or should we think of the pain inflicted on her as in some sense self-inflicted (either by her giving up on her own attempts to escape, or by her failing to resist the move to Worcester in the first place)? In the latter case, we would have a powerful example of the sadomasochistic structure of slave morality and the ascetic ideal.

And what of John's relation to this structure? In the case of the hens, he identifies with them and identifies his mother as an inflictor of suffering; but when she takes up the position of the hens, he identifies with his father, and so with his mother's position in relation to the hens. So ascetic sadomasochism structures his own position in this opening scene of the narrative; and of course, it also informs the telling of it, insofar as the protagonist of the tale and the teller of it are presumed to be one and the same, in which case its telling amounts to a confession of guilt and an expression of the desire to be punished for wrongdoing.

The book's ending works by suggesting that a certain perspective has been attained on that initial, utterly helpless imprisonment in the machinery of asceticism. In the penultimate chapter, immediately after the revelation of his father's shameful condition, the narrator tells us that John's gloom lifts.

> The sky, that usually sits tight and closed over his head... opens a slit, and for an interval he can see the world as it really is. He sees himself in his white shirt with rolled-up sleeves and the grey short trousers that he is on the point of outgrowing: not a child, not what a passer-by would call a child, too big for that now, too big to use that excuse, yet still as stupid and self-enclosed as a child: childish; dumb; ignorant; retarded. In a moment like this he can see his father and his mother too, from above, without anger; not as two grey and formless weights seating themselves on his shoulders, plotting his misery day and night, but as a man and a woman living trouble-filled lives of their own. The sky opens, he sees the world as it is, then the sky closes and he is himself again, living the only story he will admit, the story of himself.

The chapter ends with a vision of his mother as she appears when the sky is still open:

> He would rather be blind and deaf than know what his mother thinks of him. He would rather live like a tortoise inside its shell.

---

[34] There is a clear connection here to Elizabeth Costello, and her tale of the role a hen's death cry played in Camus's campaigning against the death penalty; cf. my *The Wounded Animal*, ch. 5.

> For it is not true that, as he likes to think, this woman was brought into the world for the sole purpose of loving him and protecting him and satisfying his wants. On the contrary, she had a life before he came into being, a life in which she gave him not the slightest thought. Then at a certain moment in history she gave birth to him. She bore him and she decided to love him; perhaps she chose to love him even before she bore him: nevertheless, she chose to love him, and therefore she can choose to stop loving him. (SPL, 136-7)

This, one might say, is the real Coetzean counterpart to Tolstoy's narration of the death of Nikolenka's mother; for John, the realization that his mother (and his father) have lives of their own amounts to the destruction of their identity as characters in the only story that he has been willing to admit and recount up to this point, the story of himself—the story in which he is the centre of the universe and all other characters in it exist only in relation to him. But that story does not in fact qualify as an autobiography, because there can only be a story about a self if that self can be distinguished from other selves (each equally autobiographically capable), and the story John has been telling before the sky split is one which deprives all those other people of stories of their own, of a voice in their own existence. It is therefore a story that also lacks a genuinely autobiographical protagonist, one in which the protagonist is genuinely disclosed as a self.

Otherwise put: the narrative climax of *Boyhood* is not a climactic event within John's autobiography, but rather the achievement on John's part of the capacity to relate to himself autobiographically, which means the capacity to relate to others biographically—as writers of themselves just as he is a writer of himself. The narrator of this tale figures this moment as the end of John's childhood (which is presumably why the tale takes its title from Tolstoy's second volume); but we might equally well take it as the moment at which a condition for the possibility of an autobiography has been established. This would entail that the narrative which culminates in this moment is a critical exploration of that condition of possibility: it is, in other words, at once a philosophical study of autobiography and a prolegomenon to one possible autobiography. And it is precisely this that solves the formal problem that the essay on confession identifies: for here the ending of the narrative is simultaneously a beginning, and both are dictated by the nature of autobiography as such. In other words, what authorizes the opening and the closure of this narrative is its arrival at an essential truth about its protagonist, its autobiographical narrator, and its genre.

One might worry that this achievement of closure is so tightly overdetermined and self-sufficient that it risks a certain airlessness—as if such a reflexive solution to the problem of secular confession is destined to float entirely free of the real world with which it aspires to make truthful contact. But here we need to recall one final touchstone of authenticity or authority that Coetzee invokes when introducing his essay on confession in *Doubling the Point*.

> The body with its pain becomes a counter to the endless trials of doubt...
>
> Not grace, then, but the body. Let me put it baldly: in South Africa, it is not possible to deny the authority of suffering and therefore of the body...not for logical reasons, not for ethical reasons...but for political reasons, for reasons of power...It is not that one *grants* the authority of the suffering body: the suffering body *takes* this authority: that is its power. (DP, 248)

I have already indicated one crucial point at which *Boyhood* invokes this mode of authority, in its opening treatment of the hens. But there is another point at which this authority is activated, and—precisely because I can't forget it—I can't forbear from citing it here, in conclusion. It occurs during a visit John makes with his brother to Aunt Annie, the relative whose death constitutes the formal end of the book:

> The best thing in the storeroom is the book press. It is made of iron as heavy and solid as the wheel of a locomotive. He persuades his brother to lay his arms in the bed of the press; then he turns the great screw until his brother's arms are pinned and he cannot escape. After which, they change places and his brother does the same to him.
>
> One or two more turns, he thinks, and the bones will be crushed. What is it that makes them forbear, both of them?
>
> During their first months in Worcester they were invited to one of the farms that supplied fruit to Standard Canners. While the grown-ups drank tea, he and his brother roamed around the farmyard. There they came upon a mealie-grinding machine. He persuaded his brother to put his hand down the funnel where the mealie-pits were thrown in; then he turned the handle. For an instant, before he stopped, he could actually feel the fine bones of his brother's fingers yield as the cogs crushed them. His brother stood with his hand trapped in the machine, ashen with pain, a puzzled, inquiring look on his face.
>
> Their hosts rushed them to the hospital, where a doctor amputated the middle finger of his brother's left hand. For a while his brother walked around with his hand bandaged and his arm in a sling; then he wore a little black leather pouch over the finger-stump. He was six years old. Though non one pretended his finger would grow back, he did not complain.
>
> He has never apologized to his brother, nor has he ever been reproached with what he did. Nevertheless, the memory lies like a weight upon him, the memory of the soft resistance of flesh and bone, and then the grinding. (SPL, 101)

Is this an autobiographical scene, or a fictional one? The few commentators who mention it, and might be in a position to know, write as if it is the former;[35] but of

---

[35] Cf. Derek Attridge, *J. M. Coetzee and the Ethics of Reading* (Chicago: University of Chicago Press, 2005), ch. 6.

course no reader of this text can be in a position to know this with any certainty. If it *is* autobiographical, it certainly outreaches Augustine's theft of pears or Rousseau's false accusation of theft against a maid in its shamefulness, and thus in its value as currency for a possible confession (according to Coetzee's reading of Rousseau). Or should we rather think of it as a way of his making an apology to his brother, at long last, and so as also an apology for his not having done so before? Or is Coetzee inventing a scene of a suffering body in response to his protagonist's own question about why such imaginings are not more often realized? Would it be less shameful if he invented this scene whilst implying that it is autobiographical? Or is the truth of the matter that this whole sequence is really meant to figure the power of words that evoke violence (whether fictionally or otherwise)—words that bear down on the bodies of his readers like the iron of the book press, so that their 'thinking is thrown into confusion and helplessness by the fact of suffering in the world' (DP, 248), whether or not the suffering body depicted corresponds to some particular body undergoing an actual episode of suffering? How shameful would that be?

B. Youth

If the end of *Boyhood* heralds the attainment of one condition for the possibility of an autobiography, the end of *Youth* suggests that other such conditions remain unattained during the events it records (which take its protagonist from 1959, when he is aged 19, to 1964). Having spent three summers in England, John is now one of two non-British people working for International Computers, developing an Atlas computer for use by the Ministry of Defence at Aldermaston; he has failed as a writer and as a lover; he has made no friends, established only the barest minimum of a social life, and repeatedly failed to treat the people with whom he does come into contact (particularly women) with even a basic moral decency. At the weekends, he kills time playing chess with himself until the working week begins, but his work is itself only a way of killing time whilst his destiny keeps on failing to arrive.

> At eighteen, he might have been a poet. Now he is not a poet, not a writer, not an artist. He is a computer programmer, a twenty-four-year-old computer programmer in a world in which there are no thirty-year-old computer programmers... He and Ganapathy [the other foreigner employed by IC] are two sides of the same coin: Ganapathy starving not because he is cut off from Mother India but because he doesn't eat properly, because despite his M.Sc. in computer science he doesn't know about vitamins and minerals and amino acids; and he locked into an attenuated endgame, playing himself, with each move, further into a corner and into defeat. One of these days the ambulance men will call at Ganapathy's flat and bring him out on a stretcher with a sheet

over his face. When they have fetched Ganapathy they might as well come and fetch him too. (SPL, 284)

In order for *Youth* to count as the autobiography of J. M. Coetzee, it would surely have to be the autobiography of an artist, a writer, and a poet; but this book's narrator presents its protagonist as none of these things—not just as someone who is *not yet* any of those things, but as someone for whom the once-genuine possibility of his becoming such a person has been flatly and decisively negated ('At eighteen, he might have been... Now he is not'). Even more fundamentally, any autobiography is a mode of life-writing, the recounting of a living being's story; but the protagonist of this book (as opposed to its narrator, whose irony discloses a humorous, and so enlivening, dimension to John's predicament, however biting or bitter, and however dependent on the wisdom of hindsight) shows no vital signs, no indication of vitality, whether artistic or human or merely animal. As he sees the life he is currently leading, he might as well be dead; and since our experience as readers is restricted entirely to his viewpoint, it too resembles being buried alive.

The protagonist of Tolstoy's *Youth* would not find this mode of death-in-life entirely unrecognizable, although his name for it might seem to underestimate its threat: Nikolenka confronts it under the heading '*comme il faut*'. As he begins his university career, and so enters the wider social world, he divides everyone he meets into those who are *comme il faut* and those who are not: the former he respects and regards as worthy of social relations, the latter he treats with scorn and contempt. For Nikolenka, to be *comme il faut* means to speak excellent French; to have properly cared-for fingernails; to know how to bow, dance and converse; and to exhibit indifference to everything by means of a constant expression of elegant, supercilious boredom. As he puts it:

Comme il faut was for me not merely an important virtue, a fine quality, a perfection that I wished to attain, but also an essential condition of life, without which there could be neither happiness nor reputation, nor anything good in the world. I couldn't respect a famous actor or a learned man or a benefactor of the human race if he wasn't *comme il faut*. The *comme il faut* person stood higher and was beyond comparison with the rest; he left it to them to paint their pictures, write their music and their books, and do good... but they weren't on the same level as he was. (CBY, 329–30)

Doing things properly or becomingly, as they should be done or as one does them, and maintaining unwavering indifference to everything done in this way: this is a version of the condition Heidegger calls 'das man'—the average everyday way of relating to others and to oneself which amounts to an occlusion of one's responsibility for one's own existence. It denies the fact that whatever one does in one's life, the form of existence that results must be owned—must not just be realized but realized in a way which manifests one's individuality, on pain of being hollowed out or empty of significance; for a human life is one to which mineness necessarily belongs, so that if that mineness is not enacted it will be disavowed. Nikolenka's circle of Russian society intensifies that disavowal by importing its conception of what one does from another country and culture (as using a French phrase to encapsulate that whole pattern of behaviour indicates); but even a more homegrown conception (whatever its specific content) would have achieved the same effect—one of shared and mutually reinforcing alienation from the deepest springs of one's individual being. And Nikolenka is clear that the worst damage effected by this syndrome is that it turns those who internalize it away from the necessity of active involvement in social life—the wholehearted commitment to living out some particular calling:

> The principal harm was the belief that *comme il faut* was an independent position in society, that one didn't have to make the effort to be an official or a carriage maker or a soldier or a learned man, if one was *comme il faut*; that in attaining that quality, one had already fulfilled one's purpose and even stood higher than most. (CBY, 330)

But this distraction from commitment doesn't, in Tolstoy's view, apply merely to vocations or social roles; it also applies to morality, or more specifically to the task of realizing or enacting one's moral principles and developing oneself more generally as a moral being. For what Nikolenka opposes to the threat of *comme il faut* is that which he opens his account by presenting as the defining characteristic of *youth*: a new view of life and its purpose and relations.

> The essence of that view was the conviction that it is the goal of each to strive for moral improvement, and that such improvement is easy, possible and lasting. The time came when the ideas [of virtue I examined in conversation with my cherished friend] entered my mind with such a fresh power of revelation that it scared me to think how much time I had wasted, and I wanted at once, wanted that very second, to apply them to life with the firm intention of never betraying them.
> So far, however, the only enjoyment I had obtained was discovering the new ideas that followed from that conviction, and making brilliant plans for an active moral future, since my life continued the same trivial, confused and idle round as before. (CBY, 213; sentence order changed)

A genuine moral future is an active one: not so much one in which intellectual affirmation is supplemented by a more passionate endorsement, but one in which one's particular commitments of mind and heart are enacted or realized in activity, and so in the shape of one's life, which thereby acquires the key signature of moral adulthood—genuine selfhood. Nikolenka's adolescence begins when it is revealed to him that one can become a genuinely moral being, one can make one's moral principles one's own, only by living them out; but he also sees that there is a big difference between realizing that one must enact one's ideas and being so excited by that intellectual realization that one keeps on making elaborate plans to do so instead of actually doing it. And the deep significance of his society's acceptance of the ideal of *comme il faut* is that it constitutes an obstacle to such sustained striving—not just because it presents itself as a superior idea, but because it presents itself as an idea that effortlessly realizes itself if it realizes itself at all. For when Nikolenka asks about the effort a friend makes to keep his fingernails *comme il faut*, he is told: 'For as long as I can remember I've never done anything to make them that way, and I don't see how a decent person could have nails of any other kind'; this is why Nikolenka emphasizes that 'one of the main conditions of *comme il faut* is hiding the effort by which it is achieved' (CBY, 329). Being *comme il faut* is thus the antithesis of a genuinely active moral future: it is a way of being whose nature depends upon those who embody it refusing to take personal responsibility for it, and so something that necessarily occludes the mineness of a genuinely human life.

The death-in-life undergone by the protagonist of Coetzee's *Youth* exhibits a condition similar to that of Nikolenka. John systematically fails to put his orienting ideas and desires into practice, instead living as if he expects his destiny to happen to him without any intervention on his own part ('Everything he has done since he stepped ashore at Southampton has been a killing of time while he waits for his destiny to arrive' (SPL, 281)); he derives his ideals from a culture other than his own, although where Nikolenka's circle import their ideals, John exports himself to their native land; and despite his fervent desire to become a morally decent human being, his commitment to those ideals prevents him from achieving any kind of moral growth (and for reasons surprisingly similar to those structuring the paradox of self-exposure to which Amis's John (Lewis) was subject).

> Death to reason, death to talk! All that matters is doing the right thing, whether for the right reason or the wrong reason or no reason at all...
>
> He could, if he chose, do the right thing with near infallible accuracy. What gives him pause is the question of whether he can go on being a poet while doing the right thing. When he tries to imagine what sort of poetry would flow from doing the right thing time after time after time, he sees only blank emptiness. The right thing is boring. So he is at an impasse: he would rather be bad than boring; he has no respect for a person who would rather be bad than boring, and no respect either for the cleverness of being able to put his dilemma neatly into words. (SPL, 280–1)

The key difference between Tolstoy's and Coetzee's young people is that, where Nikolenka conceives of being *comme il faut* as a superior existential alternative to that of being an artist, John has internalized a *comme il faut* version of being an artist. Indeed, if one regards Coetzee's *Youth* as a recounting of the conditions for the *impossibility* of an autobiography of its protagonist—as an account of how and why someone's potential for enacting a genuinely autobiographical relation to himself not only remained unrealized but (to all appearances) also withered away—then the really fundamental such condition is John's desire to be an artist, or rather his conception of the object of that desire.

The book's opening chapters underline the extent to which John's vision of being an artist derives from a source that is external both to himself and to his native culture: the anglophone modernist poets Pound and Eliot.

> Ezra Pound has suffered persecution most of his life: driven into exile, then imprisoned, then expelled from his homeland a second time. Yet despite being labelled a madman, Pound has proved that he is a great poet, perhaps as great as Walt Whitman. Obeying his daimon, Pound has sacrificed his life to his art. So has Eliot, although Eliot's suffering has been of a more private nature. Eliot and Pound have lived lives of sorrow and sometimes of ignominy. There is a lesson for him in that, driven home on every page of their poetry—of Eliot's, with which he had his first overwhelming encounter while he was still at school, and now of Pound's. Like Pound and Eliot, he must be prepared to endure all that life has stored up for him, even if that means exile, obscure labour, and obloquy. And if he fails the highest test of art, if it turns out that after all he does not have the blessed gift, then he must be prepared to endure that too: the incontestable verdict of history, the fate of being, despite all his present and future sufferings, minor. Many are called, few are chosen. For every major poet a cloud of minor poets, like gnats buzzing around a lion. (SPL, 159–60)

Pound and Eliot are both great poets; Pound and Eliot have lived lives of sorrow and ignominy; therefore if John is to be a great poet he must be willing to endure exile, obscure labour, and obloquy. And no sooner has John constructed that invalid inference (conflating the correlation of two potentially independent variables with the instantiation of a general law of nature) than he takes the further, equally illegitimate step of assuming that if all As are B, then all Bs are A. That is, he assumes that if he does endure exile, obscure labour, and obloquy, he will certainly enhance his chances of igniting the inner fire of art, and perhaps even validate his perception of himself as possessed of that fire.

> If for the time being he must be obscure and ridiculous, that is because it is the lot of the artist to suffer obscurity and ridicule until the day when he is revealed in his true powers and the scoffers and mockers fall silent. (SPL, 145)

The facts about Pound's and Eliot's work and life do not, then, teach the lesson that John derives from them—although he is not alone in having derived such a Romantic lesson from such facts: indeed, the further fact that he nevertheless thinks of this lesson as driven home on every page of their poetry (that is, that he approaches these two exemplars already assuming that the work can and does reveal something about the life, that they are two sides of a single coin) shows only that he has begged this question before any individual artist's work and life might be in a position to pose it. He is, on other words, haunted or possessed by a trope for the artistic life that is so pervasive and so familiar that it presents itself to him as just what artists do, what one does as an artist—in short, as *comme il faut*.

What, however, of the lesson's content? There is a strong flavour of the ascetic ideal in the conception of life as an artist upon which John is staking his existence. The true artist must be willing to sacrifice everything that is of value in human life for the sake of his art; more precisely, he must suffer persecution and mockery, and even sacrifice moral self-respect, for the sake of the bare possibility that he possesses this divine gift. For the truth is that few do; and if John turns out not to belong to that happy few, he must simply reconfigure his sadomasochistic impulse for suffering so that he can now endure the fate of lacking the one thing that makes life truly meaningful.

This vision of the artistic vocation as a species of self-stultifying mortification positively declares its genealogical affiliations in the prose with which John articulates it to himself. For in its concluding peroration, he evokes not only the Socratic daimon, but three biblical references: 'Many are called...' comes from Jesus' parable of the banquet; the 'cloud of minor poets' evokes St Paul's reference to 'clouds of witness' in his Letter to the Hebrews; and the insects buzzing around the lion distantly echoes the solution to Samson's riddle from the Book of Judges: 'out of the strong came forth sweetness' (by which he refers to a lion's carcass inhabited by honey-making bees). So when the narrative of John's youth comes so fully and painfully to incarnate the life-denying arc of exile (from South Africa), obscure labour (with computer programming companies), and obloquy (as a foreigner, as an ungenerous host and friend, as an egotistical and unsatisfying lover) that was so excitingly revealed to him by his heroes' poetry, to the point of failing even to realize the gnat-like status of the minor poet, the resultant mode of death-in-life (and in particular its unremitting infliction on the reader) is as much the articulation of a Nietzschean symptom as it is a variation on Tolstoyan themes.

It's worth recalling at this point, however, that despite his inability to produce any substantial items of poetry or prose with which he is satisfied, Coetzee's account makes it clear that John is continuously producing one kind of text—a diary; reference is made to him writing it both in South Africa and in London (and Coetzee thereby alludes to a realistic documentary resource from which the highly detailed narrative of *Youth* might have been drawn). But those references also bring out something distinctive about his understanding of what that writing signifies, or more precisely how it signifies, which in turn helps to explain why he could so easily internalize that ascetic cultural vision of the artist.

The diary first surfaces in the text in its first chapter: having fallen into an affair with a beautiful but unstable woman named Jacqueline who moves in with him, he finds that he cannot bear sharing his living space with her, but proves incapable of raising these (and other) disquieting issues with her. Then:

> It all comes to a head when, while he is out of the flat, Jacqueline searches out his diary and reads what he has written about their life together. He returns to find her packing her belongings.
> 'What is going on?' he asks.
> Tight-lipped, she point to the diary lying open on his desk.
> He flares up in anger. 'You are not going to stop me from writing!' he vows. It is a non sequitur, and he knows it.
> She is angry too, but in a colder, deeper way. 'If, as you say, you find me such an unspeakable burden', she say, 'if I am destroying your peace and your privacy and your ability to write, let me tell you from my side that I have hated living with you, hated every minute of it, and can't wait to be free.'
> What he should have said was that one should not read other people's private papers. In fact, he should have hidden his diary away, not left it where it could be found. But it is too late, now, the damage is done. (SPL, 149)

The reader of Coetzee's text is probably more surprised at the materialization of this diary than either character, since no mention of it (or of making entries in it as one of John's activities with his books that Jacqueline's presence disrupts) has hitherto been made. But one does not have to be a Freudian to interpret the idea that he simply left such a supposedly private set of papers lying around; John himself admits that he might well have wanted her to find it, so that he could use it to tell Jacqueline what he really feels about her, but without taking responsibility for their direct expression (SPL, 150). Her discovery of it certainly leads to the consummation he devoutly wishes (her ceasing to live with him), whilst ensuring that she appears responsible for bringing it about, and even leaving room to doubt whether her expression of hatred is sincere or rather an artefact of her discovery of his feelings about her (a self-protective reflex rather than a sober indictment).

What, however, of his own immediate reaction, the non sequitur that precedes any such reflective self-questioning? Why does he respond to the fact of her having read what he has written (as opposed to her response to its specific content) as something that threatens his ability to write? Why would the bare knowledge that another person will read, or might read, what he has written constitute an obstacle to his writing? It's as if John inhabits a fantasy of writing in which its possibility and value for him requires that it be severed from the idea of its being directed to a recipient or addressee; his ability to write depends upon his occluding the possibility of its communicating anything to anyone else.

Anyone familiar with Wittgenstein's later work will recognize this as the fantasy of a private language: a language whose words are meaningful for their user, but essentially unintelligible to others. And against this background, the second explicit reference to John's diary-keeping—much later in the book—takes on a fascinating aspect.

> About quitting IBM he has no regrets. But now he has no one at all to speak to, not even Bill Briggs. Day after day goes by when not a word passes his lips. He begins to mark them off with an S in his diary; days of silence.
>
> Outside the Underground station he bumps by mistake against a little old man selling newspapers. 'Sorry!' he says. 'Watch where you're going!' snarls the man. 'Sorry!' he repeats.
>
> *Sorry*: the word comes heavily out of his mouth, like a stone. Does a single word of indeterminate grammatical class count as speech? Has what has occurred between the himself and the old man been an instance of human contact, or is it better described as mere social interaction, like the touching of antennae between ants? To the old man, certainly, it was nothing. All day long, the old man stands there with his stack of papers, muttering angrily to himself; he is always waiting for a chance to abuse some passer-by. Whereas in his own case the memory of that single word will persist for weeks, perhaps for the rest of his life. Bumping into people, saying 'Sorry!', getting abused: a ruse, a cheap way of forcing a conversation. How to trick loneliness.   (SPL, 239–40)

At the heart of Wittgenstein's famous discussion of the fantasy of a private language, he tries to imagine a world in which people showed no natural outward signs or expressions of pain (or indeed of any other inner state); then he takes a further step.

> Let's imagine the following case. I want to keep a diary about the recurrence of a certain sensation. To this end I associate it with the sign 'S' and write this sign in a calendar for every day on which I have the sensation.   (PI, I: section 258)

Wittgenstein's question is: could this diarist use 'S' as a name for his sensation even though no one else can understand what it refers to? His attempts to answer it quickly raise the question of whether the diarist could remember aright in the future his original association between sign and sensation—more specifically, whether he could distinguish even in principle between a correct and an incorrect memory of the associated sensation; and his negative answer to that question—his suggestion that accurately picking out 'memories of S' cannot determine the meaning of 'S' because it presupposes a grasp of that meaning as part of grasping what the notion of 'a memory of S' is—is illuminated by a comparison between that task and a peculiar use of newspapers ('As if someone were to buy several copies of today's morning paper to assure himself that what it said was true' (PI, I: section 265)). My question is: could the author of the second diary passage in *Youth*, with its own circling around ideas of words that aren't really words, pain and suffering, memory, newspapers, privacy and isolation, have been unaware of this?

Of course, the points of difference between Wittgenstein's diarist and Coetzee's are as important as the similarities. In particular, although one might argue that John's diary-sign 'S' tracks or marks a particular feeling (the pain of loneliness), it is more explicitly meant to indicate the absence of speech: it's a kind of meta- or anti-sign—an indication that no linguistic exchanges have occurred between its user and other language users that day. And since it is the only specific sign John is described as using in his diary, it invites interpretation as metonymic of every sign in that diary: it tells us, in other words, that everything in John's diary is at once expressive of pain, loneliness, and suffering, and a registration or mode of silence. Just as his public use of the 'S' in 'Sorry!' seems not really to count as speech, let alone as an expression of sorrow, so all the words in his diary present themselves as attempts to give expression to pain which fail to achieve their goal. This is why John's way of generalizing from his encounter with the newspaperman also appears to fit his earlier fight with Jacqueline. In retrospect, was his furious exchange with her genuine human intercourse, or was it just another exemplary instance of his bumping into another person, grunting and getting abused: 'a ruse, a cheap way of forcing a conversation'—an essentially doomed attempt to trick loneliness into expressing, and thereby assuaging, itself?

That John suffers from anxieties about the privacy of the meaning of his words is confirmed when he explains why he sees no point in publishing one of the few pieces of non-diary prose writing he produces during his English exile, despite the fact that he regards this short story about two people visiting a lonely South African beach as not bad, as genuinely minor:

> The English will not understand it. For the beach in the story they will summon up an English idea of a beach, a few pebbles lapped by wavelets. They will not see a dazzling space of sand at the foot of rocky cliffs pounded by breakers, with gulls and cormorants screaming overhead as they battle the wind. (SPL, 195)

Both the presence of the fantasy of privacy, and its emptiness, are manifest in this chain of reasoning. Since, as he immediately points out, 'prose seems naggingly to demand a specific setting' (SPL, 195), there is no reason why the story can't exclude the misunderstanding he fears—if not simply by specifying that the beach is South African, then by spelling out which features of a specifically South African beach he wishes to convey. He has just, after all, spelt that out to the readers of the passage that articulates this fantasy, and there will be English readers amongst them. In the same way, although anyone who comes across his diary entries might not initially grasp the significance of his use of the sign 'S', and so it might initially say nothing to them, that lack of meaning could easily be rectified (as it immediately is for readers of the relevant passage in *Youth*) by explaining its function.

One might stay within the fantasy by reiterating its underlying scepticism: for who is to say that the ideas a reader associates with an explanatory phrase such as 'dazzling spaces of sand' or 'no human contact' resemble those that John associates with them? What comes out here is the idea that the network of associations called up by a word in one person is *necessarily* different from that called up in another whose course of life was different; not just likely to differ in certain respects but certain to differ radically, to the point at which mutual understanding is fated to fail. To deny the necessity of that difference can then seem to deny the uniqueness of individual lives, and so the uniqueness of the individuals who live them; so defending a necessary privacy of meaning can appear to be essential to defending the uniqueness of persons. Wittgenstein works to dispel this appearance by distinguishing the uniqueness of persons from the uniqueness of their feelings: I might be suffering exactly the same headache or sense of acute loneliness as you are, right here and now, but that wouldn't make us one and the same person—it wouldn't reduce the number of suffering people from two to one. Separateness of persons can and must be establishable independently of sameness and difference of inner states, or else writing of the kind that John (and Coetzee, and I) are doing would be impossible.

This is one point at which the issue of a private language touches upon issues of the conditions for the possibility of autobiography. What we saw in *Boyhood* was that one such condition was the autobiographical subject's ability to distinguish others from himself, and so himself as one inhabitant of the world amongst many; but it is easy to think that establishing that separateness as a subject requires that the contents of one's narrative of oneself be uniquely one's own, a sequence of thoughts and feelings that no other person could possibly have experienced, on pain of loss of individual reality altogether. Wittgenstein's aim is to show that such an assumption amounts to letting the conceptual pendulum swing too far in the opposite direction; and *Youth* shows its protagonist suffering from having done precisely that.

Why might anyone succumb to such a temptation—to the thought that a speaker's full and genuine presence to himself in his words about himself depends upon their meaning being present to themselves (and so to him) in a manner that ensures its necessary absence from or beyondness to any other selves? In Wittgenstein's work, the significance of the fantasy of privacy is that it relieves or assuages a variety of anxieties, of which two seem directly relevant here: the anxiety that one is accountable for failing to make oneself understood, and the anxiety that one cannot help but give expression to one's inner states (that one's subjection to embodiment and to language makes one subject to exposure, as if all expressions of oneself are confessions, hence inherently shameful). If expressions of inner states (linguistic and otherwise) really were metaphysically resistant to others' understanding, one could not be blamed for failing to express oneself honestly, and one could more generally deny that anything one says or does honestly gives expression to oneself. We might call these ways of tricking loneliness (by making it seem either part of the human condition, hence a given point of commonality with others, or else a valuable means of avoiding the shame of exposure): it seems clear that the protagonist of *Youth* is subject to both anxieties.

When discussing his love of Eliot's dictum that 'poetry is not an expression of personality but an escape from personality', John is given the following response:

> He has a horror of spilling mere emotion on to the page. Once it has begun to spill out he would not know how to stop it. It would be like severing an artery and watching one's lifeblood gush out. Prose, fortunately, does not demand emotion... Prose is like a flat, tranquil sheet of water on which one can tack about at one's leisure, making patterns on the surface.   (SPL, 194)

If giving expression to one's inner life is like severing an artery, then (like spilling) it hovers between an act for which one is responsible and one which one suffers (as with any act of the self upon the self); but either way it initiates a process which cannot be controlled, hence one for which assignments of responsibility become otiose, and the ultimate consequence of it is that the self annihilates itself. Poetry, we are told, averts such lethal rendering of oneself intelligible by the emancipatory transfiguration of emotion into impersonality; whereas prose has no need to avert the spillage of a resource it does not require. The ascetic bent of both characterizations is clear enough, since both attribute to art a constitutive aversion from lifeblood. But John's ascetic vision of poetry overlooks the fact that (as Eliot's formulation implies) words designed to escape the personal are inevitably marked by that from which they are escaping; their trajectory is projectible in both directions—in their end is their beginning. And his equally ascetic vision of prose is not only transparently dubious in itself (think of the feeling given expression in this piece of prose's invocation of slitting one's wrists); it has already been undercut by the revelatory force of his earlier diary entry when Jacqueline comes across it.

Someone desperate to hold onto the fantasy of privacy might, however, have one further bolthole; and John's early confrontation with Jacqueline shows him reaching for it, in the achieved loneliness of the immediate aftermath of her departure:

> What are his true thoughts anyway? Some days, he feels happy, even privileged, to be living with a beautiful woman, or at least not to be living alone. On other days he feels differently. Is the truth the happiness, the unhappiness, or the average of the two?
>
> The question of what should be permitted to go into his diary and what kept forever shrouded goes to the heart of all his writing. If he is to censor himself from expressing ignoble emotions... how will those emotions ever be transfigured and turned into poetry?... Besides, who is to say that the feelings he writes in his diary are his true feelings? Who is to say that at each moment while the pen moves he is truly himself? At one moment he might truly be himself, at another he might simply be making things up. How can he know for sure? Why should he even *want* to know for sure?
>
> *Things are rarely as they seem*: that is what he should have said to Jacqueline. Yet what chance is there she would understand? How could she believe that what she read in his diary was not the truth, the ignoble truth, about what was going on in the mind of her companion during those heavy evenings of silence and sighings but on the contrary a fiction, one of many possible fictions, true only in the sense that a work of art is true—true to itself, to its own immanent aims—when the ignoble reading conformed so closely to her own suspicion that her companion did not love her, did not even like her?
>
> Jacqueline will not believe him, for the simple reason that he does not believe himself. He does not know what he believes. Sometimes he thinks he does not believe anything. (SPL, 150–1)

In its most familiar forms, the denial that others can grasp the meaning of one's linguistic and non-linguistic expressions goes together with the assumption that the inner states to which they give expression are transparent to their owner: others may not grasp my pain and suffering, but I certainly know whenever I am feeling something, and I know exactly what feeling it is—how, after all, might I mistake a sensation of pain for an intention to travel to London? Coetzee's John doesn't exactly reject that assumption, but he does considerably complicate it, in two stages. First, he claims that even if what he is thinking or feeling at any given moment is transparent to him, they shift from moment to moment, so the question remains which captures what he truly, deeply thinks and feels. Then second, he describes even the uncensored private entries in his diary as having the status of a fiction. This is not because he knows them to be false in the sense invoked in the first step of his argument: it is rather that he claims to lack any criterion for distinguishing entries that truly express himself from ones that are wholly made-up. It's not that he knows that most or all of those entries are lies (which would mean that he knows the truth about himself that they deny); it is that he claims not to know whether any given entry is an authentic expression of himself or not, or even whether any entry could constitute such a thing.

There are clear points of contact here between the logic of John's position and that of the protagonist of Rousseau's *Confessions* (as analysed by Coetzee in his essay on the topic), when he tells us that he has often committed theft in order to possess objects that he had more than enough money to buy. According to Coetzee, by proffering money to satisfy his desire for a given object, Rousseau poisons that desire by bringing it into the public realm, and thereby equalizing it with the 'I want' of anyone who enters the shop; it loses its uniqueness.

> To Rousseau, his own desires are *resources* as long as they remain unique, hidden—in other words, as long as they are potentially confessable. (DP, 271)

On this account, Rousseau sees a conflict between the economy and the economy of confession. To engage in a lawful public transaction to satisfy a desire declares both that the desire lacks uniqueness and that it is not inherently shameful; so if that desire is to have potential value in the economy of confession, its possessor must keep it private. If, however, he steals the object of this undeclared desire, he gives the act of satisfying that desire a value in the economy of confession that it would not otherwise have, since theft is a criminal, hence a shameful, and so a confessable act.

Now imagine Rousseau confronted with this explanation of his declared but unexplained preference to take rather than to ask for. Either he was aware of this deeper truth about his behaviour but failed to declare it, in which case he was being deceptive; or he was unaware of it, in which case the coin of his honest confession was fake, and a deception has occurred despite his efforts. Either way, there is fresh cause for confession; but there is also fresh room for sceptically interrogating the new coin of that reiterated confession—and we enter the infinite regress of self-deception with which Coetzee is primarily concerned in the essay.

> If the confessant is *in principle* prepared to shift his ground with each new reading as long as he can be convinced that it is 'truer' than the last one, then he is no more than a biographer of the self, a constructor of hypotheses about himself that can be improved on by other biographers. In such an event, his confession has no more authority than an account given by any other biographer: it may proceed from knowledge, but it does not proceed from self-knowledge.
> (DP, 273)

Can we avoid the infinite regress simply by acknowledging this risk—by confessing, but with an avowedly open mind about the truthfulness of that confession?

> But there is something literally shameless in this posture. For if one proceeds in the awareness that the transgressions one is 'truly' guilty of may be heavier than those one accuses oneself of, one proceeds equally in an awareness that [they]

may be lighter... To be aware of oneself in this posture... is already a matter for confession; to be aware that the posture is not a guilty one (because it is inevitable) is a matter for further shame and confession; and so on to infinity.

(DP, 274)

John's first step in response to Jacqueline's reading his diary amounts to the concession in principle to which Coetzee refers: and it is enough on its own to disable any possibility of relating autobiographically to himself, because it places his own accounts of himself on exactly the same level as accounts provided of himself by others. If John is no more than one constructor of hypotheses about himself, then there is no eligible candidate to occupy the position of potential autobiographer of John's self, and that implicitly casts doubt on the assumption that John really possesses a self of the kind of which there might even be multiple biographies (for what, then, would these biographies be competing accounts of?).

These difficulties are reinforced when John takes his second step, that of claiming to regard any and all accounts he offers of himself as equally and essentially fictional. For such open-mindedness about the truth (and so the true ethical weight) of anything he says about himself makes it impossible to take anything he says as genuinely confessional, and to that extent genuinely autobiographical. If it doesn't matter to him which account he presents (whether because every account misrepresents its putative subject, or because every such account is equally saturated with confession-worthy shame simply by virtue of being an account), then neither does the specific ethical self-evaluation each embodies; and if he fails to take that seriously, no one to whom he communicates these accounts can take them seriously as putative confessions, hence as revelations of a self by a self capable of seeking and supplying necessarily evaluative accounts of how things stand with itself.

John's desire to preserve the hiddenness or privacy of the self here compels him to render it necessarily hidden, not only from others but from himself (not just something that might as easily be characterized truthfully by others as by himself); he stakes the reality of his existence on its necessary recession beyond anything he might present as a revelation of it (which is why something must be kept forever shrouded even from his diary, and why that goes to the heart of all his writing (SPL, 150)). To render his own reality invulnerable, he deprives himself of the possibility that any of his expressions of himself really do give expression to that self: to adapt the words of Jesus (Matthew 16:25), to gain himself absolutely, he must lose himself. For if one can be metaphysically assured that no expression of oneself can truly express oneself, then anyone subject to the anxiety that anything and everything one says and does risks shameful and potentially annihilating self-exposure need no longer struggle to refrain from giving expression to themselves—for no mark they make on the world can (on this account) truly betray its maker, genuinely be a sign of life.

Unfortunately, however, John's ascetic shame-avoidance strategy is inherently unstable. For suppose, taking into account the circumstances in which he gives expression to this scepticism about self-knowledge and selfhood, we follow the logic of his own position and ask: is John here telling us what he really thinks, or is he finding a way of avoiding the shame of exposure and the burden of responsibility consequent upon Jacqueline's discovery of his diary? Does he really believe that he is lacking in any inner states sufficiently concrete or stable to merit calling beliefs, thoughts, or feelings; or is he rather constructing for himself an account of selfhood that is true only to its own immanent aim—that of escaping accountability for the all-too-concrete consequences of what he says and does in the world he shares with other vulnerable human beings? Suppose that this really is what John believes: then, since he believes that all expressions of himself amount to confessions, and so to forms of shameful self-exposure, this expression of his real belief would itself be shameful. If, however, all expressions of belief are really just one of many possible fictions, then so too is this professed belief about selfhood and its expressions; so its profession, here and now, must invite the sceptical question about its motive that I just raised, and at the very least cannot confidently dismiss the shameful answer I supplied. Either way, then, John's strategy exposes him as behaving shamefully.

This may well constitute a paralysing existential problem for the would-be writer who is the protagonist of *Youth*; but it amounts to an indispensable resource for its narrator, because the narrator is writing an autobiographical text, and insofar as autobiography has an ineliminably confessional aspect, it requires the currency of confession, which is shameful thoughts, words, and deeds. One might say that the pivotal issue of *Youth* is how what paralyses its protagonist enables its narrator; and understanding this requires understanding the internal relation between—hence both the separateness and the relatedness of—these two textual positions or functions (which we earlier encountered in McCabe's Aquinas, as well as the phenomenological tradition).

The protagonist of *Youth* is someone who has not yet become a writer, and has not yet begun to live; this is because his only desire is to live as a writer, but his conception of writing is such that it requires him to dissociate his writing from his life. His conception of literary art demands that he produce words that aspire to escape from personality, and that he sacrifice ordinary human satisfactions and comforts to the task of producing such words; his conception of language as such entails that any speech act he sincerely performs will—by virtue of the way words at once expose their users and confine them to the commonalities of common speech—promise to give expression to his individuality and threaten to annihilate it.

He does keep a diary throughout the events recorded in *Youth*; but—as we have seen—his understanding of the relation in which that account stands to himself ensures that it fails to meet the conditions for being autobiographical, and the radical scepticism about self-knowledge and selfhood that informs that relation also ensures more generally its failure as writing (insofar as writing may not be about the self, but must be by a self and constitutive of the self that results from that writing). In short, the protagonist's life-denying conception of art, language, and self produces only lifeless art and a deathly form of life.

By contrast, the narrator of *Youth* is a writer, and so has been leading the life of a writer for a certain length of time; but he does not provide us with an account of that life. Instead, he provides an account of its prehistory, which means at once a recounting of its conditions of impossibility and its conditions of possibility. It is not quite an account of how the protagonist became the narrator, since strictly speaking the protagonist hasn't yet become a person at all, and 'becoming' doesn't seem the right word to characterize the transition into personhood (as opposed to processes of change and development that a given person undergoes, or even the quality of self-overcoming that differentiates genuine personhood from its simulacra). So perhaps one should call it an account of the protagonist as a kind of necessary precursor to, a site or field for the constitution of, the narrator.

If *Youth* is the autobiography of a writer, then the narrator of *Youth* must have become a writer before writing *Youth*; so the book's protagonist is being investigated or constructed (anyway presented) as the precursor of the narrator's career as a writer as well as of his current writing project—hence as the precursor of a career that began with the publication of *Dusklands* and currently culminates in the publication of *Youth*. This, one might say, is the crucial internal relation between protagonist and narrator: the protagonist of this autobiographical text is always the narrator's protagonist—always the version of the protagonist that is visible to this particular narrator, with his particular interests and needs.

And the narrator of *Youth* duly acknowledges the gradual culmination of the raw material that will provide the academic preconditions for and the basic content of that first novel, as well as one of the enduring thematic obsessions that underlies it and its successors. Towards the end of the book, his protagonist discovers the novel by Samuel Beckett that will prompt his academic doctoral work (SPL, 273); he is captivated by the British Library's collection of accounts of reconnaissances by ox-wagon into the desert of the Great Karoo (SPL, 258–60) and by the traumatic fate of the Americans in Vietnam (SPL, 271)—the twin topics of his first published novel; and his work with the Atlas computer prompts him to pursue the intuition that logic is a human invention rather than part of the fabric of being (SPL, 276). Call these conditions for the possibility of *Dusklands*, and so conditions for the possibility of *Youth* as an autobiography of the author of *Dusklands*.

The narrative of *Youth* is designed, on this level, to explain what initially prevented its protagonist from becoming the writer of *Dusklands*, and what ultimately made it possible. What prevents him is his absorption in a deathly, *comme il faut* or *das man* mode of life, the key conditions of which are his commitment to an ascetic vision of literary art, and the fantasies of privacy and exposure that intertwine around his vision of writing and self-expression more generally. And since a key indicator of someone's immersion in a *das man* mode of life is his conviction that it could not be otherwise, that this way of living just is what living is, then a key indicator that its hold is beginning to loosen is the recognition by the one living it that this is their condition—that is, that their condition is antithetical to a genuinely individual life and that it could be otherwise. As we saw earlier, it is this recognition that the narrator of *Youth* attributes to his protagonist in the very last sentence of the book; and his ability to see this about himself facilitates and is facilitated by his loss of conviction in his poetic vocation as he has previously understood it, and his faltering reorientation towards more genuinely individual resources for literary prose (both academic and fictional)—ones which reflect literary, political, and socio-cultural investments that really mark his life as his, his to own. In this respect, *Youth* brings us to the point at which its protagonist is (despite himself, and in particular his perception of himself) becoming capable of realizing his distinctive potential as a writer: in that sense, it is a precursor to an autobiography rather than an autobiography.

However, given that protagonist's increasing hostility to binary logic, and his search for 'the moment in history when *either-or* is chosen and *and/or* discarded' (SPL, 277), we should not be too quick to impose an either-or analytical framework here. After all, in another sense, *Youth* is genuinely autobiographical: or perhaps one should say that concerning itself with these conditions for the possibility of an autobiography of the author of *Dusklands* is its way of being autobiographical, because it realizes a particularly powerful inflection of the confessional dimension inherent in all autobiography. If the indispensable currency of autobiography is shame, the protagonist of *Youth* is not only responsible for a number of shameful acts—shame seems to be his basic mode of existence. This is one reason why the narrator's portrait of the protagonist is so sustainedly unforgiving, and the experience of reading it so relentlessly discomforting. But this narrator's portrait of his protagonist is designed to show us that this fact about him both disables and enables the autobiographical stance.

It disables it, insofar as no one consumed by such a relation to himself counts as a self, and so as a possible autobiographical subject; indeed, since such a self's sceptical, anxiety-induced absence to itself is the antithesis of the modernist ideal of presentness, it doubly excludes him as the subject of a modernist autobiography. It enables it, insofar as it allows the narrator to express in every word of his text his shame at his precursor's shame—to confess both to the prior reality of that shame and to his present shame at that prior reality. And it also allows him to show that becoming ashamed of shame must not slip into shamelessness—into an attempt to rid oneself of shame altogether (for that would be both morally and aesthetically inept in a genre which requires confessional currency, and whose writer must acknowledge his prior self as no longer who he is and so as having been judged to stand in need of transfiguration).

The solution is for this text to show that, and how, inhabitable territory between these poles of absolute shamelessness and absolute shame can emerge. This is the quotidian domain of directed and local manifestations of shame, of careful discriminations between genuinely shameful thoughts, words, and deeds and their mere appearance, and between degrees of shame. It means, for example, discriminating between a commitment to art and a commitment to an ascetic ideal of art; between acknowledging the internal relation between the personal and the impersonal, collapsing one into the other, and severing each from the other; between preserving the freedom to write and rejecting the presence of any other in one's life. Any such discriminations will always be subject to question; but unless concrete reasons for questioning them are advanced, the person making them can and must take a stand on them, and thereby constitute themselves as occupying a particular point in the process of self-overcoming that is human selfhood. It is in this way that this autobiographical narrator aims to achieve presentness, at once to his past self, to himself, and to his audience.

C. Summertime

Although the premise of *Summertime* is that John Coetzee is dead, the text that incorporates his fictional absence delivers a readerly experience that abounds in vitality in comparison with its predecessor. If the protagonist of *Youth* achieves an ascetic mode of death-in-life whose incarnation achieves a correspondingly sado-masochistic impact on its readers, the literal death of the subject of *Summertime* gives life not only to the multitude of other characters it presents, but also to the deceased person towards whom their words are all ostensibly directed, and so rewards the reader's initial investment of interest by compounding it. In McCabe's terms, the removal of the author-as-character seems magically to restore the creative, life-affirming powers of the author-as-author; and it thereby implies that it is in the latter's capacity to confer life on fictional beings that the true life of the former is to be found. However, this fundamental autobiographical truth about Coetzee the writer is disclosed by means of a formal aversion from generic autobiographical conformity—by deploying the resources of the cognate genre of biography in a flamboyantly fictional manner.

Taken at face value (that is, focusing first on the textual dimension inhabited by the author-as-character), the main body of *Summertime* consists of transcripts of interviews conducted between 2007 and 2008 by Vincent, a would-be biographer of Coetzee, with five people he has selected on the basis of their apparent importance to Coetzee himself during the short period of his life in which Vincent is specifically interested: 1972–7. Those transcripts are book-ended by two short selections of extracts from Coetzee's notebooks from that same period (amounting overall to roughly 10 per cent of the whole text), presumably made by Vincent himself, since he uses them to attempt to stimulate many of his interviewees' memories. Each extract typically consists of a short passage written by Coetzee in the 'third-person present-tense' style familiar from *Boyhood* and *Youth*, together with a brief italicized note to himself about how to expand or revise the passage to bring out its thematic relevance to a volume of memoirs that he contemplated writing in 1999–2000 but quickly dropped.

In effect, then, elements of the raw material for an aborted autobiography of Coetzee at once frame and serve partly to constitute the raw material for an aborted biography of him. Since Vincent seems to be responsible for selecting and arranging the notebook excerpts, we have reason to think that they are primarily contributions to the biographical project rather than amounting to an independently authoritative and contextualizing autobiographical project; but they nevertheless allow the reader to appreciate that Coetzee himself had earlier tried and failed to engage autobiographically with the very period upon which Vincent is now trying and failing to engage biographically. Otherwise put, *Summertime* begins and ends with an apparently unfruitful dialogue between the Coetzee of 1999–2000 and his 1972–5 counterpart; in between, we encounter five people prompted by a sixth in 2007–8 to remember what they can of the Coetzee they knew between 1972 and 1977, hence five people in memory- and interview-mediated dialogue with their 1970s counterparts in ways that appear to be equally unfruitful for their interviewer's intended biography. And the availability of both types of material is occasioned by the fact that somewhere in the space between them—speaking chronologically rather than textually, somewhere between 2003 and 2007 (since more than one interviewee knows that Coetzee was awarded the Nobel Prize, hence was still alive in 2003)—the subject of their recollections died.

Even in its truncated, excerpted condition, however, the autobiographical raw material gives us a different picture of its subject from the one we acquired from *Boyhood* and *Youth*: less solipsistic, less passive, more fully involved in a broader range of real relations to other human beings. He is living with his father after the death of his mother, and accompanies him to rugby games, as well as meeting some of his fellow employees at the business for which his father remains the accountant; he describes himself meeting neighbours who are also old friends from secondary school, as well as someone in need of his linguistic expertise to contest a will; and he throws himself into a physically demanding regime of renovating his shared house against the ravages of damp. In these respects, the John Coetzee of 1972–5 appears to have found inhabitable territory between the extremes marked by *Boyhood* and *Youth*—between lacking any appreciation of the independent reality of others and anxiously defending the inviolacy of his inner life against public expression. In particular, his relation with his father appears to have overcome the murderous hostility with which it had become imbued by the end of *Boyhood*: their shared life is plainly limited in a variety of ways, emotionally and intellectually, but they are at least living it together.

Of course, there are also deep continuities with the earlier John Coetzee—and not just his persistent interest in the extent to which South Africa's apartheid political system continues to invade and pollute everyday life in ways that people work hard to deny. The second block of notebook fragments is particularly reminiscent of the earlier books: it contains a savagely punitive memory of his earlier hatred of his father (when he deliberately scratched one of his favourite Italian opera recordings), and another version of *Youth*'s fantasized diary whose sole function becomes the recording of private pain; and it ends with his father's diagnosis with cancer of the larynx and his immediate sense of the dilemma this creates for him:

> It used to be that he, John, had too little employment. Now that is about to change. Now he will have as much employment as he can handle, as much and more. He is going to have to abandon some of his personal projects and be a nurse. Alternatively, if he will not be a nurse, he must announce to his father: *I cannot face the prospect of ministering to you day and night. I am going to abandon you. Goodbye.* One or the other: there is no third way. (SPL, 484)

Each of these reminiscences has its sharp edge a little dulled: the memory of damaging Tebaldi in order to promote Bach comes with an acknowledgement that the former now calls as much to his soul as it did to his father's; the diary is presented as part of an idea for a story, hence as a more distanced fictional device or vehicle for the fantasy so directly enacted in *Youth*; and *Summertime*'s ending at least leaves it open which of his two alternatives John will take. On the other hand, even its denial of a third way should remind us of one of the few traces of life that the final pages of *Youth* allowed its protagonist: his commitment to the project of undermining Western culture's worship of the logic of either-or, his search for a logic of and/or. Should we take this concluding deployment of resolutely binary thinking as John's coming to appreciate the flimsiness of his earlier vision in the face of reality's refusal to conform to it, or should we rather assume that later reflection will allow him to recover that earlier insight, and realize that his sense of his situation as purely binary is itself a symptom that blinds him to the fact that reality always offer more than two exclusive alternatives?

However one draws up the balance-sheet between growth and stagnation or stasis, the fact that there are substantial items on the former side of the ledger is itself significant; for it gives greater weight to the question of why the John Coetzee of 1999–2000 abandons his project of constructing a third volume of memoirs from this notebook material (presumably, in exactly the manner of the first two books). We know from internal evidence that his first two works of fiction were published in the 1970s, so in that sense he has become a writer, and so a possible subject of a writer's autobiography; and the notebooks suggest that he has also overcome his previous failure to meet other crucial conditions for the possibility of such life-writing—namely, his lack of a genuinely individual life lived amongst other acknowledged individuals. Why, then, is this precisely the point at which the John Coetzee of 2000 abandons, or is abandoned by, his autobiographical impulse?

Two answers suggest themselves immediately, and we do not have to choose between them. First, since the material in the 1972–5 notebooks suggest that Coetzee had by then become a possible subject of autobiography, they cannot help explain how he did so. If *Boyhood* and *Youth* map out what make their protagonist ineligible as an autobiographical subject up until 1964, and *Summertime* reveals that this ineligibility has been overcome by 1972, then the three volumes mark out the intervening period as the crucially transformative one, but they define it purely negatively. During John Coetzee's time in America, the vital change—that of access to human vitality—was undeniably effected; but how remains essentially elusive, residing in the textual gap between the first two volumes and the third. More precisely, it is in the failure of that third, intended volume to come into being—insofar as its would-be author comes to appreciate its ineliminable belatedness, and so its inability to contribute to the project of achieving autobiographical closure by articulating the conditions of its own possibility—that the reality of the change is affirmed. In other words, the formal mode of its presence in *Summertime* is the gap between each third-person present-tense not-yet-authorial notebook fragment and its italicized, would-be authorial commentary.

The second answer is that the Coetzee of 2000 comes to realize that the moment John Coetzee's life as an author begins, the truth of that life is to be found in his writings rather than his life. In its simplest version, this answer would direct our attention in the first instance to the published fiction, and then perhaps to any other published writings, as opposed to unpublished writings such as diaries or notebooks. In its less simple version, this answer would include all of Coetzee's writings, both published and unpublished, whatever their genre, as constituting the domain in which the truth of his life is to be found. Hence, both the notebooks and their later italicized commentaries would form part of the relevant evidential domain; but they would have no greater autobiographical significance than any other of his writings. Either way, on this account, Coetzee abandons the projected third volume of memoirs because he realized that everything he had written since *Dusklands* was itself part of his autobiography—he had appreciated what he expressed in *Doubling the Point* in his claim that 'all writing is autobiographical'. And the formal mode in which this truth is acknowledged is the transcript material that holds apart (and holds together) the notebook fragments—the enacted disruption of the documentary by the extravagantly fictional.

To fully appreciate the meaning of that acknowledgement we have to bear in mind not only that it is fictional, but also what kind of fiction it is. For beginning from the ineluctable impossibility of its author's death, it constructs an elaborate representation (and deconstruction) of one way of envisaging the possibility of a truthful biographical perspective on Coetzee-the-character, and of the possibility of its being an alternative to or substitute for the aborted autobiographical perspective that frames it. Vincent embodies both aspirations: he feels that the image of Coetzee dominant in the public culture, and to some extent reinforced by his unpublished and autobiographical writings, was unduly critical and unrepresentatively narrow, hence essentially untruthful, and he seeks out his five interviewees with a view to countering it. As he puts it to Sophie Denoël, his final interviewee:

> There was an image of him in the public realm as a remote and supercilious intellectual, an image he did nothing to dispel. Indeed, one might even say he encouraged it.
>
> Now I don't believe that image does him justice. The conversations I have had with people who knew him well reveal a very different person, not necessarily warmer in temperament but more unsure of himself, more confused, more human...
>
> I have been through the letter and diaries that are available to me. What Coetzee writes there cannot be trusted, not as a factual record—not because he was a liar but because he was a fictioneer. In his letters he is making up a fiction of himself for his correspondents: in his diaries he is doing much the same for his own eyes, or perhaps for posterity. As documents they have their value, of course; but if you want the truth, the full truth, then surely you need to set beside them the testimony of people who knew him in the flesh, who participated in his life...
>
> Of course, we are all fictioneers, more or less... But which would you rather have: a range of independent reports from independent perspectives, from which you can then attempt to synthesize a whole; or the massive, unitary self-projection comprised by his oeuvre?   (SPL, 462, 453–4)

Vincent is here virtually transcribing one central part of the dialectic of Heidegger's early thinking on the kind of self-knowledge and individuality available in distinctively human modes of existence that I outlined in the first section of this essay. Just like Heidegger's resistant interlocutor, he posits the perspective of others on the self under examination as a likely resource for establishing a potentially superior perspective on the truth of that self compared to the one to which the self itself has access—one which can incorporate the self's own narrative and correct for its partialities, in part by locating it in a larger totality of distinct but complementary perspectives provided by those who participated in his life. And in one way, Vincent succeeds in his task. Each interviewee reveals aspects of Coetzee's character that do undermine his public image, and not only reveal more humanity but offer potentially significant glimpses of the underlying philosophical stances that find expression in his way of living. Particularly interesting here are the reports of his reasons for privileging manual labour (SPL, 331), his visceral attachment to the Karoo (SPL, 358), his vision of the body, music, and dance (SPL, 458), and most pervasively his Platonic philosophy of teaching (SPL, 408); it is tempting to link any one of them with elements of his published fiction, as Vincent (and his creator) are very well aware.

On the other hand, of course, one central way in which these insights into Coetzee's background thinking enrich the picture of his character is through the tragicomic ironic outcome of his attempts to embody them in his life—their power to unsettle as well as to enhance his integrity; and his interviewees also provide much testimony that reinforces the validity of the public image of Coetzee that Vincent wishes to problematize, by undermining Coetzee's dignity on a regular basis (particularly with respect to his romantic life, even if the flavour of their witness is more one of pity than [self-]disgust). Rather more worryingly for Vincent, however, each interview transcript reveals to the reader some essential flaw or limitation in the image of biographical access with which he is working; and when these individual issues are synthesized, they add up to a counter-position that strongly resembles the one Heidegger develops in response to his interlocutor (his version of Vincent).

To begin with, each interviewee is relying on her or his memories of the relevant period, and those memories are specifically prompted by Vincent's selection from the Coetzee character's notebooks; so what he transcribes is doubly refracted testimony. Furthermore, since each interviewee did have a relationship of some kind with Coetzee, their accounts are all informed by their non-literary perspectives, and so vulnerable to the charge of being (as Martin J. puts it) 'no more than a settling of scores, personal scores' (SPL, 449). Then there is Vincent's tendency to revise the original transcripts of the interviews: he repeatedly promises to allow the interviewee the final edit, but since several transcripts contain passages that the interviewee wanted to remove, the implication is that the promise was not fulfilled. In the case of Coetzee's cousin Margot Jonker, he even recasts her transcript into Coetzee's third-person present tense, embellished with fine writing and even with purely speculative passages on her private life. He claims, with striking implausibility and in terms that in effect disqualify him as a student of literature, that giving a narrative 'new form has no effect on the content' (SPL, 353); and if he engages in such transformative recasting in Margot's case, we cannot be sure whether or how he did so in any other case. Hence, each interviewee's perspective is unknowably informed by the interviewer's perspective, and the reader loses any confidence that what she is given is what each interviewee really meant to give.

The most fundamental problem of all, however, is emphasized by the therapist, Julia Frankl:

> [T]he only story involving John that I can tell, or the only one I am prepared to tell, is...the story of my life and his part in it, which is quite different, quite another matter, from the story of his life and my part in that. My story, the story of me, began years before John arrived on the scene and went on for years after he made his exit...Mark [her husband] and I were, properly speaking, the protagonists, John and the woman in Durban members of the supporting cast...
>
> You commit a grave error if you think to yourself that the difference between the two stories...will be nothing more than a matter of perspective—that while from my point of view the story of John may have been just one episode among many in the long narrative of my marriage, nevertheless, by dint of a quick flip, a quick manipulation of perspective, followed by some clever editing, you can transform it into a story about John and one of the women who passed through his life. Not so. Not so. I warn you most earnestly: if you start playing around with your text, cutting out words here and adding in words there, the whole thing will turn to ash in your hands. I *really* was the main character, John *really* was a minor player. (SPL, 317–18)

Julia not only rejects Vincent's conception of the external relation of narrative form and narrative content, but brings out a particularly fateful entailment of that rejection for the practice of biography. John's place in a narrative in which he is a minor player is radically different from, and essentially discontinuous with, his place in a narrative in which he is the protagonist; and since John's life is a narrative in which he is essentially the protagonist, then any narrative provided by others—being ones in which he is essentially a minor player—will necessarily omit a crucial aspect of John's distinctive mode of being-in-the-world: what Heidegger calls the mineness of human life. Vincent's hope of constructing a more authoritative perspective on Coetzee by interviewing the minor players in his life is thus doomed to failure; and since Coetzee's own perspective on his life has been shown to be lacking in other (although equally fateful) ways, the very idea of a truthful portrait of a single human life, as Vincent envisages that ideal, falls to ash in his hand.

Why ash? Because that is one canonical mode of the being of the dead—after cremation. Coetzee's death might initially seem to make Vincent's biographical project easier to execute, since it permanently immobilizes an otherwise-moving target with its own elusive but authoritative perspective on the subject matter; but as the perspectives of Coetzee's others expand into this newly available space, they only confirm his continuing elusiveness. At his death, Coetzee-the-character's life presents itself to us as a whole, as all that it will ever amount to; and that turns out to mean that we represent it as absent. It's almost as if the underlying motive of the biographical impulse is not so much to bring its subject back to life, but rather to confirm (to affirm, even partly to constitute) its departure from it.

Here Heidegger's perception of the necessary opacity of the mineness of any human life overlaps with Sartre's perception of the otherness of others as not simply misrepresenting one's life but threatening to negate it. If I can only ever appear as a minor player in the life story of any and all the others I meet, then acknowledging the reality of those others appears to require denying my own reality; and of course, the same applies in reverse. Anyone who asserts their centrality to the narrative of their own lives exiles others to the status of minor players; whereas if they attempt to acknowledge the centrality of those others to their own lives, he must reduce himself to a minor player. In Nietzsche's terms: this Heideggerian vision of biography, autobiography, and human life amounts to the assertion that there is no human life without denying the lives of others—no life without life-denial.

To think, however, that this is Coetzee-the-author's conclusion about autobiography and biography would be to conflate the ascetic ideal of knowledge of self and others embodied in Julia's inversion of Vincent with *Summertime*'s attempt to diagnose and overcome that ideal without giving up on the very idea of self-knowledge or knowledge of others. After all, Vincent is only the self-subverting fictional author, or rather composer, of *Summertime*: its non-fictional author is John Coetzee, and he is not dead (or at least, he wasn't dead when he wrote and published *Summertime* in 2009: using the tripartite model of *Doubling the Point*, we might call him the Coetzee who emerges from the Coetzee of 2000's critical engagement with the Coetzee of 1972–5). It is only within the fictional world of *Summertime* that Coetzee (that is, Coetzee-the-character) is dead, and so functions as an allegory of the fate awaiting anyone who hands over the narrative of his life to the fictioneering of the others in his life. But that fictional world is itself the creation of Coetzee-the-author: so any putative truth attributed to that representation is an effect of fiction, which means that there is no essential opposition between telling the truth and telling a story. More specifically, this fiction is abundantly successful in representing all of its characters who are Coetzee-the-character's others as possessed of vivid, individual life—not just as strongly individualized, particularly in the longer transcripts, but also as bringing with them an equally vivid and rich portrayal of the specific stratum of South African society to which each belongs (suburban adultery, subsistence farming, Brazilian immigrancy, and academic life).

It is precisely through being asked to contribute to a narrative about Coetzee-the-character that each of these characters conveys the narrative texture of their own lives, and so conveys a truthful sense of themselves as the protagonists of those lives; and since Coetzee-the-character really was (and like all of us, has to be) a minor player in the lives of some or other others, then their narratives simultaneously disclose part of the truth about Coetzee (a truthful representation of Coetzee-as-minor-player, and of the unrepresentability within this fictional world of Coetzee-as-protagonist). But by framing the transcript material with the notebook material, *Summertime* simultaneously shows that being the protagonist of one's own life and being a minor player in the lives of one's others and being the protagonist in one's own life are also internally related conditions of any human life—that no one can be the one without being the other.

If the truth of human subjectivity is to be properly acknowledged, what is required is a simultaneous acknowledgement of the mutual implication and the mutual exclusivity of the roles of protagonist and minor player in the narrativity of our lives. Echoing the ideas of the protagonist of *Youth*, we might say that insofar as all narrative frames—in this respect resembling the for-itself structure of consciousness—always make someone the protagonist and others the minor players, they impose an either-or logic; but insofar as one can deploy or contextualize such frames in a way which acknowledges that fact about them (as opposed to either denying it or absolutizing it), one can thereby acknowledge the internal relatedness of those contradictory stances, and so incorporate an and/or logic. Echoing the analysis of Herbert McCabe, we might say that this is where Coetzee-the-author as opposed to Coetzee-the-character comes in, or rather discloses his absent presence. For both the framing and the framed elements of *Summertime* are his work: Coetzee-the-author creates them all, and all the protagonists and the minor characters, female and male alike, within them. So it is the sheer existence of this aesthetically successful fictional world (beyond, but in necessary conjunction with, the specific configurations of what it contains) that shows that it is possible for one person properly to acknowledge the reality of others, and that participating in such worlds is the only—and the best—way through which to acknowledge the reality of the real John Coetzee: by acknowledging the truthfulness of his fictioneering.

The absent presence of Coetzee-the-author-of-*Summertime* is not merely a melodramatic description of an unsurprising consequence of John Coetzee's inhabitation of the real world—as if John Coetzee obviously couldn't be present in or to *Summertime*'s fictional world because he occupies a Coetzee-shaped gap in reality. That authorial absence doesn't and couldn't constitute a space that could conceivably be filled by the presence of a real person, because the former is an effect of textuality ('Coetzee-the-author' is an essential structural node or point of reference in our experience of the book we are reading), whilst the latter is not ('John Coetzee' is a proper name). Hence, when readers of *Summertime* succumb to the inevitable tendency to bring to bear established facts about the real John Coetzee (as articulated in Attwell's archival studies or Kannemeyer's biography) as part of their attempt to understand the aesthetic object for which he is (at least legally) responsible, they must avoid simply identifying the author-function with the flesh-and-blood human being; but at the same time, they must avoid treating them as essentially unrelated (since a flesh-and-blood human being did indeed create the aesthetic object, including its author-function).

Suppose, then, that someone points out that the fictional world of *Summertime* appears to conflate some aspects of the real John Coetzee's life in the 1970s with some aspects of his life between 1986 and 1988.[36] On the one hand, since none of this information is made available by *Summertime* itself, we cannot simply read across from it to Coetzee-as-author, as if such data could mitigate or eliminate our sense of his absence; on the other, it might indirectly contribute to a deeper understanding of the text itself by inviting us to look in more detail at those aspects of the fictional world whose existence or salience is here presented as a result of deliberate authorial contrivance. The interest of the information would then lie not in its establishing the sheer counterfactuality of the fictional representation, but in its underlining certain potentially significant aspects of its internal structure (in its emphasizing which counterfactual world is represented, and asking why).

Such biographical invocations might therefore legitimately motivate us to consider what, if any, concrete, specific truths about himself Coetzee-the-author is able to establish and explore by eliminating his wife and children from *Summertime*'s version of the 1970s, by substituting for that family life a reconstituted and diminished version of life with his parents that he actually undergoes in the late 1980s, or by deferring his entry into university teaching. And a further biographical fact that may cast helpful light here is that in 1987 the real John Coetzee first begins, and then temporarily abandons, the project of writing a memoir—the memoir that will eventually become *Boyhood*. One effect of the conflation is thus that it closes the circle between that first volume of memoirs and the present one, and thereby achieves the formal closure (the presentness of himself to himself, and to his readers) that he has been seeking for more than twenty years; and this implies that the origin and the telos of the autobiographical impulse—its alpha and omega—lies in what Freud called 'the family romance'.

---

[36] Attwell, *Coetzee and the Life of Writing*, 180.

Essay Three
Knowing, Framing, and Enframing

1. The Inner and Outer Worlds of Christopher Nolan

As I pointed out in the Introduction, Christopher Nolan's films will function at the beginning of my third essay as my (historically belated, and so dialectically distinct) contemporary candidate for the role played in Nietzsche's third essay in his *Genealogy* by Wagner's opera *Parsifal*. There are three main reasons for this. First, certain themes running through Nolan's films engage with aspects of Nietzsche's thinking that have a bearing on his critical evaluation of the ascetic ideal, but which have not yet been fully developed in my account (in particular, his conception of selfhood and its links to a perfectionist vision of ethics and politics, and his obsession with the limitations and distortions of our practical knowledge of ourselves—our many and varied ways of failing to know what we have done or are doing, and so to appreciate the limits of our capacity to know[1]). Second, Nolan's films show a recurrent interest in technology, understood as an expression of modern scientific world-views, which (given the highly technological material basis of cinema) also amounts to an exercise in reflexive self-criticism that provides a route into a Nietzschean understanding of the mutual imbrication of modern scientific truth-seeking and the ascetic ideal. And third, at least one of Nolan's most acclaimed and influential films circles around themes of scepticism; we have already seen (in Essay Two) how the ascetic ideal can generate sceptical (this is, modernizing rather than modernist) accounts of individual artworks and their media, and Nolan's treatment of scepticism will allow us to generalize that connection.

Putting together those three points, we might say that Nolan is interested in the ways in which we (mis-)conceive of ourselves as knowers, as men and women of knowledge; and this should remind us of the note Nietzsche strikes in the first sentences of the Preface to his *Genealogy*, as if sounding the central concern of the whole study:

---

[1] Robert Pippin has argued that this is a central theme in modernist literature, and in early Hollywood cinema: see his *Henry James and Modern Moral Life* (Cambridge: Cambridge University Press, 2000), and *Fatalism in American Film Noir* (Charlottesville, VA: University of Virginia Press, 2012).

> We are unknown to ourselves, we knowers, we ourselves, to ourselves, and there is a good reason for this. We have never looked for ourselves—so how are we ever supposed to *find* ourselves? How right is the saying: 'Where your treasure is, there will your heart be also'; *our* treasure is where the hives of our knowledge are. As born winged-insects and intellectual honey-gatherers we are constantly underway towards them, concerned at heart with only one thing—to 'bring something home'...
>
> We remain necessarily strangers to ourselves, we do not understand ourselves, we *must* confusedly mistake who we are, the motto 'everyone is furthest from himself' applies to us forever—we are not 'knowers' when it comes to ourselves
>
> (GM, P. 1)

Why are we knowers not only unknown to ourselves but necessarily so self-estranged? Why *must* we be confused or mistaken over who we are? If the problem were just that we have never hitherto looked for ourselves, it could easily be solved: we could simply start looking, and thereby overcome our ignorance of ourselves. But how would born intellectual honey-gatherers go about such a task? They would think of it—as they think of all knowledge—as something that is to be gathered or collected, something to be brought home. But then seeking to know ourselves would require us to regard ourselves as essentially capable of being brought home, hence as presently (and perhaps forever) not-at-home to ourselves; to gather knowledge of ourselves, we must first be willing to conceive of ourselves as necessarily self-estranged or self-distanced.

So if Nietzsche thinks that we knowers are condemned to misunderstand ourselves, that must be because he thinks we are condemned to resist any understanding of ourselves as in need of gathering or collection, hence as dispersed or disseminated or internally differentiated, call it non-self-identical. The unattainability of self-knowledge thus manifests the depth of our commitment to a conception of ourselves as always already at-home to ourselves—as self-identical, hence essentially transparent to ourselves (both from moment to moment—no sooner thinking something than knowing that we do—and with respect to our essence, which is of course our capacity to gather knowledge). We are essentially unknown to ourselves because we think of ourselves as essentially known; we will never look for ourselves because we think we have always already found ourselves, and have done so without ever really having to look. For when all is said and done, what there is to know about ourselves—the full depth and extent of our nature—is that we are knowers, essentially cognitive creatures, born collectors.

And yet the very conditions of our lives as intellectual honey-gatherers declare the underlying truth of our condition to be otherwise. For if knowledge, including self-knowledge, is inherently to-be-gathered, then we knowers are constantly making towards the hives of our knowledge, hence always returning from journeying away from those homes, and so never actually residing in them: we are, in short, always on the way to or from home but never at home—always not-at-home. And if knowledge is a phenomenon of the hive, to which we make one essential contribution (even if not the one Nietzsche's words attribute to us, since what foraging bees gather is not honey but pollen, honey's raw material), then its emergence or creation is also essentially collective—an achievement of the group and its dynamic hierarchies and divisions of labour. And the point of this shared enterprise is not the piling up of treasure as an end in itself, but the production of something useful to the survival and reproduction of the group (and the wider natural world). So if our treasure really is where our heart is, and our heart is with the hive, then our heart is itself dispersed or disseminated, residing essentially outside ourselves, something in relation to which we are always either no longer or not yet there.

What, however, is it that such honey-gatherers really treasure? Is it the knowledge, or the gathering of it—the collection or the collecting? If they really treasured the collection, why would they never stay with it but rather dedicate themselves to the unending task of enhancing it, which inevitably means maintaining their distance from it in order to look for (more of) it? Such a creature is either mislocating her treasure and her heart; or else she truly prefers seeking knowledge to having it, and so treasures being underway above being home. More exactly, her form of life suggests that her true home is to be found, is indeed a matter of her being, underway—that her creaturely essence lies in seeking or voyaging. She is, after all, a winged thing.

This does not exactly mean that we are wrong to think of ourselves as knowers (since the term captures the process of collecting as naturally as it does the product). It rather shows that we do not really understand what it means to say this of ourselves—that the true significance of that self-description is not something we have as yet brought home to ourselves, or allowed ourselves to be struck by, something we have not yet properly experienced. And indeed, in the portion of the first section of his preface that we have so far passed over (the sentences connecting the two paragraphs I began by quoting), Nietzsche connects our confusion about knowing to a certain estrangement from our own experiences:

> As far as the rest of life is concerned, the so-called 'experiences'—who of us ever has enough seriousness for them? or enough time? I fear we have never really been 'with it' in such matters, our heart is simply not in it—and not even our ear! On the contrary, like somebody divinely absent-minded and sunk in his own thoughts who, the twelve strokes of midday having just boomed into his ears, wakes with a start and wonders 'What hour struck?', sometimes we, too, *afterwards* rub our ears and ask, astonished, taken aback, 'What did we actually experience then?' or even 'Who *are* we, in fact?' and afterwards, as I said, we

count all twelve reverberating strokes of our experience, of our life, of our being—oh! And lose count, (GM, P. 1)

It is the human being immersed in his own thoughts, apparently at one with his mind, who is truly absent-minded, because he is in fact lost to his experiences, incapable of being struck by them even when they boom into his ear. If one is seriously to experience each reverberating stroke of the world's impact, one must count them or rather recount them—take the time to provide a recounting. So being present to my experiences is a matter of first suffering their impress, and then offering an account of them: the fulfilment of any impression lies in its expression, and thus requires a capacity and willingness on my part to make that impression other to me, to actively distance myself from it in time and thereby allow it to re-verberate—that is, to reappear in verbal form, to find words for it for which I am willing to be accountable, and thereby to take responsibility for my own experiences, in the absence of which my experiences, and so my life and my being, will remain absent or lost to me, something in which I am simply immersed or sunk.

Properly recounting our conception of 'experience' thus reveals two things about ourselves as beings possessed of an inner world or interior life as well as a place in nature, what one might call genuine subjectivity. First, we are necessarily capable of distancing ourselves from ourselves—of taking a perspective on our experience; and second, this capacity is inseparable from a capacity to articulate our experiences—which means both finding words for them and taking responsibility for doing so in the sight (or rather the hearing) of others. It follows that properly to know ourselves as knowers—no longer being simply immersed or sunk in my being as a knower but genuinely experiencing what it means to be a man or woman of knowledge—will involve distancing ourselves from that state, getting underway on a journey or transition from it to whatever state lying beyond it allows us to gain perspective on it by providing a recounting of it. Only those who no longer wholly inhabit that mode of being can properly bring it home to themselves as it really is, or rather was.

From what perspective, however, could anyone advance the claim that 'We are unknown to ourselves, we knowers...'? The problem here is one of time, or say tense: using the present tense seriously in such a self-description appears to be either beyond us or behind us, depending on whether we truly remain self-unknown knowers or have gone beyond that state or condition. Or one might say that it is a problem of pronouns: someone who is no longer a self-ignorant knower might coherently describe those who remain so in such terms, but then the third person or the second person would be the appropriate mode of address—and yet this speaker talks not of 'they' or 'you' but of 'we' (that is, him and us, the author and his readers) being knowers who are unknown to ourselves.

Suppose, however, that we treat the claim not as a neutral or dispassionate assertion, but as a mode of testimony, a way of testifying to the existence of a possibility as yet unknown to those addressed but not essentially beyond them. For the claim's presupposition (that we are simultaneously both self-ignorant knowers and beings who no longer inhabit that mode of being) would in a sense be valid if we were underway from the former state to the latter—that is, inherently between states, transitional, becoming, but also inherently between just those two states, beings whose aspiration to go beyond the condition of self-ignorant knowing was engendered and oriented by some aspect of that condition. We would then be in (an internal relation to) both states: we would be moving away from the first and towards the second, and the latter precisely because of the former. And what, after all, is more calculated to stimulate a knower's energies than the insinuation that her knowledge is not only somehow deficient, but is so with respect to the one domain of her knowledge that she has hitherto assumed to be beyond doubt—her knowledge of herself?

The real point of saying something to us whose apparent point presupposes that we are simultaneously both self-ignorant and becoming otherwise is thus not that Nietzsche thinks that that presupposition currently holds true of us, his readers; it is that he hopes thereby to encourage us to *make* it true. For if our commitment to knowing does drive us to figure out this presupposition of Nietzsche's address, then in so doing we will come to realize not only that he apparently believes that our relation to ourselves might be other than it currently is, but also that only someone who was already underway in just that sense—already effecting this transformation in his own case—could have attained the perspective from which to offer such encouragement. If Nietzsche can do it, and if, having done it, he addresses us in a way which identifies himself with us, quite as if—as far as he can see—he is essentially indistinguishable from us in the relevant respects, then why can't we?

We might accordingly say that, for Nietzsche, an appropriately calibrated scepticism about our self-understanding as knowers will make it possible for us to overcome that failure of self-knowledge, and thereby generate a properly grounded confidence in our general capacity for knowledge as such. This in effect inverts modern philosophy's assumption that self-knowledge is inviolable but knowledge of the external world is inherently subject to sceptical doubt. And the Nolan film with which we shall begin our account of his work offers a thought-provoking variation on precisely that modern theme, as well as its Nietzschean inversion.

A. Scepticism, Plagiarism, and Fanaticism: *Inception*

When a film projects a world in which people can not only shape and inhabit one another's dreams but follow one another into dreams undergone within those dreams (and even into dreams undergone within *those* dreams) in order to exploit our proneness to take our dreams for reality, in which these manipulative protagonists themselves require a means of private reassurance in order securely to distinguish reality from the nested dreams in which they operate, and in which two central characters are driven to the point of madness by a quarrel over whether their world is real or merely a dream, then I hope I can take it for granted that it has an interest in what philosophy calls scepticism—famously epitomized in the Cartesian meditator's attempt to subvert our conviction in the reality of the world as revealed to our senses by asking us to consider whether we have any way of distinguishing these revelations from what presents itself to us as reality when we are dreaming, and so whether we have any reason to accept our current sensory testimony as veridical, or indeed to keep faith with the very idea of a world external to our experience which that experience might either reveal or conceal.

As I pointed out earlier, my understanding of the architecture of philosophical scepticism has been shaped by Stanley Cavell's Wittgensteinian conception of it as demanding the availability of what he calls best cases for knowledge, and as under study in Shakespeare as tragedy; but at this point in our investigation, it is important to note that Cavell also takes it to be under study in some of the best comedies and melodramas of Hollywood's Golden Age.[2] So what struck me most forcibly on a first viewing of *Inception* was the extent to which its projection of scepticism appeared responsive to the contours of that Cavellian reshaping, to the point at which even when it exhibited inversions or reversals of key conceptual polarities in Cavell's vision, it proved the general validity of that vision precisely by extending it fruitfully in unforeseeable directions; for only a vision of the sceptical field that was deeply inward with Cavell's own could subject it to such fatefully precise contestation.

As I explained in Essay Two (Section 2), on Cavell's reading of Wittgenstein, the philosophical sceptic presumes that the human relation to the world is fundamentally one of knowing (or of failing to know). Cavell attempts to clarify the erroneousness of that presumption by introducing the distinction between treating objects generically as opposed to specifically (as exemplars of objecthood rather than of individuality, and so as potential best cases of knowledge), and arguing that the sceptic is required (incoherently) to treat the exemplary objects of his doubt as if they were simultaneously generic and specific. Given the importance of the notion of generic objects in what follows, it may prove helpful if I dwell in a little more detail on the inner logic of the sceptic's dilemma.

---

[2] For those wishing to explore in more detail the background to these interconnections, the relevant Cavell texts are, respectively: *The Claim of Reason* (Oxford: Oxford University Press, 1979); *Disowning Knowledge: In Seven Plays of Shakespeare* (Cambridge: Cambridge University Press, 2003); *Pursuits of Happiness* (Cambridge, MA: Harvard University Press, 1981); and *Contesting Tears* (Chicago: University of Chicago Press, 1996).

Imagine someone being brought to claim that she knows there is a tennis ball on the table in front of her, to which the sceptic responds by pointing out that she does not in fact see all of it, for the back half of the ball is hidden from her. This putative ground for doubt seems to supply everything needed to generate universal doubt about knowledge acquired through the senses; for if we regard the back half of an object (e.g. a ball) as that part of it which is established by imagining an outline drawn around it whose plane is perpendicular to the perceiver's line of vision, then any object's back half will always be hidden from the perceiver's view regardless of her position, since every shift in her position will involve a corresponding shift in what will count as its back half.

At the same time, however, any given region of the object that is hidden from a perceiver's current position is always one that they *can* see, simply by shifting their position; so this mode of determining an object's back half cannot determine a region of it that we can never see. On the contrary: this way of determining 'the back half' of an object is such that there is no particular part of an object that is invariably its back half, that is *the* back half of that object, and so no determinate part of it that is visually inaccessible. In order to think otherwise, one would have to be imagining objects and subjects as unchanging in their orientation to one another; for it is only if objects always presented the same face to a given subject that the region our projection method determines as its back half would really never be seen. As Cavell puts it:

> Thus this sceptical picture is one in which all our objects are moons. In which the earth is our moon. In which, at any rate, our position with respect to significant objects is *rooted*... The moment we move, the 'parts' disappear, or else we *see* what had before been hidden... This suggests that what philosophers call 'the senses' are themselves conceived in terms of this idea of a geometrically fixed position, disconnected from the fact of their possession and use by a creature who must *act*. (CR, 202)

Nietzsche would already detect the scent of life-denial in this occlusion of the perceiving and knowing subject's agency, and hence her embodiment, which means her participation in a world of independently existing objects amongst which she is capable of moving in ways that are internal to any realistic assessment of her cognitive capacities and status. The frozen natural world that results from the sceptic's need to impose his geometrical diagramming is as perfect an example of denying Becoming in favour of Being as one could wish for. And for Cavell, the fact that this is the imposition of a fantasy finds expression in the fact that the method that imposes it needs to, but cannot, specify a determinate region of the objects we encounter that retains an independent identity throughout our shifting interactions with it. If the necessary determinacy is achieved, the region's invisibility is merely contingent; but if its invisibility is to be rendered necessary, that can only be at the price of failing to determine a specific region that is subject to that fate.

As I also explained in Essay Two, Cavell sees such external-world scepticism as internally related to scepticism about other minds, by virtue of the fact that there can also be a best case of knowledge of another mind—a case in which a given other embodies my view of psychic reality as such, an other who is (not generically or unexceptionably other but) exemplary of all others, of humanity as a whole, upon whom I stake my capacity for acknowledgement (which means my capacity for acknowledging the existence of others and for revealing my own existence to those others) altogether. If we were to acknowledge the existence of such an exemplary other, then the very singularity of the relationship would allow scepticism to generalize (rather than disallowing it, as it seems to do in putative best cases of knowledge of the external world): for if I cannot credit what *this* other shows and says to me, then the remainder of the world and my capacities in it will become irrelevant—will become matters not beyond my knowledge but past my caring. This is why Cavell claims that what philosophy encounters as an intellectual difficulty is dramatized by Shakespeare in the relationships between Lear and Cordelia, or Othello and Desdemona, as a matter of psychic life and death.

For my present purposes, the most significant of Shakespeare's stagings of scepticism for Cavell is *The Winter's Tale*, and for two reasons. First, in that play, Cavell understands scepticism to be presented as inflected by gender: for if we accept Leontes as giving expression to sceptical doubt in the form of jealousy, then that jealousy takes the form of a doubt about whether his child is really his (a doubt he recites in good Cartesian fashion by looking for specific physiognomic features possessed by both, then ruling out the testimony of others, then considering his dreams, all the while insisting that he is being reasonable). But such a doubt is not one to which the child's mother has access (as Cavell puts it, 'What would it look like for Hermione to doubt whether her children are hers?'[3]): it is the doubt of a father, a man's anxiety. Does this mean that scepticism as such is not a female business at all, or at least not the business of the feminine aspect of human character more generally? Or does it rather mean that sceptical doubt will, in the female or feminine case, take either another object (say, the father of the child rather than the child) or another passion (say, fanatical or unconditioned love rather than hyperbolic doubt)?

The second reason for giving priority to *The Winter's Tale* is that Cavell cites it (and in particular its presentation of Hermione's death and resurrection at the hands of Leontes and Paulina) as one of two canonical theatrical sources for the genre of remarriage comedy that he identified through an interpretation of seven films made in Hollywood's Golden Age. The notion of a genre—as invoked when

---

[3] Cavell, *Cities of Words*, 425.

we think of film genres such as 'the Western' or 'the horror film'—is most commonly interpreted as a form characterized by a certain range of features, as an object is characterized by its properties; membership in such a genre is established by establishing whether the relevant film possesses the requisite features (or a sufficient number of them), just as identifying an object as belonging to a particular kind is envisaged as a matter of establishing whether it has the features that all objects of that kind necessarily possess.

With respect to his comedies of remarriage, Cavell interprets the notion of genre very differently: the generic relationship of these films depends not upon their each exhibiting a feature or set of features that all possess, but upon their common inheritance of certain conditions, procedures, subjects, and goals that are subject to critical study in each of the films. One might think of this inheritance as a myth of which each film provides an interpretation (and thereby an interpretation of other films in the genre). It may do so by emphasizing a certain aspect of that inheritance, or even by omitting one such aspect altogether (we might call this testing its claim to essentiality); but if a particular film does lack an established clause or feature of the myth, then it must compensate for that lack by the provision of another feature, which will itself contribute to a further, more fruitful interpretation of the original myth. So understood, a genre of film functions as an artistic medium.

The founding myth of the medium of remarriage comedy emerges by contrast with that of Old and New Comedy; its goal is not to get two young people together despite the obstacles in their path, but rather to get two rather less young people together *again*, back together in the face of a quarrel which has pushed them apart. In order to do so, the woman must receive a certain kind of transformative education that will allow her to awaken again to her desire, and the man must prove his right to provide that education by manifesting a certain willingness to suffer humiliation in the pursuit of his desires, and more generally by a capacity to sustain a meet and happy conversation with the woman, one through which they acknowledge a mutuality of desire and a shared imagination of a diurnal mode of existence that would constitute its satisfaction.

If membership of this genre is primarily constructed by the operation of compensation, then an adjacent (that is, a different but internally related) genre can be constructed by the operation of negation—that is, by positively cancelling clauses or features of the founding myth of remarriage comedy without providing anything resembling recompense for their absence, anything that might be thought of as forging even a radical reinterpretation or recounting (hence a continuation) of that myth as opposed to the founding of a new (but of course not entirely unrelated) myth. And the genre Cavell called 'The Melodrama of the Unknown Woman' is derived by just such an operation. For whilst it retains a concern with the legitimization of marriage, it focuses upon women who could neither manage nor relish relationships with men of the kind their comedic sisters construct, and so must achieve genuine existence (or fail to) apart from marriage. They lack a common language with the (always inadequate and often villainous) men of their world, so that their words are pervaded with an isolating irony, often rising to arias of severance from all around them, to which those around them react with bewildered hostility.[4] This vision of the crippling, self-lacerating, and mutually victimizing loneliness of such (mis-)marriages is at the heart of Milton's sustained pleas for divorce, and finds canonical theatrical expression in Ibsen's *A Doll House*; and the route to re-creation or recovery canvassed by the women of the melodramas involves a systematic negation of the existing world's claims upon them, in the name of a higher, unattained state of society in which alone genuine individuality is attainable for them, and apart from which that society's claims upon them lack any real authority.

The connection between the preoccupations of these related genres of film and those of philosophical scepticism depends upon taking marriage (call it the inhabitation of the domestic) as the artistic equivalent of the domain of the ordinary or the everyday towards which sceptical doubt directs its anxieties. Then we should expect the threat to the ordinary that scepticism represents to show up in art in the form of (most likely melodramatic) threats to marriage such as divorce, and to see the issue of the legitimization of marriage as a figure for the issue of legitimately overcoming scepticism's desire for a divorce from one another and from reality. Seen this way, the men and women of the remarriage comedies manage to overcome scepticism, even if they can do so only by constructing a domain of domesticity whose ratification by mutual acknowledgement remains a private rather than a public matter (its validation being something over which the state exercises no authority, despite the fact that its validity amounts to a ratification of the society whose arrangements tolerate it). By contrast, the women of the melodramas either succumb to sceptical fantasies of revenge and fanaticism induced or reinforced by those around them, or they manage to refuse those temptations and keep private faith with the reality of their own existence as unknown, as currently unacknowledged although capable of acknowledgement in some as yet unrealized future; but either way, they suffer divorce from their world—from its arrangements, its inhabitants, and its words.

Suppose we think of the complex and ramifying material I have just recounted as Stanley Cavell's evolving myth of scepticism (part of which tells us that scepticism finds different mythological expression in different fields of culture—philosophical, theatrical, cinematic); then we can think of the world of *Inception* as Christopher Nolan's cinematic revision of that myth. But one of the ways in which Nolan revises Cavell is, one might say, methodological: he creates his revision to the content of Cavell's myth by means of operations that are not

---

[4] We can now see that Eliot's Prufrock (cited in Essay Two) envisages the object of his impotent desire as just such an unknown woman.

properly characterized either as ones of compensation or of negation—at least not as Cavell employs those terms in recounting his conception of cinematic genres. Nolan's characteristic mode of operation is indeed to negate specific articulations of Cavell's myth, but in ways that do not appear to generate an adjacent myth so much as a revision of the original—so that one appears forced to call it negation as compensation, or compensation as negation. I can best illustrate what I mean by tracing the significance of two elements that are central to the world of *Inception*, and showing thereby the extent to which they become fully comprehensible only against the background of Cavell's myth of scepticism. The two I have in mind are the role of the totem, and the figure of Mal.

The central members of the team that Dom Cobb has assembled for his current work as an extractor (which involves introducing targeted individuals into dream worlds constructed by other team-members—known as architects—with a view to locating and extracting commercially valuable secrets) have adopted a rather theatrical means of establishing the reality of any world in which they find themselves, one that was invented by Cobb's dead wife Mal: they use a totem—a small, everyday object that they have altered in a way that they reveal to no one else (Arthur has a loaded die, Ariadne a fractionally unbalanced chess piece, and Cobb makes use of Mal's original totem—a pewter cone that can revolve on its axis like a miniature spinning top). However painstaking the architect of a dream world might have been, he cannot have reproduced in his dream-representation of a totem any feature of its real original that is known only to its possessor; so any extractor can always tell whether she is inhabiting a dream designed and realized by someone else simply by checking whether her totem possesses its talismanic property.

Of all the seductive images projected by *Inception*, Cobb's totem is the one most viewers will carry away with them—if only because of the film's ending, in which the camera first shows us Cobb reunited with his children, then tracks back to reveal the top he has set spinning on the kitchen table, as it continues to spin, then begins ever so slightly to wobble, or at least to sound as if it is wobbling slightly, or might be doing so; but the screen fades to black without allowing us to see whether or not it falls, and so without allowing it to determine whether or not this reunion scene is real, or merely something in a dream. In a film which has managed to present us with a dream-within-a-dream-within-a-dream, each dreamworld the setting for a distinct narrative that is nevertheless cunningly interwoven with the other two narratives, all of which culminate in the inhabitants of these dreams re-emerging into the reality of a long flight from Sydney to Los Angeles, what could be more vital than establishing the reality of that reality? Hence the pleasurable frustration of so many viewers, deprived of this crucial piece of information; hence also the question of whether Nolan's refusal to supply that information amounts to an evasion of his responsibilities (a failure to resolve an absolutely fundamental issue in the world he has created) or an acknowledgement of the viewer's autonomy (whether because the film elsewhere provides everything we need to work out the answer to this question, or because it means to leave us with the room to determine for ourselves what the answer should be).

Anyone familiar with Cavell's Wittgensteinian way of envisioning scepticism will, however, already be suspicious of what is being presupposed by both the makers and the viewers of Inception in assigning such anti-sceptical power to its totems. For to believe in such power would be to believe that the difference between reality and dream might be established by establishing whether an object possesses or lacks a particular feature—that one might tell the difference by means of the satisfaction or otherwise of specific criteria; it would, in other words, amount to assuming that the possession of a piece of criterial knowledge might constitute a definitive rebuttal of sceptical doubt. Whereas on Cavell's view of the matter, the truth of scepticism lies precisely in its revelation of the fact that the difference between reality and dream, whilst critical, is not criterial; it is not a matter of knowledge but of acknowledgement (understood in this case as acceptance).

Matters are not quite so simple, or so simply un-Cavellian, as they may appear, however. For the film foregrounds, and so apparently takes as exemplary of its various totems, the one Cobb inherits from Mal—the spinning top; it thereby invites us to consider just how generic of totemhood that instance really is, and the moment we take up that invitation, specific differences emerge. Most fundamentally, whereas the die and the pawn work by instantiating one very specific value of a perfectly everyday property (of mass or proportion), the top works by transgressing such ordinariness. One might initially think that (like Arthur and Aridane) Cobb makes use of his knowledge of his totem's specific weight and balance, which determines that it should only spin for a particular amount of time. But that seems an inherently unreliable prophylactic against doubt (since the relevant length of time is also determined by the force Cobb applies, which it would be very difficult to keep perfectly constant); it runs counter to the grain of the final scene (whose suspense would be nullified if what mattered was the precise time the top takes to stop spinning); and it is flatly contradicted by the fact that Cobb is later shown (in a crucial scene to which we shall return) to have compelled his wife to acknowledge that she was living in the dream world of Limbo by setting her top to spin endlessly. In short, unlike the die and the pawn, the top's tell-tale property reveals unreality by revealing the capacity of dreams to suspend or violate basic physical laws. Its modus operandi allegorizes existence in a dream in just the way exploited by the nested-dream architecture and plotting of the film as a whole—that is, as frictionless free fall, so that the world of a dream not only lacks weight or substance, but is essentially limited in its ability to make a real impact on its inhabitants, as if its ways of constraining them (and so declaring its independent reality) are fundamentally attenuated.

In other words, whereas the die and the pawn do their revelatory work by virtue of properties that distinguish them from other objects of the same kind, the top does its work solely by virtue of a capacity that it shares with all other such cones, and indeed with all other physical objects (its subjection to physical law). Hence, whereas Arthur and Ariadne use their totems by exploiting a private cognitive resource that sharply distinguishes their position in relation to the totem's criterial property from that of any other human knower, what Cobb knows about his totem is not only knowable but actually known by anyone who knows what it is for an object to inhabit the spatio-temporal system of nature. It is something that no one who grasps what it is for an object to be an object (who grasps the concept of an object) could possibly fail to know, something of which no competent worder of the world (a group which includes not only every other person in the world of the film, but also every viewer of it) could conceivably be informed.

Put in Cavellian terms, whereas Arthur and Ariadne attempt to ward off sceptical doubt by means of specific objects, Cobb does so by means of a generic object; only his top might be thought of as exemplary of objecthood as such, sheer externality. Hence only Cobb is confronted with a best case of knowledge: only with respect to his totem might its possessor intelligibly think: 'If I don't know this, then I don't know anything.' And the film makes it clear that Cobb suffers the consequences of this singling out: for whereas Arthur and Ariadne are never shown to make use of their totems, let alone to display anything resembling sceptical anxiety about the existential status of the real world or any of the nested dreams they inhabit, Cobb is obsessively anxious to spin his top after every exit from what he believes to be a dream world (whether in Japan, in Mombasa, or in the USA). In other words, and exactly as the terms of Cavell's myth would predict, of all the extractors, only Cobb suffers from—indeed, is increasingly disabled by—sceptical doubt, until its climactic overcoming in his encounter with Mal in Limbo.

So should we say, on reflection, that Nolan's revisioning of scepticism is not essentially anti- or un-Cavellian but rather absolutely Cavellian in its architecture? Even to pose the question in such terms is to fail to register a further reach of significance in the film's apparent assignment of totemic significance to its totems in relation to scepticism. For although it has seemed almost impossible for its viewers to take this in, the film makes it clear at the moment of their introduction that the extractors' totems are designed to address a problem essentially distinct from the one that philosophy attempts to raise by asking how we know that the world we currently experience is not a dream. The problem totems are intended to solve is that of establishing whether or not one is inhabiting the world of *another* person's dream (an issue that is of pressing importance to people whose working lives are devoted to passing off dream worlds created by others as dreams of the subjects inserted into those worlds). They are not intended to, and they patently could not, solve the problem of establishing whether or not the possessor of the totem is currently inhabiting a dream of their own (since in that case, the dreamer—who in this case is also the architect of the dream—knows everything about the totem that its possessor does, given that dreamer, architect, and totem-possessor are one and the same person). But it is precisely the latter problem that the phenomenon of dreaming, as canonically invoked by the Cartesian meditator, is meant to raise.

It would seem to follow that the significance of the film's culminating and teasing preoccupation with Cobb's spinning top cannot be what it appears to be. For at that point, if the film's viewers experience any sceptical anxiety, it surely concerns the canonically philosophical doubt about whether Cobb has actually succeeded in returning to his actual children, or merely in inhabiting a wish-fulfilling dream of his own devising (the anxiety voiced by his father and teacher Miles during their interview in Paris). But if he were, then he (or rather, his subconscious) would know that in order to convince himself of the dream's reality he must dream that the top stops spinning; so we could expect it to stop no matter what the truth of things is. Indeed, even if he were instead inhabiting the world of another dreamer, that dreamer would no more contemplate realizing a world in which tops went on spinning for ever than would Cobb himself (it's not as if such unearthly behaviour—unlike that of paradoxical structures like Penrose staircases—would serve any pragmatic architectural purpose); so again the top is bound to stop spinning. Either way, then, Cobb's totem evinces an ineptness to which neither Arthur's die nor Ariadne's pawn are subject; it necessarily fails to perform the task apparently assigned to it—that of giving him, and so us, assurance as to the reality of his world.

Can Christopher Nolan simply have misunderstood so basic a point about the original shape of philosophical scepticism? I would prefer to consider another possibility: that it is only by appreciating the failure of totems directly to address the primary or primal form of sceptical doubt that we can properly appreciate their significance as elements in Nolan's attempt to revise Cavell's myth of scepticism. For what the film encourages us to do is to conflate (and so to reflect upon the internal relatedness of) two anxieties about the existential status of our current experience: a doubt about whether we are confusing reality with a dream world of our own devising, and one about whether we are confusing it with a dream world of another's devising. Canonically understood, scepticism is a doubt that tries to address an essentially isolated subject, that attempts to engender anxiety about the deliverances of the subject's senses solely by invoking resources internal or private to the subject himself; scepticism about the external world could not, after all, consistently engender itself by means which presuppose the reality of someone other than the subject, some other subject (who would have to be external to the subject of the doubt). But in the world of *Inception*, the subject's anxiety about the unreality of his experience derives from a suspicion that it possesses only the reality of another's dream. And Nolan's reason for so reformulating it may be to suggest that the canonical Cartesian expression of sceptical doubt by the invocation of dreaming is a cover for the form it takes in *Inception*.

So taken, it would reinforce the Cavellian assumption that external-world scepticism is allegorical of other-minds scepticism, so that the privacy of the resources deemed permissible in the canonical Cartesian recital of scepticism is an expression of the human desire to deny the reality of other minds; and it would further suggest that a primary reason for that denial is that one primarily experiences other minds as always already internal to one's own, as having designed and realized the world that one's subconscious wishes to think of as its own, to the point of striving murderously to eradicate any elements of that world that it deems to have their origin outside itself (as Robert Fischer's militarized projections devote themselves to doing at every dream-level of the central heist scenario).

The devotion of the protagonists of the world of *Inception* to their totems is thus not an expression of a concern with something other than scepticism; it is an expression of Christopher Nolan's Cavellian reinterpretation of scepticism as primarily a doubt about the reality of other minds, a doubt which in turn conceals a vision of the reality of other minds as undeniable, more precisely as undeniably threatening to dispossess the subject of his own mind, to claim ownership of that which is most intimately his, possession of himself in all his privacy or interiority. In this way, scepticism disguises and discloses an anxiety about whether the innermost contents of our minds are ours, something we possess inalienably, or rather essentially the possessions of others—whether because they can dispossess us of them (extraction) or because they can deceive us into accepting what originated with them as having originated with us (inception). It thereby inverts the epistemological polarities of the Cartesian cogito (according to which only immediate self-certainty escapes sceptical doubt), so that certainty about the independent reality of other minds is not only given but also deprives us of any certainty about the independent reality of our own. And it also reinterprets Descartes's sense that a perception of God as Creator will alone permit us to recover the world from our bastion of self-certainty—for (in the light of God's death) the idea of our world as another's creation acquires a paranoid tinge, promising only a threat to its and our integrity. This is a vision of sceptical anxiety as concealing (and so betraying) a conception of ourselves as inveterately either plagiarizing or plagiarized, hence of human beings as the site of crimes against intellectual property.

This connection allows us to move from the first to the second of the two elements I earlier itemized in Nolan's revision of Cavell's myth of scepticism—from the image of the totem to the vision of a cursed marriage that grounds the film's elaborate heist scenario in human reality. For Cobb's attempted inception of Robert Fischer is motivated by his client's promise to make the criminal charges that currently prevent him from re-entering the United States (and returning to his children) disappear permanently. Hence, as the heist scenario unfolds in a broadly linear way, we are also given (by means of episodic flashbacks) the key fragments of the story of how and why he has been left responsible for those children on his own, and invited to fit them together into the following portrait of a marriage.

Cobb trained as an architect in the traditional sense before being introduced by Miles to the chemical-induced business of dream-sharing, which his father valued as a way in which architects might not only realize even their most fantastic ideas but also share them with others.[5] Mal was another such student, of French extraction: they got married and had two children, whilst continuing to explore the world of dream-sharing, and in particular the concept of dreams nested within dreams.[6] On one of these joint explorations, they went down so many dream levels that they encountered Limbo—'raw, unconstructed dream space—infinite and empty'. On the one hand, this realm maximized their joint capacity for creation, rendering it godlike in its scope; on the other, because at each succeeding dream level brain function speeds up (and hence the perceived passage of time slows) by a factor of twenty, Cobb and Mal experienced their residence in Limbo as lasting for fifty years (and as capable in principle of continuing without any perceivable end). Mal's response to this offer of infinite scope in space and time was to accept it: already equipped with her totemic top, she created a safe within her Limbo-reproduction of her childhood home in which to lock it away, thereby (as Cobb puts it) 'deciding to forget that our world wasn't real'. Cobb's response was, by contrast, to tire of this divine mode of being because he either couldn't or wouldn't forget its unreality. In order to get Mal to agree to return to reality (something that could only be achieved, as any upward transition between dream levels must be achieved in the world of *Inception*, by killing themselves), he hunts for and locates her safe, opens it, finds the top sitting on its side, and sets it spinning again. Thus recalled to Limbo's unreality, Mal lies with her husband on a set of train-tracks, and the two are catapulted back to reality by an onrushing freight train of their own creation.

However, Mal brings with her the resilient idea that her world is not real, an idea which applies itself parasitically to the real world of their marriage and even to their children, whom she interprets as projections in a dream of her husband's to which she is currently being subjected, with her real children out of reach on the next level up: 'I'm their mother; don't you think I can tell the difference?' After failing to get Cobb to acknowledge the truth of her idea, she tries to compel him to join her in another joint suicide pact, the necessary means of their reaching the

---

[5] This is one of the very few points at which this reading of *Inception* draws on information contained in the shooting script of the film rather than a transcript of the dialogue contained in its theatrical release; cf. Christopher Nolan, *Inception: The Shooting Script* (San Rafael, CA: Insight Editions, 2010).

[6] The reality of the children's presence before their descent into Limbo is implicit in the fact that Cobb tells Ariadne of their creation of a facsimile of the apartment to which they moved upon the arrival of their first child.

'real' real world. She sets the scene of their usual wedding anniversary celebrations in an elegant hotel room as the site of a violent struggle with her husband, whom she has described in a letter deposited with her lawyers as having threatened to kill her; so if he refuses to join her when she leaps from a window, he will be arraigned as her murderer, and so lose the children whose need for him she knows he will cite as his reason for staying in this dream of reality. She jumps, but he does not; and he manages to escape to Europe just before his arrest, although only by abandoning his children and abandoning himself thereby to a peripatetic lifestyle in which he attempts to earn the money needed to overcome his legal difficulties by using the only talent he possesses. But every time he enters a dream world for extraction purposes, his projection of Mal bursts through from his own (supposedly professionally self-disciplined) subconscious to disrupt the team's manipulations with an extremity of violent but calculated hostility.

A more concise recounting of this narrative might run as follows: Cobb and Mal awake from a shared dream in which they grew old together, to find that their marriage no longer enables the fulfilment of reciprocal desire. Mal's loss of faith finds expression in a sceptical paroxysm: she turns their previously meet and happy conversations into a mutually uncomprehending argument about the reality of their present world, in the course of which her sceptical hypothesis turns out to be irrefutable by her husband, and she finds herself capable of doubting that her children are hers; her passion to reach a genuinely real reality is such that she is willing to abandon her children and force her husband to choose between suicide, incarceration, and exile in order to attain it. More specifically, she wants Cobb to choose death (and so real life) with her over life with their children (but without her); and in so doing, she recapitulates in reality what she had already declared in Limbo, by locking away her knowledge of its unreality in order fully to inhabit a world of unending, mutually satisfying creative collaboration with her husband alone—a world in which it appears there is simply no room for children. This is the fanaticism of love: Cobb can truly be hers only if nothing and no one else stands between them—only if they are everything to each other, exemplary of the world as such in a world that is utterly subject to their essentially single will. In comparison to this, the real world of independent others (including the autonomous offspring of their love) becomes as toys; she chooses to die to a world that has gone dead for her, and in a manner calculated to make chaos come again for her family.

The pervasiveness of Cavellian tropes and turns of phrase here is uncanny, and overwhelming; and the shape and trajectory of Cobb's and Mal's relationship draw upon the founding myths of remarriage comedy and their companion melodramas with fanatically loving attention to detail. For their story pivots around the point at which the two people's prior willingness endlessly to remarry one another (in effect renewing their vows every time they return from dream to reality) runs out, in which their meet and happy conversation is negated by sceptical irony and mutual victimization, and the root motive for their subjecting themselves to the accelerating threat of divorce (one person's passionate refusal to accept the other's independence, or the independent reality of the world they inhabit, or the internal relation between the two as that finds expression in the natural consequence of their sexual satisfaction) is apparently death-dealing.

So taken, *Inception* might be seen as addressing a question that the adjacency of the comedies and the melodramas invite us to pose: what happens to the spouse who appears immune to, or at least capable of resisting or overcoming, scepticism when the spouse who succumbs to it has definitively removed herself from the scene? How might someone whose self-legitimizing marriage was transformed into a mutually lacerating travesty of itself survive the experience when the other partner to the marriage has placed herself absolutely beyond recall, and so has placed the marriage essentially beyond recovery? In the comedies, the irruption of sceptical anxiety proves overcomable in light of the couple's continuing willingness to remain available to educate one another; in the melodramas, when the unacknowledged woman divorces herself from the villainously inadequate man (even removes herself from the scene altogether, as Lisa does in *Letter from an Unknown Woman*), she reveals their relationship as never having been (or even having had the potential to be) mutually satisfying, hence not something that could be recovered or redeemed. The issue Cobb faces in *Inception* is (related but importantly) different: it is how to accept the incomprehensible and unalterable transformation of his marriage from a state in which it realized the best aspirations of the comedies to a state in which it realized the worst fears of the melodramas.

This film can thus be read as creatively revising the founding myths of these genres in order to address questions that are essentially continuous with, and so expressible in some revised version of the basic terms of, Cavell's myth of scepticism. One might even accommodate in this way one of the film's more pointed revisions of the myth of remarriage comedy, in which children are generally absent from the couple's lives, which Cavell interprets as making it possible for them to devote themselves more purely or exclusively to the mutuality of their imaginations of one another (which in part means keeping lines open to their own shared childhood, hence facing the challenge of parenting one another—a feature that *Inception* correspondingly negates by imagining its couple as having rather grown old together). On the one hand, *Inception* implies that Cobb and Mal initially and for some time succeeded in incorporating children into their meet and happy conversations, which suggests a certain narcissistic shallowness in the mutuality of the comedic couples; but on the other, their later presence proves to incite and concentrate lacerating tensions between them in just the manner predicted and studied in the companion melodramas (in which, as Cavell emphasizes, the women's maternal relation to children is insisted upon).

But the issue of children carries a further, more problematic charge in *Inception*: for the film utilizes that issue positively to negate a fatefully central clause or provision of the sceptical myth as it finds expression in the Shakespearean source of its cinematic incarnations, *The Winter's Tale*—the clause which states that insofar as scepticism finds expression as a doubt as to whether your children are yours, it is not a feminine business. For *Inception* positively underlines the fact that Mal is someone whose scepticism finds expression in that form, and thereby dictates the basic shape of events in her world: the fate of her children is the fundamental issue for its protagonist, and its resolution provides the climax of the film. One might say that it provides an answer to the rhetorical question I earlier reported Cavell as posing in this vicinity, showing it thereby to be something other than purely rhetorical: Mal is what it would look like if Hermione doubted whether her children were hers.

Might we say that the apparent conflict here between Nolan's and Cavell's ways of seeing things dissolves if we utilize the latter's distinction between the female (as opposed to the male) and the feminine (as opposed to the masculine), and conclude that Mal is giving expression to the masculine side of her (and of human) character? Matters cannot be quite that simple: for in response to his revelation of scepticism as a gendered business, Cavell canvasses two possible ways of distinguishing its feminine from its masculine inflections—by reference to the object of the doubt, and by reference to its prevailing passion. The object of Mal's doubt is definitely masculine (the children as opposed to their father, and as subject to the telling of specific differences); but her passion—being an exemplary instance of obsessive or fanatical love, a drive towards an unconditioned form of its fulfilment that amounts to a refusal of finitude (as manifest in her devotion to the Limbo version of her marriage)—is equally definitely feminine. And yet Cavell also ends his discussion of the fanaticism of love understood as the refusal of finitude with the (far from transparent) declaration that 'this...is what permits me to describe Leontes as a portrait of the sceptic as fanatic'.[7] Perhaps, then, we should say that Mal is a projection of the actual Leontes rather than of an imaginary Hermione— that she is the cinematic realization of a Cavellian interpretation of Leontes' scepticism as combining masculine hyperbolic doubt with feminine hyperbolic love, hence of each inflection of scepticism as internally related to the other (and so as available either as a proxy or as a disguise for the other), as the feminine is to and for the masculine.

There is, however, a further complication—and one that connects the film's way of envisioning other-minds scepticism most closely to its way of envisioning external-world scepticism: the issue of plagiarism. For if Mal becomes possessed by the sceptical idea and destroys her husband and children as a consequence, how does it first come into her possession? The film's answer is clear: she brings it back with her into the real world because her husband devoted all of his energies

---

[7] *Disowning Knowledge*, 17.

in Limbo to the task of implanting it in her (achieving its inception by locating and manipulating the tell-tale cone which she had consigned to irrelevance out of love, so that it might once again activate her desire to reinhabit the everyday reality of their marriage and family life). Mal's subjection to scepticism, and her family's subsequent subjection to it, is thus ultimately the responsibility of her husband: the idea is his, although she gives it expression and application. In other words, Mal's fate is to live her husband's scepticism—the scepticism that he alone lives out after her death, as if having been always already made for it; and his simultaneous persecution by the monstrous hostility of his projections of Mal whenever he subsequently enters a dream world amounts to a further acknowledgement of his own guilt about the consequences of that originally sinful act of inception.

One response to this realization would be to transfer absolute responsibility for the cursing of the Cobb marriage from wife to husband, so that Mal is transformed from malignant demon to unknowing victim and Cobb from noble warrior against a lethal intellectual virus to ignoble manipulator and disseminator of it. And there is certainly a Cavellian case to be made against Cobb the inceptor of scepticism, since to a striking extent he exemplifies Cavell's conception of the villainous male of the melodramas—perhaps most directly the character of Paula's husband, Gregory Anton (played by Charles Boyer) in *Gaslight*, whose attempts to locate a hoard of jewels lead him to implant ideas in her mind which loosen her grip on reality, deprive her of words for the world of her experience, and threaten to destroy the psyche they inhabit. Nolan's film presents us with a comparable image of marriage as vampirism, of cursed or curdled intimacy as a matter of one life's sapping of another; and it elaborates its version of that image by touching upon another key reference point in Cavell's explorations of this topic—his deployment of texts from Freud and Henry James to suggest that the masculine inflection of other-minds scepticism takes the form of wanting to know what the woman knows.[8]

The male sceptic pictures the woman's unknownness as a matter of her knowing something that he does not, something she prevents him from knowing by withholding it, locating it somewhere inaccessibly private; and he devotes himself to gaining control over it, whether by penetrating that privacy or by ensuring that whatever it contains never finds expression—both approaches being routes for mastering the woman's voice, more precisely for depriving her of a voice of her own. But this obsessive desire to open or close the woman's private chamber or closet is in fact a projection: it pictures her individual reality as posing a problem of knowledge rather than of acknowledgement, and it externalizes a secret about himself that he cannot not know but that he nevertheless

---

[8] Cf. 'Postscript: To Whom It May Concern', in *Contesting Tears*, 151–96.

refuses to acknowledge—Cavell calls it the feminine register or tone of his own (human) voice, a register that he thinks of as essentially private in order (according to circumstances) either to account for his failure to use it, or to deny that it finds expression despite himself in everything he says.

Cobb's act of inception against his wife involves him in penetrating and manipulating the contents of just such a private space; he does so in order that she do what he wishes without doing it because she wants to do it, so that from that point on her life and her voice are no longer her own; and even after her real voice is silenced, she endlessly reappears within him as a persecutory self-projection, more specifically as someone who knows everything he does (from whom nothing can be hidden) and whose implacable hostility must therefore give expression to a feminine aspect of himself that he experiences as essentially beyond his control, and as having lethally violent designs on his subjectivity. His initial response to this incessant self-betrayal is to attempt to imprison his wife in a chamber of memories of their marriage before its encounter with Limbo, an unstable stack of self-serving scenarios in which he claims in effect to know that she is happy, and nothing but happy (as wife, as mother)—to tell her what there is to know about herself, to determine who she is.

This is why Cobb's redemption comes only when he allows himself to engage in an increasingly emancipatory relationship with another woman (Ariadne), whose conversational thread leads him through his internal labyrinth to acknowledge what he did to initiate Mal's scepticism, which brings him to acknowledge both her and him, and so to acknowledge the Minotaur of their marriage as a thing of the past—available to memory and in unaccommodated subconscious drives, but essentially beyond recovery or redemption, to be mourned but not to be fixated upon. As for the children: they get their father back in the end, but hardly free of guilt—not only in relation to their mother but in relation to them. After all, in the aftermath of Mal's suicide he wasn't willing to risk his own liberty in order to stay close to them; and the primary effect of Mal-as-projection during his sojourn in exile from America is to disrupt his extraction plans, and thereby to defer his return to his home and his offspring. To blame those delays on Mal would be to conflate her projection with her real self; Mal-as-projection is in truth Cobb's way of delaying himself, of maintaining himself at a distance from his children, converting them into a fantasy.[9]

---

[9] Leonardo DiCaprio's role as Cobb is thus strikingly analogous to his role as 'Teddy Daniels' in Martin Scorsese's *Shutter Island* (2010), in which DiCaprio's status as husband and father is also positively insisted upon, in which he kills his wife in response to her drowning of their three children, and in which he constructs and inhabits a world of fantasy in which to evade acknowledgement of his sense of responsibility for all four deaths (since his problems with alcohol led him to ignore his wife's mental instability). What is it about DiCaprio's lengthy and challenging screen transition from beautiful youth to mature male that engenders so close and tense a tie between marriage and parenthood, and between paternal love and maternal murderousness? I try to elaborate this connection

In the end, however, to demonize Cobb would be no more accurate to the film's perception of things than to demonize Mal. After all, it is Mal who first creates the private safe, and invents its resident (not to mention investing it with totemic status); and Cobb violates that safe only in response to her hyperbolic attempt to make their relationship infinite and all-consuming, thereby denying their finitude. It would accordingly be more accurate to say that attempts to assign responsibility for the corruption of their marriage to one party or the other fail to appreciate the most significant thing about it—the fact that the boundary between Mal and Cobb is one that neither finds it possible to draw, or to acknowledge. Just as their creations in Limbo are essentially joint affairs, so neither seems in a position confidently to claim any idea about themselves or their world as theirs as opposed to their partner's. Ownership of the sceptical idea is not ultimately settleable—not because ideas possessed of such resilience transcend the idea of personal ownership, and not because the origin of an idea is as nothing compared to the uses to which they are put, but primarily because neither Mal nor Cobb has succeeded in acknowledging the separateness of each others' minds, and so their individual agency and independent reality.

The Cavellian reference point here is his reading of *Macbeth*, according to which the Macbeth marriage is one in which each reads the other's mind so readily and exhaustively—each constantly articulating what the other has it in mind to say, or not saying what the other will not say, each imagining the other to have conceived of the idea on which he or she is acting, hence thinking of himself or herself as the embodiment or externalization of that other's thoughts—that they seem to be trapped or imprisoned in one another's minds, quite as if the idea that there are two such minds at issue remains unacknowledged or unrealized (and of course, in a way that raises questions about their children). This inflection of the cursed marriage as a species of vampirism is reflected not only in Nolan's presentation of Cobb's inability to mourn as a matter of his mind's being ineradicably inhabited by Mal, but also in the means of his redemption being his willingness to acknowledge that the Mal he encounters in his nested dream worlds all the way down to Limbo is not Mal herself—not the real, independent person whose separateness is definitively established by the fact that her death does not cause or constitute his. Only when Cobb acknowledges himself as alive can he free himself from the limbo of his current existence, and confront the existing consequences of his love for his dead wife.

It didn't require Leonardo DiCaprio's adoption of Christopher Nolan's hairstyle and goatee beard to tell us that *Inception*'s gang of thieves offer a projected image of a team of film-makers with Cobb as its director. Just like Cobb, Nolan is

---

in 'Martin Scorsese's Screening Room: Theatricality, Psychoanalysis and Modernity in *Shutter Island*', in C. Barnett and C. Elliston (eds.), *Scorsese and Religion* (Leiden: Brill, 2019).

deeply collaborative in working out the financing and production logistics, the script and the set design of their dream worlds; the vast majority of his films are adaptations of other's work (whether films, novels and graphic novels, or short stories and scripts originally written by his brother); and he draws heavily throughout upon the conventions of various popular film genres which have already shaped his audience's perceptions of reality to the point at which their deployment will facilitate the reality effect of the dream-narratives. Ultimately, however, both directors shape all of these elements in ways that betray their individual signatures—both when that shaping is under conscious control and when it is subconsciously conditioned.

The film's theme of plagiarism is thus particularly relevant to its reflexive concerns: for it suggests that its director is anxious properly to acknowledge the nature and limits of creative originality in an artistic medium that is inherently collective, and whose history records an unprecedentedly successful colonization of the interior lives of its audience, including those who inherit the history of the enterprise as its present practitioners. Against this background, the film's myth of inception and extraction provides a conceptually precise and interestingly original way of thinking through this issue of cinematic originality, from the perspective of the director and from that of the critic.

Suppose, for example, that we imagine *Inception* as one of the dream worlds it contains; then on my reading Stanley Cavell's philosophical consciousness would be the subject of that dream, and Christopher Nolan its architect. This discussion would then amount to an attempt to determine whether, and if so at what points, Cavell's subconscious might realize that it did not design or create the world in which it finds itself, and deploy its defensive projections in order to combat the foreign nature of the dreamer, like white bloods cells attacking an infection. In general, I have found that Nolan's revisions of the Cavellian myth of scepticism tend to diverge far less straightforwardly or significantly than might at first appear to be the case, or at least that the most central of these divergences can be seen as unfolding ideas that were either implicit in Cavell's myth or that function to elaborate its underlying economy in fruitful directions; others may find that a more highly militarized response is appropriate.

But we might equally well regard the conceptual articulations of this essay as the architecture of a dream world of which Christopher Nolan is the subject. Would he sense the Cavellian dispositions I impute to that world as essentially foreign in nature to his own designs and goals—perhaps even as so distant from his concerns as to constitute an essentially unrecognizable backdrop for his dreaming mind? The risk my interpretation of *Inception* runs is that of becoming an act of inception on the film's maker—attempting to pass off another's idea of scepticism as his own, thereby simultaneously denying Nolan's originality and assigning a godlike status to Cavell (as if he were the first cause of anything cinematically creative, essentially omnipresent and incapable of being transcended or outstripped). Put otherwise: is this reading's elaboration of a moment of critical inspiration more creation than it is discovery (to displace the film's own schema for creativity, as sketched by Cobb for Ariadne)?

How might I tell the difference between being enabled by Cavell's originality to acknowledge the originality of others, and being disabled by it, to the point of denying the autonomous creativity of others (by finding that any world they construct amounts to an extraction from a Cavellian vision of reality) and losing the autonomy of my own experience (of this film, and of film more generally)? One way of doing so is to test the extent to which this reading of *Inception* enables complementary readings of other Christopher Nolan films, thereby strengthening the claim that emphasizing these features of *Inception* identifies features that characterize his body of work as a whole, and so constitute distinguishing features of his cinematic subjectivity. Another is to test the extent to which those features individually and collectively engage with themes that have been identified by thinkers other than Cavell, thereby strengthening the case for regarding them as having a genuine purchase on reality independently of one's allegiances to any one of those thinkers. In the present context, Nietzsche's thematization of the ascetic ideal (and its vicissitudes in thinkers such as Wittgenstein or Coetzee) is an obvious candidate for the third reference point in such a process of intellectual triangulation.

Consider, for example, Nolan's use of the totem as a vehicle for reflecting on external-world scepticism. If my Cavellian reading of the relation between its apparent and its real significance is right, then it also amounts to a vehicle for interrogating what Nietzsche would call the will to truth. For when—if—we come to appreciate that totems cannot provide a bastion of certainty against external-world scepticism, we thereby catch ourselves having previously assumed that our fundamental relation to reality must be a cognitive one—a matter of knowledge and certainty (hence truthful apprehension) or its absence, rather than one of acknowledgement: that is, acceptance (or rejection) of one's responsibility for maintaining the shared grammatical horizon within which knowledge-claims are possible and intelligibility can be sought. In one sense, then, our ascetic will to truth is here shown to overreach itself; but in another sense, this overreaching discloses the truth—about the conditionedness of human orientation in the world and our drive to deny it, and about the will to truth's participation in that drive. This is what Cavell calls the truth of scepticism: and he thereby identifies in epistemology the same paradoxical expression of the will to truth's self-overcoming that Nietzsche enacts in the *Genealogy* (expressing his indebtedness to that will by disclosing a genuine difference between its evaluation of truth and what truth's value might otherwise be or become).

So there is nothing self-undermining about Nolan's cinematic exposure of the truth of the sceptical will to truth. His therapeutic designs on his audience—his attempts to get them to see their own entanglement in that will to truth—rather show that one of the things from which the truth can and should set you free is the ascetic valuation of truth. After all: to think that emancipation from the will to truth requires relinquishing the very idea of truthful apprehension of reality is to conflate truth with the ascetic valuation of it, and so amounts to one more manifestation of the will to truth that is under critical interrogation in the work of both philosophers and in this film-maker.[10]

The rest of this portion of my third essay will attempt to establish whether that kind of intellectual triangulation can be applied to Christopher Nolan's body of work as a whole.

B. Two Become One Flesh: Marriage and Love's Alteration in *Memento*

Nolan's second film, *Memento* (2000), is at least as inviting an interpretative object for the philosophically inclined as *Inception*, although most commentators have tended to see the former as preoccupied with issues (principally, the role of memory in the constitution of personal identity) that have only a tangential relationship with those foregrounded in the latter. And yet, in *Memento*'s final scene, as Leonard speeds away from the hidden corpse of his most recent victim to set in train the process which will result in the death of the person who enabled that murder, and whose image is diminishing in his rear-view mirror, his glance falls on a tattoo on the back of his hand which says 'Remember Sammy Jankis', and this prompts an internal monologue (which reaches us as a voice-over) that makes the following declaration:

> I have to believe in the world outside my own mind. I have to believe that my actions still have meaning, even if I can't remember them. I have to believe that when my eyes are closed, the world's still there.

Then he closes his eyes, driving blind through the traffic, as he continues speaking:

> But do I? Do I believe the world's still there?

---

[10] This is my fundamental point of disagreement with Todd McGowan's powerful and influential Lacanian reading of Nolan's body of work, epitomized in his book *The Fictional Christopher Nolan* (Austin, Texas: University of Texas Press, 2012); hereafter FCN. Although we agree in seeing various ways in which Nolan critically evaluates the nature of truth and knowledge, my Nietzschean lens suggests that Nolan positively and repeatedly denies what McGowan claims that he affirms: 'the ontological primacy of the lie' (FCN, 1). I hope that what follows provides reason for accepting my finding with respect to each film in Nolan's oeuvre.

We see cars fly past him, horns blaring:

> Is it still out there?!
> (beat)
> Yes.

At which point he opens his eyes, straightens up the car, and begins looking for a tattoo parlour. But he also offers a final observation before the screen goes blank, and he loses his recollection of the resolution whose realization (we now realize) the preceding film has been exclusively preoccupied with tracking:

> We all need mirrors to remind ourselves who we are. I'm no different.

This sequence strongly suggests that Leonard's condition as he interprets it fundamentally forces him to engage with the problem of external-world scepticism; more specifically, it prompts him not only to perform what Cavell would call a sceptical recital, but also to put the sceptical proposal to a practical test—one in which the exercise of his agency (what Kant would call practical rather than theoretical reason) reveals that the world contains at least enough independent reality to refuse to accommodate itself frictionlessly to whatever eccentric trajectory he pursues through it. Leonard is not convinced of the world's existence by an argument, but by its ability to protest audibly against his scepticism, and thereby to promise a potentially lethal form of material resistance to it. He tries to live his scepticism, and he fails, at which point scepticism appears to fail. Except...

For one thing, does his inability to shake his belief in the world's externality to him amount to a proof of that externality, or just to a proof of the unshakeability of that belief? If seeming to see other cars on the road isn't enough to convince him that the world exists, why should seeming to hear their protesting horns? It's almost as if only an auditory response from the world can adequately rebut a scepticism whose mode of expression is itself intended for the ear—a recital, a doubt that we know is voiced within Leonard's head only because it is voiced over Nolan's screened projection of it. In Nolan's world, the world answers back to the sceptical human voice, and thereby betrays the way scepticism places it in the position of an interlocutor, an other to the sceptical human subject.

And as if to confirm the Cavellian hypothesis of the allegorical relation of external-world scepticism and other-minds scepticism, the final scene which culminates in Leonard's silent sceptical aria has painstakingly laid out the true source or narrative origin of his predicament. As viewers, we were quickly made familiar with Leonard's current beliefs about that origin: his memory was impaired as the result of an assault by two men in which his wife Catherine was killed, and for which he seeks vengeance against the second attacker (who initially evaded capture). But the final scene offers us a very different version of that story: for according to Teddy, Catherine was not killed in the assault, but was sceptical of the reality of Leonard's resulting impairment, to the point at which she was willing to test its authenticity by repeatedly inviting Leonard to inject her with the insulin she needed to counteract diabetes, as a result of which she received a lethal dose.

At this point in the film, we only hear Teddy's version of events: the flashbacks that his words briefly induce in Leonard only show him remembering one occasion in their pre-assault lives on which he injected Catherine—or more precisely, show him first seeming to remember this and then seeming to remember it otherwise, as he resists the authority of Teddy's account. But in another sense, the entire tragic drama that Teddy's words summarize has already been threaded through the film before we hear his testimony: for much of the material in the black-and-white sequences with which Nolan intersperses his reverse-chronology colour narrative involves Leonard relating exactly the same story on the phone, but presenting it as another's—as the story of Sammy Jankis and his wife, whom Leonard encountered in his previous life as an insurance claims investigator. According to Teddy, however, Sammy Jankis was simply a con man who unsuccessfully pretended to be suffering from Leonard's post-assault condition; and Leonard's compulsion to tell his version of Sammy's story to all and sundry is an attempt to occlude the truth about the end of his own marriage by repetitively conditioning his own memory to accept it as the truth about another's. In short, on this account, at the heart of *Memento* lies another conjunction of our Cavellian articulation of scepticism in terms of a cursed marriage, plagiarism, and defensive projection.

Although it's just about possible that Teddy is lying—by his own admission, he lies to Leonard about a lot of things, and he is perfectly willing to use Leonard's weakness and his strengths for his own purposes—there's no obvious reason for him to do so, at this point in their shared form of life and about this particular topic. Moreover, if he were lying, much about the film that contains him would lack any obvious rationale—not just the long-drawn-out telling of Sammy Jankis's story (which doesn't add anything to its hearers' understanding of Leonard's condition, despite his claims to the contrary), but also the fact that Leonard is driven to take murderous measures against Teddy in response to his telling of that tale (as if his ability to live with himself in the future depends not just on ensuring that Teddy cannot treat him as a useful tool, but also on eliminating the sole possible source of that tale's retelling). If we further recall that Leonard's sceptical recital is prompted by the tattoo that exhorts him to remember Jankis, and concludes with a reference to seeing himself in a mirror (just moments after we have seen him watching Teddy in his rear-view mirror), then we have good reason to proceed on the assumption that Teddy is telling the truth.

In which case: what is it about his marriage that Leonard is both concealing and revealing by displacing it onto Sammy Jankis? Is it that he wants to disavow the fact that he killed his wife (even if he did so unintentionally)? But the truth is that she deliberately brought it about that he repeatedly injected her with those individually innocuous but collectively lethal doses, and that she equally deliberately failed to take numerous opportunities to prevent him from doing so. So what he is more specifically disavowing is the fact that Catherine was willing to put him to the test in this way, and thereby her reasons for doing so. For if we are to take Mrs Jankis's confession as our guide, Catherine is sceptical of her husband's claim to be suffering from short-term memory loss (Korsokoff's syndrome); but that is because she is more fundamentally sceptical that the person she married has really gone:

> When I look into Sammy's eyes, I don't see some vegetable, I see the same old Sammy. What do you think it's like for me to suspect that he's imagining this whole problem? That if I could just say the right thing he'd snap out of it and be back to normal? If I knew that my Sammy was truly gone, then I could say goodbye and start loving this new Sammy. As long as I have doubt, I can't say goodbye and move on.

This confession tells us that the wife takes herself not only to have a superior means of cognitive access to the continued existence of her old husband than is available either to medical science or to the husband himself, but also to have the means to rescue him from the delusion he is currently inhabiting. In other words, she treats him as her own best case of knowledge of another mind, and regards herself as the ground of his own continued existence—as perhaps his only opportunity to exchange the fantasy he currently inhabits for the renewed contact with reality that she exemplifies for him (as his best case for knowledge of another mind).

This is confirmed by her chosen way of effecting his self-recovery, and so her own: for that turns out to involve staking her existence as such on her conviction that the man she married and whom she knows beyond doubt loves her could not continue to inhabit his fantasy if that would cause her harm. This redemptive strategy is thus not a matter of her finding the right thing to say, and it is not exactly a matter of her finding the right thing to do: it rather involves her creating a situation in which she allows something to be done to her by her husband—in which she is passive and he is active—and in which what he takes to be a health-giving act becomes a death-dealing one. So it turns out that what is at stake is not just her own continued existence, but also her husband's condemnation to continued existence as his wife's murderer.

Cavell would call this sadomasochistic scenario—in which both parties relate to each other and to themselves as at once victimizer and victim—a manifestation of the fanaticism of love; and *Memento* makes it clear that this fanaticism is based on Catherine's driving desire to regard her relation to Leonard as fundamentally a matter of knowing something about him rather than acknowledging him. More specifically, although she expresses a willingness to bid farewell to the old Leonard and start loving the new one, it is conditional upon her coming to know with certainty that the old Leonard has gone; indeed, her need for that cognitive basis goes so deep that in order to acquire it she is willing to risk rendering it impossible for her to acknowledge Leonard at all (whether as unchanged or as changed), let alone for him to acknowledge her.

This extremity of risk-taking strongly suggests that Catherine would prefer her own non-existence to the obligation to acknowledge that the man she married was vulnerable to or capable of alteration—vulnerable to havoc wreaked by the independent external world, and capable of transforming himself for reasons of his own (a capacity whose acknowledgement would accordingly require acknowledging her husband's independent reality as another person). She would rather die than acknowledge that (as Nietzsche would put it) her exemplary other's mode of being is one of becoming—perhaps because that would require acknowledging that the same is true of her. It isn't an accident that Leonard's only substantial memory of their marriage concerns a conversation in which she criticizes him for questioning her habit of repeatedly rereading the books she likes—hence of seeking pleasure in the reassurance of change's absence.

So Leonard's refusal to acknowledge the true story of his marriage is not just a way of disavowing his unwitting role in his wife's death. It also occludes her unwillingness to acknowledge the reality of his condition, and so of his survival of radical change; and it permits him to avoid acknowledging her willingness to make him responsible for her own demise and that of their marriage, rather than to take responsibility for maintaining that marriage in the face of alteration. After all, if love is not love which alters when it alteration finds, then to acknowledge any of this would be to acknowledge that his marriage was not what it appeared to be, and that his wife's inability to sustain her standing as his best case for knowing (and being known by) another mind had condemned him to a world of chaos that unendingly comes again, within which his ability to know himself seems unsustainable.

However, given the symmetrical logic of acknowledgement, embodied in marriage's making of two into one, can Leonard fully acknowledge Catherine's responsibilities and inabilities without fully acknowledging his own real but indeterminable contribution to her condition of vulnerability to them? Leonard's awareness of this point is encoded within his transposition of his own story onto that of Mr and Mrs Jankis: for according to that narrative, he plays a crucial enabling role in Mrs Jankis's transition from theoretical doubt about her husband to practical action. She seeks out Leonard's opinion of the genuineness of Sammy's condition, and it is only when he declares that there is no physical reason why Sammy couldn't create new memories that she gives Sammy his final exam. So presenting the story of his own marriage as the story of two other people allows Leonard to admit some degree of complicity in its tragic ending without having to acknowledge it to himself; and the nature of his real guilt makes it all the more appropriate that his imaginary role in bringing about

Mrs Jankis's fate is correspondingly unintentional (since he meant only to suggest that Sammy's condition was mental rather than an illusion or a deception, without realizing that Mrs Jankis took herself to be the privileged adjudicator of her husband's inner life).

So is Leonard's narrative of Mr and Mrs Jankis a truthful account of the nature and fate of his own marriage? Can a narrative be autobiographical if its narrator does not mean it to be, or believe that it is? But embodied beings such as ourselves can give expression to what we're thinking and feeling even when we don't realize that we are, and sometimes even when (indeed precisely by virtue of the means we employ when) we attempt to conceal it: as Freud puts it, betrayal oozes out of us at every pore. On the other hand, what is thereby betrayed is open to interpretation, and interpretation is conditioned by context. Leonard appreciates this:

> My job taught me that the best way to find out what someone knew was to let them talk... throw in the occasional 'Why?', but just listen. And watch the eyes, the body language. It's complicated. You might catch a sign but attach the wrong meaning to it. If someone touches their nose while they're talking, experts will tell you it means they're lying. It really means they're nervous, and people get nervous for all sorts of reasons. It's all about context.

Taken at face value, Leonard's own story about Sammy Jankis appears to be a confession of guilt, and it still appears that way when reconsidered in the light of the film's conclusion; but the context supplied by Teddy radically reconfigures what the reason for, and hence the nature of, that guilt really is. This does not show that there is no such thing as truth, only interpretations; it shows rather that the truth will out, and often by means of our best attempts to conceal it. The trouble with our ability to suppress how things really are with us is that our modes of suppression, rightly interpreted, are also modes of expression. So Leonard's story is both a false confession and a true one, and it is the latter by virtue of being the former: the specific form and content of its falsehood is what reveals the truth its narrator both wants and does not want to acknowledge.

What, then, of the specific and notorious form of *Memento* itself—and in particular, its presentation of Leonard's story between the deaths of Jimmy and Teddy in the form of a chronologically reversed sequence of smaller, chronologically linear sequences? Nolan has said that this strategy aspires to ensure that his audience's experience of his film mimics as closely as possible Leonard's experience of his own post-accident form of life. In other words, this is Nolan's way of achieving his usual goal of intensifying cinema's distinctive capacity for generating an immersive experience for viewers of this particular narrative. But does it?

The reverse chronology form of the general narrative certainly ensures that the film's viewers begin each smaller episode in as disoriented a state as Leonard does: this is perhaps most clearly exhibited in the episode which begins with Leonard finding himself running, but not knowing whether he is chasing or being chased. On the other hand, once he figures out that it's the latter, his experience begins quickly to diverge from ours: in particular, we know—having already seen a number of chronologically succeeding episodes—that he will survive this chase essentially unscathed, whereas he must remain in ignorance of that fact until he manages to make it one. Correspondingly, whereas each new chronologically prior episode eliminates more and more of our initially complete ignorance of Leonard's short-term past, Leonard's knowledge never extends beyond the boundary of each episode as he undergoes it (and doesn't always extend that far).

The stringent limits of mimesis in such a context should not be surprising: a film-maker may be able convincingly to present a protagonist who has lost his short-term memory, but he can hardly create such a loss in those watching. But the issue here is more specific. For the nature of this protagonist's relation to his own experience and existence is deeply and necessarily non-immersive: from Leonard's point of view, his lack of short-term memory makes an untroubled engagement with the flow of his experience something that can only be achieved after a great deal of interpretative effort, hence typically only at the end of each episode in his discontinuous mode of being. Being immersed in, call it owning, his life is precisely what his condition deprives him of. Hence, in order for our experience as viewers to mimic his, Nolan must attempt to counter cinema's massive bias towards the immersive—its overwhelming power to compel its viewers to inhabit the world of the film.

This is precisely what the general reverse-chronology form achieves; for it results in the systematic disruption of narrative immersion—repeatedly forcing viewers to renew their attempts to acquire enough of a grasp of context for them to be drawn smoothly into an identification with the character's current concerns and goals. But in so doing, it makes manifest, and so acknowledges, two determining features of cinema as a distinctive aesthetic medium: its reliance upon succession, and its projection of pastness. Each frame of a film is at once distinct from every other, and part of a continuous, always already present strip of such frames; Leonard's condition dramatizes the first of these features, and our relation to him—insofar as each wrench away from one episode to its predecessor nevertheless progressively overcomes our ignorance of what has happened to him—presupposes the second. Leonard's endlessly renewed reconstruction of presentness is something that his viewers relate to as part of something that has already happened; the tense of his story—like that of any screened fictional narrative—is that of the past.

C. Film as Confession: *Following*

Nolan's first film was *Following* (1998): *Memento*'s immediate predecessor, it shares its successor's interest in disarticulating narrative unity; and once the audience have put together the scattered pieces, its plot hangs together with the same precision-engineered elegance.

When a woman's relationship with a club-owner ends, she retains evidence of his criminal tendencies (a bloodstained rug) with a view to blackmail; but unknown to her, the club-owner hires a man named Cobb to kill her. Cobb begins a relationship with this woman (identified in the credits only as 'The Blonde'), and asks her to help him with a difficulty he claims that he's currently having with the police. He tells her that he is a burglar, and that the police suspect him of involvement in the brutal death of an old lady who was a victim of burglary. He protests his innocence, but says that the only way to convince the police to leave him alone is to set up someone else as the real killer.

Cobb has recently noticed that he is being followed around by a young man who calls himself 'Bill'. Bill is a writer at a loose end, who has gradually become obsessed with following people he picks randomly from the London crowds. Cobb confronts him, and then inducts him into what he presents as his equally intrusive but rather more clinically conducted life as a burglar. One of the flats they break into together belongs to the Blonde, and Bill's voyeurism (triggered by seeing photos of her) leads him to steal some of her possessions, follow her and inveigle himself into her life—much to Cobb's apparent fury when he finds out, since he says that it puts them both at risk; so he ends their fledgling partnership forthwith.

Meanwhile, the Blonde tells Bill about the club-owner, and asks Bill to rob him—in order, she says, to retrieve compromising photographs with which he is blackmailing her. Bill duly breaks into the club and opens the safe, to find both photographs and a substantial amount of money; but he is discovered by one of the owner's henchmen, and defends himself, leaving the henchman for dead when he makes his escape. Then—contrary to his promise—he looks at the photos and sees that they are nothing but unexceptional modelling portraits; so he demands an explanation from her. She reveals to him Cobb's plot as she understands it, and her willingness to help implicate him as a potentially violent burglar. He departs in disgust, abandoning the stolen items and the hammer he used on the henchman.

The next day, he goes to the police to confess the whole story; but he there learns that the Blonde has herself been killed, and that the murder weapon was Bill's hammer (now marked with two dead people's blood). The policeman interviewing him knows of no old lady killed in the course of a burglary, nor of a habitual burglar whom they supposedly suspect of the crime; no such person lives at the address that Cobb presented to Bill as his transient dwelling. On the other hand, they have found a number of the Blonde's possessions in Bill's flat, as well as the dead man beside the emptied safe in the club. So they conclude that Bill murdered the woman after torturing her for the combination of the safe, which he then robbed for the money. Bill desperately claims that Cobb must be the one responsible for her death (and the film shows Cobb explaining his real plan to her before killing her and taking the stolen money as his agreed payment); but since

Cobb has vanished without trace, Bill's confident sense of knowing exactly what he was doing throughout his adventure has been definitively undermined, and his unforeseen fate sealed.

Whatever the elegance of Cobb's double deception, however, the formal fragmentation of its means of presentation in Following (1998) doesn't have any obvious justification in the aberrant memory or mode of existence of its protagonist, Cobb's second unwitting dupe and the narrator of the tale. The film begins with Bill's first words of confession to the policeman, and then stays resolutely with his limited and belated point of view as it plunges us into a mélange of glimpses of various stages in Bill's gradual manipulation by Cobb and the Blonde, to which he later returns in longer internally coherent sequences that nevertheless continue to leap forwards and backwards in time. Bill's appearance is the key reference point by means of which we begin to work out the underlying order of events, since he begins casually dressed, then smartens up his act in imitation of Cobb, and then sports the bruises left by Cobb's violent dissolution of their partnership. But the question is: why should we have to? Bill's underlying narrative certainly involves him entering new worlds whose terms of reference it takes him time to master, and which ultimately mean something very different to his initial impression of them: but imposing temporal discontinuities in the telling of it seems a pointlessly extravagant way of signalling that there is a mystery to be solved.

Suppose we take seriously Bill's ownership of the overall frame of the film. As his first voice-over words declare, 'the following is my explanation... my account... of what happened': that is, what he goes on to say is that account, but so also is the film whose title is 'Following'. This would allow us to regard the initially extreme but gradually moderating temporal discontinuities as a reflection of his initially anxious mental state, as he struggles to digest the implications of the Blonde's revelations and so to radically recalibrate his conception of what he thinks is the real significance of what has happened to him, of how these people and places really hang together. The discontinuities then settle down as he establishes a calmer, more confidently comprehending narratorial relation to them—before the final twist asks him and us to rearrange them once more.

But if we also take seriously the fact that Bill's explanation or account is more specifically a confession to a policeman, then another possible explanation for these temporal jumps begins to emerge. For why, after all, are we so confident that the policeman's concluding scepticism about his narrative is misplaced? What exactly are our grounds for believing the confession that Bill has just made? Suppose that he had befriended, tortured, and killed the Blonde in order to rob the club-owner, as the policeman believes: wouldn't it make perfect sense for him to invent Cobb and his baroque schemes as a last-ditch way of deflecting responsibility? Indeed, what gives us any reason to believe that Cobb exists at all except what Bill has told us, and what the film has shown us as it obediently answers to the sinuous complexities of his voice-over?

If we were to confine ourselves to the traces left on the external world by what has happened—to what we have evidence for beyond Bill's word—all we would have to go on is a robbed safe, two dead bodies, and a mass of incriminating evidence in Bill's flat. Moreover, the tale he tells is exactly the kind of genre-dependent, double-crossing and triple-crossing plot that any budding writer might be well placed to dream up (particularly if his voyeuristic tendencies had led him into criminal temptation). From this sceptical perspective, the film's frenetic but gradually diminishing temporal discontinuities would then mimic Bill's efforts to construct an exculpatory fiction—a tissue of pure invention that might articulate the few obdurate, objectively establishable facts of the case in such a way as to raise reasonable doubt in the minds of a jury, even if not in the more experienced mind of a policeman.

It certainly seems to have worked on most of Bill's listeners—that is, Nolan's viewers; and that success merely confirms Coetzee's perception of the ascetic genre of the confession as one that constantly runs up against the limits of its capacity to underwrite its own sincerity. But we don't need to believe that the policeman's reading is superior to the one which takes Bill's word for it: Nolan's point is made simply by his ensuring that two equally defensible readings of what happened are made available by his film—one according to which its narrator is as radically unreliable as the formal conditions of narrative (that we examined in the early part of Essay Two) allow, the other according to which he is as helplessly truthful as he is generally hapless. For when any member of his audience comes to realize that possibility, they find themselves in exactly the position of anyone who is the subject of an attempted confidence trick—the position of both Bill and the Blonde (if we believe his account), or that of the policeman (if we do not). The film viewer has no epistemological superiority here: she, too, must rely on our defeasible ability to negotiate the ways in which the content of a confession and its motives interact with and subvert one another.

D. One Flesh, Two Minds: Marriage and Love's Alteration in *The Prestige*

In *The Prestige* (2006), tricks of various kinds are also to the fore, in a tale of two magicians whose dispute over the ownership and the perfecting of an illusion stages a confrontation between two modes of doubling or duplicity (one of which requires two men to pretend to be one man over a long lifetime, the other of which requires one man to destroy himself in order to create a copy of himself, night after night). But since marriage is an equally salient concern, this film (like *Memento*) links that state or condition to issues involving appearance and reality, both between subject and world and between subjects, and to a perception of the self as becoming or non-self-identical, as an unceasing dialectic between self-constancy and self-transformation.

Angier is the first of the two protagonists to be married; indeed, we barely have time to register its reality before a trick involving his wife, Julia, goes wrong, and she drowns on stage in a sealed tank of water because she can't slip free from the knot securing her hands. Angier is convinced that this is because Borden, the other protagonist, has used a knot (the Langford double) that holds tighter (and so gives better support when Julia is hoisted into the tank) but is harder to slip under water. When pressed afterwards, Borden claims not to remember which knot he used—a peculiar defence that only becomes comprehensible retrospectively, when we realize that the Borden being asked the question is not necessarily the Borden who tied the knot that night. But the film makes it tolerably clear what actually happened: after carefully registering Julia's belief that she can slip a Langford double under water, and Borden's admission that they have been practising the manoeuvre, during the fateful performance the camera captures Borden reconsidering which knot he should use, looking enquiringly at Julia, and Julia nodding conspiratorially—that is, licensing the use of the Langford double.

Although the film's audience accordingly have good reason to believe they know what happened, only one person in the film can share that confidence. The Borden brother who wasn't on stage that night can never know whether what he has been told by the brother who was is true or not; and although Angier has strong circumstantial evidence implicating Borden in the death, he has equally strong reason to suspect that his wife had been collaborating with Borden over the matter of the knot, and so to suspect that she was complicit in her own fate—perhaps to the point of being primarily responsible for it. And Nolan makes it clear that it is this constitutive uncertainty about what Borden did (what knot he tied, and for what reason) that sets the whole complex plot machinery into motion. For when Angier begins the feud by sabotaging Borden's 'bullet catch' trick and damaging his fingers in the process, he intends the threat of the loaded gun to force Borden to satisfy his desperate desire to know what really happened, and he is baulked by Borden's bewildering inability to supply an answer to that question. 'How can he not know what he did?' Angier asks himself, and us: but if he were to ask himself whether he really intended to shoot Borden if he failed to tell him, or when his search for Borden's knowledge about his wife's death becomes a quest to know the secret of his 'Transported Man' trick (and so to know what Borden knows about what it means to be Borden), would he be able to answer?

Against this background, it is hard to overlook the fact that the mode of despatch Angier employs each night against the version of himself who enters the Tesla machine precisely mimics the way in which Julia died. Would a husband who was genuinely haunted by his wife's death create a stage act whose mechanism requires that he subject himself to the same agonizing fate, every night? If we take seriously Angier's earlier admission to Olivia (that he doesn't care about his wife—he cares about the secret of Borden's Transported Man trick), his choice of method would seem to confirm its truth. But if we also take seriously the fact that the person who is killed every night is (a version of) Angier himself—and a version who knows that this is the inevitable consequence of entering the Tesla machine— we might rather conclude that Angier has finally realized that his mimetic rivalry with Borden has prevented him from acknowledging his wife's death, and is regarding these one hundred performances as his way of atoning for that failure.

It wouldn't follow, of course, that they constitute a genuine acknowledgement of Julia's and his marriage; for that would involve acknowledging that she is dead, hence that he is a widower rather than a husband, and so that grieving for her is not incompatible with—and may even require—going on from that relationship, being open to new ones without repressing the significance of the old. Angier's version of the Transported Man trick, by contrast, amounts to a self-punishing, sadomasochistic way of commemorating his wife—a way of taking her death upon himself, and thereby identifying himself with her, that refuses to relate to it as past. It is a nightly re-enactment of his own inability to recover from her loss: it is an apotheosis of asceticism that turns the potentially emancipatory human capacity to become other than oneself (to die to one's actual array of cares and concerns) into a means for reducing the future to the reiterated inscription of the past upon the present. Freud would diagnose it as melancholia rather than mourning; Nietzsche might call it a vengeful refusal to accept time and its 'it was', a denial of the pastness of the past that equally denies the present and the future.

Borden's way of pulling off the 'Transported Man' trick is importantly different: rather than making use of cloning-at-a-distance and thereby creating two from one, he makes use of his status as a twin to create one from two. He and his brother spend a lifetime secretly alternating on a daily basis between two personas—Borden the magician and Fallon his *ingénieur*—so that they can then secretly alternate between being the man who enters the first door and being the Prestige (the one who emerges instantaneously from the second door to the audience's acclaim) in such a way as to make it appear that Borden alone performs it. In other words, the Borden brothers each subordinate their distinct lives to the achievement of a single creative goal (as the apparently disabled magician Chung Ling Soo did with his): but their way of becoming the magician who can perform that specific trick ensures that neither of them actually becomes that magician, because there is no such person—not because it isn't really magic, but because there isn't really a (single) person who performs the trick. More precisely put: for either to achieve that goal, they must be willing to deny their difference from their twin, which would amount to denying the distinctness which is the condition for the possibility of performing the trick their way, the distinctness without which neither would be capable of setting and attaining goals of his own in the first place.

This subsumption of two people into one project is thus not only as striking a case of aesthetic asceticism as is that of Angier; it is equally punitive, sadomasochistic, and self-subverting, as the film makes clear in its presentation of Borden's marriage (and of the love affair he conducts with his assistant Olivia). Sarah, his wife, is not fooled by the trick: or rather, she can tell the difference between the two occupants of the role of her husband, although she interprets it as a difference between the days when her husband's expressions of love are sincere and those when they are not. Sincerity here functions as a criterion of identity because the brother who doesn't love Sarah does love Olivia; hence, each brother spends half his life giving expression to a genuine love for one woman he shares it with, and the other half pretending to have the same feelings for the other.

But this does not, as one of the brothers claims at the film's climax, amount to each having to be satisfied with half a life, and half of the satisfactions available in it. For what Sarah understands as the inconstancy of her husband results in the gradual but entire destruction of their relationship and her own suicide; and what Olivia understands as her lover's cold willingness to marry a woman he doesn't love leads her to break off their relationship. So neither brother can honestly comfort himself by saying that he attains half of the satisfactions of love: the truth is that their deception ensures that none of those satisfactions is available to either of them.

Both Angier's and Borden's ways of performing 'the Transported Man' thus confirm the essentially non-self-identical nature of human being, but only by realizing its self-negating rather than its self-overcoming possibilities. Little wonder that the trick they perform is called 'the Transported Man': for the notion of transport encodes not only the idea of travel (say, process or becoming) but also that of imprisonment (as when criminals from the Old World were transported to the New), and that of ecstasy—the idea of ec-stasis, of standing outside oneself, a condition that one might turn either to confining or to emancipatory use. And these ideas are all vital in articulating a vision of selfhood that Cavell has long argued is internal to Nietzsche's (although not only Nietzsche's) thinking, and which is central to a tradition or dimension of moral concern that might be called perfectionist. One might think of it as a genealogical conception of personhood.

Cavell's version of moral perfectionism—which he distinguishes from others to which that label is often applied by calling it 'Emersonian', thereby declaring its distinctively American physiognomy—cuts across more familiar moral preoccupations with doing one's duty or maximizing the general happiness or cultivating one's virtues. It understands the self or soul as on a journey that begins when it finds itself lost to the world, and it requires a refusal of the present state of society in the name of some further, more cultivated or cultured, state of society as well as of the soul. Such perfectionism further assumes that there is no final, as it were absolutely or perfectly cultivated, state of self and society to be achieved; rather, each given or attained state of self and society always projects or opens up another, unattained but attainable, state, to the realization of which we might commit ourselves, or alternatively whose attractions might be eclipsed by the attained world we already inhabit. In that sense, every attained state is (that is, can present itself as, and be inhabited as) perfect—in need of no further refinement; hence, the primary internal threat to this species of moral perfectionism is that of regarding genuine human individuality as a realizable state of perfection (even if a different one for each individual), rather than as a continuous process of self-perfecting (selfhood as self-improvement or self-overcoming). The most extreme version of that threat is realized when an individual's investment in her attained self is so unquestioning that the very possibility of her present state being otherwise is occluded: this amounts to her living out a false sense of perfect self-coincidence, as if her selfhood were exhausted by and so identical with its current state. Overcoming such self-inflicted falsity may require a relationship with an other—one who exemplifies in her own life the possibility of things being otherwise, and exhibits an impersonal interest in recalling particular others to their own ways of becoming other than they currently are.

The perfectionist self is thus internally split or doubled, essentially non-self-identical even when it relates to its attained state as if it could not be otherwise (for to adopt such a relation is itself something that could be otherwise). Existing as a self is thus a processual or active business of perpetual nextness to or neighbouring of oneself (or its failure)—what Emerson's disciple Thoreau calls being beside ourselves in a sane sense, and what Nietzsche (himself a lifelong venerator of Emerson) might express as a matter of Becoming (or its refusal) rather than Being. And Cavell pointed out that Nietzsche's call for a philosophy of tomorrow and the day after tomorrow deploys a German construction (*morgen und übermorgen*) which parallels his more familiar invocation of the overman (*übermensch*). If we assume that that self-overcoming human being is Nietzsche's way of articulating the Emersonian vision of an individual who privileges her unattained over her attained self, and recall the former's intimate neighbouring of or nextness to the latter, then we can infer that the day after tomorrow—the day in which we realize our own and our society's self-overcoming—is itself not a measurable distance away from our present moment, but rather haunts each such moment as its better or higher self, from which we are separated by nothing (nothing substantial, no external obstacle, only our own unwillingness to realize it).

Returning to *The Prestige* against this background, Angier's use of the Tesla cloning machine can be seen as incarnating the self's capacity to identify itself with an existing state of itself to the point of occluding the possibility of becoming otherwise (reducing self-relation to self-mimesis). Borden's alliance with his brother results in a life in which two essentially self-sufficient selves alternate without relating—each promising a possible life but neither being able to realize itself precisely because the other is simultaneously trying to realize itself (treating non-self-identical becoming as if it were a succession of distinct selves). Nolan's point is not that creativity requires such life-denying forms of self-sacrifice; it is rather that although the nature of human being makes such ascetic deformations of itself possible, it also makes possible their overcoming (and indeed, that being brought to appreciate Angier and Borden as deformations in this sense is a particularly forceful way of articulating what those counter-possibilities are).

The film's ending—more precisely, the culmination of its plot—gestures towards one such counter-possibility, when events force the Borden brothers to separate once and for all, so that the surviving brother becomes capable of wholehearted commitment to a genuinely singular life. Its primary preoccupation turns out to be Jess—Sarah's child, whose future had otherwise threatened to belong to Angier, who had attempted to complete his revenge on Borden by combining coerced access to his version of the trick with equally coerced adoption of Jess (thereby literalizing the etymological point that 'plagiarism'—the form under which scepticism is so often studied in Nolan's work—originally referred to the kidnap of a child). Since the death of one Borden brother signalled the annihilation of their version of that trick, it also made possible Jess's escape from the hollow mockery of family life in which she had thus far been imprisoned. A projected image of life-denying creativity is thus replaced by its life-affirming counterpart: more precisely, newly created life finally comes to take priority over the creations of art, and that demands acknowledging its genealogical nature. For each new life is flesh of another's flesh, emerging from a hybrid network of biological and cultural relations, and ensuring their projection into the future: and the dispute between Angier and Borden could not have begun had either acknowledged the equally genealogical (historically and socially conditioned) originality of artistic creativity.

Of course, Angier's and Borden's competing forms of doubling also have a reflexive significance: for they embody a study of acting as much as one of selfhood, and more specifically imply that the former is an allegory of the latter. In the context of cinema, a study of acting includes the question of how to understand the relation between actor and character; but it is further complicated by the question of how to understand the relation between the human being before the camera and the human something projected on the screen (as the American citizen Humphrey Bogart makes possible the star 'Bogie' whose various incarnations include Philip Marlowe and Rick Blaine). In the film's theatrical world, Borden lacks any capacity for the showmanship essential to a successful magic act, whereas Angier is an effortless performer who lacks the real qualities of the true magician. But Nolan is, naturally enough, primarily interested in what their different modes of self-enactment in the world of the film as such might tell us about cinematic acting. So understood, in the Borden mode of acting, actor disappears into character, although each actor finds that different aspects of the two roles both essay come more naturally to them ('husband', 'lover', 'parent'); whereas in the Angier mode, character dissolves into actor, or more exactly his personae on stage and off amount to versions of himself writ large (even when—as was temporarily the case with his recruitment of Root as a double—that self is another person altogether).

In other words, Angier embodies a conception of acting as self-cloning, as the endless reiteration of the self of the actor; Borden a conception of acting as self-effacement, as the unceasing incarnation of the self of the character. What Borden finds is that absolutely ceding self to the emancipatory othernesss of character is impossible—that the actor's individuality will inevitably limit his range; and what Angier discovers is that absolute or literalized self-cloning amounts to the death of the actor. Taken together, their contrasting fates suggest that, although in cinema the actor will always have priority over the character (insofar as the camera always privileges the embodied individual before it), he can properly exercise that power only if he is willing to acknowledge the camera's unpredictable but decisive power to transfigure him into a screened projection of himself that is created by and determinative of his characters, hence at once confining and ecstatic. In this sense, all cinema actors are Transported Men; and in another but related sense, so are we all.

E. Losing Your Way: Perfectionism, Education, and Individuality in *Insomnia*

As well as returning to the moral complexities of self-examination and confession touched in in *Following* and *Memento*, *Insomnia* (2002) also offers another projection of the doubleness of human being: but whereas the protagonists of *The Prestige* essentially relied on themselves to turn that non-self-identity to emancipatory purposes, this film emphasizes that such self-overcoming is more easily achieved in relation to exemplary others.

Long before the unceasing daylight of the Alaskan town that he's flown into induces debilitating sleeplessness, Will Dormer has already become psychologically and morally disoriented. Despite a long, successful, and spotless career as a detective, he has recently planted evidence in order to ensure the conviction of someone named Dobbs who committed appalling crimes; now Internal Affairs is investigating him, and in particular trying to get his partner Hap Eckhart to betray him in exchange for a lighter punishment. Eckhart obdurately refuses to reject the deal, unconvinced by Dormer's claims that his own conviction would lead to the release of many dangerous criminals; and in the course of their investigation into the case that has brought them to Alaska (the murder of a teenage girl, Kay Connell), Dormer shoots and kills Eckhart when they are chasing the suspected murderer on a foggy beach. When the local police assume that the murderer fired the fatal shot, Dormer doesn't disabuse them, and is consequently forced to cover up his role in various ways; but the murderer saw him shoot Eckhart, and threatens to make this public unless Dormer helps to ensure that the local police don't catch him.

The film presents Dormer as genuinely uncertain whether his shooting of Eckhart was purely a matter of mistaking him for the murderer in the fog (thereby establishing his internal relation to Dom Cobb, Leonard Shelby, Bill, Borden, and Angier). It's clear that he didn't deliberately seek to kill him; and the film leaves it perfectly open for Dormer and us to regard what happened as a terrible accident that was essentially due to factors beyond Dormer's control—a piece of bad moral luck. This would not leave him morally unscathed, since—despite the contributory role of the fog, Eckhart's own carelessness about his position in relation to the other police, and the murderer's already-demonstrated willingness to shoot at his pursuers on sight—Dormer could also have taken more care to identify the figure at which he was firing. Rather than simply accept this limited mode of self-indictment, however, Dormer finds it impossible to exclude the possibility that on a subconscious or unconscious level he meant to do what he did. In part, this is because he is well aware that Eckhart now poses a threat to his own reputation and career (with all the collateral damage that would go with it); in part, it is because he knows that he has already acted in a manner contrary to everything he stands for as a policeman (with respect to Dobbs), and so he can no longer rest confidently in a sense of his own integrity. And this latter issue is more fundamental, for it puts in question the reliability of any of the deliverances of his own self-scrutiny.

The Dormer who planted evidence on Dobbs is not the Dormer whose career and life preceded that case: he's someone who has shown himself willing to do his job in ways that he had always hitherto regarded as absolutely out of the question, as morally (rather than psychologically or physically) impossible—one of those courses of action whose exclusion from consideration regardless of their feasibility or potential benefits partly constitutes his identity as a moral being. It is to this sense of necessity and possibility that Luther was adverting when he said 'Here I stand: I can do no other'. So the Dormer we encounter in Alaska, who knows that he actually did what he was and continues to be absolutely opposed to doing, cannot exclude the possibility that he could do such things again. He no longer knows who he is, morally speaking.

Two people Dormer meets in Alaska embody answers to that question. Ellie Burr is a young local police officer for whom Dormer is a hero: he represents her career ideal, the kind of detective she aspires to be; and, both in the Connell investigation and in her later assignment to write up a report on Eckhart's death, she seeks to apply Dormer's example. Walter Finch is a writer of crime novels, and the murderer Dormer has come to catch: he represents his killing of Kay as something less than a murder, as caused by her humiliation of him when he expresses his attraction to her and then by his fear of her screaming. On this basis, he claims kinship with Dormer, repeatedly aligning himself with his supposed pursuer as he blackmails him into ensuring his own safety (for example, when he attempts to frame Kay's boyfriend Randy, just as Dormer proved willing to leave Finch in the frame for Eckhart's death).

Finch thus represents the possibility that Dormer will become the kind of person for whom a denial of responsibility for individual error, and a more general willingness to let the end justify the means, is not only morally possible but morally requisite: it would be a mode of self-exculpation understood as a mode of self-improvement—as access to a deeper understanding of self and world that depends upon a refusal properly to scrutinize the roots of one's thoughts and deeds in ways that allow for potentially radical self-criticism. Burr, by contrast, embodies the attraction of recovering Dormer's currently lost best self: her willingness to regard him as her educator sustains his ability to stay in touch with his earlier self-understanding, and thereby fulfil his role as exemplar for her despite his inability to realize its demands elsewhere in his life.

As the film unfolds, Dormer struggles to hold open his capacity to be educated by Burr, which the film presents as a matter of maintaining his continuing ability to educate her—as when he deliberately invites her to dig deeper into Eckhart's death despite the fact that she was initially willing to exonerate him, and so unwittingly put her name to a falsehood because of her respect for him. It is thus only when his falling away from his best self threatens to induce a similar fate in another that he can recover the capacity to resist it. At the same time, he struggles to resist conforming to Finch's malign purposes. Whilst feeling unable simply to reveal what Finch has done and is doing, since it will entail revealing what he has done and is doing, Dormer first attempts to apply a version of his Dobbs tactic against Finch (planting the gun with which Eckhart was shot in Finch's apartment), only to discover that Finch not only finds it but uses it to frame Randy. This illustrates exactly the weakness that Kantians see in consequentialist moral thinking: if one stakes one's moral standing on getting the causal consequences of one's actions to come out right, one opens oneself to the ineliminable risk of their coming out catastrophically wrong (since they work themselves out in a territory that is subject to sheer contingency, to luck beyond the self's control), and in ways that affect others as well as oneself.

The fact that the actual outcome in this case is not just a failure to indict the guilty man but a successful framing of an innocent one finally leads Dormer to end the agonizingly purgatorial condition of suspended animation that he has endured for days, and to side with the state of the self that Burr exemplifies and sustains rather than the one Finch instantiates. Dormer risks his life to save Burr from Finch, and his dying words—which conclude the film's conclusion—instruct Burr to reveal the full truth about himself rather than to sacrifice her principles for the sake of preserving his reputation: 'Don't lose your way.' But he is only in a position to offer this advice because she has embodied for him the possibility of reoccupying the perspective on self and others from which alone such guidance can be issued; and neither he nor we will be in a position to see whether, and how, Burr responds to it.

On this depiction of the matter, then, perfectionist self-overcoming crucially depends upon a pedagogical relationship between those who aspire to it. Prioritizing Becoming over Being in this sense will involve a willingness to help others to do the same, without demanding that the way that opens up for them must be identical with one's own. What Burr must not lose is the direction that is truly hers, her own way of being the kind of police officer that Dormer originally and ultimately was, in his own way.

For many viewers of this film, of course, it is precisely the nature of this ending—and the foregrounding of the relationship between Burr and Dormer that prepares for it—that reveals its relative weakness within Nolan's body of work. More specifically, it is taken to reflect the malign forces that inevitably work upon an independent director when he first enters the Hollywood mainstream, especially when he does so in order to remake a successful European film. For in the original version of *Insomnia*, which was directed by Erik Skjoldbaerg and starred Stellan Skarsgård, the Swedish police officer who flies into Norway to help with the hunt for a murderer is named Engström, and his nature and experiences differ from Al Pacino's Dormer in a number of ways.

Most evidently, Engström carries with him no prior moral failing: an embarrassing tale is told of his being caught up at the wrong end of a police raid, but otherwise his shooting of his partner, Erik Vik, and his consequent failure to correct the Norwegian police's assumption that the murderer was responsible, are presented as his first moral misstep. Having taken it, however, he then heads speedily and decisively towards the dark side as his insomnia intensifies: he covers his own tracks by shooting a local dog (where Dormer uses one that is already dead) and by straightforwardly attempting to deceive the officer who is investigating his partner's death, who is roughly his age and who shows no signs of hero worship; he collaborates with the murderer with far less hesitation and scruple than Dormer does; he attempts to rape the friendly manager of the hotel in which he is staying (where Dormer simply talks to her); and he leaves Norway physically intact, having killed the murderer and escaped official responsibility for killing his partner, but his concluding stare into the camera strongly suggests that his soul has suffered irreparable damage.

One way of reading Nolan's adaptations of this original tale—or at least the adaptations in the script with which he had to work—is as standard Hollywood ways of smoothing away its psychologically and morally rough edges so as to make the protagonist more palatable both to the narcissistic star who is playing him and to the audience's presumed aversion to challenging material, at the familiar cost of sacrificing whatever made the original sufficiently distinctive and aesthetically interesting to generate the desire for a remake. Another way is to see them as intelligently responsive to real limitations in the original—to what one might call its unearned bleakness of spirit: to its apparent belief that demotivating, accelerating, and absolutizing Engström's moral disintegration makes the film's vision courageously realistic as opposed to cheaply nihilistic.

What makes Nolan's version superior is his much more nuanced and complex handling of Dormer's predicament. Two features of this handling stand out, but the crucial one is his decision to present Dormer as having already suffered an inexplicable moral lapse before the events portrayed on screen. Call this Dormer's original sin: although that idea is often taken to be Christianity's transparently unsuccessful attempt to explain the human tendency to commit sin (an attempt which simply leads us to ask what motivated this original fall into sin), it would be better understood as Christianity's way of saying that it lies beyond explanatory representation in terms of the psychological and moral resources we usually employ in grasping human behaviour. It is, in other words, a way of acknowledging rather than denying the inexplicability of human evil.

Because Skjoldbaerg's film makes Engström's shooting of Vik into his original sin, it presents itself to us as attempting to represent that which is by its nature beyond representation; more specifically, it embodies the mythically shallow suggestion that there is a moment in our lives when we fall into sinfulness, rather than the mythologically deeper suggestion that we have always already so fallen. By displacing Dormer's original fall beyond or before his film's representational grasp—more precisely, by presenting a moment from it (in which blood soaks into white fabric) as the film's originating moment, and so ensuring that its significance reveals itself to us only retrospectively, hence as having always already happened—Nolan makes it clear that he cleaves to the deeper myth.

And as a result, he can offer a more sophisticated presentation of what that fallen state is actually like. For when Dormer shoots Eckhart, his ensuing paralysis reveals the constitutive limits of the techniques of scrupulous self-examination that Christianity offers as a mode of response to its perceptions of our fallenness. I said earlier that Dormer can't be sure whether on some level he meant to shoot Eckhart; but it would be more accurate to say that there is nothing here—no spiritual fact of the matter about this or any other specific action—for him to be certain (or uncertain) about. First, because—given that no determinate period of self-examination could suffice to exclude the possibility of further blame-relevant revelations—nothing could count as establishing a conclusion with certainty (this is a version of Coetzee's point about confession and closure); and second, because if we are all originally sinful, then nothing we do can ever be entirely free of moral taint. Nolan's Dormer haunts his own existence in Alaska in such a way that he affirms the constitutive indeterminacy of our responsibility for each specific thought and deed, and the equally constitutive overdetermination of that responsibility (by virtue of our fallen nature). Such a carefully projected image of the human condition is more than enough to generate sleepless nights in its audience.

F. Asceticism, Morality, and the Will to Truth: The 'Dark Knight' Trilogy

As Quentin Tarantino famously emphasized, Superman and Batman are anomalous in the comic book superhero milieu: Superman is not human (Clark Kent being merely the human guise of an alien from the planet Krypton), and Batman has no superpowers—he is the alter ego of the extraordinarily wealthy but human, all-too-human Bruce Wayne (who is not a mutant, has not been bitten by a radioactive spider, has not been scientifically enhanced...). One might say that Batman's real superpower is the interweaving of technology and theatricality: in order to turn fear against those who prey on the fearful, and more specifically to defend the forces of law and order against those who oppose them—hence, to defend justice (and so the good) against injustice (or evil), Wayne constructs a persona whose capacities seem to outstrip what is humanly possible—flight, invisibility, invulnerability to weapons, overwhelming physical force—but are in fact the application of cutting-edge technological advances and age-old magician's tricks (techniques of dazzlement and distraction).

Unsurprisingly from a Nietzschean point of view, this last-ditch defence of the values of slave morality requires that Wayne take on an exceptionally ascetic form of life. In order to be Batman, and so to appear essentially invulnerable to the worst that criminals can throw at him, he has to be in the best possible physical condition, and to be extremely skilful in the use of his technological and theatrical methods. In other words, he has to devote the best resources of science and art to the defence of morality, and undergo an immensely demanding self-disciplinary regime. On the physical level, this entails a punitive training schedule whose purpose is for him to reach the point at which the physical punishment he takes from Batman's enemies becomes manageable. But it also entails continuing to live a form of life as Bruce Wayne which will ensure that he is never connected to Batman (thus protecting his loved ones). So he acts the part of a self-indulgent playboy, but it is made plain throughout that he derives no real pleasure from the wine, women, and fast cars to which he exclusively devotes himself when in the public eye. His indulgence in bodily pleasures is thus merely apparent: in reality, it is a mode of monkish life-denial which distances him from the only woman he loves, and which further denies him any of the recognition due to his willingness to put his life on the line for his fellow citizens each night as Batman.

Rachel worries whether Bruce's commitment to that symbol has turned the rest of his existence into a mask for his real identity as Batman; but the truth is rather different. It is not that one side of his identity is real and the other a symbol, with his (and our) task being that of determining which is which: that would imply that self-knowledge is a matter of establishing which single description of oneself is the correct one. The question is not: 'is Bruce Wayne Batman or a playboy?' For in order to be Bruce Wayne, Bruce has to be both Batman and a playboy, which means that he has to be neither. To be who he is he has to present himself as, and to be absent from, both halves of his new sadomasochistic mode of existence (as the Borden brothers were from theirs)—quite as if he has to vanish altogether if his moral vision is to be sustained. The challenge for him is to find a way of turning that self-abnegation to positive account, to discover a mode of absenting himself that will make possible the recovery of a genuinely human life for himself. But it will take three movies for Bruce Wayne to realize that this is the conclusion his story demands, and then to find a way of realizing it—of making it real.

Why, however, construct this particular persona in the service of the ascetic ideal? Why create and manipulate this kind of fear—the fear of bats? The first film in Nolan's trilogy (*Batman Begins*, 2005) offers an explanation that reformulates the mythology established in his graphic-novel sources. For Nolan's Bruce Wayne is shown to have acquired a particular fear of bats as a result of a childhood accident, when he falls down a disused well in the grounds of the Wayne mansion, and disturbs a bat colony whose members flutter around and fly past him in an apparently endless stream before he is rescued. This primal trauma is then shown to play a crucial role in the event that is usually regarded as the canonical origin of Wayne's fearsome alter ego. For Bruce's phobia is reactivated by the demonic creatures he sees during a performance of Boito's opera *Mefistofele* (not the film *The Mask of Zorro*, as in the original graphic novels); this is why his father brings the family out of the opera house early, and into the hands of the mugger who kills him and his wife.

This revision of his sources allows Nolan to tie together Wayne's desire to avenge his parents' death and the bat-persona he chooses as a vehicle in a number of ways. First, it means that Wayne feels personally responsible for his parents' death: if he had properly mastered his fear of bats, they wouldn't have needed to leave the opera house. Second, it ties together the bats and the inhabitants of Gotham's criminal underworld, ensuring that in Wayne's psyche the threat of lawlessness is akin to that of the bats—it has overwhelming weight of numbers, it lurks in the dark, it sucks the lifeblood of its victims, and it attacks indiscriminately, without moral justification or psychological provocation. Moreover, since the bats are linked to the criminals through the demons, Wayne's phobia with respect to both acquires a supernatural dimension, and more specifically a religious one (as if both the animals and the lawbreakers are the devil's disciples).

This operatic inflection is reinforced by the narrative context Nolan presents for Wayne's childhood accident. For in the film's first sequence, we see him chasing Rachel in order to discover what she has come across somewhere in the grounds (to know what she knows). When he catches her, she reveals that it is an arrowhead; he then claims it as his possession and runs off with it, as Rachel gives chase, until he tumbles into the well and has to be rescued by his father. In other words, the young Bruce Wayne falls because he takes an archaic or archetypal item of knowledge offered to him by a young woman in a hitherto-paradisal garden; he then has to be rescued by his godlike father; but the mark of this original sin re-expresses itself later in his life and in such a way as to deprive him of his intimate connection with that divine source of authority. It's the origin story from which all Western origin stories derive—straight from the book of Genesis (and recognizably reworking the strategy employed in *Insomnia*).

Matters are, however, further complicated by the moral his father encourages him to draw from his traumatic experience. Echoing an idea of Rousseau's about the primal encounter of any solitary human being with other such beings, Thomas Wayne tells Bruce that the bats attacked him because they were afraid of him—because he was so much bigger than them; and he further claims that all creatures feel fear, especially the scary ones. On the surface, this guides Bruce towards his anti-criminality strategy: if scary creatures are especially prone to fear, then embodying an appropriately fearsome object will be a particularly effective way of disabling them. But if Thomas is right about this, it also follows that bats are not genuinely fearsome, and so that the human creatures who for all the world resemble bats are not genuinely fearsome either. Indeed, if they prove to have the same disabling fear of bats that Bruce Wayne has, then what exactly is the difference between him and them?

Little wonder that one of Wayne's first outings as Batman concludes with him using the gangster Falcone's unconscious body strapped against a spotlight in order to project his Bat-symbol onto Gotham's night sky. And this invocation of the idea of projection as well as identification seems entirely fitting. After all, if what seems fearsome to you is acting in a fear-inducing way only because you induce fear in it, then the external objects of your fear are only proxies for something fearsome about yourself: and since what goes proxy for that internal feature is their misinterpreted expressions of fear, then what you're afraid of in yourself must be your own expressions of fear.

Taken one way, this amounts to the claim that in Batman's world, no genuinely fearsome things are to be found—that it is only our mutually reinforcing fearful responses to one another that generate a collective hallucination of one another as fearsome. This is why the plot of *Batman Begins* is threaded through with hallucinogenic experiences, whose source is the blue flower that Wayne brings to the training temple of the League of Shadows: it provides the drugs that the Scarecrow uses to manipulate his allies and enemies during his rule over Arkham Asylum, and that Rā's al Ghūl intends to employ to spread chaos amongst the populace of Gotham. Taken this way, the solution to our problems is to dissipate the hallucination—to reveal the threatening aspect of people and things as mere appearance, and to disclose the still-problematic but essentially mundane and manageable reality underneath. Taken another way, however, this hallucinatory logic of fear tells us that there is one thing that we find truly fearsome: our fearfulness—our vulnerability to fear. And if Bruce Wayne and his criminal adversaries are alike in this respect, then the primary threat to law and order in this mythology is the fact that we terrify ourselves—that we are terrified by our capacity to be traumatically marked by our experiences, and so by our more general vulnerability to the world we inhabit: it is a fear of our finitude (a fear that we are now in a position to see may be lurking beneath Nietzsche's recurrent, ferociously expressed, contempt for the weak and feeble amongst the human herd: this aspect of his aversion to the advocates and beneficiaries of asceticism would then itself amount to an aversion to life). And the solution to this problem is far less easy to identify, since nothing is more human than our desire to deny the human.

Although Batman's response to the League of Shadows plainly works with the first interpretation, aspiring only to dissipate hallucinated fears in the name of a sane reality, *Batman Begins* has an epilogue which identifies the possible limits of this strategy. Lieutenant Gordon acknowledges what Batman has achieved, but he also notes that many of the liberated Asylum residents remain uncaptured, and that he expects the criminal underworld to mount an escalated response to Batman's arrival on the scene. When the police get Kevlar vests, the criminals get armour-piercing rounds; so when a man starts wearing a mask and jumping off rooftops, his adversaries can confidently be predicted to turn an enhanced version of the same tactics against him. Then Gordon shows Batman a new criminal's calling card—a Joker.

In other words, the Joker is what happens if you create in others the very thing that creates fear in you: a man whose mode of being mimics your own, but in a way which heightens and thereby undercuts everything on which you are staking that self-denying divided existence—the sharp division between mask and face (the Joker's mask is gradually disintegrating make-up, with his clown's smile carved into his flesh), the belief in the value of goodness and truth (as essentially opposed to evil and falsehood), and a sense of the absolute, world-consuming seriousness of all these things. *The Dark Knight* (2008) tracks the traumatic consequences of Wayne's confrontation with this parody of his modus operandi.

There is clearly a Nietzschean aspect (or rather, an aspect of what everyone thinks of as Nietzschean) to the Joker. It's not so much that he opposes to Batman's identification with self-denial, goodness, and truth an equal and opposite identification with self-indulgence, evil, and falsehood; it's more that he treats all these binary oppositions as imposters—as essentially ludicrous, part of a game that preoccupies the bad guys as much as the good guys, but that has no basis in reality. Perhaps most fundamentally of all, however, he objects to the idea of system as such: as he explains to Harvey Dent, his power over his opponent is at root dependent on his lack of interest in plans, methods, rules, and schemes. He is a dog chasing cars, an agent of chaos: if acting presupposes a set of nested reasons for acting, or a secure knowledge of why he is doing what he does, then he denies being an agent at all. As Alfred puts it, such people can't be bought, bullied, reasoned, or negotiated with: they just want to watch the world burn. The Joker represents the idea that there is no meaningful structure inherent in things, by aspiring to embody the negation of agency, and so the meaninglessness of selfhood.

On the other hand, this same person plainly feels the need to educate Gotham in what he takes to be the real way of the world. He stages his ferry version of the prisoner's dilemma to teach its citizens that ordinary morality crumbles when confronted with the animal imperatives of survival, and he corrupts Harvey Dent in order to show that even the most shining white knight is capable of switching allegiance to the dark side when the world's randomness—its independence of the human will or of any other mode of significance—causes sufficient harm to himself and those he loves. And although it is the real prisoners on the ferry who show Gotham's citizens a solution to their dilemma, Dent's degradation is successfully engineered: having previously utilized the mere appearance of chance to bring about moral outcomes (by using a two-headed coin), he now uses its reality (the same coin, but with one side blackened by the fire that disfigured him) to wreak vengeance on all who contributed to his suffering, and on the very idea of moral meaning (since their guilt now leads to punishment only if a coin-toss licenses it).

But Dent's reaction is an overreaction: having previously assumed an absolute ability to make the world bend to his moral will, he now assumes the absolute pointlessness of any attempt to do so. And such a vision of morality's necessary impotence will appear compulsory only from the perspective of someone previously possessed by a fantasy of its necessary omnipotence. From the fact that the rain falls on the just and the unjust alike it does not follow that there is no real difference between justice and injustice, or between justice and chance: it simply shows that justice and morality are not written into the nature of things—that their authority is inextricable from human investments in them (although not reducible to those investments), and their implementation accordingly depends upon our willingness to continue to act upon them in the face of the inevitable risk of the world's resistance. It is the citizens and prisoners on the ferries who learn to appreciate this more naturalistic perspective on morality and its demands: they give us reason to believe that our sense of one another as truly fearsome is a hallucination generated by our fearful responses, rather than a disclosure of how things really are.

Although the Joker tries to shrug off the failure of his ferry plot, this turn of events makes it clear that his position is not really any more internally stable than Dent's. After all, he utilizes a great deal of careful planning in order to bring about this version of the prisoner's dilemma (as well as in reducing Gotham to chaos); when those on the ferries fail to act as he requires, he steps in so as to try to ensure his preferred outcome; and most importantly of all, in doing all this, he regards himself as revealing the truth about Gotham, morality, and human nature to its citizens. In other words, his insistent hostility to Batman's incarnation of the will to truth is itself a manifestation of it: he wants to reveal the truth about the truth on which Batman's existence is predicated, but he doesn't seem to appreciate that that could only be his goal if it is possible—at least in principle—to criticize the ascetic, life-denying will to truth without abandoning the very idea of truth.

Given this kinship between the Joker and his adversary, it isn't surprising that *The Dark Knight* ends at a point which suggests that Batman's position embodies a complementary kind of internal instability. For in order to obviate the damage that might be done to the forces of law and order in Gotham by the revelation of Dent's Joker-induced criminality, Batman and Gordon conspire to conceal it. They jointly agree to hold Batman responsible for Dent's villainy and his death, and thereby to maintain Dent's heroic persona with a view to introducing exceptionally stringent laws against Gotham's underworld as a memorial to his self-sacrifice. Here, the ascetic ideal of the scapegoat is deployed in such a way as to utilize falsehood as a means to supposedly good and truthful ends: the will to truth finds itself having to consort with its own worst enemy in order to maintain its own absoluteness. *The Dark Knight Rises* (2012) investigates the consequences.

And what it suggests is that substituting Dent's legend for that of Batman contained the seeds of its own destruction.[11] Commissioner Gordon has spent eight years living with a guilty conscience over his part in this deception: he tries and fails to confess the truth at a celebration of Harvey Dent Day, but the text of that speech falls into the hands of Bane, who broadcasts it to Gotham's population as the climactic element in his overthrow of Gotham's system of law and order. By showing that those in positions of authority have violated their own principles in order to impose draconian penalties against criminals and more generally to preserve the status quo, allowing the rich to live large and leave so little for the rest, Gordon's words work to undermine the moral basis for their imprisonment, and so license Bane to open the jails and place the justice system in the hands of the Scarecrow and his like—a parody of law that facilitates the lawlessness that Bane wants to use to bring the decadent civilization of Gotham to the fiery end that his League of Shadows has long sought.

The resultant anarchy (bounded by a ferociously policed martial law) could be taken to show that the Joker was right after all—that when shown the full truth about the social order and its roots in human nature, human beings will return to a violent, brutish, and essentially self-interested state of nature. But it might rather show that what causes such chaos is a sense of disillusionment entirely created by

---

[11] This, I take it, is why McGowan's recent paper 'Stumbling over the Superhero: Christopher Nolan's Victories and Compromises' (in J. Furby and S. Joy (eds.), *The Cinema of Christopher Nolan* (London: Wallflower Press, 2015])) expresses a rather stronger sense of Nolan's having been cinematically and philosophically compromised by his involvement with this franchise than his earlier book allowed. For although the ending of the second 'Dark Knight' film might plausibly have seemed to express a sense of the ontological primacy of the lie, the third film gives the lie to that appearance.

our inability to cleave to the truth even when what it might reveal—about us, about our heroes, and so about our values—proves hard to accept. Could the forces of law and order have overcome Gotham's criminal underworld without the benefit of the draconian Dent Act, and so without canonizing Dent himself? Or would a Gotham less prone to place its faith in a fantasy of moral heroism also have proved less open to manipulation by Bane?

It's clear what Commissioner Gordon believes. He blames himself for contributing to the cover-up; and his confessional speech praises Batman as the true exemplar of moral heroism, not just for avoiding Dent's pathological excesses but for being willing to accept responsibility for them himself in order to allow Gotham to retain Dent as a symbol of hope. Gordon certainly tries to atone for his sins by leading the resistance against Bane's martial law. But he doesn't make his confession willingly; and the assumption on which that confession is based in fact replicates Dent's misconception of good and evil, for it amounts to the belief that in order for a man to exemplify goodness, he must be absolved of any taint of evil—as if continued faith in morality depends upon occluding the possibility that a good man might also have vices, and even be destroyed by the injurious unfolding of sheer contingency.

What does Batman—or rather Bruce Wayne—believe? The evolution of his self-understanding is articulated and tracked in the film in terms of his shifting relations with three women. Rachel Dawes died at the hands of the Joker, but Wayne continues to be haunted by her memory—or more precisely, by his false belief that she continued to be in love with him and would have chosen him over Dent had she lived. When Alfred (declaring that 'Maybe it's time we all stopped trying to outsmart the truth and just let it have its day') reveals that she had in fact decided to marry Dent—and said as much in a letter to Wayne that Alfred burnt to save him further pain—Wayne initially reacts to this confession about Rachel's confession by banishing him. But he also begins to explore the possibilities of a more intimate relationship with Miranda Tait and Selina Kyle, which suggests a deeper inability to deny the truth of Alfred's revelation, or its potentially redemptive (life-preserving and life-enhancing) power. Since Rachel not only preferred Dent to Wayne, but in doing so underlined the extent to which she embodied the same uncomplicated, absolute relationship to goodness, Wayne's willingness to move on from her memory suggests that he is beginning to appreciate the damaging limitations of the conception of moral heroism that Dawes and Dent shared.

In one sense, the remainder of the film concerns itself with Wayne's way of working towards the choice of Kyle over Tait—a choice that is admittedly partly made for him when Tait tries to kill him and reveals herself as Bain's partner and master. Nevertheless, the success of his attempts to save Gotham from their depredations importantly depends on his continued identification with certain qualities Miranda represents. For she was the only other person who proved able to escape from the prison to which Bane consigns Wayne; so his return to Gotham depends upon his ability to do what she did—to make the leap to the top of the vast well without a rope, and so the willingness to recover his capacity for fear: the fear of death that drove her, and that will drive him. But since Wayne's creation of Batman was his means of mastering the primal fearfulness he first suffered at the bottom of another well (by embodying it in order to turn it upon others), then when he reinhabits his Batman persona after his escape from the prison well, it must be on a rather different, and potentially unstable or provisional basis.

That basis certainly retains its indebtedness to the ascetic ideal that has always driven him. If anything, the events of *The Dark Knight Rises* intensify that indebtedness: for at this point in his life, Wayne's body is giving up on him (he needs a caliper on one knee even to walk properly), and Bane is anyway more than capable of helping that process along. Immune to Wayne's theatricality, and able to turn his technological resources against him (by simply stealing the contents of Fox's armoury), he reduces his opponent to a broken-backed creature whose spirit is being tortured by Gotham's descent into chaos and his own inability to save it. But Wayne responds to this meticulous dismemberment of his realization of the ascetic ideal by doubling down on it. So he embarks on an intensified sadomasochistic regimen to restore his body and liberate himself from enforced impotence; he defeats Bain in physical combat in classic slave morality style, by turning his immensely strong body against itself (damaging his anaesthetic mask, and thereby returning him to a state of continuous, internally generated agony); and the way in which he saves Gotham is by flying the nuclear bomb out to sea in the Bat before it explodes, and apparently perishing in the explosion himself—an apotheosis of self-sacrifice.

On the other hand, this martyrdom turns out to be mere appearance. As Lucius Fox discovers, Wayne had secretly repaired the Bat's autopilot function, and so was able to eject from the plane before the bomb went off; and as Alfred discovers, this makes it possible for him to leave Batman behind, and to lead an anonymous but normal life in Italy. In other words, Wayne uses all his technological and theatrical skills to produce a performance of pure altruism: he thereby creates an ascetic legend that is set in stone (a granite statue that becomes the object of civic worship), but he liberates himself from the necessity to continue enacting or embodying it.

Why is this not simply a reiteration of the fatal strategy that Bane exploited— that of grounding civic virtue on a falsehood? Because there are falsehoods and falsehoods; more precisely, one might say that there are myths which are mythically false and myths which are mythically true. We have seen why the Dent legend was mythically false—damaging to the values it claimed to embody and to the people who prized them, insidiously disorienting, and impossible to live with (to live) over the long run. In what ways is the Batman legend mythically true? To begin with, there is a significant sense in which this event does constitute an act of existential self-sacrifice on Wayne's part. His feigned death entails that he has to give up the wealth that facilitated the combination of technological and theatrical resources that made Batman possible, and more generally to give up whatever satisfactions his own inhabitation of that persona gave him. But at the same time, his strategy frees the Batman persona from its essential personal connection to Bruce Wayne, and so leaves it open to inhabitation by others—in particular, by the police officer Blake, to whom Wayne bequeaths the Batcave and all that it represents, and whose first name turns out to be Robin. And this moment of potential inheritance realizes one of Wayne's most significant initial goals when he constructed this persona—the idea that anyone and everyone could be Batman, that this persona embodied a possibility of moral exemplarity that could in principle be realized by any citizen (rich or poor). For Bruce utterly to relinquish the belief that only he could rescue Gotham, or represent hope for its citizens, is truly an act of radical self-transformation for the orphaned boy so long in thrall to his childhood playmate's fantasy of moral omnipotence and purity (the ancient arrowhead of her mode of cognizing good and evil).

And what permits this achievement of perfectionist self-overcoming is the woman with whom Alfred finds him sharing a drink in Italy, the woman now wearing his mother's pearl necklace—Selina Kyle, otherwise known as Catwoman. For Kyle is someone who is neither absolutely good nor absolutely evil: she is a burglar who was willing to betray Batman to Bane for her own purposes, but she is also someone who spurns the chance of escape from Gotham's anarchy in favour of allying with Batman against the League of Shadows, and so shows her ability and willingness for self-transformation (for achieving a clean slate not by trying to erase the past but by atoning for it, rather than refusing to let go of it, as Dawes refuses to allow Wayne to put Batman behind him, and Tait refuses to move on from her punitive father's death). She is, in other words, an ordinary person, with an everyday mixture of virtues and vices, always capable of moral improvement but never deluding herself into thinking that she might be perfect. In choosing an unremarkable and unpredictable life with her over life with Batman, that embodiment of his fear of his own fearfulness, Bruce Wayne finally achieves the kind of non-ascetic mastery over himself, the sane reality beneath the hallucinogenic appearances, that he has been seeking all his life.

One might say the same thing about Nolan's adaptation of his sources in this trilogy: what he seeks to present above all is the comprehensible reality behind the comic novels' hallucinogenic appearances, or more precisely, to present the fantastic as real—to show that what appears to be utterly fantastic is the carefully controlled effect of credible technological and theatrical resources driven by recognizable psychological causes, hence grounded in reality rather than in whatever one takes the opposite of reality to be (the supernatural, or the superhuman). And Nolan has his own version of technological theatricality, or theatrical technology, to rely upon in achieving this reality effect: not just very high quality cinematic resources of the familiar kind (acting, scriptwriting, production design, and costume) but a commitment to analogue rather than digital film, to increasing use of IMAX cameras, and to achieving as much as possible of the film's effects in-camera rather than by CGI.

Those joint commitments place demands on Nolan (and his collaborators) that are as intense and unremitting as those placed on Bruce Wayne by his desire to bring his Batman persona into existence. Just as Wayne has to convince his criminal audiences that they really are encountering a cross between a bat and a man, so Nolan's action sequences actually have to be realized in front of a camera that captures images with very high resolution (rather than being produced by manipulations of their content). There is plainly something ascetic about these practices, especially when they are applied to a subject matter whose nature is essentially fantastic: it is, after all, no accident that the advent of CGI has fuelled a virtual colonization of mainstream Hollywood movies by superhero genres deriving from graphic novels—a medium whose capacity to represent violations of nature and logic seemed to defy convincing adaptation by means of predigital cinematic resources. It is thus particularly clear in the case of the Batman trilogy that Nolan's methods close off far easier ways of achieving what many would call the same result, and they make sadomasochistic demands on everyone involved, not just the director—and yet his collaborators keep on coming back for more of the same excessive expenditure of painful effort.

But of course, Nolan and his team would deny that digitally captured and manipulated images would provide the same experience for the viewer as his own practices do. Take the opening sequence of *The Dark Knight*, which opens with a travelling shot over the rooftops of daytime Gotham that closes in on a wall of high-rise windows as one pane of glass is shattered to reveal criminals initiating a complex assault on a bank. Given that this sequence was the first one in the trilogy to be shot in IMAX, that exploding pane also looks very much like the film's acknowledgement of an indebtedness to the medium of the graphic novel that it intends to transcend (as this array of static panels becomes genuinely animated by moving pictures) and its declaration of war against the digital (for which images consist of grids of pixels, each of which is discontinuous from the others and so is subject to independent manipulation or even obliteration). It's as if Nolan is saying that no image with an underlying structure akin to that grid of panes could possibly have the depth and texture, and hence the immersive reality effect, that this presentation of such a grid effortlessly achieves—that he proposes to meet the intensified technical challenges that are posed by his aesthetic decision to take his creature of the night from the gloomy shadows of its comic-book origins (captured in *Batman Begins*) into the bright light of the sun flooding into business offices or the neon that illuminates subterranean concrete bunkers: into the supposedly transparent and affectless (but in truth fantasy-infused) environments of modernity.

By offering such a realistic portrayal of narratives whose medium is that of fantasy, Nolan declares that fantasy and reality are not, or not simply, opposites. As Cavell points out:

> It is a poor idea of fantasy which takes it to be a world apart from reality, a world clearly showing its unreality. Fantasy is precisely what reality can be confused with. It is through fantasy that our conviction of the worth of reality is established; to forego our fantasies would be to forego our touch with the world. And does someone claim to know the specific balance sanity must sustain between the elaborating demands of self and world, some neat way of keeping soul and body together?   (WV, 85)

It is not hard to see how Bruce Wayne's narrative arc tracks his struggle to sustain some, or any, kind of balance between the demands of self and world, or to see how he and Selina Kyle find one another, and so find worth in their existence, through their willingness to inhabit and enact their fantasies of themselves (as well as their best imaginings of each other). It may be less easy to see that Nolan's IMAX-centred practices imply a critique of digital cinema as something which so clearly shows the unreality of the fantasies it so frictionlessly depicts that it blocks us from appreciating the extent to which reality is deeply infused with our own projections of fantasy.

This leads Nolan to question the extent to which we are, and are not, screened from fantasy by the screen on which such fantastic tales (and the fictional worlds of narrative cinema as such) are projected—to query the absoluteness of the division between the world of the film and the world of its viewers (a division to which his career-long commitment to immersive cinematic experience was always likely to bring him into conflict). Take the Batmobile: it's well known just how much time and effort Nolan and his collaborators devoted to constructing a working vehicle that could convincingly withstand the camera's gaze as Bruce Wayne's adapted military prototype. We can accordingly take it as a figure for the extent to which, as one might put it, Wayne's and Nolan's resources aren't so much aimed at the creation of two corresponding things (the vehicle and its cinematic representation) as at the creation of one thing that exists both in the world of the film and in the world in which that film is projected. And this amounts to a critical interrogation of one of the usual structural conditions of viewing the world of a film—that since the objects and people that inhabit it can always be presented as having whatever properties are possessed by those inhabiting the real world (and with extreme ease in the case of digital manipulation), the only essential difference between them is that the former do not exist. With respect to Nolan's work, it's as if he aspires to a cinematic mode of presenting an object or event as part of the film world which will engender in its viewers the conviction that that very object exists in the real world (even if not with every property or feature it possesses in the world of the film).

G. Pure Cinema, Realism, and Modernism: *Interstellar* and *Dunkirk*

The pivotal sequence in *Interstellar* (2014) concerns Cooper's attempts to communicate quantum data acquired from a black hole (by the articulated machine TARS) to his daughter, Murph, on Earth. She is trying to establish a theoretical scientific grounding for the technology required to build the ships that will allow the dying planet's population to be evacuated into space, but cannot effect the necessary reconciliation of relativity theory with that of quantum mechanics without that information. The problem Cooper, and the film, confronts in getting that data to Murph is that his interstellar journey (attempting to identify humanly habitable planets) has taken him via a wormhole to regions of space from which standard means of communication are impossible, and near to a black hole whose gravitational strength has slowed time for him. During the months of his voyage, years have elapsed on Earth, so that the 10-year-old child he left behind is now a 40-year-old woman, and the food-supply problems to which she is attempting to facilitate a last-ditch response are now critical. Since Nolan has constructed his narrative thus far so as to respect our best available scientific understanding of the effects of space travel on those undergoing it, and indeed to create accurate cinematic presentations of the phenomena that generate those effects (*Interstellar*'s portrayal of a black hole is unprecedented in its fidelity to the ways in which its light-distorting nature would affect its appearance to the human eye), his solution to Cooper's problem also has to stay within the bounds of what is scientifically possible. He does so by means of a tesseract.

A tesseract is a hypercube—a cube with four rather than three spatial dimensions: its construction is envisaged on analogy with the construction of an ordinary cube. If we take a line and extend it by its own length into a dimension perpendicular to itself, we get a square (with four faces, each of which is a line); if we take that square and extend it into a dimension perpendicular to itself, we get a cube (with six faces, each of which is a square); so, by analogy, if we take that cube and extend it into a dimension perpendicular to itself, we get a hypercube—it has eight faces, each of which is a cube. Of course, our world has only three spatial dimensions, together with a fourth temporal dimension. But for several decades now, physicists struggling to establish laws of quantum gravity have found that they could make progress on this only by constructing theories whose best interpretation treats our universe as a membrane (a 'brane') contained within a 'bulk'—a hyperspace with at least nine spatial dimensions and one temporal dimension. Since the same hypothesis is required to make sense of the way wormholes connect very distant parts of the universe, and a wormhole is needed to make Cooper's prospecting mission feasible, Nolan's film is necessarily committed to the existence of the bulk—although his version restricts it to four spatial dimensions. But that is enough to allow him to consider the possibility of a tesseract as the kind of object that could inhabit the bulk. He can then exploit two further possibilities: first, that Cooper might occupy one of the tesseract's (three-dimensional) faces; and second, that the tesseract as a whole might intersect with our brane.

Imagine, to begin with, a two-dimensional brane embedded within a three-dimensional universe such as our own. How would it look to the inhabitants of such a brane if a three-dimensional object passed through it? A cube would look like a square (the two-dimensional cross-section of a cube); a sphere would look like a point which expands into a circle whose diameter gradually expands, then gradually decreases until it becomes a point and then vanishes. So now imagine a hypercube intruding into our three-dimensional brane: since each face of the hypercube is itself three-dimensional, each could reside in a three-dimensional portion of our brane in just the way the circular cross-section of a sphere might reside within a two-dimensional brane. Otherwise put, one face of a hypercube could contain—more precisely, could intersect or interface with—a given portion of our universe.

And this is how Nolan brings Cooper into contact with his daughter. Cooper inhabits one three-dimensional face of a hypercube which is then introduced into our brane in such a way as to incorporate his 10-year-old daughter's bedroom into another of its faces. Cooper will be able to see Murph and her bedroom because rays of light from the objects in it will reach him indirectly via the other faces of the tesseract: indeed, since he inhabits a face with six sides (since it's a cube), each side will display the contents of that room to him as they would look from each of its sides. But Murph can't see Cooper: for the light which would allow her to do so would bring her information from (his present, which is) her future—exactly the kind of backwards-in-time information flow within our brane that is forbidden by our current understanding of the laws of physics. Cooper doesn't face this problem because he is not currently inhabiting our brane, but the bulk in which it's embedded; the light by which he sees his daughter is always travelling from young Murph's present to her future (which is when Cooper enters the tesseract).

However, the laws of physics do allow for the possibility that gravitational signals can go backwards in time. More precisely, whilst those signals must go forward in local time (whether the time dimension of the bulk or that of our brane), if they reach our brane by means of travel through the bulk, they can be propagated forwards in bulk time and yet arrive in brane time before they set out. So Cooper is in a position to send a message to young Murph—by means of a gravitational signal that is sent through the interior of the tesseract. Everything that happens to Cooper and to the young Murph happens within different three-dimensional faces of the tesseract: but being a hypercube, it also has an interior dimension—one that belongs to the bulk. This is invisible, since light can't travel through four dimensions; but gravity can. Hence, Cooper can affect events in the young Murph's bedroom: first by pushing books off her shelf, then by creating dust patterns containing coordinates expressed in binary code, and finally by manipulating the second hand of a watch so that its flickering conveys in Morse code the quantum data acquired by TARS.

Of course, we know from earlier scenes in the film that there are several such mysterious events in the young Murph's bedroom; so they occur in temporal sequence within our brane, and that means that Cooper must be able to move between different temporal moments at that particular spatial location in order to cause them all. Since this is exactly what a hypercube's interaction with a three-dimensional brane would involve, that is not a theoretical problem; but its presentation in a film requires that Nolan and his collaborators devise an intelligible means of screening it. In other words, he needs to find a way of representing the dimension of time within our brane spatially—that is, within the three-dimensional space of the screened world that contains the tesseract face Cooper occupies.

Nolan does this by means of a coordinated bundle or tube of individual coloured lines, each of which corresponds to one of the material particles that make up Murph's bedroom, and which radiate in three spatial dimensions from each of the six images of the room that are currently visible on the walls of Cooper's face of the tesseract. If we think of each line as the world line of one particle in the room (delineating its passage through space-time), then every point at which one of these radiating bundles intersects with two others will display another three-dimensional image of the room, but one which shows it at another moment in time—either earlier or later in its spatio-temporal career. And since each such intersection is an image potentially visible on one of the six walls of a tesseract face, any six of those images that occupy the appropriate spatial relations to one another also define a different possible position for the tesseract face Cooper inhabits. Otherwise put: the tesseract can allow Cooper to travel backwards and forwards along the timeline of Murph's bedroom by moving diagonally between appropriate combinations of intersections so as to apprehend the images they constitute.[12]

Most immediately then, the tesseract sequence permits Cooper to communicate with his daughter in such a way that, when she returns to her bedroom at the age of 40, she will find the watch still flickering (its pattern of movements presumably stored by the tesseract in the bulk) and so acquire the data with which she can facilitate the evacuation from Earth. One might say, in the light of our

---

[12] My explanation of the scientific theories underlying the tesseract sequence is deeply indebted to Kip Thorne's account in his *The Science of Interstellar* (London: Norton and Company, 2014).

consideration of Nolan's earlier films, that it represents the overcoming of an extreme instance of a failure of practical self-knowledge on Cooper's part: for it is only at this very late stage that he finds himself in a position to recognize the mysterious events in Murph's bedroom as his own actions (more precisely, to bring to bear the intentions in the absence of which those events would have remained instances of mere matter in motion rather than the realization of an agent's goal). But the situation that enables this also speaks directly to a number of more specific themes in the film.

To begin with, it constitutes a moment of reconciliation between Murph and her father: in order to fulfil his mission, he has to leave her behind when she is 10, and he couldn't explain his motive (to make possible a future for her and the human race more generally) without forcing her to interiorize a vision of the all-but-inevitable end of the world. When the vicissitudes of space-time ensure that decades pass on Earth during the months of Cooper's mission, his child spends decades nursing her resentment at his presumed abandonment; and when Professor Brand finally confesses that he has known all along that he can't make the crucial theory work, Murph suspects that her father left her despite knowing that all hope was lost (instead placing his faith in the alternative possibility embodied in the population bomb their spaceship carried—charged with five thousand fertilized human eggs, to be implanted and brought to term by surrogates once a viable planet was found). It is only when the older Murph returns to her bedroom and realizes that its ghost was in fact her father that their decades-long rupture is healed.

But the ruptures at issue here are not just between father and daughter, but within both individuals. For Cooper, his time in the tesseract enables him not only fully to acknowledge the harm he caused by leaving Murph, but also to find a means of redeeming it. The scenes he watches are those we've already seen earlier, which culminate in his rejecting her plea to stay; but to begin with (not yet having heard from TARS, and so believing that his attempt to save the human species has failed) he despairingly berates his earlier self for what he sees as his selfishness, his refusal to see that the fact that the mission fulfilled his deepest, hitherto-frustrated desire (to be an astronaut) did make it wrong—or at least that he hadn't properly appreciated the extent to which luck (and so factors outside his control) might deprive him of a retrospective justification for his abandonment of her. At this first stage, then, he literally argues against himself: he is the source of the ghost's message to 'STAY', a message that the young Murph decodes and passes on, but that his earlier self still chooses to ignore.

Then, after TARS makes contact, he realizes that he has a way of redeeming that earlier decision, which of course requires that he be enabled to make it in the first place. So he uses gravity to encode the NASA coordinates in a dust pattern, which puts them both on the path which leads to his departure, and consequent occupation of the tesseract face; and finally he encodes and stores the quantum data in the watch which he gave Murph to remember him by on his departure—one that embodied his promise to return. It is only because she kept the watch despite her resentment that she will be able to save everyone on the planet; so it is only because she never lost faith in his promise that he will prove able to fulfil it (by communicating with her through the watch, and in the film's conclusion, when he meets Murph on her deathbed, in one of the space vessels she helped to build).

Nolan's editing of the tesseract sequence (which intercuts Cooper's views of what happened to the young Murph with views of what happens when the older Murph revisits her bedroom) also emphasizes Murph's internal divisions. Where Cooper confronts his earlier self by means of the bulk, Murph remains within the brane, and so cannot directly encounter her earlier self. But she can remember her, and in particular she can remember her earlier self's relation to the ghost in her bedroom. She tells us that she was never afraid of that ghost, because it always felt to her like a person trying to tell her something (we might say someone with the authority to testify): this is what leads her to return to that room, to identify that person as her father, and so to look for some way in which he might have been able to pass on the information she desperately needs.

The implication seems to be that Cooper and Murph are each capable of fulfilling their unattained selves, but only by virtue of the enabling intervention of the other. Murph can solve the critical scientific puzzle only because her father helps her to do so; and Cooper can make a success of his mission only because his daughter helps him to do so. But neither could attain their individual self-overcoming unless both do. In more Nietzschean perfectionist terms, one might say that both fulfil their promise, realize their nature as promising animals, but each does so only because the other does. As with the question of whether it is Cobb or Mal who originates the sceptical hypothesis in *Inception*, it is impossible to say whether it is Murph or Cooper who saves the world, or even to say which of them brings the idea of doing so into being. In both films, then, issues of originality and indebtedness, hence of plagiarism, find expression in ideas about sceptical relations to others, and about the loss and recovery of children. But in *Interstellar*, that loss and recovery is not tied up with the fate of a marriage: like Cobb, Cooper's wife is dead, but her absence has not cursed his present existence and created a distance between him and his children. It rather allows Nolan to treat the parent–child relationship in isolation—as a purely intergenerational and mutually pedagogical matter.

The words that this film finds to attest to its vision of Murph's and Cooper's (quantum) entanglement as the world's redeemer—its linguistic equivalent for the visual logic of the tesseract sequence—confirm this. They are laid out in two exchanges between father and daughter, the first of which occurs just before Cooper departs. Because, as we later learn, he refuses to make her internalize a vision of the world's end, he cannot explain his motives; instead, he says this:

COOPER: Murph, a father looks in his child's eyes and thinks—maybe it's them... maybe my child will save the world. And everyone, once a child, wants to look into their own dad's eyes and know he saw how they saved some little corner of their world. But, usually, by then, the father is gone.

MURPH: Like you will be.

COOPER: No. I'm coming back.

Cooper begins to repeat his initial set of remarks later in the film, at Murph's deathbed, but there Murph voices the second half of his thought:

MURPH: And everyone, once a child, wants to look in their own dad's eyes and know he saw.

This pair of exchanges implies a highly charged vision of the father–daughter relationship. All fathers inevitably convey to their children a vision of the world as such, and so must choose between its being a vision of that world's ending or of its redemption—an epitome of despair or of hope. Since their key imperative is to make their child feel safe, any father will choose the latter, and grasp the child's existence in relation to it; this perception of her implants that orienting ideal in the child, who then strives over a lifetime to realize it, but feels that it can never be fully enacted in the inevitable absence of the father's confirmatory gaze; this in turn leads them to gaze in this way at their children; and so on. We might call this a melodrama of inevitably insufficient inheritance—each child constituting herself by internalizing a conception of her higher self that is in fact her parent's unattained higher self, which then becomes her own unattained self, which she bequeaths to her children.

We could read this as an essentially sadomasochistic structure, in which each parent's sense that the fate of the world is at stake in their child's flourishing always already condemns each child to a sense of inevitable failure of self-realization. Or it could be an essentially enabling one, the natural way in which the family romance makes possible our individual attempts to become all that we might be. Either way, in *Interstellar*, that structure appears to be itself overcome, or transfigured; for in the case of Cooper and Murph, the father not only sees the child's achievement of self-realization but also acknowledges it directly to her, and that proves to complete not only her self-overcoming but also his own. And this fantastic achievement is presented as not only consistent with our best scientific understanding of reality but also as something that its embedding of our brane in the bulk of hyperspace positively enables.

But it turns out that Murph's and Cooper's way of redeeming the world is not so much an alternative to its ending but a way of turning that ending into a new beginning. For of course, in one sense, the world does end: planet Earth ceases to exist as a humanly inhabitable environment. The new beginning is for the human race, and this requires not only their transplantation to a new world (presumably Edmund's planet, on which Brand is beginning to stake a claim), but also a willingness to undergo transportation from the old world to the new—to realize an essentially transitional mode of human being. This is a vision of the human species as capable of enacting an analogue of the perfectionist structure in which its members participate—one whose mode of Being is Becoming. And it is confirmed by another insight Cooper achieves in the tesseract sequence.

We know from the outset that the NASA project in which he is participating has been stimulated by an outbreak of gravitational anomalies, and in particular by the sudden appearance of a wormhole near Saturn which can give them speedy access to a distant region of space that contains a number of likely alternative homes for humanity. Since the probability that the wormhole occurred naturally is virtually zero, NASA's scientists have been assuming that beings who inhabit the bulk have created it in order to help the human race escape Earth; and when Cooper finds himself in the tesseract, he assumes that those same beings created it to further that plan. It is only when he realizes that the messages he received from the ghost in Murph's bedroom were in fact sent by him that he comes to see that the bulk beings are not an alien species but a more advanced version of the human species—people who have evolved beyond our four-dimensional brane, and who are helping their evolutionary predecessors to avoid an extinction event. At both the individual and the collective level, then, *Interstellar* posits a perfectionist perception of our higher, unattained but attainable states as exerting a gravitational force on us, thereby attracting us away from our attained state—indeed, having to do so if we are not to succumb to a mode of being that amounts to annihilation.

The tesseract sequence thus crystallizes this film's instantiation of every major theme in Christopher Nolan's body of work: the nature of time and its distortions, the nature of the self (divided, transitional, capable of self-overcoming), the active and passive registers of femininity in marriage and family, plagiarism and originality, and scepticism. But it also constitutes an extreme expression of his cinematic signature—with its concern for immersive experience, its commitment to realism, and its preference for IMAX analogue film rather than digital alternatives. This may seem a perverse claim about a film which depends more extensively upon CGI than any other in his oeuvre, but Nolan's characteristic desire to face down digital cinema here takes a more precise target.

As we have seen, the whole narrative of *Interstellar* is predicated on taking seriously one of the most counter-intuitive deliverances of modern science—its claim that our necessarily three-dimensional spatial mode of experiencing reality is (if not exactly illusory, then certainly) partial, for that reality is just the reality of the brane, whose nature can only be grasped if we relativize it, treating it as a layer within the bulk of a four-dimensional hyperspace. And the tesseract sequence is the climax of Nolan's attempt to be faithful to this vision of reality: for on the face of it, it finds a cinematic way of presenting (that is, a way of showing rather than telling) what it would be like to inhabit a four-dimensional spatial entity, and to experience the kind of relation that it would have to locations and people occupying a three-dimensional space if it were to pass through a brane containing that space. We might think of it as a stunningly ingenious and technologically sophisticated three-dimensional projection of the diagrams that so often accompany popularizing scientific explanations of these matters, a moving image of the reality they attempt to delineate.

And the one thing Nolan doesn't need in bringing off this feat is what current digital cinema is pleased to call '3-D' technology. In fact, the films produced and projected in this digital format do not bring a third dimension to a medium that had hitherto only been able to generate two-dimensional images. For of course, the worlds of previous films, both analogue and digital—the worlds projected onto the screen and perceived by their viewers—were always possessed of three dimensions: they could hardly be worlds containing people and buildings if they did not. To be sure, the screens on which those worlds were projected are (virtually) two-dimensional, so the image projected on them could be described in two-dimensional terms—as an array of colour-patches; but then, so could what are now called '3-D' films. There is certainly a difference between our experiences as viewers of '3-D' films and our experience of other films: in the former case, what is projected on the screen generates images which appear to us to reach out towards us from the screen, and so to occupy the space between us and the screen—the three-dimensional space of the world in which we view the film. But this is a different difference: the world of a non-'3-D' film—the world in which its characters go about their business—is fully three-dimensional even though their projected images remain securely screened off from us.

However that may be, one way of understanding Nolan's tesseract sequence is as a declaration that non-'3-D' film is capable not only of presenting genuinely three-dimensional worlds, but also of presenting four-dimensional ones. After all, Cooper's relation to the events in Murph's bedroom is all-but-explicitly presented as that of a viewer to a screened cinematic image. Every side of his face of the tesseract acts as a movie screen, and the three-dimensionality of the world thereby depicted is trebly emphasized—because the images are plainly of the real world of the film, because there are always six of them which present that world from six different but integrated perspectives, and because each of those images is given the kind of hologrammatic depth that '3-D' films are so proud of achieving (except that this depth is disclosed behind the screen rather than between it and Cooper).

Thus far, the reflexive implications of the tesseract sequence are consonant with Cavell's understanding of cinema and its worlds, which he summarizes in two claims. First, he denies that the photographically generated world of a film differs in any particular respect from the real world: any criteria we employ to distinguish real objects from one another can be employed to distinguish objects in a photograph, so there is no feature an object in a photograph lacks which the real object has, or vice versa (no specific respect in which Jessica Chastain in a photograph differs from Jessica Chastain in the flesh). But of course, seeing an object and seeing an object in a photograph are two different things; it's just that the distinction must be specified not in terms of visible differences but in terms of the different relationships in which we stand to them. So Cavell's second claim is that the viewers of a film share neither a space nor a time with the objects in the world of a film: there is no route from our location to theirs, and the moment at which they were captured by the camera is not present to us (and cannot be made present by us). In short, 'the reality in a photograph is present to me while I am not present to it; and a world I know and see, but to which I am nevertheless not present (through no fault of my subjectivity) is a world past' (WV, 23).

But if the motion picture camera causes live human beings and real objects in actual spaces to appear to us when they are in fact not there, presenting our senses with nothing less than reality but nothing more than an image, then our relation to a screened world exemplifies scepticism's understanding of our relation to the world itself. In this sense, film is a moving image of scepticism.

It therefore becomes important to note a crucial point of difference between Cavell's vision of cinema and Cooper's relation to the world screened on the sides of his face of the tesseract. For Cooper learns how to interact with that world, and so appears to contest what Cavell sees as the wholly mechanical screening of the viewer from it—a contestation that continues the mode of realism Nolan pursued in the 'Dark Knight' trilogy, in which the projected world's being screened from us can come to seem provisional or porous. More specifically, he uses his fists to move various objects in the young Murph's world: he uses the gravitational force of his body to make those objects means of extending his physical presence into that world, making that presence primarily a material rather than a visual matter.

Cooper's interaction still respects the pastness of that world (since what he does in the young Murph's bedroom was always already done in the older Murph's world), and presents his own relation to that past world as a mode of absent presence; but Nolan's scientifically authorized reconception of space and time as internally related and hyperdimensional gives him a means of access to it that allows both him and Murph to realize the true meaning of their shared past for the first time—to make its hitherto-ghostly presence real and to appreciate it as such (quite as if each had previously been excluded from that common inheritance by a corrosive scepticism about its enduring significance, and only now can fully immerse themselves in it). In Cavell's terms, this would make their joint achievement a scientifically buttressed means by which cinema's capacity to reinforce scepticism can be overcome.

Can it really be said, however, that Nolan makes good on his attempted declaration of superiority over '3-D' film? There are reasons to doubt it, which might emerge if we adopt a Nietzschean perspective on the extravagance of Nolan's commitment to the cinematic realization of what modern science calls the true nature of reality. For Nietzsche would regard any such commitment as participating in the ascetic ideal, insofar as it locates truth in a realm that lies beyond the blooming, buzzing deliverances of the senses, and situates us in relation to that truth in just the way inhabitants of a two-dimensional universe would relate to the reality of the three spatial dimensions we inhabit—that is, as essentially incapable of grasping the larger environment in which we nevertheless have our being.

One way of resisting such an asceticism of knowledge would be simply to deny that we really can make sense of this aspect of science's way of making sense of reality. For example: when—following the guidance of scientific popularizers such as Kip Thorne, the physicist who was also the film's key adviser—I earlier explained the nature of a hypercube by suggesting that it related to a cube in just the way that a cube related to a square, it would be entirely reasonable to question the legitimacy of analogical reasoning in this context. There is no problem in explaining the relation between a line, a square, and a cube along these lines, since we are familiar with all three entities from our experience of a three-dimensional world and our grasp of geometrical theory. It is because we know how to project a three-dimensional cube onto a two-dimensional plane that we think we know what it would be like for an inhabitant of a two-dimensional universe to encounter a cube passing through it.

Even here, however, we are passing over deep conceptual difficulties in the idea of the inhabitant of a two-dimensional universe (since a two-dimensional entity is not something that is really, really thin but one lacking the dimension of depth altogether—in other words, a pure shape: a geometrical entity rather than a material one). And when someone goes on to say that 'a hypercube is what you get if you take a cube and extend it into a dimension perpendicular to itself', this kind of explanation uses the very notion it attempts to elucidate, since it is precisely the idea of a spatial dimension that is supplementary to the three dimensions in which a cube exists—'a dimension perpendicular to those of length, breadth and depth'—that lacks any sense within the terms of our experience and our geometry. We know what it means to regard a square as a line extended into a second spatial dimension, and to regard a cube as a square extended into a third; but since we don't have any conception of what a spatial dimension distinct from those three might be, we cannot make any sense of the suggestion that we envisage a hypercube as a cube that is extended into it.

Might Nolan's tesseract sequence be seen as a convincing counter to this line of criticism? After all, I said earlier that it realizes cinematically exactly what it would be like to inhabit a four-dimensional spatial entity, and to experience the kind of relation that it would have to a three-dimensional space. One immediate problem with this suggestion is that it is far from obvious on a first viewing of the sequence (or indeed, on repeated viewings) that, or rather how, it is attempting to project these scientific notions. The dialogue between Cooper and TARS offers some terse words of guidance, with its references to bulk beings and the spatial representation of time; but—as my own earlier attempts to explain what is going on in this sequence illustrate—unless one is already equipped with some knowledge of the relevant scientific ideas, it's all but impossible to appreciate the exquisitely detailed virtuosity of Nolan's attempts to provide a cinematic analogue to them. This, it seems to me, is one of the main reasons why the initial reception of *Interstellar* carried a clear tinge of disappointment—a sense that Nolan had fallen away from the fully achieved combination of intellectual complexity and dramatic propulsion embodied in his preceding film *Inception*. In Nolan's terms, this lack of immediate legibility radically limits his ability to generate the immersive experience he is always committed to providing, and at precisely the point at which the ultimate fate of the film's characters and themes hangs in the balance.

Moreover, even when the viewer *is* intellectually equipped properly to appreciate the virtuosity of the sequence, it cannot provide any independent grounds for dismissing doubts about the intelligibility of the ideas it aspires to embody. Nolan is certainly able to present us with the contents of two faces of the tesseract, each of which is of course possessed of just three spatial dimensions; but the relation between them—which must involve the fourth hyperspatial dimension—is also presented as a three-dimensional one, since the environment within which both are contained in this aspect of the world of his film is of course possessed of three dimensions. Furthermore, as the dialogue of the sequence acknowledges in its characterization of the intentions of the bulk beings, he can only capture the dimension of time by treating it as spatial—as represented by a certain direction taken within this three-dimensional presentation of one face of one object inhabiting the bulk.

In both these respects, Nolan is in effect deploying a visual analogue of Thorne's explanation by analogy: but since he is inevitably restricted to the intelligibility of the three-dimensional in just the same way as Thorne, he can only appear to have presented an intelligible image of hyperspace if he either resorts to the unintelligible (treating time as if it were a spatial dimension), or refrains from presenting the very thing that reveals its unintelligibility (as he doesn't present the interior or fourth dimension of the hypercube, the medium through which Cooper's communicative acts are supposed to be effected). This is why the diagrams in popular science textbooks are constantly accompanied by references to the (supposedly innocent) fact that their author is treating time as a spatial dimension, or is suppressing one or more of the dimensions that the reality they purport to depict actually has. For that is the decisive move of the conjuring trick: that is the point at which the understanding that such images purport to convey is shown to be mere appearance.

This doesn't mean that there is nothing at all to understand here—that there is no sense to be made of the idea of a fourth spatial dimension (let alone nine of them), or of the idea that time is not distinct from three-dimensional space but is rather internally related to them. But the only intelligible expression of these ideas is to be found in the mathematics of the theories whose substance is inevitably distorted by its attempted translation into systems of representation that are inherently incapable of embodying them. The only way of grasping what all this might mean is to master the mathematics of superstring theory: and that brings us right back to the Nietzschean anxiety that modern science is fundamentally committed to locating truth and reality in the timeless mathematical realm of being, and thereby to privileging Being over Becoming.

So it is worth noting that one feature of Nolan's way of cleaving to Thorne's science suggests an underlying disagreement with its evaluative thrust; and it becomes clearer if we compare Nolan's achievement with that of his obvious modernist predecessor—Stanley Kubrick, and his *2001: A Space Odyssey*. Kubrick's film certainly tries to conform to the best contemporary scientific understanding in its presentation of the solar system; but even though he uses human beings (and protohuman beings) as his protagonists, they are wholly dwarfed by the technological and astronomical domains they inhabit, and their evolutionary progress is wholly facilitated by their uncomprehending relationship to the technology of an alien race. Nolan's film, by contrasts, depicts humanity's survival and evolution as primarily facilitated by itself, and this species-level self-reliance is condensed in the film's central concern with the way in which Cooper's and Murph's divided selves facilitate their own redemptive self-transformations. Insofar as the hyperspatial complexities of the tesseract sequence are ultimately in the service of making this individual and collective process of self-overcoming possible, one might interpret Nolan's film as declaring that the only way of making sense of the supposedly impersonal and absolute perspective of modern science is by making human sense of it—by finding a way in which its gravitational mathematics articulates the truth of love (a way that here depends on perfectionist figurations of self-reliance, aversion from conformity and self-overcoming in terms of attraction and repulsion). As Simone Weil might put it, in Nolan's hands Kubrickian gravity discloses grace.

In many ways, *Dunkirk* (2017) is closer to the Kubrickian model than *Interstellar*, and indeed is more generally antithetical to its predecessor. It reconstructs a real historical event; it is geographically and temporally confined; it massively privileges the visual image over dialogue, and is consequently able to maximize its use of noisy IMAX cameras (in which some 70 per cent of the film is shot, with the remainder being 70 mm); and it situates individuals within larger human groups that are dependent upon, vulnerable to, and dwarfed by the vicissitudes of larger technological, natural, and geometrical conditions (weapons-delivery mechanisms and boat draughts; tides and weather; the vast flat expanse of a beach and the thin extrusion of a mole reaching out through the chaotic waste of water to nowhere). But Nolan's distinctively modernist signature lies in the organizational principles through which he tells this overfamiliar tale: he follows three distinct viewpoints within his unified space (that of a pilot, the sailor of a small boat, and a soldier awaiting evacuation on the beach), but imposes a different timescale on each—one week on the mole, one day at sea, and one hour in the air.

This tripartite structure has a specific impact on the world of the film. In particular, it at once insists on and denies differences in the nature of the three kinds of experience that it intercuts. Immediately, it implies that one intense hour on board a Spitfire engaged in a series of dogfights might, phenomenologically speaking, be the equivalent of a day on a slow boat and a week marooned on a beach. More specifically, it suggests that the proportion of terror to boredom shifts significantly towards the latter as we shift from air to sea to land; but in making that suggestion, it implies an essential commonality, in that each mode of experience is made up of just those two elements, as the experience of *Dunkirk* is itself elemental (comprising air, water, earth, and a climactic manifestation of fire—and so makes up a world whose building blocks are simple, various, but essentially interrelated).

But this structure has a more insistent and complex impact on our relation to the world of the film. In the first instance, it makes possible the construction of a narrative equivalent to the musical phenomenon of the Shepard Tone, which is a way of creating the illusory impression of a tone that endlessly rises (or descends) in pitch without actually getting any higher (or lower). Nolan has used that musical effect in earlier films—in *Prestige*, and in *The Dark Knight* (where it permits the Batpod to sound as if it is continuously accelerating); here, the distinct temporal scale of his three storylines allows him to construct a series of phases in which one story is reaching a climax, the second is halfway there, and the third is just beginning to build towards one. This is not just an innovative means of creating virtually continuous narrative suspense and propulsion; it amounts to an interrogation of the differences between—and hence the internal relatedness of—music and narrative, and so of the relation between a film's story and its soundtrack.

At the same time, however, the need to follow relatively long sequences within any one storyline (in order to make its order of events comprehensible) means that there are various points in the film in which events derived from the other two storylines have an impact upon the one in which we're currently immersed that we have either not yet experienced in that other storyline or have experienced so long ago that we have to recall its significance. So these chronological discontinuities create difficulties of intelligibility for both the characters and the viewer: the characters find that the significance of their actions depends unpredictably but decisively on the unfolding consequences of actions and events elsewhere, so that what they have done—a failed or pointless effort, or an essential contribution to a rescue—becomes knowable to them (and so to the viewer) only retrospectively. And even when all three storylines converge so as apparently to determine this (when the pilot's downing of a German fighter sets alight the oily water through which the soldiers are swimming towards the sanctuary of the Dawsons' small boat), the memory of these difficulties undercuts any tendency on the viewer's part to view this convergence as a meaningful climax as opposed to sheer happenstance (to view it as inherently shaped by its narration rather than as possessed of the shapelessness of that which is narrated). And by emphasizing the discontinuity between narrative order and the (dis)order of the events narrated, Nolan forces his viewers to acknowledge the conventional nature of the former, and so to acknowledge that their immersive cinematic experience is made possible by an ineliminable element of construction, hence choice, and so the threat of arbitrariness.

The significance of the distortions and occlusions that the gap between events and their narration makes possible is doubly underlined at the film's conclusion—in a minor key, when we see the local newspaper's report of the young man George's death at sea, and in a major key when the rescued soldier Tommy reads out another newspaper's report of Churchill's famous speech to Parliament across images of Dunkirk beach littered with wrecked vehicles and dead bodies. Both exemplify the way in which the meaning of what one has done, and so one's standing as an agent and a self, is at once subject to external control and never immune to later reinterpretation. But they equally show the pervasiveness and depth of our desire to clothe accident in meaning, and so support the artistic purpose of the alienation effect more generally achieved by the film's own deliberately baroque narrative structure; for that anti-immersive device paradoxically works to reimmerse the viewer in the film's primary concern—the ineliminable element of arbitrariness in the fate of the film's characters.

Which among the large cast of characters lives or dies is essentially a matter of chance: a hair's-breadth difference in the accumulation of contingent conditions and causes is all that it takes to ensure that a boat is on hand to rescue a pilot from his sinking plane, or that a traumatized soldier's panic attack results in the death of a young boy who shouldn't have been on board in the first place.

Nolan's hand-held, tight-focus, high-resolution examination of one very specific series of events thereby delivers a metaphysical perception of the human condition as inherently subject to sheer chance which is as far as it could be from *Interstellar*'s vision of human meaning as always already infusing bare materiality, and as close as he has yet come to matching the clinical brutality of Stanley Kubrick. And the way in which this cinematic work conveys an Aeschylean vision of tragic moral luck through narratival structures that aspire to incarnate an inherently musical phenomenon makes it hard to avoid comparison with Wagner's achievement in opera. It's as if Nolan's long apprenticeship in sophisticated manipulations of cinematic time and space have here reached a certain kind of provisional telos: for it is in *Dunkirk* that his exceptional powers of aesthetic ordering first prove capable of fully acknowledging what lies beyond their grasp, and so of acknowledging their own limits rather than hermetically sealing his viewers within them. Nietzsche might recognize such a synthesis of the Apollinian with the Dionysian.

2. Physics as Metaphysics: Philosophy, Science, and Technology in the Modern Era

A. The Under-labourers of Asceticism

Nolan's recurrent interest in the intellectual and technological deliverances of science provides a helpful reminder of, as well as a point of entry into, Nietzsche's own linkage of science and the ascetic ideal. Towards the end of the third essay of his *Genealogy*, he anticipates and disdains the suggestion that science might constitute a centre of resistance to the persistent deforming in-formation of secular morality, art, and philosophy by the JudaeoChristian value system.

> [I] am told [that modern science] not only has...fought a long, successful fight with [the ascetic] ideal, but...has already mastered that ideal in all essentials... [A]s a genuine philosophy of reality, [it] obviously believes only in itself, obviously possesses the courage to be itself, and has hitherto got by well enough without God, the beyond and the virtues of denial.
>
> Precisely the opposite of what they are declaring here is the truth: science today has absolutely *no* faith in itself, let alone in an ideal *above* it—and where it is still passion, love, fire, *suffering*, it is not the opposite of the ascetic ideal but rather the latter's own *most recent and noble manifestation*... They themselves are its most intellectualized product, its most advanced frontline troops and scouts, its most insidious, delicate and elusive form of seduction...*because they still believe in truth*   (GM, 3.117–18)

'Belief in truth' is not merely a matter of participating in practices that are designed to seek it out and are (unprecedentedly) successful in so doing: it is a species of faith, an existential orientation that assigns truth to the place once occupied by God, and thereby maintains the valuation of truth woven so deeply into the lives of religious believers, for whom after all God *is* the Truth (as well as the Way and the Life). It is, in other words, a manifestation of what we have been calling the will to truth, and so shares in the peculiar grammatical articulation of Nietzsche's counterpart will to power: for just as the will to power seeks power not as a means to achieve some other end but as a means to the unending accumulation of more power, so the will to truth unceasingly deploys accumulated truths in order to drive towards ones as yet unattained, from which we will then turn away in the name of attaining further truths.

So the moral Nietzsche would draw from the mythological status of Galileo's conflict with the Church is not that modern scientific theory and practice precipitates (initiates and crystallizes) Western culture's decisive break from religious domination, but rather that the concept of martyrdom provides an attractive way of making sense of themselves even to those who take themselves to be contesting the system of values that incubated it. These heroic founding narratives of the rise of science supply new saints rather than subverting the concept of sainthood; and the criteria for canonization—a willingness to risk not only one's creature comforts but one's entire existence for the cause—extrapolate from more everyday modes of disinterest in and seclusion from worldly things (the absent-minded scientist uninterested in keeping body and soul together) whose religious variants (in cloisters and churches across the planet) came to elicit condemnation as modes of self-denial that are also denials of life. Hence, what Nietzsche sees more generally when he views science physiologically (or physiognomically) is a certain impoverishment of life:

> the emotions cooled, the tempo slackened, dialectics in place of instinct, *solemnity* stamped on faces and gestures (solemnity, that most unmistakable sign of a more sluggish metabolism and of a struggling, more toiling life)...times of exhaustion, often of twilight, of decline—gone are the overflowing energy, the certainty of life. (GM, 3.121)

These claims about scientists and science need involve no scepticism about the hard-won truths embodied in scientific theories validated by observation and experiment; Nietzsche was no more interested in critically engaging with scientific practices on that level than he was interested in approaching religious practices by critically evaluating the truth of their credal and dogmatic claims. He rather intends to analyse the evolving meaning or significance of science and its results as they shape individual forms of life, and our culture's self-understanding—that is, as an existential value-system. His focus is accordingly on how scientific insights are interpreted to and for the wider culture (by philosophers and artists, as well as by many scientists themselves), and then are fed back into the institutions and practices of science; it is on how the scientific world-view informs the genealogical development of modern Western European forms of life. And in this respect, for Nietzsche, the defeat of theological astronomy by Copernicus primarily ensured that human existence has come to look more arbitrary, idle, and dispensable—it enhanced the human will to self-deprecation (and the work of Darwin and Freud hardly diminished our sense of cosmic demotion).

All science... is seeking to talk man out of his former self-respect as though this were nothing but a bizarre piece of self-conceit;... its own pride, its own austere form of stoical ataraxy, consisted in maintaining this laboriously won *self-contempt* of man as his last, most serious claim to self-respect. (GM, 3.122)

Two further, closely related, characteristics of the modern scientific world-view reinforce this denigration of self and life: its dependence upon the language of mathematics, and its sceptical relation to the deliverances of the senses. The massively enhanced power to predict and control material reality that grounds the claims of modern physics to superiority over its Aristotelian predecessor is inseparable from its identification of natural laws whose articulation presupposes essentially quantitative characterizations of matter and the forces acting upon it. The truth about the material world is thus expressible only in mathematical terms—in terms of unchanging relations between abstractly defined quanta. This is a world beyond the world of our experience, beyond the world as it makes itself manifest to us through the senses, as it impresses itself upon the bodies through which we in our turn act upon it. And it has proven all too tempting (for scientists, and for philosophers deeply impressed by modern science's achievements) to conclude that the explanatory power of these quantified laws doesn't just enhance our understanding of the manifest properties of the world and of our capacities for grasping them, but justifies us in denying reality to the former and condemning the latter as inherently deceptive. It's as if the discovery that the surfaces of things depend upon their depths were taken to show that those depths don't really have surfaces at all. What begins as an attempt to explain devolves into a drive to explain away, to interpret this epochal world-disclosure in terms which ontologically prioritize Being over Becoming; and this drive finds paradigmatic expression in modern philosophy's denigration of secondary qualities.[13]

Galileo and Descartes began a tradition that was continued by Boyle and Locke—that of assimilating secondary qualities (colour, sounds, tastes) to sensations, and thereby denying that they are real properties of objects. Galileo pointed out that a feather passed repeatedly over the nostrils causes us to feel 'an almost intolerable titillation', which is a sensation of the creature being tickled rather than a property of the feather; and he argued by analogy that sound is a sensation caused by the impact of vibrations on our ears. Descartes chose a related model: he pointed out that the painful sensation of a strap pressing harshly into our flesh or a sword cutting into it is not a property of the strap or the sword—that nothing exists in either object resembling the pain it causes, and that by analogy, colours,

---

[13] In the ensuing discussion, I am extensively indebted to two sources: P.M.S. Hacker's *Appearance and Reality* (Oxford: Blackwell, 1987) and John Hyman's *The Objective Eye* (Chicago: University of Chicago Press, 2006).

sounds, and tastes are merely sensations caused in us by objects which lack any properties resembling those sensations. By contrast, our perceptions of primary qualities—those of size, shape, location, and motion—were held to resemble properties really possessed by the objects whose impact upon our senses generated the relevant impressions.

The analogy between perceiving secondary qualities and feeling pain was eagerly taken up by Boyle and Locke; and it is worth at least raising the question of why pains are so uncontroversially taken as exemplary of the realm of sensation when that realm is being equated with the human animal's fundamental modes of commerce with reality—why Galileo imagines even his feather as intolerably titillating (rather than playfully pleasurable). For it pictures our openness to the world as a species of vulnerability—as if reality essentially aspired to make us suffer, and our senses were the primary site of the trauma consequent upon its impositions. Little wonder that we reach gratefully for early modern science as a way of turning the tables: for by way of its stringent regimes of experimentation, its increasingly powerful methods of forcing reality to confess to its hidden patterns, the knowing subject can now torture its torturer.

But even if we (comfortably ensconced in our more technologically advanced and so secure forms of life) were more willing than the progenitors of the Enlightenment to acknowledge that not all sensations are injurious, it wouldn't rescue the general equation of perception with sensation—in large part because that involves acquainting an essentially active aspect of the human endowment with a broadly passive one. A creature who can see is one equipped with a perceptual faculty—with the ability to discriminate phenomena in its environment in terms of their visible properties, or more generally the ability to acquire knowledge by the use of the relevant sense organ. This is an ability the creature can typically choose either to exercise or refrain from exercising, and one that it can refine or improve—making it better at achieving certain cognitive goals. But although vision is one of the five senses, and those who possess it are thereby vulnerable to suffering a certain distinctive range of sensations and visual experiences (from aches and itches in the eyeballs to being painfully dazzled by a bright light or pleasurably immersing oneself in the rich colours of a Barnett Newman painting), being able to see is not a matter of undergoing a continuous sequence of visual sensations—as if seeing the visible properties of its environment were a matter of enduring an onslaught of psychological episodes of varying degrees of intensity located in our visual apparatus. Such a conception is phenomenologically awry and conceptually confused. We can certainly have sensations as a result of, and even in, our organs of perception; but they are not organs of sensation, because there is no such thing as an organ of sensation—unless we want to call the human body such an organ.

It should, however, be acknowledged that Locke did not—or at least did not always—take his equation of secondary qualities with sensations to justify the flat dismissal of secondary qualities as real properties of objects; for his considered position appears to have been that secondary qualities are powers—a capacity or disposition that some objects have to cause a certain kind of sensation in human observers (more precisely, in normal human observers under normal conditions). The role of sensation or visual experience remains indispensable in such an account, insofar as the nature of the relevant power can be specified only by specifying what it is a power to do; but whether or not an object possesses that power is as much a fact about it as is its possession of any other property (and hence is something we may attribute to it rightly or wrongly, as well as being a property an object might possess even when it is not being exercised—that is, even when no one is experiencing the sensations it can cause). On this understanding, it is not that every time we predicate a colour of an object we say something false (since colours are in fact sensations in the mind); but what it is about the object that makes those predications true, when they are true, is something other than we take it to be.

There are, however, two strong reasons to reject any such dispositional analysis. The first is that, since powers are potencies rather than acts, although we can see the exercise of a power (and in some cases see the material constitution that gives someone or something that power), we cannot see the power itself—because we cannot see *cans* or *woulds*, any more than we can taste them or hear them. In other words, if colours were powers, they would not be visible properties of bodies, and none of our experiences of colour would be perceptions. Second, a dispositional analysis of colour conflicts with the fact that our use of colour terms to characterize mental phenomena is parasitic upon our use of them to describe non-mental phenomena; for someone is only in a position to identify red visual experiences if they can successfully apply the term to red objects, and more generally we can only explain what we mean by saying that something looks red by inviting our interlocutor to look at an object that is red.

This point does not directly block a dispositional analysis: for if colours were dispositions, we might still say that the experiences they are disposed to cause in us are ones which precisely consist in representing the world (rather than some subjective state) as being a certain way. In other words, it might seem that we could characterize the experiences used to specify the disposition which causes them in a way that acknowledges the semantic priority of non-mental attribution over mental attribution. But if the dispositional analysis of colour is right, then the colour property these experiences represent the world as having must be the disposition to cause such experiences—that is, a disposition which can itself be specified only in terms of the kind of colour experience it causes: and that makes the attribution of colour to non-mental phenomena secondary to (logically dependent upon) its attribution to mental phenomena. Once again, we reach the conclusion that, if colours were powers, they could not be visible properties of the objects we perceive.

The basic shape of dispositional analyses of secondary qualities reinforces a further questionable assumption we often make about our ordinary concepts of colour and our related practices of applying colour terms—namely, that they amount to a primitive analogue to scientific theorizing, in that their primary purpose is to postulate properties of objects that might account for the fact that they appear to us to have colour, to explain our having the sensations and experiences we do when we look at them. According to this assumption, attributing colours to objects is an explanatory postulate—not just in highly specialized cases (as when, having observed that a white shirt emerges from my washing machine pink, I infer that I must have mistakenly included a red item of clothing in the load), but in any and every attribution of colour to an object that I make. This is absurd: noting or describing an object's colour is an epistemically basic exercise of our visual sense that can be done for an indefinite variety of purposes, only some of which might contribute to an explanatory goal of any kind, and very few of which form part of any kind of explicitly scientific exercise in theory-building. It is particularly bizarre to think that our practice of attributing colours to objects might be an attempt to explain why they look coloured: for that would suggest that first comes our encounter with visual experiences of colour, and then comes our collective positing of colour as a property of objects, which is not only phenomenologically awry but would amount to another violation of the principle that public uses of colour terms are logically prior to their application to mental phenomena.

That is not to say that there aren't genuine scientific explanatory questions to be answered in this vicinity: in particular, if one accepts that colours are subject to what Hyman calls the epistemic jurisdiction of the senses (that the acid test of an object's colour is to look at it), one might wonder how the human visual apparatus is capable of detecting the colours of objects. Although most of the scientists and philosophers of the early modern period lacked any worked-out theory to account for this (that would have to wait for further advances in optics), the relevant explanation invokes both the object's capacity to reflect light of certain wavelengths and the physiological structure of the human visual system, amongst other things. The truth of such theories does not show that colour is, after all, a dispositional property; it shows only that certain dispositional properties of objects help to explain how human observers are capable of perceiving the colours of those objects. And since we have already canvassed reasons for doubting that attributing colours to objects might coherently explain why they look coloured, it will hardly be surprising to learn that the explanatory mechanisms invoked in these scientific accounts of the basis of colour perception do not themselves involve attributions of colour. That fact gives us no reason to be sceptical of the idea that objects really have colours—any more than an explanation of vodka's capacity to intoxicate by reference to its chemical composition and the physiological structures of the human body gives us reason to doubt that vodka really is an intoxicant.

Might it, however, suggest that our colour attributions are relative in some sense that impugns their reality? They certainly involve a frame of reference, in the sense that they presuppose a system of colour concepts; and that system reflects various aspects of the human visual apparatus—the fact that we have trichromatic colour vision, and that our photoreceptors function in such a way as to make certain differences in spectral reflectance more salient than others. In this sense, our gross colour concepts are anthropocentric: creatures with other kinds of visual apparatus could not employ them. But since any colour attributions must presuppose some system of colour concepts or other, it is hardly surprising that we use one which fits with our nature; and it certainly doesn't follow from that fact that, when we judge that a grassy bank is green, the truth is that it is green relative to human observers. What follows is that it is green without qualification, and 'green' is an anthropocentric concept. Far from the colour of an object being relative to observers, observers qualify as such only relative to some specific frame of reference: a normal trichromatic human being qualifies as an observer relative to our anthropocentric system of colour concepts, and a very differently equipped creature would only do so relative to a system of colour concepts that reflects its nature in the corresponding respects.

This last point indicates that defending the reality of colour is entirely consistent with acknowledging limits to its explanatory range or efficacy. For we could hardly explain the responses of bulls to red capes by invoking their colour, since they aren't equipped to perceive red; and more generally, we should expect the primary explanatory role of the colours humans are equipped to perceive to lie in explanations of human behaviour, and that of animals equally capable of perceiving those colours. Since the primary instruments that detect colours are sentient animals, it is their behaviour with respect to which the presence of colours should be expected to have explanatory force; as Jonathan Bennett puts it, the behaviour of sentient animals is the bottleneck through which we should expect secondary qualities to affect the world, and so to count as explanatory causes. And since, as we have seen, our best explanations of the nature and preconditions of sentience do not themselves invoke secondary qualities, and the same holds true more broadly of our best explanations of non-sentient nature, then we have every reason to expect that secondary qualities will have a much more significantly restricted explanatory range than, say, primary qualities. Colours, sounds, and tastes do not, then, wield global explanatory power; but neither are they causally inert. Their significance is local, but it is not at all nugatory, so this fact about their role in the scientific enterprise offers no reason for querying their ontological status, unless one mistakes a point about the role of a concept in physics for a point about its role in metaphysics.

B. The Age of Technology

Nietzsche's suspicions about the way in which a mathematically grounded physics pushes truth beyond the realm of sensory animal existence, and thereby invites us to privilege Being over Becoming, would only have been intensified by recent developments in that field. As we saw earlier in this essay, many contemporary physicists struggling to establish laws of quantum gravity claim to have found that they could make progress on this only by constructing theories whose best interpretation—they tell us—treats our universe as a membrane contained within a hyperspace with at least nine spatial dimensions and one temporal dimension. The temptation to treat this as a ground for dismissing our perceptions of a three-dimensional world as illusory is one to which many (whether scientists or not) have found it easy to succumb, despite the fact that even the most skilled and self-aware attempts to translate the complex demands of this mathematically driven theorizing into intelligible discourse result in forms of words to which we struggle to attach sense. We must assume that the relevant mathematics is internally coherent; but the theorizing about the material world that it informs is widely acknowledged to have gone beyond not just any practical, but quite possibly any conceivable, means of testing its empirical validity. So to regard it as an unquestionably authoritative account of reality (as a substantial scientific theory, let alone a metaphysical breakthrough) when its ties to both evidence and extra-theoretical intelligibility have been, if not decisively cut, then radically attenuated—when the only sense we can currently make of it is mathematical—amounts to exhibiting a particularly virulent form of the will to truth.

The later Heidegger—best known as a respectful but radical critic of Nietzsche—is here in deep agreement with his influential interlocutor. For such hyperspace hypotheses exemplify the current culmination of a long modern transition from a mode of physics that deploys mathematics as a powerful supporting technique, to one in which physics becomes essentially incapable of developing its own explanatory powers without drawing on those of mathematics, to one in which it is drawn helplessly along in its erstwhile ally's slipstream (Nietzsche might say that the master is now enslaved). Contemporary physics appears to be in thrall to increasingly sophisticated, massively complex, and internally motivated extensions of mathematical structures that were originally capable of being related back to experimentally verifiable modes of making sense of the world we inhabit, but which have now taken us decisively beyond such relations, and into a realm of increasing, and increasingly self-sufficient or hermetic, abstraction that is nevertheless continually presented to us as the truth about material reality. This priority of the mathematical does not exclude the human being from truth: but it presents us to ourselves as capable of accessing it only by virtue of our possession of calculative rationality, and more specifically by an elaboration of that capacity that at once denigrates other aspects of the human endowment and threatens to thrust the grounds of that capacity (the basis of its supposed ability to disclose reality) entirely beyond the understanding of its possessor. And Heidegger's famous diagnosis of the relation between science, technology, and mathematics in modernity offers a deeply complementary interpretation of the inner logic and existential consequences of this trajectory.[14]

Heidegger begins with the most culturally salient of his three phenomena—technology; and he declares that his interest lies not in the sociology or the history of technology, but in its essence—in what other philosophers might call the metaphysics of technology, which he declares is nothing technological: in other words, he believes that its essence will not show up if we approach the phenomenon of technology in ways that are indebted to that very phenomenon. If, for example, we began by defining technology as an array of instruments, of increasingly sophisticated means towards independently given ends—and perhaps go on to argue that its powers for good or ill will depend upon which ends we choose and how we apply technology in achieving them—then we are looking at technology technologically; we are attempting to grasp the technological world or age in the manner in which we might legitimately grasp specific technologies within that world. But the technological era is not itself a piece of technology: a world which increasingly orders things in terms of means and ends is not itself a means to any end, but rather a fundamental way in which we encounter worldly things, and ourselves amongst them.

Heidegger characterizes this mode of world-disclosure as one of enframing (*Gestell*), in which the real appears as standing-reserve (*Bestand*). A simpler term for *Bestand* might be 'resource': most obviously, nature is primarily or predominantly encountered as a source of energy to be extracted and stored; but that energy is then itself a means to other ends, which are themselves primarily appropriated as means (as the earth yields ore, which then yields uranium, which yields atomic energy, which yields power, which yields electricity and weaponry, and so on). *Gestell* is standardly translated as 'enframing', when it might more simply be translated as 'framework'; but that English term would be appropriate only if we stressed the idea of activity in '-work', and in particular avoided its primary invocation of a static structure (such as a rack or skeleton). It is meant to capture the thought that the technological mode of ordering objects is not so much towards some particular end as towards further—more specific, more flexible or finely grained or efficient—orderability: its end is the enhanced

---

[14] In expounding this diagnosis, I rely on two essays—'The Question Concerning Technology' and 'The Age of the World Picture'—collected in English translation in Heidegger's *The Question Concerning Technology and Other Essays*, trans. W. Lovitt (New York: Harper and Row, 1977); hereafter QCT and AWP respectively.

availability of means, the proliferation of resources. Nietzsche's idea of the will to power is plainly in the vicinity.

Albert Borgmann has helpfully attempted to capture the spirit of Heidegger's thinking by advancing the concept of 'the device' as a paradigm of the technological age.[15] But it's worth being clear from the outset about the distinctive features of employing such paradigmatic or paradeictic modes of accounting for social reality. They are not exercises in apodeictic reasoning—ones which aspire, as do the natural sciences, to explain by subsuming particular cases under general laws; they rather address the prior question of how to identify those features of a complex phenomenon an account of which (whether apodeictic or otherwise) is most likely to help account for the nature of that phenomenon. Invoking a paradigm works as a mode of pointing or indicating (of para-deixis) specifically designed for the field of social theory: it picks out a concrete entity, and invites us to view it as a particularly clear embodiment of a pattern that is realized more broadly, in a range of different but analogously related and equally concrete ways, such that recognizing its pervasiveness allows us to grasp something fundamental about the form of life it orders.

Such a mode of explanation thus depends crucially on two things: the extent to which using the indicated concrete entity as a centre of variation around which others might be organized actually provides a deeper understanding of the broader social phenomenon to be explained (as I claimed that 'conversation' functions with respect to language in Essay One); and the extent to which the one picking out a candidate paradigm has the practical wisdom needed to identify specific details that might have more general import from an otherwise unmanageably complex field of phenomena. Such exercises of right judgement are thus ineliminably personal—they testify to the individuality of the judger, and amount to appeals that we cede authority to the synthesis of experience and insight that generates their pointing gesture; but those gestures must prove themselves by proving to illuminate the phenomenon to be explained—to disclose or reveal something that penetrates to its essence.

Borgmann anchors his device paradigm in social experience by comparing a stove to a central heating system. A stove of the kind belonging to houses in nineteenth-century Montana made warmth available: but it did not do so instantaneously (since its fire had to be built and lit each morning), it required a range of interlocking, complex activities (felling trees, sawing, hauling and stacking logs, feeding the fire as it burned) in order to do so, and it could only provide that warmth in a specific area, and in a manner to which risks (of burns and accidental conflagrations) were attached. Hence, it formed the centre of a world of embodied and social engagement—as the inhabitants of the house worked together to feed

---

[15] *Technology and the Character of Contemporary Life* (Chicago: University of Chicago Press, 1984), esp. ch. 9.

and maintain it, and so regarded it as a focus of that group's labour and leisure, hence as a locus around which its own unity was declared, maintained, and celebrated, and situated within the wider world, both social and natural: the neighbourhood and the landscape (within which wood was either plentiful or not), the climate and the seasons.

Now consider a contemporary central heating system: it too provides warmth, but it also disburdens us of the (genuinely burdensome) further elements within which stoves functioned, which are taken over by the machinery of the device, which not only places fewer demands on our skill, strength, or attention, but also tends to become more and more concealed as technology advances. What defines it is thus the function it serves, the commodity that it makes so commodiously available; and the means by which it does so recede further from our grasp with every iteration of its hidden machinery. Hence every device has structural equivalents, and equivalent devices might have very different underpinnings; broader ranges of raw materials thereby become interconvertible as resources for the provision of a given commodity, and any such commodity itself becomes a more commodiously available resource.

The device paradigm is thus one in which radical variability of means combines with relative stability of ends, and the increasing concealment of the former with the increasing prominence of the latter. And this pattern can extend far beyond what one might call technology proper—beyond the realm of machines, tools, or pieces of equipment. Borgmann uses the example of wine, which he sees as becoming not simply a commodity with distinctive machinery involved in its production, but as internally divided—between a particular aggregate of taste, colour, and smell that it is intended to provide regardless of time and place, and the complex chemical machinery that constitutes its delivery vehicle. Wherever such a structure of prominent commodity and concealed machinery prevails, goods such as warmth or wine are stripped of their pre-technological interwovenness with other goods, and with their broader context of nature, culture, and community; and those who avail themselves of such increasingly self-sufficient, disaggregated commodities do so as increasingly isolated and interchangeable consumers of them.

Borgmann published his analysis in 1984, at a time when the computing revolution and the rise of the internet had barely begun to penetrate everyday life; but one result of more recent technological advance would surely confirm the incisiveness of his device paradigm: the smartphone. Smartphones are, of course, not phones at all: the ability to make a phone call is simply one (decreasingly prominent) app amongst an indefinitely large array of such apps that it makes available to its users. In this sense, smartphones are not devices but meta-devices: they are miniaturized computers, whose theoretical basis (as exemplified in the concept of a Turing machine) is that of infinitely adaptable software—meta-programs capable of realizing or running whatever specific program their user wishes to employ at any given time. The smartphone touch-screen gathers and presents as interconvertible, hence amounts to a commodity that massively enhances the already-considerable commodiousness of, the various applications hitherto made available to us only by desktop or laptop computers operating in conjunction with the World Wide Web (itself made possible only by virtue of the global network of computers known as the internet). And this cornucopia of availability is matched by the exceptionally recessive nature of the machinery that makes it possible—not just the sealed hardware of the device, but the nested hierarchies of incomprehensibly complex proprietary code that run on it. Moreover, as we are belatedly beginning to realize, these meta-devices have been particularly influential in allowing the companies who provide its first-level devices to become consumers of its consumers—to transform those who use its apps (or at least the bundle of data-points that constitutes their presence on the web) into a commodity to be sold to those who wish to sell them commodities.

The information age, the age of surveillance capitalism, is thus a further, devastatingly powerful, iteration of the age of technology—a further step in the de-substantialization or devolution of nature, society, and individuality into infinitely malleable resources. And if we maintain Borgmann's paradeictic stance, we can trace a direct line between the contemporary smartphone and the piece of wax to which Descartes turns—huddled near his own stove, alone in a secluded house near the sea—at a pivotal point in the six meditations that inaugurated Western Europe's modern self-understanding, when he wants to disabuse us of our belief that we clearly and distinctly understand the wax's nature because our senses immediately reveal to us its colour, shape, and size, its scent and its taste. But he only has to bring it nearer the fire for every one of those properties to alter or vanish; and yet the same wax remains. So its real essence, as revealed to experimentally informed exercises of reason that each must perform for himself but which all are equally capable of performing, is something extended, flexible, and changeable. In short, in this little meditative exercise we can see in embryo precisely the mutually reinforcing themes—the denigration of the senses (and so the body, and so the realm of becoming), the isolation and interchangeability of human subjects, and the infinite malleability of all matter—to the full flowering of which Heidegger's work attempts to point us.

How does that work envision the relation between technology and science? Whilst fully acknowledging the dependence of technological progress on scientific advances, Heidegger claims that the essence of modern science is in fact technological:

> [M]an's ordering attitude and behaviour display themselves first in the rise of modern physics as an exact science. Modern science's way of representing pursues and entraps nature as a calculable coherence of forces. Modern physics is not experimental physics because it applies apparatus to the questioning of nature. Rather the reverse is true. Because physics, indeed already as pure theory,

sets nature up to exhibit itself as a coherence of forces calculable in advance, it therefore orders its experiments precisely for the purpose of asking whether and how nature reports itself when set up in this way...

Hence physics... will never be able to renounce this one thing: that nature report itself in some way or other that is identifiable through calculation, and that it remains orderable as a system of information. (QCT, 21, 23)

Heidegger's sense of the distinctively technological nature of modern science has a number of facets. Most fundamentally, the questions it asks of nature—as with any mode of science, and indeed any mode of questioning—presuppose a prior conception of that which is being questioned, and of that which might result from the questioning: and on Heidegger's view, modern physics approaches nature as being essentially a self-contained system of motion of spatiotemporally related units of mass.

> Motion means change of place. No motion or direction of motion is superior to any other. Every place is equal to every other. No point in time has preference over any other. Every force is defined according to—ie *is* only—its consequences in motion, and that means its magnitude of change of place in the unity of time. Every event must be seen so as to be fitted into this ground-plan of nature. Only within the perspective of this ground plan does an event in nature become visible as such an event. (AWP, 119)

Defined in the terms of this ground plan (as Heidegger calls it), all natural events must be essentially identifiable through measurement, with the help of number and calculation. Hence their objectivity—their reality over against our experience of it—is made out in terms of the susceptibility of the forces which constitute them to exhibit constancy within their unceasing change, in other words to manifest inherently calculable modes of alteration, hence rule-governedness, or subjection to law. Scientific research is informed by the presupposition that one grasps the facts by establishing their constitutive laws; and its experimental method of verification is articulated correspondingly. Aristotle was well aware of the importance in acquiring empirical knowledge of the practice of observing things in a variety of conditions to establish how different kinds of things behave as a rule; a medieval schoolman such as Roger Bacon was perfectly sensitive to the difference between acquiring knowledge of things by expounding authoritative doctrine and by direct observation, and to the value of the latter. But neither way of emphasizing the fruits of attending to objects presupposes the laying down of a law as its essential first step.

> To set up an experiment means to represent or conceive the conditions under which a specific series of motions can be made susceptible of being followed in its

necessary progression ie of being controlled in advance by calculation. But the establishing of a law is accomplished with reference to the ground plan of the object-sphere. That ground plan furnishes a criterion and constrains the anticipatory representing of the conditions. Such representing in and through which the experiment begins is no random imagining.   (AWP, 121)

This creates an immediate feedback loop, since the more nature's testimony responds to questions asked of it on these terms (whether negatively or positively), the more precisely the scientist can reformulate her postulated natural laws, which will then constitute a more refined set of conditions on the basis of which future experiments will be set up. And as ever more specific and rigorous laws emerge from this experimental method, so its continued application will presuppose increasingly sensitive and complex devices with which to conduct it—devices whose construction presupposes the validity of the scientific theorizing (and its grounding projection of nature as inherently calculable) that it simultaneously enhances, and which thereby unceasingly refine and reinforce the dominance of that ground-plan. And this drive towards increasing specificity and rigour results in the internal diversification of the scientific enterprise, as each field of inquiry generates subfields governed by specific subsystems of natural law, which in turn generate further subfields, to each of which will belong a distinctive methodology that facilitates and is facilitated by corresponding arrays of experimental technology.

This articulated diversification of fields, methodologies, and procedures constitutes a context within which scientific research takes on a dual capacity for unceasing self-elaboration: within each methodologically specific field (as its laws, experimental devices, and results feed back on one another), and between fields (as their diversity raises the question of how their research methodologies relate to one another, and so how each field's laws, devices, and results might feed back productively on those of another such field). What becomes increasingly necessary is what Heidegger calls 'a plannable conjoining of types of methodology, that further the reciprocal checking and communication of results, and that regulate the exchange of talents' (AWP, 124). It is this internally generated coordinative need that elicits the institutionalization of science, and so of scientific research as an ongoing activity carried out by people whose primary task increasingly becomes that of generating further research opportunities, in crucial part by coordinating globally with other researchers engaged in parallel tasks—primarily through conferences and publications.

In Borgmann's terms, one might say that the institutionalizing of scientific research not only facilitates and presupposes technological devices; it is itself a technological device. It is a device not only for ordering, but also for enhancing the orderability, of scientific knowledge, conceived of as a system of communicable information. It generates that knowledge in such a way that its (undeniably increasing) practical value for society is increasingly independent of, and (certainly for those active in acquiring it) occluded by, the value of its enhanced availability as a resource for the generation of further such knowledge, by virtue of its ability to reorder the laws, experimental devices, and results of given fields of research in ways which facilitate ever more research activity. And the increasingly complex mechanisms which make this knowledge an increasingly commodious commodity fade ever further into the background, beyond the grasp not just of laypeople but of any individual scientist, whose horizon of practical experience is increasingly specialized and whose means of access to other subfields of science is accordingly reduced to the increasingly limited range of potentially relevant data they generate that might be applicable to her own subfield. In short, the ongoing activity of modern science is a device for the increased production of ongoing scientific activity; indeed, since such science contains a multitude of self-enhancing subsciences, and naturally finds application in the production of technology (both for society in general and for itself), it might better be regarded as a meta-device.

C. 'Where the World Becomes Picture...'

On Heidegger's account, then, at the root of modern science lies the same calculability that Nietzsche identifies as a fundamental aspect of its implication in the ascetic ideal; and both philosophers are equally sensitive to the ways in which modern philosophy draws upon and reinforces that emphasis. Heidegger puts it this way:

> This objectifying of whatever is, is accomplished in a setting-before, a representing, that aims at bringing each particular being before it in such a way that man who calculates can be sure, and that means be certain, of that being. We first arrive at science as research when and only when truth has been transformed into the certainty of representation. (AWP, 127)

Heidegger attributes this transformation to Descartes, who he understands as seeking to emancipate human beings as knowers from Christian revelational truth, according to which the salvation of our souls is guaranteed:

> Hence liberation *from* the revelational certainty of salvation had to be intrinsically a freeing *to* a certainty in which man makes secure for himself the true as the known of his own knowing. That was possible only through self-liberating man's guaranteeing for himself the certainty of the knowable. Such a thing could happen, however, only insofar as man decided, by himself and for himself,

what, for him, should be 'knowable' and what knowing and the making secure of the known...should mean. (AWP, 148)

Just as a Nietzschean genealogical approach would expect, the emancipatory impulse of the Enlightenment can justify its turning away from Christianity only by transposing its key predicates onto purportedly secular equivalents. It understands the self's freedom from the legislative authority of others as requiring its acquisition of such legislative authority over itself; and it understands the authority under which it thereby places itself as genuinely obligatory only if it possesses the unconditionality, the absolute and self-grounding certainty, of divine law. Hence, Descartes's metaphysical project seeks, above and before all else, self-guaranteeing self-determination—the self-certifying indubitability of the *cogito ergo sum*; and when it turns its attention to that which is not itself, to external objects, it continues to seek the self-guaranteeing certainty that it has already secured in relation to itself. And the obvious way to achieve that is to relate that which is not oneself unconditionally or absolutely to the self—that is, to conceive of what it is to be an object as a matter of being essentially knowable by that self (representable by it as it really is), and for that self to be capable of knowing this with the same certainty with which it can know anything and everything. Of course, Descartes continues to see an indispensable role for God in securing this knowability, but only a God of whose existence the self can be assured, and from its own resources (rather than, say, by divine revelation).

Kant's critical philosophy offers a purer expression of such a metaphysical vision—in which to be is to be representable to a cognizing subject. For his first *Critique* explicitly tells us that to be an object is to be a possible object of experience, and that the realm of experienceable objects and the realm of contentful empirical thoughts are coextensive. More precisely, it gives an account of empirical knowledge as a conjunction of brutely given sensory input with conceptual form: indeed, the very idea of the given as a body of object-related intuitions—of mere affections as potential representations, candidates for informing us of how things might be outside the experiencing subject—is itself the product of an ineliminable contribution from the subject, being the first stage in a complex and ongoing process of synthetic intellectual activity in accordance with the demands of its rational nature. This activity essentially takes the form of imposing order (or the possibility of order, orderability in Heidegger's terms)— filling out the spatio-temporal field of experience with a system of objects necessarily capable of standing in law-governed relations with one another (of just the kind of which Newton had given a scientific account).

That this must be so—that knowledge of objects, and so what it is to *be* such an object, must take this form—can itself be demonstrated by reason; hence, that knowledge is possible, and that objects are objects of possible knowledge, are themselves deliverances of the very intellectual faculties involved in the acquisition of knowledge, and so ground both knowledge and objectivity in reason's ability to render itself transparent to itself. Such a critique of pure reason is, one might say, its way of redeeming itself; but the price of that redemption is its attribution of a metaphysical priority to the subject over the object that threatens to build the idea of the object's enslavement to the subject into the very idea of objectivity as such. And the history of German Idealism after Kant exploits more systematically his implicit acknowledgement that this synthetic activity of the knowing subject is an aspect of its will, since thinking is a mode of doing and all actions count as such by virtue of giving expression to the orientation of the subject's rational will, whose reality is undeniable despite lying beyond the realm of possible experience. In this respect, cognitive mastery appears as part of the human being's more general drive towards mastery of the world as an environment for achieving its purposes—hence part of our transformation of reality into a standing-reserve, a reservoir of resources.

As is well known, Heidegger argues elsewhere that this post-Kantian trajectory culminates in Nietzsche's own notion of the will to power, and so implicates him in the technological orientation that the former is criticizing. Nietzsche's analysis of modernity undeniably complicates this picture, but it doesn't straightforwardly rebut it. On the one hand, he argues that the orderability sought by modern science embodies the will to truth, which—as an expression of the ascetic ideal—is the object of his criticism; but on the other, he conceives of the drive to truth as in effect a mode of the will to power: truth in the age of the institutionalization of modern science is increasingly sought for the sake of seeking more truth, as power is sought for the sake of enhancing one's ability to seek power. So what are we to make of his apparent endorsement of the latter? If we take the will to power as a cosmological hypothesis or vision, as Heidegger appears to, the threat of an internal contradiction would loom large, and Heidegger's critical distancing of himself from Nietzsche would seem well merited. But such a resolution of the situation fails to appreciate its full complexity.

To begin with, it would be difficult for Nietzsche to have missed the fact that his own genealogical inquiry into the value of truth is itself a further expression of the phenomenon it criticizes—an expression of his desire to seek the truth about truth. Hence his criticism of it is also, and necessarily, a form of self-criticism, and one which at least implies that the will to truth might generate its own internal way of transcending itself. So perhaps we should think of this as the point of acknowledging that the will to truth participates in what it takes to be its opposite (the will to power); after all, if this is so, then furthering the will to power might not be essentially incompatible with the pursuit of truth, suitably reconfigured.

Such an intuition of compatibility is furthered if we recall Cavell's suggestion that our relation to the external world is allegorical of our relation to other minds (or to the otherness of our own minds), and consider the will to power as being in the first instance not a cosmological hypothesis but a vision of human selfhood.

According to that vision, as we saw earlier in this essay, selfhood is essentially a matter of Becoming or transitionality, in that every subject is stretched out between its attained and its unattained but attainable states, always tempted to remain with its current array of cares and concerns but always capable of turning away from them in the name of a more attractive transfiguration of itself. According to this perfectionist vision, the self always points beyond itself; but it always does so from a concrete situation and towards the realization of an equally concrete alternative. This kind of self-perfecting requires a capacity for truthful self-accounting, but one which presupposes Becoming rather than Being; and it requires maintaining the power of self-enhancement, but that power is not an end in itself so much as a means of realizing concrete gains in particular circumstances—of becoming something specific by relinquishing something equally specific. So transfigured, our drives for truth and for power take on a decidedly life-enhancing aspect; and they would not only put Nietzsche's thought decisively beyond the range of Heidegger's critique of the age of technology, but confirm the suspicion that Nietzsche might comfortably incorporate its central thrust into his own critique of modern culture.

In the essay with which we're currently concerned, however, Heidegger doesn't follow up the Kantian and post-Kantian elaborations of representational metaphysics directly; instead he takes guidance from another facet of the concept of representation, and develops a conception of modernity as the age of the world picture (or *weltbild*). We might most naturally take this as a way of claiming that we moderns all think of ourselves as subjects representing how things are in the world, and so as depicting the world as such; but Heidegger wants to be understood otherwise.

> With the word 'picture' we think first of all of a copy of something. Accordingly, the world picture would be a painting, so to speak, of what is as a whole. But 'world picture' means more than this. We mean by it the world itself, the world as such, just as it is normative and binding for us. 'Picture' here does not mean some imitation, but rather what sounds forth in the colloquial expression 'We get the picture' [literally, we are in the picture] concerning something... 'To get into the picture' [literally, to put oneself into the picture] with respect to something means to set whatever is, itself, in place before oneself just in the way that it stands with it, and to have it fixedly before oneself as set up in this way. But a decisive determinant in the essence of the picture is still missing. {That}'We get the picture' concerning something does not mean only that what is, is set before us, is represented to us, in general, but that what is stands before us—in all that belongs to it and all that stands together in it—as a system. 'To get the picture' throbs with being acquainted with something, with being equipped and prepared for it. Where the world becomes picture, what is, in its entirety, is juxtaposed as that for which man is prepared, and which, correspondingly, he therefore intends

to bring before himself, and have before himself, and consequently intends in a decisive sense to set in place before himself. Hence world picture, when understood essentially, does not mean a picture of the world but the world conceived and grasped as picture. What is, in its entirety, is now taken in such a way that it first is in being, and only is in being to the extent that it is set up by man, who represents and sets forth.
> (AWP, 129–30: square-bracketed interpolations by translator; curly-bracketed ones by me)

The conceptual and figurative logic of this passage is complex: but at its heart is Heidegger's claim to detect a certain tension or duplicity internal to our everyday conception of a representational picture—understood as something exhibiting systematicity of a kind that allows it both to stand over against us and yet be something we can envisage inhabiting or entering into. Heidegger wants to exploit that perceived duplicity in order to develop his claim that in modernity man achieves an unprecedentedly powerful but implicitly unstable precedence over what is; and his way of elaborating it suggests that he sees a similarly paradoxical structure—according to which the human being must stand simultaneously within and without the systematically structured scene of representation—in the Kantian critical settlement.

> [I]n that man puts himself into the picture in this way, he puts himself into the scene ie into the open sphere of that which is generally and publically represented, [and t]herewith ... sets himself up as the setting in which whatever is must henceforth set itself forth, must present itself i.e. be picture.
> (AWP, 131–2)

In other words, the human being doesn't just represent how things are with objects; it sets itself up as (the source or origin of, and thus *as*) the systematic setting within which subjects can set up objects representationally.

In more directly Kantian terms, we might say that a given human subject can successfully represent specific objects as they are, but only if we assume that some aspect of itself is prior to, and so transcends, the world within which such cognitive transactions could occur. This is because its transcendental or noumenal powers must be involved if it is to conceptualize its sensory affections as those of an embodied subject inhabiting a doubly systematic world of independently existing objects—doubly systematic, in that both subjects and objects are subordinate to laws of nature (as opposed to behaving chaotically), and in that particular natural laws are systematically subsumable under more general ones (exhibiting a single, self-sufficient architectonic essentially modelled on Newton's theory). Hence, the subject is at once inside and outside the world of its experience:

> What is decisive is that man himself expressly takes up this position (in the midst of what is) as one constituted by himself, that he intentionally maintains it as one constituted by himself, and that he makes it secure as the solid footing for a possible development of humanity.   (AWP, 132)

That last phrase quietly implies that it was precisely Kant's hopes for the unceasing self-Enlightenment of human civilization that helped to make possible their devolution into endless technological advance. As Heidegger puts it, with an eye to the simultaneously pragmatic and death-dealing connotations of the idea of 'execution':

> There begins that way of being human which mans the realm of human capability as a domain given over to measuring and executing, for the purpose of gaining mastery over that which is as a whole.   (AWP, 132)

However that may be, I want to go back to the figurative logic that makes possible this Kantian conceptual reading of Heidegger's central point. For what Heidegger is exploiting, in order to deny that his characterization of modernity as the age of the world picture simply amounts to claiming that we picture the world, is in fact a characteristic feature of representational paintings, and of our relation to them (so his initial, studiedly casual, denial of the relevance of actual paintings is on my reading of it a typically Heideggerian device for inviting us to consider their pertinence to the task). Such things are at once objects and depictions: as framed expanses of paint-smeared canvas, they stand over against us as objects—just like any other objects in our world; but as depictions, they present us with a world-within-our-world (one populated by an interrelated array of objects and people that might be fictional or real). To talk of a representational painting or picture is thus always to talk of a world—the world of that picture, the world we see when we look at it; hence, to regard the picture as a representation (a copy or imitation, a mimesis) always implicitly raises the question of what our relation to that depicted world might be. Is it one into which we can look but from which we are excluded, or is it one we are invited to enter? Is the painting a window or a door?

Some twenty years earlier (in the first of his three lectures on *The Origin of the Work of Art*), Heidegger exploited this same duplicity—and to equally complex effect—when he invoked a Van Gogh painting of a pair of shoes.[16] The vexed question of the significance of that canvas has of course dominated much of the best commentary on those lectures, including the notorious exchanges between

---

[16] Published in *Poetry, Language, Thought*, trans. A. Hofstadter (New York: Harper and Row, 1975); hereafter OWA. For a more detailed discussion of this set of lectures, and of Van Gogh's place within it, see my 'Two Shoes and a Fountain: Ecstasis, Mimesis and Engrossment in Heidegger's *Origin of the Work of Art*', *Proceedings of the Aristotelian Society* 119/2 (2019), 201–22.

Schapiro and Derrida. They engage simultaneously with the question of which actual shoes were the occasion or model for Van Gogh's painting, to whom they belonged, whether they formed a pair, whether they are shoes of the peasant or the urban kind, and so on, and (at least in Derrida's case) with the rather more important question of whether the answer to any of those questions can help in grasping the role of Van Gogh's painting in Heidegger's thinking.

I want to pick up one strand of these exchanges in the present context—the fact (emphasized by Derrida) that the proximate reason for the painting's appearance in Heidegger's argument is its apparent handiness as a prompt for a phenomenology of the equipmentality of equipment.

> We choose as example a common sort of equipment—a pair of peasant shoes... Everyone is acquainted with them. But since it is a matter here of direct description, it may be well to facilitate the visual realization of them. For this purpose a pictorial representation of them suffices. We shall choose a well-known painting by Van Gogh, who painted such shoes several times.
> (OWA, 32–3)

The treacherousness of this moment is not underlined, but it is surely hard to overlook. For by this point in his text, Heidegger has already castigated Western philosophy for attempting to grasp the thinghood of things in terms of three conceptions that do violence to it. The subject-accident model forcefully keeps us at arm's length from it, by placing the bearer of the artwork's perceptible properties beyond our direct apprehension; the 'aggregate of sensations' model makes it press too hard upon us, by dissolving the work into the totality of its affections of our subjectivity; and the most prevalent form-matter model amounts to misinterpreting thinghood as such in terms appropriate to specifically equipmental things—this, indeed, is precisely why Heidegger presents himself as requiring a proper understanding of equipmentality. But in order to gain that understanding, he proposes to treat Van Gogh's painting as a piece of equipment—as a (representational) tool to be made essentially subservient to the needs of his intellectual project, a means to the end of achieving supposedly thoughtful engagement with the work of art. In the terms provided by my present discussion, we might say that Heidegger presents himself as treating this artwork as an intellectual resource for metaphysical inquiry—as a device.

So we ought not to be surprised that the painting proves recalcitrant:

> As long as...we simply look at the empty, unused shoes as they merely stand there in the picture, we shall never discover...the equipmental being of the equipment...From Van Gogh's painting we cannot even tell where these shoes stand. There is nothing surrounding this pair of peasant shoes in or to which they might belong—only an undefined space. There are not even clods of soil from the

field of the field-path sticking to them, which would at least hint at their use. A pair of peasant shoes, and nothing else. And yet—

From the dark opening of the worn insides of the shoes the toilsome tread of the worker stares forth. In the stiffly rugged heaviness of the shoes there is the accumulated tenacity of her slow trudge through the far-spreading and ever-uniform furrows of the field swept by a raw wind. On the leather lie the dampness and richness of the soil. Under the soles slides the loneliness of the field-path as evening falls. In the shoes vibrates the silent call of the earth, its quiet gift of the ripening grain and its unexplained self-refusal in the fallow desolation of the wintry field. This equipment is pervaded by uncomplaining anxiety as to the certainty of bread, the wordless joy of having once more withstood want, the trembling before the impending childbed and shivering at the surrounding menace of death. This equipment belongs to the earth, and it is protected in the world of the peasant woman. From out of this protected belonging the equipment itself rises to its resting within itself. (OWA, 33–4)

The painting's recalcitrance manifests itself in two phases or forms: first, it flatly refuses to perform its representational task of conveying the equipmental nature of the two shoes, and then—well, then it transports or translates its viewer into the world of the peasantry, inducing an ecstasis that finds expression in one of Heidegger's most notorious passages of prose. The first corresponds to the fact that such paintings can stand over against their viewers; the second amounts to an extreme expression of the fact that viewers of a representational painting can find themselves inhabiting the world it depicts—to the point of being possessed by it, and giving voice to it in a way that many readers might find hard to take seriously. Derrida, for example—or at least one of his interlaced voices—finds Heidegger's outburst to be ridiculous and lamentable, at once impoverished and overloaded, the snigger-inducing kitsch of a Swabian museum guide.[17] And yet—

One can take such outbursts seriously without taking them at face value. Reflecting on this passage a few pages later, Heidegger says: 'By bringing ourselves before Van Gogh's painting [t]his painting spoke. In the vicinity of the work, we were suddenly somewhere else than we usually tend to be' (OWA, 35). The reflective form of these remarks necessarily distances Heidegger, and so us, from the person before the painting who spoke in such a 'ridiculously lamentable' way: and that in turn makes it possible for us retrospectively to consider his outburst as indicating not how he really thinks the truthful work of an artwork is meant to happen, but rather what happens when a certain violence is done to it, and what we might learn about it from the form that its resistance to such violence takes.

---

[17] 'Restitutions', in *The Truth in Painting*, trans. G. Bennington (Chicago: University of Chicago Press, 1987), 291.

So understood, Heidegger's reflections suggest that the result of attempting to make philosophical use of a work of art that supposedly represents a piece of equipment is that it refuses either to be so used or to be defined by a particular (representational) mode of use, and instead assaults that which attempted to assault it. This diphasic response effects a break or discontinuity in the thinker's line of thought, one which displaces him from an initial, inordinate distance from the painting (situated as an observer with essentially technological designs on it from whom the world of the painting turns away) by placing him into inordinate proximity to it (as it speaks from his location, which is another way of saying that he speaks from its location—within or out of the world it depicts). And such a displacement is only possible because a representational painting is both an object in the world and the bearer of a world.

So the painting's resistant response to Heidegger holds open a certain possibility of genuine understanding; and one textual registration of this lies in his resorting to three variations on the word 'nothing' in as many sentences when characterizing the shoes in the painting—nothing surrounding them, no clumps of soil, the shoes and nothing else. This will remind some readers of Heidegger's inaugural lecture, in which he attempts to displace our attention from science to ontology by emphasizing the extent to which science concerns itself with objects 'and nothing else'. As that lecture emphasizes, genuinely ontological insight comes from our willingness to stay with that 'nothing' as it is in itself—to patiently attend to the nullity that science presupposes and overlooks. But his first lecture on art makes it abundantly clear that this is more easily said than done. For Van Gogh's painting no sooner draws Heidegger's attention to nothingness (despite his desire to appropriate it as a resource) than he produces an uncannily overloaded painting in words of the world that is absent from the shoes in the painting, and so is absent from the painting—quite as if he cannot bear to suffer that absence, and so attend to what is truly present in the painting.

The ecstatic outpouring that gives expression to this unwillingness is thus set up or staged by Heidegger not as an indication of the truth set to work in the painting, but as an exemplification of the misapprehensions that can be unleashed by the painting's being set to work in the wrong way, and of the genuine guidance that can nevertheless be elicited from what makes such misapprehensions possible. It amounts to a short stretch of Heidegger's longer path of thought about art that dramatizes or enacts what it is not to think about art, and in such a way that what it might be to think about art more fruitfully comes more clearly into focus.

For my present purposes, it's crucial that that self-dramatization involves Heidegger playing the role of a technologically minded metaphysician—someone who, according to his later essay of that name, inhabits the age of the world picture (as we all do). But it's also worth pausing over the fact that the particular painting around which the drama is staged is one by Van Gogh—that is, a painting that inhabits the initial stages of the development of modernist painting in the wake of

Manet. I have adverted more than once in these essays to the orienting influence of Michael Fried's account of the prehistory of modernism in French painting—an account which uses Diderot's writings to help identify a crucial break or discontinuity in the development of painting in France in the 1750s and 1760s, between the work of Chardin and that of Greuze. So it strikes me as significant that what Fried takes to be revealed and set in motion by that break depends on the very properties of representational painting upon which Heidegger's invocation of the medium turns both in his lectures on art and in his essay concerning world pictures.[18]

According to Fried, Diderot implicitly recognized that the primordial convention that paintings are made to be beheld was no longer something that could be taken for granted, as it had been in the work of Chardin. The nature of Greuze's work showed, by contrast, that for him the presence of a beholder must rather be earned, accomplished, or at least powerfully affirmed by the painting itself. In short, paintings must attract, arrest, and enthral their viewers, hold them there as if spellbound; but if, in so doing, the painting betrayed too blatant an awareness of the beholder's presence, it would thereby court theatricality, making the beholder aware of the illusion of reality by means of which she had been halted in front of the painting, and so breaking its spell.

Resolving this tension depended upon finding a means of securing the beholder's presence by establishing the fiction of her absence; and one such means was to depict people wholly absorbed in their pursuits or purposes within the world of the painting, for they in effect declared themselves to be oblivious of the gaze of others, including those beholding the paintings which depicted them. It is the anti-theatrical value of such absorptive themes and scenes in the post-Chardin world that explains Diderot's particular advocacy of history painting as the highest of the medium's genres. The inherent drama of the scenes represented in such paintings could match the beholder's increasingly demanding need to be enthralled; and its orientation to past events made more plausible the illusion that the dramatis personae had determined their own positions and groupings, unlike work in such genres as landscape and still-life painting. Both features helped to ensure a painting's success as a dramatically unified composition or 'tableau': for they bequeath a strong, coherent, and self-sufficient systematicity to the world of the painting, one which captures the attention of the beholder precisely because she forms no part of that system, and so experiences herself as being excluded from the depicted world in a way which can only convince her of its independent reality—hence, of the painting's success as the representation of a world.

---

[18] *Absorption and Theatricality* (Chicago: University of Chicago Press, 1980); hereafter AT.

But Diderot was willing to recognize a second such strategy—and one which he encountered primarily in works of what he considered less elevated genres: those of still life, and particularly of landscape. For Fried shows Diderot responding to certain works in such genres as if he were inhabiting the depicted scene: he writes from the perspective of someone taking a walk through the depicted landscape, or deriving solace from sitting next to a depicted river; and in one case, he writes about six separate landscape paintings by Vernet as if they formed snapshots of a single long walk that he took in the company of a sensitive guide to the terrain. Deploying such a fiction of inhabiting the world of the painting became an indication of Diderot's sense of their success as paintings; it's remarkably similar to Christopher Nolan's career-long sense that cinematic success depends upon creating an immersive experience in viewers, in which the screen does not so much screen us from its projected world as allow us to project ourselves into it (as Cooper is presented as doing from his tesseract in *Interstellar*).

However that may be, Fried emphasizes that what he calls Diderot's pastoral strategy is just as much a way of de-theatricalizing the painting–beholder relationship as is the essentially dramatic strategy employed in history painting. For the former also works to remove the beholder from in front of the painting (not by representing absorptive states, but by absorbing her into its represented world); and in doing so, it too exploits a strong sense of the systematicity of its depicted worlds—it's just that in the pastoral strategy this effect is achieved by capturing the causal systematicity of nature that underlies and makes possible its human inhabitability, rather than the dramatic unity of concentrated and poised human action and passion.

On Fried's analysis, then, it was increasingly assumed that the beholder's desired absorption in a painting's fictional scene of representation could be achieved only by deploying representations of absorption which negated or neutralized her presence before the canvas depicting that scene—her position in what one might call the literal scene of representation, in the world that contains both her and the painting. But of course, any such achievement could itself only be a supreme fiction. For the dramatic illusion of reality in painting can only operate in the context of the literal scene of representation, so the beholder's existence before the canvas could no more be successfully negated or denied than could the canvas's existence before the beholder; indeed, to aim for the one would be to aim for the other. Consequently, the anti-theatrical tradition Fried sees as emerging with the painters who share Diderot's understanding of their situation in effect commits itself to the entirely incoherent aim of denying the material reality of its own works as well as the material reality of those who behold them. It isn't difficult to see in such a drive towards de-realization or disincarnation a mode of life-denial akin to that of the sceptic's incoherent desire to relate to his best cases of knowledge at once specifically and generically.

Nevertheless, the proponents of this tradition were responding to a real problem. The very medium of an easel painting emerged only after paintings ceased to be primarily encountered as part of larger, primarily religious contexts (the walls and ceilings of churches and chapels), or as part of the primarily decorative schemes of aristocratic buildings. An easel painting was thus something essentially portable and self-sufficient—removable from any surface or environment with which it could be conjoined, and hence not able to rely on a given larger context to draw and gather people who might then attend to it. That task of drawing and gathering now became something it had to execute itself; hence the importance of its presenting itself as a self-sufficient and instantaneously accessible unity—something that could immediately be apprehensible as an authentic whole, by exhibiting a compellingly meaningful relation of its parts. And this was why genuinely fundamental anxieties were generated when painters began to sense that the beholders of their work were becoming alienated from them—no longer absorbed or enthralled by canvasses qua paintings, qua fictional scenes of representation. For they rightly saw such alienation as a sceptical threat to painting's capacity to maintain its status as a major art form.

Their (metaphysical) error was to attribute this scepticism to beholding as such, rather than to the increasingly exhausted powers of traditional modes of creating absorption in the dramatic illusions of painting. That is, they assumed that what was undermining the beholder's capacity to be absorbed by the dramatic illusion of any painting was the ineluctable fact of her existence as an embodied being standing before a pigment-smeared canvas, rather than some developing loss of conviction in a prevailing system of painterly conventions for creating this illusion. Consequently, they took their painting's continued capacity to create compelling dramatic illusions as dependent upon those works embodying denials of the literal or physical reality of both beholder and painting—strategies of negation that became increasingly extreme as previous ones necessarily failed to achieve their incoherent purpose, and thus ironically contributed by their resultant theatricality to the beholder's intensifying loss of conviction in the dramatic illusions of painting.

There are, however, alternatives to this metaphysically confused anti-theatrical strategy; and Fried credits Manet with the initiation of one, and thereby with the initiation of painterly modernism in Europe. Manet's version of anti-theatricality still aims to defuse the threat of scepticism; but it does so by acknowledging rather than denying the metaphysical constraints of the literal scene of representation—by producing work which finds a source of new artistic convention in the necessary physicality or embodiedness of painting and beholder, in the fact that the two face one another in space and time, and that any fictive or dramatic encounter they facilitate depends upon that fact and its implications. Since a painting is both canvas and depiction, its beholder is at once the beholder of a physical object and of a fictional scene of representation: in this sense, beholding is an inherently doubled or dual subject-position. One mode of anti-theatricality interprets this duality as self-cancelling: either literal beholding negates its fictional counterpart, or vice versa, so painting must commit itself to the production of works which deny their own literality and thereby attempt to constitute a beholder whose literality is negated. The other interprets the duality as ineliminable, and therefore aims to produce convincing representational works which simultaneously acknowledge their own literality and thereby construct a beholder capable of acknowledging her own literal presence.

Of course, paintings exist not just as physical objects and as fictional scene of representations, but as products—as the result of meaningful human activity; the beholder not only perceives an object and is absorbed in a dramatic illusion, but confronts the work of another human being. So, fully acknowledging a representational painting also requires acknowledging it as a scene or site of the artist's representational efforts. Accordingly, Fried contrasts what he sees as incoherent attempts within the Diderotian anti-theatrical tradition to negate or deny the fact that paintings are the intentional product of human activity from attempts to produce work which acknowledges its origins in human action, and thereby makes it possible for a beholder to acknowledge her role as beholder of an intentional or worked object.

Manet achieves this in part by his unprecedented emphasis on the reality of the painter's model, and hence of the studio she occupied. But to achieve this whilst also acknowledging that his paintings are both physical objects and representations forced him to revise the Diderotian ideal of the *tableau*. On this new conception, what Fried christens 'facing' rather than absorptive closure would be the *tableau*'s operative principle: the instantaneity and strikingness which most contemporary critics saw as achievable only through absorptive closure would still be aimed at and achieved, but through strategies of a fundamentally opposing kind.

Thus, Manet systematically avoids depictions of people absorbed in what they are doing, tending rather to depict figures gazing directly out of the painting; he makes use of unintelligible subject matter and internally disparate *mise-en-scène*; he combines strong figural gestalts with abrupt tonal contrasts in a way which stamps out the depicted image; he executes his paintings with a marked lack of finish, and so on. In these ways, he does all he can to dramatize or underscore, and thereby to acknowledge, the fact that paintings present their viewers with a representation consisting of marks placed on a physical surface by their maker; in short, his paintings simultaneously acknowledge the three dimensions of beholding or of the scene of representation (the painting qua physical object, painted object, and/or depiction).

Manet's work does not presuppose that these elements necessarily eclipse or negate one another; but neither does it assume that they form self-contained parts of a self-sufficient whole. In that sense, where absorptive *tableaux* aim for a mode of closure which stands opposed to the fragmentary (to *morceaux*), his antiabsorptive *tableaux* might also be called assemblages of *morceaux*—or better, as placing the *tableau/morceau* contrast in question. Fried's Manet thus sees the three conditions or dimensions of painting as engaged in a constant mutual confrontation or facing-off, each constraining and being constrained by the others, and each standing in need of acknowledgement by and through the others in a kind of productive and open-ended dialogue which can be brought to a provisional conclusion in particular works of painting, but for which no final, totalizing closure can ultimately be imagined.

For my purposes, what matters most about Fried's account of Manet's avoidance of Diderot's anti-theatrical strategy is understanding why that strategy emerged and became so salient in the century before Manet. A clue resides in the fact that the incoherence it turns out to embody has an essentially metaphysical cast; for that implies that the roots or form of the alienation that it rightly apprehended and aimed to combat were also as much metaphysical as aesthetic— that is, that they concerned not only aesthetic objects but objecthood as such. As Fried has it:

> [T]he criticism and theory we have been considering expressed an implicit apprehension of the beholder' alienation from the objects of his beholding (and therefore...from himself, both in his capacity as beholder and as a potential object of beholding for others)...
>
> In Diderot's writings on painting and drama, the object–beholder relationship as such, the very condition of spectatordom, stands indicted as theatrical, a medium of dislocation and estrangement rather than of absorption, sympathy, self-transcendence; and the success of both arts, in fact their continued functioning as major expressions of the human spirit, are held to depend on whether or not painter and dramatist are able to undo that state of affairs, to *de-theatricalize beholding* and so make it once again a mode of access to truth and conviction, albeit a truth and conviction that cannot be entirely equated with any known or experienced before. (The antidualistic implications of this project are consistent with the dominant tendency of Diderot's thought in all fields.) What is called for, in other words, is at one and the same time the creation of a new sort of object— the fully realized *tableau*—and the constitution of a new sort of beholder—a new 'subject'—whose innermost nature would consist in the conviction of his absence from the scene of representation. (AT, 105, 103–4)

Since easel painting is a medium that emerged by severing painting's preceding internal relatedness to religious, social, and political power, it exemplifies the Enlightenment's general tendency to separate out the hitherto tightly intertwined strands or dimensions of Western European culture, and accordingly participates in the broader metaphysical trajectory of modernity. So it is unsurprising that the crisis of aesthetic integrity that Fried identifies by means of Diderot should turn out to be internally related to a broader cultural crisis—that these specifically aesthetic struggles appear on the one hand to reflect broader anxieties, and on the other come to be regarded as a privileged location in which to identify and resolve them. But Fried's Diderotian lens also allows us to make more specific sense of that assignment of privilege, and in ways that seem deeply compatible with (and so help to illuminate and render more plausible) Heidegger's general analysis of the ascetic technological essence of modernity, as well as his specific suggestion that modernity is that age in which the world becomes picture.

If the being of objects in modernity increasingly comes to lie in their being represented, the specific worldly objects whose function is to provide self-sufficient visual representations of worlds are likely to attain paradigmatic or paradeictic status—to act as a kind of cultural lightning-rod. But the structure of the aesthetic crisis that begins in mid-eighteenth-century French painting reflects the broader metaphysical scene in more specific ways. To begin with, the core problem is the one identified in Cavell's essay on Kierkegaard's portrayal of Adler—the subject's increasing alienation from its objects and itself; and that alienation here takes the form of those objects no longer attracting or compelling that subject's attention. Most immediately, this is a matter of the subject's loss of interest in these objects: but that loss of interest is experienced as consequent upon the object's excessive interest in the subject (the increasing transparency of its designs upon its putative beholders), and since these objects are explicitly acknowledged to be products of the subject (the result of human labour), their designs upon the subject are in fact the subject's own, which means that the aesthetic subject is losing interest in these objects primarily insofar as these products of his subjectivity betray an intense awareness of those standing before them (not just all the beholders for whom they are made, but also their makers, who are after all their first beholders). But since, on Heidegger's account of modernity, all objects are increasingly attaining that status—being set up over and against the subject by the subject and for the subject—this crisis in art is at heart an aesthetic inflection of a more general metaphysical anxiety underlying Western European culture.

If we turn to the structure of the resolution offered by the Diderotian tradition to this sceptical crisis, we find further ways in which the nature of representational easel painting shapes and is shaped by its broader metaphysical background. Two features of that resolution seem particularly to invite comparison with Heidegger's characterization of a world picture: the fact that successfully anti-theatrical paintings in the Diderotian line negate the beholder's presence before the canvas either by wholly absorbing him into his role as beholder of the world of the painting, or by fictionally absorbing him into that world; and the fact that both strategies of negation depend upon creating worlds that exhibit a compelling mode of systematic unity (whether dramatic or pastoral).

The first feature depends upon the fact that the beholder of an easel painting can with equal justice regard the world it depicts either as one into which she looks from the outside, or as one into which she can enter. For such a painting—framed, portable, immediately visually accessible—necessarily represents its world as a bounded whole, hence as something to which any beholder of it is essentially external; and yet, insofar as it presents a convincing or truthful representation of some aspect of the real world (whether human or natural), it can be experienced as holding open a world that the beholder might imaginatively or fictionally inhabit precisely because it presents itself as continuous with the world she actually inhabits along with the painting. And this dual subject-position is establishable only insofar as the worlds a painter makes successfully realize a strongly systematic inner unity—whether primarily dramatic or primarily pastoral (itself a matter of emphasis rather than opposition, since—as Kant acknowledged in his *Critique of Judgement*—the systematic unity of nature must be such as to accommodate the achievements of human purposes, and so must be inherently capable of exhibiting dramatic unity). For this kind of systematicity is correspondingly Janus-faced: it makes possible both the beholder's sense of being excluded from the world of the painting, and her sense that there are stable positions within it that she might conceivably take up.

In other words, the anti-theatrical strategy that Diderot advocates aspires to establish exactly the kind of beholder–painting relationship, and so exactly the kinds of beholders and paintings, that Heidegger argues are encoded into the more general mode of subject–object relationship that dominates the age of the world picture. Paintings that embody the Diderotian ideal of the *tableau* would present worlds whose inner unity situates their beholders as either outside them or inside them. And such objects constitute their corresponding subject-position as at once constitutive of the world they represent (since it is those subjects who make these worlds, and with an eye to their being taken in as a whole by beholders such as themselves) and subject to it (capable of being drawn within, and thereby subordinated to, its systematic unity).

In more Nietzschean terms, such a beholding subject is at once master of and enslaved by its aesthetic object; and Heidegger's notion of 'a world become picture', with its equally emphatic focus upon systematicity and upon the dual or duplicitous situating of the modern subject within the world it sets up, can then be seen as his way of saying that the basic subject-position of modernity amounts to a more general or pervasive inflection of that synthesis of master and slave. The fact that this Diderotian ideal of the beholder is fundamentally unstable and ultimately incoherent further suggests that the modern subject's self-interpretation is likewise beholden to fantasy, hence vulnerable to internal collapse, and perhaps to disclosing the possibility of its overcoming.

On Fried's account, it is Manet's reconfiguration of painting's ideal of the *tableau*, and so of the objects and subjects of painting, that embodies the genuinely emancipatory and essentially modernist alternative to Diderot's project in aesthetics. And that is why it is significant that Heidegger chose a Van Gogh painting when considering the nature of art and its works in his earlier lectures on that theme— that is, a painting which was produced in a context deeply determined by Manet's achievement, and so on the other side of painting's doomed investment in the construction of paintings whose modes of world-construction disclosed and reinforced modernity's life-denying self-interpretations.

I noted earlier that Heidegger dramatizes his encounter with that modernist work as having two phases—one in which the painting refuses his attentions, leaving him absolutely external to its world, and one in which it displaces him from in front of itself by compelling him to speak on behalf of its world (as if not so much taking his place within that world as merging with it). We are now in a position to say more about why this encounter goes wrong, and wrong in this particular way; for what we see in beholding Heidegger's drama is an attempt on his part to relate in the manner appropriate to a Diderotian beholder to an object whose principles of construction are essentially antithetical to that mode of apprehension.

It is, after all, far from implausible to interpret Van Gogh's various paintings of peasant shoes as further developments of Manet's revolutionary deconstruction of the Diderotian idea of a *tableau*. In the terms I laid out earlier, where absorptive *tableaux* aim for a mode of closure which stands opposed to the fragmentary (to *morceaux*), anti-absorptive *tableaux* amount to assemblages of *morceaux*—or better, are intended precisely to place the *tableau/morceau* contrast in aesthetically productive question. Accordingly, those following in the wake of Fried's Manet will have to find their own ways of acknowledging the three constitutive conditions or dimensions of painting as engaged in a constant mutual confrontation or facing-off, staging thereby a kind of productive and open-ended dialogue which can be brought to a provisional conclusion in particular works of painting, but for which no final, totalizing closure can ultimately be imagined.

If Van Gogh's shoe paintings aspire to just such a provisional internal stability, they will lack the strongly delineated inner unity that Diderot admired. They will rather exhibit a kind of self-absorption that belongs more to Manet's anti-theatrical modernist project than that of its ill-fated predecessor, insofar as the painter's intense affirmation of their fictionality—their representational status— intensifies our sense of the reality of that which they represent. The paintedness of this particular Van Gogh painting of two shoes shows us what it might mean for pieces of equipment (as opposed to persons) to be absorbed in their own nature; and that self-involvement—insofar as it involves their turning away from their usual accessibility to users—isolates the shoes from each other (leading some to question whether they form a pair), hence from their equipmental world, and so from their viewers (whose suddenly problematic access to that world is the painter's way of acknowledging them as inevitably located outside it, before the canvas).

This means that paintings such as this simply will not accommodate the doubled or duplicitous subject-position that Diderotian *tableaux* are made for. On the contrary: they are made precisely in order to emphasize or reveal a rift, a radical instability, within the subject-position from which Heidegger looks to engage with it—a position that he deliberately stages as an essentially technological one, according to which the painting is approached as a resource for metaphysical investigations. This is why his encounter with the Van Gogh painting begins with an absolutized and unsatisfying inflection of the beholder's sense of exclusion from the world of the painting, and immediately transitions into an equally absolutized and unsatisfactory inflection of the beholder's sense of inclusion or absorption within that world.

The encounter can thus be read as a dramatized acknowledgement of how a modernist reconception of Diderot's thematics of absorption actually works on its beholders: first by attracting their attention despite their distractedness, and then by rebuking its inevitable inappropriateness or misdirectedness. Heidegger approaches the painting simply as one amongst many appropriate depictions; then his attention is caught by its particularity—initially by the shoes' absorption in themselves as that declares itself in their refusal of their implied pictorial world, and then by their resultant refusal of his presence and interest in them; and finally, he finds himself transported into the absent world of the painting, as if its presence as a material object to which he is present has been obliterated.

His deliberately theatrical conjuration of the peasant woman's world thus dramatizes the Diderotian beholder's aversion from the painting's attempt to acknowledge rather than to deny the fictionality of its shoes; and his equally theatrical dissolution of such a beholder into the absent scene of representation dramatizes its equal aversion from the literal scene of representation, rendering beholder and canvas so inordinately proximate to each other that their separateness (and so their relatedness) vanishes. In other words: this elaborately dramatized encounter amounts to an attempt on Heidegger's part to allow an artwork that is struggling to transcend the basic aesthetic logic of the technological age to help him (and so his readers) in their struggle to transcend its metaphysical logic, and thereby (by means that are at once aesthetic, ethical, cultural, and philosophical) to overcome what Nietzsche would call the ascetic ideal from within.

D. Photography as a Technology of Artistic Modernism

Heidegger's (and Fried's, and Cavell's) sense of the redemptive dimension of modernist painting may or may not be attractive; but it is very likely to seem obsolete. For it is now an art-critical commonplace to regard artistic modernism as outmoded or dead, as having been theoretically and practically outflanked after the mid-twentieth century by what might be called postmodernist modes of artistic endeavour in which the artist's relation to the history of their enterprise appears to be an eminently dismissable problem. If that were true, then the present value of this case study of Nietzsche (like that of Cavell's case study of Kierkegaard) would lie in its helping us to measure what we might have lost (let's say spiritually) in losing that form of artistic life; but since concepts that have migrated once might do so again, we should also consider the possibility that the categories needed to comprehend modernist painting and sculpture in the 1960s (and so to comprehend its long and winding prehistory) are now needed in other artistic media, or in other spheres of culture.

Michael Fried's *Why Photography Matters as Art as Never Before* argues that this possibility has been recently realized in the domain of photography.[19] More specifically, he claims to have identified a new photographic regime—an epochal development in art photography engendered by the recrudescence of issues of beholding and pictorial ontology that were central to Western painting from 1760 to 1960.

In my view, any useful critical response to his claim has to recognize that the representational strategy Fried deploys in arguing for it mirrors a representational strategy that is central to the regime it aspires to acknowledge. For his account of that regime repeatedly returns to the ways in which contemporary art photographers employ versions of portraiture to confront issues of absorption and theatricality; and the account itself is organized as a kind of group portrait—a sequence of intensively elaborated, perspicuous presentations of the distinctive physiognomy of specific pictures and sequences of pictures by individual photographers, through which a sense of their family resemblances (the complex overlapping and interweaving of themes, concerns, and strategies within and between their individual bodies of work) might gradually emerge.

This consonance of content and form is apt to baffle certain familiar interpretative strategies. We cannot, for example, expect any simple or even single definition of what unifies the regime in terms of what philosophers might call necessary and sufficient conditions for belonging. Nor should we expect to acquire a full understanding of what Fried wants to say about any particular element of the regime by concentrating exclusively on a single portion of his book (either a chapter or some part thereof). For pretty much every concept deployed to relate a particular photograph or photographer to that regime is deployed elsewhere in the book in relation to various other photographs and photographers, and thereby acquires various inflections and elaborations that inevitably deepen our sense of its full significance in our initial context. And these matters are further

[19] Cf Fried, *Why Photography Matters as Art as Never Before* (New Haven: Yale University Press, 2008); hereafter WPM.

complicated by Fried's willingness to regard the work of his chosen photographers as illuminated by, and illuminating, the work of certain philosophers. For even if we accept the very idea of such achievements of cross-disciplinary insight, their proper acknowledgement requires that we acknowledge the apparently stark differences of context, presupposition, preoccupation, media, and method at work on each side of these conversations.

Nevertheless, these complexities have to be negotiated if we are to address the question that his book raised more insistently for most of his readers than any other: what conception of the nature of photography underlay its overlapping accounts of various bodies and series of photographic works of art? After all, those accounts continuously declared Fried's conviction that some contemporary art photography could be understood only in relation to topics that determined the nature of pictorial modernism; and as we have seen, his account of modernist painting, and in particular of the value of the works of high modernism in American painting of the 1950s and 1960s, located it in the way such works acknowledged the essential features of their medium, and so its distinctness as one artistic medium amongst others.[20] Even if that idea of the essence of a medium was, as it were, historicist—adverting not to the irreducible, ahistorical essence of all painting, but rather that which, at a given moment, is capable of generating (in both artist and audience) the conviction that the relevant work is a great painting, despite e.g. its refusal to provide representational content or traces of brushwork on the painted surface—it still involves the disclosure of some features as essential to its being a contemporary exemplar of that long artistic tradition, as opposed to any other. It would seem to follow that any photographs produced by artists understood to be grappling with the conditions of modernism would necessarily constitute acknowledgements of the essential nature of photography, and so must amount to disclosures of what essentially distinguishes photography from, say, painting (or video or cinema), here and now.

An immediate difficulty with this conclusion is that Fried's own account aims to disclose a deep continuity between modernist, and in particular high modernist, painting and the relevant strands of contemporary art photography; hence it appears to require that he apply a range of concepts (beholding, absorption, worldhood, objecthood, theatricality) whose sense he had worked out as part of working out how modernist painting came to be able to acknowledge the conditions of its own medium to works of art that appeared to belong to a very different medium. A further difficulty is that the relevant photographic works were largely produced under a very different technological regime than that of analogue photography (involving the registration of light on film): both their scale and their content were a function of (sometimes quite radical) advances in a variety of

---

[20] The key works are AT; *Courbet's Realism* (Chicago: University of Chicago Press, 1990); and *Manet's Modernism* (Chicago: University of Chicago Press, 1996), hereafter MM.

primarily digital photographic techniques (relating to the capture, manipulation, and printing of the relevant images), and so they inevitably raised the question of whether the concept of a photograph, and so that of a distinctively photographic medium, still retained a univocal sense. Might not those differences of technology and technique even be sufficient to license the judgement that a photograph by Jeff Wall and one by Cartier-Bresson were essentially different kinds of object—even that what Wall calls a photograph is closer to a painting than it is to a photograph produced by analogue means?

This might address the immediate difficulty I raised, although only at the cost of jettisoning Fried's patent conviction throughout his book that he is disclosing the nature of a new photographic regime rather than a new phase in a long (related series of) regimes of painting; but it would only heighten the bewilderment induced by Fried's apparent lack of interest in explicitly confronting this issue in his book. That is to say, although his discussion of any given photographer's body of work (or portion of a larger such body) always brings out the way in which it acknowledges some determining condition or conditions of its own possibility, he offers no general account of how each such condition relates to those acknowledged in other such bodies of work (that is, no account of what kind of work these contemporary works actually are, if indeed they are a single kind, as opposed to being each a kind unto themselves), or of how they stand—aesthetically and ontologically speaking—in relation to photographic works produced under analogue conditions.

It's worth emphasizing that this sense of something missing from Fried's account will persist even if one takes fully on board the Wittgensteinian warning enunciated in my critical response quoted above, and avoids either demanding or expecting a *merkmal* definition of the relevant kind(s). For one might still reasonably expect the composer of this group portrait to say at least as much about the overlapping family resemblances making up the kind(s) of photographic artwork his book aspires to disclose as he did (and assigned great importance to being able to do) with respect to the evolving collective ontological self-understanding embodied in the kinds of modernist and high modernist paintings that formed the subject of so many of his previous writings.

My orienting suggestion is that Fried does in fact confront the frustrated expectation I have just articulated, or rather provides a justification for frustrating it, in the final chapter of the book itself—where he gives an account of the work of the Bechers, photographers of the highest interest in their own right, and extremely influential figures for many of the German photographers discussed in other chapters (Gursky, Ruff, and Struth were students of Bernd Becher). Beginning in the 1960s, Bernd and Hilla Becher travelled extensively across Europe and the United States to photograph various structures—water towers, cooling towers, gasometers, lime kilns, and so on—on industrial sites. Using analogue cameras with long exposures or fine-grained film to capture real detail and depth of field, the resultant black-and-white photographs were taken from raised, head-on vantage points, with each structure's environment cropped to a minimum but in such a way as to capture its rootedness in the ground. As their first book's title indicates, their concern was typological: from each category of structure, they selected a small number of photographs and arranged them in a grid, whose point—as Fried emphasizes—is 'above all comparative: the viewer is thereby invited to intuit from the... individual instances the latent "presence" or operation of a single type and at the same time to enjoy a heightened apprehension of the individuality or uniqueness of the particular instances relative both to one another and to the latent or implied type' (WPM, 309).

Fried interprets this typological concern in the light of Hegel's distinction between the genuine or true infinite and its spurious or bad counterpart, which is designed to help us grasp the finitude or determinateness—call it the genuine individuality—of objects. By virtue of their typological mode of presentation, the objects depicted in the Bechers' work are made internally contrastive with one another, so that our perceptual mode of address to their individual instances is strongly but non-coercively structured or directed, both within a given group and between different groups. (Heidegger might call this a non-technological mode of orderability.) This format prevents us from attempting to perceive any individual object of a given type 'in itself', as it were: for so encountered,

> the category of water tower would implicitly be contrasted with every other category of object, man-made and natural, large and small, opaque, translucent and transparent, solid, liquid and gaseous, and so on, to be encountered in the universe; and ... *all* the specific features of that particular water tower... would in principle be equally important and moreover would implicitly stand in contrast with everything that might be truly predicated of every other object in the universe... (the water tower, one might say, would be a bare particular and nothing more, and so would every discernible feature of its construction)
> (WPM, 326)

For Hegel, such sheer particularity is chimerical—a fantasy of objecthood rather than its underlying essence. One might think of it as a fantasy of what it might mean to relate to an object specifically rather than generically (in the terms of Cavell's articulation of external-world scepticism).

What the Bechers' typological tableaux supply that is missing from what Fried calls a mere world of real things encountered in the course of everyday life 'is a showing of the grounds of its intelligibility, which is also to say of its capacity for individuation, *as* a world. Or, as a *world*, one bearing the stamp of a particular stage in history' (WPM, 327–8). For Hegel (or at least for Pippin's Hegel as interpreted by Fried), this field of relations, contrasts, and oppositions is a collective, greatly mediated, and deeply historical field maintained by human subjects; so it is subject to evolution and to contestation about its proper articulation and interpretation. Hence '[i]t goes without saying that the project of creating... typologies [that bring some aspect of that field to consciousness] can never be final, both on the typological level and on that of the individual instance... which is to say that the project is always... open to further discoveries and arrangements. [As Pippin puts it] "The infinity at play in such incompleteness is of the kind Hegel calls 'true' or genuine" ' (WPM, 327).

In the first instance, this Hegelian interpretation of the Bechers' typological practice implies that the two dominant analogies in the literature deployed to grasp its significance (Linnean comparative morphology and Galtonian composite photography) miss something vital. However that may be, I want to suggest that this concluding chapter also has a reflexive significance; for it provides an illuminating model for understanding the internal structure of Fried's book and so the mode of address it tries to establish to its readers. Just as the book as a whole might be thought of as a group portrait of the various photographers whose work so often assigns prominence to the role and nature of portraiture, so its successive alignment of more than a dozen different kinds of (series of) photographs—Wall's near-documentaries and his street photographs, Struths's museum photographs and family portraits, Demand's allegories of intention—can be thought of as a typology of a certain kind (more precisely, of a certain kind of kinds) of photographic object. What Fried calls the genuine individuality of that which is produced by the members of this group is 'a kind of ultimate "deep" relationality... a "deep" contrastiveness or oppositionality' (WPM, 325–6). The necessarily linear typological mode of their textual re-presentation brings out both their generic similarities and their specific differences (without absolutizing either or absolutizing their opposition); and it thereby discloses the historically specific grounds of their intelligibility as the kind of aesthetic object they are.

This relationality is not the result of conscious reflection by the human subjects who make them, but they are nevertheless responsible for them; their collective efforts have established the field within which their photographic objects are themselves established and grasped as inseparable from each other, hence as part of a larger whole, one which is itself open to further articulation and reflective rearrangement as it makes possible the making of further, new, similar but different such objects. Here, it matters that the Bechers are the earliest of the practitioners Fried discusses: their typological practice is thoroughly analogue, and it is the generation of students they influenced (both directly and indirectly) who followed their example into territory opened up by new photographic technology and techniques of presentation. This suggests that what Fried is bringing to our consciousness in his book is the emergence of a new kind of photographic entity; it is one made possible by more traditional photographic entities, or more precisely by an aesthetic possibility disclosed by a creative practice of analogue photography, without which the new aesthetic possibilities established by the work of contemporary philosophers employing new photographic technologies would not have been graspable, but which outreaches them and both extends and reconfigures the photographic field those analogue practices helped to establish and maintain.

In that sense, Fried's characterization of the Bechers' photographs is (just like those photographs themselves) an attempt to document the inhabitants of a rapidly vanishing, historically and technologically specific realm. But precisely by presenting them in such a way as to emphasize that they belong to a particular spatio-temporal location, he also brings to consciousness that which replaced them, as well as the fact that the originality of those replacements is ultimately dependent on that which they replaced. But it is vital to appreciate that their photographic successors are emerging rather than, as it were, fully realized—that Fried's sense of the contemporary arrangement of the photographic field is that something is, as it were, struggling to be born within it.

It is not that he is struggling clearly to perceive what has already been solidly established and needs only to be brought to critically reflective consciousness. It is rather that the Bechers have helped him more clearly to perceive that their successors are struggling to establish an aesthetically satisfying successor to their kind of analogue photographic work of art, which accordingly means a kind of photographic entity that possesses genuine individuality—a concretely specified, deeply relational, and internally articulated mode of photographic objecthood (and that it is only his dim, initial, and provisional perception of that struggle that enables his perception of the Bechers' typological practice as one of its enabling conditions).

So understood, Fried's avoidance of any explicit general or generic account of the new kind of photographic object that is his concern in *Why Photography Matters* is multiply determined. To begin with, that object is still subject to determination—because all typological modes of presentation show rather than say, and so leave the work of articulating the understanding they embody importantly in the hands of the viewer; and because these photographic objects are still in the process of being brought into existence by the subjects of his group portrait. In that sense, the question of what this new kind of object might be is itself a matter of debate between those involved in making it, part of the work in which they are involved in creating their works.

There is a clear analogy here with Cavell's conception of the internal relatedness manifest by films that belong to his conception of a genre of film (such as comedies of remarriage), according to which what unites the members of the genre is itself a matter of discussion between them; and that shared willingness to converse about what relates them to one another is not only the mode of their generic unity, but also entails that the unity or individuality of each film is itself deeply relational—impossible to grasp except as internally articulated, hence as a specifically different inhabitant of a shared cinematic world whose own individuality is grounded and manifest in that of its inhabitants. And Fried is of course also tapping into his and Cavell's broader conception of an artistic medium as something whose aesthetic possibilities are not read off from its material ones, but rather constituted over time by our ability to make meaningful works within it.

So Fried is not best understood as approaching his group of contemporary photographers with an independently established conception of the material basis of this new photographic medium (understood in terms of new technologies and techniques of capturing, manipulating, and enlarging images), and then arguing that the work of certain individuals constitutes great art because it exploits precisely those features of this new photographic medium. Rather, he takes the striking success of a given work to disclose (that is, to determine) an aesthetic possibility of its new medium, and thereby to acknowledge something about that medium as being of essential aesthetic significance, there and then. It amounts, in effect, to a currently convincing but inherently contestable partial specification of the historical essence of the new photographic medium.

For this reason, aesthetic appraisal of each new work in the terms best able to make sense of its claim on our experience and judgement is necessarily prior to any more general characterization of the ontological field each individual entity inhabits. Hence a second reason for Fried's apparent failure to provide such a general account is that his reflective critical appraisal of the relevant works was still at the stage of (as it were) compiling authoritative individual depictions of the relevant works and asserting their interrelatedness, rather than being confidently able to step back, assemble, and present a stable and perspicuous typology of the field (something that the Bechers after all achieved only with respect to types of object always already receding into history). In this sense, Fried is still touring his sites, taking his pictures, and selecting his candidates; the presentational grid is to-be-realized.

A third factor determining Fried's refusal of generality becomes visible once we acknowledge (in the spirit of qualitative dialectics) that no individual critic experiences such photographic objects in a vacuum. If the objects must be understood in relation to their socio-historical location, so must the subjects they address; and Fried's subjectivity has a very specific genealogy whose pertinence to his critical appraisals is explicitly acknowledged throughout the book. For (as I noted earlier) the terms he reaches for in understanding the work of these photographers are essentially those through which he has previously attempted to grasp the high modernist paintings of the 1960s, and the prehistory of modernist painting from Chardin to Manet and the impressionists.

According to Fried, the moment that these photographers disclosed the possibility (inherent in various technical developments) of making photographs primarily and essentially intended to be framed and hung on a wall—to be looked at like paintings rather than merely to be examined up close by single viewers—they were bound to confront a new question, or rather a question long familiar to painters newly transposed into a photographic context, concerning the relation between the photograph and its beholders. This led them to engage with a range of concerns familiar from the context of modernist painting—absorption, facingness, the relationship between beholder, artist, and subject—in ways that acknowledge, and so are inflected by, the specific characteristics of (this kind of) photography (a photographic subject's awareness of the camera, the photographer's distinctive ways of declaring his or her hand in the staging of the presented scene, the distinctive ways in which photographs present a world, and so on). Most fundamentally, it led them to confront the problem of theatricality and its avoidance—the issue that, as we have seen, Fried associates with the Diderotian origins of the prehistory of modernism, and that pressed so deeply on his own art-critical writings of the 1960s.

Given the pervasiveness with which Fried's readings of these photographs reach for this familiar conceptual regime, readers could be forgiven for thinking that Fried had fallen upon this new artistic territory because he understood it to provide a surprising but straightforward continuation of the historical-critical narrative of modernism that most (including himself) had judged to have come to a decisive end when minimalism prevailed over high modernism in the art world of the 1970s and after. But then he would surely confront a devastating dilemma (of a kind touched on earlier in this book): either these photographers are engaging with the very same issues as those faced by modernist painters, in which case those issues float free of medium-specific constraints in exactly the way that Fried's own narrative denies; or the distinctive character of the photographic medium does have the significance Fried's approach would presuppose, in which case these photographers can't really be confronting the same problems that modernist painters and Minimalists faced.

But certain aspects of *Why Photography Matters* suggest that Fried would not accept the terms of this dilemma. Take his concluding chapter on the Bechers: the immediate significance of the contrast that their typological practice discloses between mere particularity and genuine individuality—or as Fried puts it, deploying a contrast he previously invoked to grasp a photograph by James Welling, between bad and good objecthood—is that it gives him a way of reformulating his 'Art and Objecthood' critique of minimalism.[21] Whereas in that essay he talked of literalists as aiming to project and hypostasize objecthood as such (whereas modernists struggled to undo or neutralize it), he now finds it more apt to characterize this as a conflict between bad and good modes of objecthood.

The crucial point here is that this is a *reformulation* of his original claim. As Fried puts it, '[t]his is a distinction that was not there to be made by me in 1967, in advance of any knowledge of the photographic practices that were already

---

[21] Collected in AO.

bringing it into being' (WPM, 328). In other words, the notion of objecthood as it was deployed in his art-critical writings, and genealogized in his subsequent art-historical work, is subjected to potentially radical, even if enabling, revision when projected into this new aesthetic and ontological context—to the point at which its reconfiguration feeds back in genuinely new ways to Fried's current best understanding of his earlier critical stance.

Two more general issues thereby become salient. First, the dilemma that Fried is supposed to confront by virtue of his venture into photographic territory depends upon assuming that the key terms of the conceptual regime he deploys in so doing must either mean exactly what they mean in the context of painting, or else they must mean something essentially different (and hence stand in need of disambiguation). Otherwise put, these terms must either be univocal or equivocal; but as we have already seen, to anyone as immersed in Wittgenstein and Wittgensteinian authors (such as Cavell) as is Fried, this will appear to be a deeply misleading picture of the nature of linguistic meaning.

Cavell's and Wittgenstein's counter-vision of words as inherently projective in fact gives us a useful analogical model for understanding the grammatical schematism of Fried's explanatory conceptual regime for painterly modernism. For coming to appreciate the projectibility of its constituent terms into a photographic context amounts to a way of disclosing further reaches of their significance, and that in turn requires that we view them as neither univocal nor equivocal but as analogically related to their mode of deployment and signification in their original context.[22] Fried's aesthetic responses to these new photographic objects accordingly disclose an essentially analogical relation between these photographs and the high modernist paintings of the 1960s (as well as the minimalist works of the same era, and of course their modernist predecessors). Insofar as we are compelled to characterize them by the same terms, we declare a conviction of the similarity of their objects; but insofar as those terms are necessarily modified by the distinctive character of their new context of application, we also declare a sense of the specific differences of their objects. And the discovery of such a new context for their application retrospectively alters our understanding of the significance of those terms (and so of their objects) in their original context; for it reveals dimensions of sense-making and significance in both that we would otherwise never have come to appreciate.

And this brings us to the second general issue bearing on the inherent situatedness of Fried's modes of critical response to contemporary photography. It is not just that his present discoveries reconfigure and deepen his understanding of the conceptual regime he had previously brought to bear on painterly modernism,

---

[22] For a more detailed discussion of analogical uses of language, and their pertinence to grasping Wittgenstein's vision of language, see my *The Great Riddle* (Oxford: Oxford University Press, 2015), esp. lecture 4.

but that this reconfigurative disclosure of past and present opened up a particular trajectory into the future. The essentially enabling and productive nature of his encounter with the photographers captured in *Why Photography Matters*'s group portrait is shown above all in the work Fried has published since that book's appearance. On the one hand, there has been another book on contemporary artists—two video artists, one of whom did make a brief appearance in *Why Photography Matters* (Sala and Gordon), together with a sculptor (Ray) and a painter (Marioni);[23] and on the other, he has published two substantial art-historical books on Caravaggio and a body of work produced in the decades after Caravaggio's death.[24]

Further exploratory work in the same vein as that embodied in *Why Photography Matters* may seem unsurprising; but *Four Honest Outlaws* is surprising in that it doesn't examine any further specifically photographic work, but does address new work in the more familiar media of painting and sculpture. This leads Fried to more explicit specifications of the ways in which *Why Photography Matters* had reshaped his sense of both the contemporary art scene and of the modernist context with which his earlier work had been so concerned. He describes the former as one in which his early commitment to a particular canon of high modernist painting and sculpture had 'left me stranded in a corner, one that I saw no way of escaping short of relinquishing a set of core values and beliefs that remained, for me, inviolable' (FHO, 22–3); but his experience of the new photography opened up work in other media, so that his current sense is 'not so much that I have finally found a way out of the corner...as that over the past three decades photography and certain other developments have reconfigured the room' (FHO, 23).

In other words, both the basic circumstances of the world of art and Fried's basic orientation or mode of address towards it have altered; on the one hand, genuinely valuable work in a variety of media has begun to repudiate the facile post-minimalist rejection of modernism, and on the other, Fried himself has thereby been enabled and compelled to discriminate more finely between those aspects of his conceptual regime that only appeared to be essential to the continuation of modernist anti-theatricality from those that really are essential (here and now). Most interestingly, he cites the three famous theses proposed towards the end of 'Art and Objecthood',[25] and specifically distances himself from the third—the one which declares: 'The concepts of quality and value—and to the extent that these are central to art, the concept of art itself—are meaningful, or

---

[23] *Four Honest Outlaws*; hereafter FHO.
[24] *The Moment of Caravaggio* (Princeton: Princeton University Press, 2010), hereafter MC; and *After Caravaggio* (New Haven: Yale University Press, 2016).
[25] Quoted in full in Essay Two.

wholly meaningful, only within the individual arts. What lies *between* the arts is theatre' (AO, 164).

Initially, this insistence on medium-specificity is only reconfigured typographically: Fried says that 'I wish I had put "between" in scare quotes instead of italics' (FHO, 10). This is hardly a perspicuous qualification, but it at least suggests that what he had then regarded as a term whose meaning was so uncontroversial he could simply emphasize its importance he now regards as one whose meaning can and should itself be held up for interrogation (a task I touched on in Essay Two). And later, he goes further: in the book's conclusion, he declares:

> Although this book singles out artists whose work seems to me to prove the current vitality of high modernist themes and issues, it also demonstrates that that vitality is not tied to a specific medium, or to put this more strongly, that the question of medium-specificity, while not exactly irrelevant to the artists I discuss—Ray's commitment to sculpture and Marioni's to painting are definitive for both of them, while Sala's pursuit of presentness finds a perfect home in video—no longer plays the kind of role that it did at an earlier moment in the history of modernism. That is, I would no longer wish to argue that for a work of contemporary art to matter deeply it has in all cases to be understood as doing so as an instance of a particular art or medium. My conviction as to Sala's accomplishment is in no way dependent on an appreciation of a standing canon of previous video art; and in the case of Gordon, it is not at all clear how the concept of a medium bears on my analyses of *Play Dead; Real Time* or *Déjà vu*.
>
> (FHO, 204)

This is, of course, a highly qualified concession, given that it really excludes only Gordon from the conceptual matrix in which the aesthetic significance of a modernist work hangs together with its acknowledgement of the possibilities of its medium. One might also wonder why Fried thinks that his analysis of *Déjà vu* doesn't involve the concept of a medium, given its argument that Gordon's treatment of *D.O.A* in that installation foregrounds the exemplary absorption of its actors in their roles, and so acknowledges the relation between actor and character that is a condition of the possibility of movies, and so of *Déjà vu*. But it certainly amounts to a reconfiguration of what Fried holds to be essential to the modernist project; and other reconfigurations hang together with it. For example, on Fried's account of what he still thinks of as modernist contemporary work, what makes it modernist is increasingly seen as its investment in the struggle to avoid or overcome bad objecthood and theatricality whilst acknowledging its relation to its beholder, rather than the more specific strategies it deploys to do this. Indeed, Fried even suggests that his present conception of the essence of modernism is even more general: that it lies in its pursuit of what he calls 'the ultimate stakes of serious art—to attach us to reality. Modernism from Manet onward aimed at nothing less, under conditions it knew to be unpromising. Presentness, theatricality and...embedment concern nothing else' (FHO, 24).

Ascending or descending to such a general characterization of artistic modernism usefully makes its internal relation to what philosophy calls scepticism unprecedentedly explicit; and it also makes it easier to acknowledge a greater variety of more specifically differentiated realizations of it in different works in different media. But such reformulations of earlier attempts to characterize the essential nature of modernism in the light of later artistic developments give us no reason to reject the earlier characterizations *tout court*. On the contrary, a willingness to engage in such retrospective revisions of an initial understanding is positively demanded of anyone who sees such characterizations as ultimately grounded in his experience of individual works, who sees the projection of the relevant terms into new contexts which require their adaptation and thereby elicit further reaches of their significance as exemplary of how words function, and who thinks of modernism not only as determining what the essential nature of a given medium is in a given historical context, but as itself possessed of an essence that is equally bound to evolve, adapt, and unfold new reaches of significance as it encounters new historical circumstances.

The other focus of Fried's post-*Why Photography Matters* work is Caravaggio— or more precisely, the work that eventually culminated in *Why Photography Matters* interrupted and was interrupted by work on Caravaggio, although the two book-length versions of the latter only appeared in print well after the former. However that may be, what is striking about the account of Caravaggio's work that Fried provides is the extent to which it employs versions of themes and terms drawn from the conceptual regime long familiar from his account of modernism. So, for example, Fried argues that Caravaggio's persistent use of the self-portrait is an attempt to acknowledge his own generative role in the production of his paintings; he uncovers a persistent interest in absorption—the depiction of figures engrossed in their own activities and hence oblivious to the viewer; and he finds that Caravaggio returns repeatedly to the question 'which way does a painting face (towards the viewer or into the depicted scene)?'.

However, Fried is quick to point out that these outcroppings of familiar concepts do not have their familiar significance. In Caravaggio's work, we see the *invention* of absorption: absorptive themes and effects emerged as central to the enterprise of painting as never before. But the concept of theatricality has no direct purchase, because, unlike the situation in eighteenth-century France, 'whatever intimation of unawareness [of the viewer] there may appear to be goes hand in hand with a new...thematization of pictorial address' (MC, 2), the repeated deployment of figures openly looking at their viewers without any hint of suspicion attaching to that stance. Likewise, the immersive thrust of Caravaggio's work is—unlike Courbet's work—balanced by a specular counter-thrust, whereby the picture is given up to visuality or spectatordom. And Caravaggio's attempts to establish the independence and autonomy of his paintings do not, as analogous struggles in Diderot's era did, generate a pursuit of ideals of dramatic unity, as manifest in the *tableau* format.

On the one hand, then, Fried is no more prone to think that disclosing pre-Diderotian contexts in which versions of his modernist conceptual regime can find fruitful application entails univocity of sense than he did when finding an equally fruitful context for their application in post-1960s photography. On the other hand, the successful projection of that regime back onto 1590s Rome does indicate a significant continuity: as he puts it, Caravaggio is revealed as the inventor of absorption, and so as a profoundly fateful historical source for the premodern phase of European painting outlined in Fried's trilogy on the roots of Manet's modernism. And what enables this perception—call it a further extension of the premodern roots of modernism—is Fried's work on contemporary photography.

For at least two crucial features of Fried's account of Caravaggio patently have their counterparts in *Why Photography Matters*. First, having appreciated that the new photography (and so a new kind of photographic object) emerges once it is made primarily for the wall, Fried can see more clearly that the problematic of absorption and address emerges in Caravaggio because he is confronting the emergence of the gallery picture—a new cultural context, importantly comprising ambitious, highly cultivated collectors and the construction of personal galleries for the exhibition of their work, which encouraged the development of framed and portable, less large and not necessarily devotional, paintings capable of bearing up under a new level of unusually close scrutiny (the precursor of the 'homeless' easel painting with which Diderot was concerned). Second, having had to resort to a concept of 'severing' in order to grasp Gursky's response to photographic to-be-seenness (WPM, 158–65), Fried then finds that a central aspect of Caravaggio's response to the gallery mode of painterly scrutiny—his mode of acknowledgement of its framed, portable independence from its surroundings—is to deploy representations of severed heads (John the Baptist, Medusa, Holofernes) to thematize the viewer's relation to the painting itself as a conjunction of decapitation and presentation.

How, then, should one understand the internal articulation of the new tripartite historical schema that results from this dual extension of the range of application of Fried's modernist conceptual regime—so that his familiar narrative of the problematic of theatricality from Greuze to Manet to 1960's high modernism is now flanked both by an account of pre-Diderotian European painting and by one concerning post-high modernist photography? More specifically, how are we to assign relative creative priority between these three phases of Fried's current narrative?

The crucial clue lies in an aspect of Fried's own account of Manet to which he gives prominence in his book of that title by devoting its final chapter to the topic.

That chapter discloses 'a complexly recursive three-part hingelike structure' (MM, 410) operative at various levels in Fried's narrative wherever questions of origins or sources are at stake—whether it be the origins of high modernism (which Fried attributes to the triad of Courbet, Manet, and impressionism), or of modernism more generally (where Fried invokes both Courbet and his post-Diderotian predecessors in accounting for Manet's achievement), or of the pre-modernist tradition of denying the beholder by dramatizing absorptive scenes (where Fried finds that Greuze's initiating achievement can be grasped only in relation to that of Chardin before him and David after him).

According to Fried, this hinge-like structure involves 'a relation in which, conceptually, the first and third 'moments' precede the second, and thus jointly determine its meaning' (MM, 411–12). Although the second moment appears genuinely determinative, it only acquires that originary status retrospectively: it can appear as originary solely from a point of view constructed by the work of those whose labours it makes possible—indeed, until that work is done the supposedly originating moment hasn't actually originated anything. But once the third moment confers originary status on the second, it inevitably reveals the second's dependence on the first; for insofar as the second moment originates a tradition, it distinguishes itself from the preceding moment and thereby reveals a shared frame of reference (as Diderot's anxious denial of the beholder is what makes it possible for Manet to break decisively with him by finding a way to acknowledge that relation without theatricalizing it).

Here we can see Fried's general sense that the development of an artistic tradition involves a continuous process of revisionary reconstitution of the nature and achievements of its past through the contemporary work that that past enables. And I want to suggest in conclusion that this is one element of his modernist conceptual regime that persists in his post-*Why Photography Matters* work, and so helps to account for its structure. For his discovery of contemporary photography as a continuation of the high modernist project not only reveals that 1960s body of work as originating or creative (rather than the final phase of a project whose origins lie far in the past, in the complex historical nexus that links Greuze, Courbet, Manet, and impressionism); it also reveals Caravaggio as an originary figure in relation to the prehistory and so the history of modernism, including that contemporary photographic work. In other words, by seeing Caravaggio and the new photography as the first and third moments which reconfigure the meaning of the second moment that is the unfolding of modernism from Diderot to Stella, we disclose a new register of significance—and a new dimension of creativity—in that second moment.

As we just saw, however, we cannot identify the origin of an artistic regime or tradition without invoking a further instance of the hinge-like historical schema. So to characterize Caravaggio's work as initiating the thematization of absorption may distinguish him from his predecessors, but it also directs our attention to them, and to the role they play in making it possible for him so to distinguish himself. And here it is hard to avoid being struck by the sheer violence implicit in the modes of severance to which Fried finds that Caravaggio is compelled to resort in asserting his own autonomy by asserting the autonomy of his works. For the emergence of the gallery picture—the ontological development that Caravaggio determines and is determined by—is primarily the displacement of painting from churches and devotional contexts; and Fried's invocation of decapitation in characterizing that process presents it as an uncannily traumatic disembedding or dismemberment.

In other words, Fried's most recent work reveals religion, or more precisely a wounding attempt to separate art from that determining matrix, as a deep-running genealogical root of the (prehistory of) artistic modernism. It positively invites us to examine more closely how and why this fateful diremption of art from religion came to seem not only possible but also necessary in the inauguration of modernity; it thereby poses the question why this made possible and definitively inflected a mode of thematizing absorption that avoids any premodernist anxiety about theatricalization; and if we recognize this as a sceptical anxiety, then we open up its cultural connections with analogous dialectical developments in metaphysics, and so in science. Only by exploring these issues further can we acquire a deeper understanding of the ease with which Fried's earlier narratives of modernism as in search of attachment to reality so often reached for a religious register—most notoriously in his citation, in 'Art and Objecthood', of a Protestant preacher's declaration that 'presentness is grace'.

References

Amis, K., *That Uncertain Feeling* (London: Panther, 1955).
Andersen, H. C., 'The Toad', English translation at http://hca.gilead.org.il/the_toad.html.
Anscombe, G. E. M., 'Modern Moral Philosophy' (1958), in *Ethics, Religion and Politics* (Minneapolis: University of Minnesota Press, 1981).
Attridge, D., *J. M. Coetzee and the Ethics of Reading* (Chicago: University of Chicago Press, 2005).
Attwell, D., *J. M. Coetzee and the Life of Writing* (Oxford: Oxford University Press, 2015).
Beckett, S., *Molloy; Malone Dies; The Unnamable* (London: Picador, 1979).
Boorman, J., *Adventures of a Suburban Boy* (London: Faber & Faber, 2004).
Borgmann, A., *Technology and the Character of Contemporary Life* (Chicago: University of Chicago Press, 1984).
Byatt, A. S., *The Biographer's Tale* (London: Chatto and Windus, 2000).
Carey, J., *William Golding: The Man Who Wrote* Lord of the Flies (London: Faber, 2009).
Cavell, S., *The World Viewed* (Cambridge, MA: Harvard University Press, 1971).
Cavell, S., 'On Kierkegaard's *On Authority and Revelation*', in *Must We Mean What We Say?* (Cambridge: Cambridge University Press, 1976).
Cavell, S., 'The Avoidance of Love', in *Must We Mean What We Say?* (Cambridge: Cambridge University Press, 1976).
Cavell, S., *The Claim of Reason* (Oxford: Oxford University Press, 1979).
Cavell, S., *Pursuits of Happiness* (Cambridge, MA: Harvard University Press, 1981).
Cavell, S., 'Being Odd, Getting Even', in *In Quest of the Ordinary* (Chicago: University of Chicago Press, 1988).
Cavell, S., *Contesting Tears* (Chicago: University of Chicago Press, 1996).
Cavell, S., 'Hamlet's Burden of Proof', in *Disowning Knowledge in Seven Plays of Shakespeare* (Cambridge: Cambridge University Press, 2003).
Cavell, S., *Cities of Words* (Cambridge, MA: Harvard University Press, 2004).
Coetzee, J. M., *Doubling the Point*, ed. D. Attwell (Cambridge, MA: Harvard University Press, 1992).
Coetzee, J. M., *Elizabeth Costello: Eight Lessons* (London: Secker and Warburg, 2003).
Coetzee, J. M., *Scenes from Provincial Life* (London: Harvill & Secker, 2011).
Conradi, P., 'Writing *Iris Murdoch: A Life*—Freud versus Multiplicity', *Iris Murdoch Newsletter* 16 (Winter 2002–Spring 2003), 1–8.
Crary, A., *Inside Ethics* (Cambridge, MA: Harvard University Press, 2016).
Derrida, J., *The Truth in Painting*, trans. G. Bennington (Chicago: University of Chicago Press, 1987).
Diamond, C., 'Losing Your Concepts', *Ethics* 98 (Jan. 1988), 255–77.
Diamond, C., 'Eating Meat and Eating People', in *The Realistic Spirit* (Cambridge, MA: MIT Press, 1991), 319–34.
Diamond, C., 'Wittgenstein on Religious Belief: The Gulfs Between Us', in D. Z. Phillips and M. von der Ruhr (eds.), *Religion and Wittgenstein's Legacy* (London: Ashgate, 2005), 99–138.

Diamond, C., 'The Difficulty of Reality and the Difficulty of Philosophy', in A. Crary and S. Shieh (eds.), *Reading Cavell* (London: Routledge, 2006), 98–118.
Eliot, T. S., 'The Love Song of J. Alfred Prufrock', in *Collected Poems 1909–1962* (London: Faber, 1963), 13–17.
Fried, M., *Absorption and Theatricality* (Chicago: University of Chicago Press, 1980).
Fried, M., *Courbet's Realism* (Chicago: University of Chicago Press, 1990).
Fried, M., *Manet's Modernism* (Chicago: University of Chicago Press, 1996).
Fried, M., *Art and Objecthood* (Chicago: Chicago University Press, 1998).
Fried, M., *Why Photography Matters as Art as Never Before* (New Haven: Yale University Press, 2008).
Fried, M., *The Moment of Caravaggio* (Princeton; Princeton University Press, 2010).
Fried, M., *Four Honest Outlaws* (New Haven: Yale University Press, 2011).
Fried, M., *After Caravaggio* (New Haven: Yale University Press, 2016).
Gaita, R., *Romulus, My Father* (London: Review, 1998).
Gaita, R., *A Common Humanity* (London: Routledge, 2000).
Gaita, R., *The Philosopher's Dog* (Melbourne, Australia: Text Publishing, 2002).
Gaita, R., *Good and Evil: An Absolute Conception* (rev. edn., London: Routledge, 2004).
Golding, W., *Darkness Visible* (London: Faber, 1979).
Golding, W., *The Paper Men* (London: Faber, 1984).
Hacker, P. M. S., *Appearance and Reality* (Oxford: Blackwell, 1987).
Heidegger, M., *Being and Time*, trans. J. Macquarrie and E. Robinson (Oxford: Blackwell, 1962).
Heidegger, M., 'The Origin of the Work of Art', in *Poetry, Language, Thought*, trans. A. Hofstadter (New York: Harper and Row, 1975), 15–86.
Heidegger, M., 'The Age of the World Picture', in *The Question Concerning Technology and Other Essays*, trans. W. Lovitt (New York: Harper and Row, 1977), 115–54.
Heidegger, M., 'The Question Concerning Technology', in *The Question Concerning Technology and Other Essays*, trans. W. Lovitt (New York: Harper and Row, 1977), 3–35.
Hopwood, M., 'Terrible Purity: Peter Singer, Harriet McBryde Johnson, and the Moral Significance of the Particular', *Journal of the American Philosophical Association* 2/4 (Winter 2016), 637–55.
Hyman, J., *The Objective Eye* (Chicago: University of Chicago Press, 2006).
Keyes, D., *Flowers for Algernon* (New York: Harcourt Brace, 1966).
Kierkegaard, S., *Early Polemical Writings*, ed. and trans. Julia Watkin (Princeton: Princeton University Press, 1990).
Kierkegaard, S., *The Book on Adler*, trans. H. V. and E. H. Hong (Princeton: Princeton University Press, 1998).
Kinkead-Weekes, M., and Gregor, I., *William Golding: A Critical Study of the Novels* (London: Faber, 2002).
Kittay, Eva Feder, 'Equality, Dignity and Disability', in Mary Ann Lyons and Fionnuala Waldron (eds.), *Perspectives on Equality* (Dublin: Liffey Press, 2005), 93–119.
Kittay, Eva Feder, 'The Personal is Philosophical is Political', *Metaphilosophy* 40/3–4 (July 2009), 606–27.
Lee, H., 'How to End It All', in *Body Parts: Essays on Life-Writing* (London: Chatto and Windus, 2005), 200–18.
McCabe, H., *The Good Life* (London: Continuum, 2005).
McDowell, J., 'Comment on Stanley Cavell's "Companionable Thinking"', in A..Crary (ed.), *Wittgenstein and the Moral Life: Essays in Honour of Cora Diamond* (Cambridge, MA: MIT Press, 2007), 299–304.

McGowan, T., *The Fictional Christopher Nolan* (Austin, Texas: University of Texas Press, 2012).
McGowan, T., 'Stumbling over the Superhero: Christopher Nolan's Victories and Compromises', in J. Furby and S. Joy (eds)., *The Cinema of Christopher Nolan* (London: Wallflower Press, 2015), 164–74.
MacIntyre, A., *After Virtue* (London: Duckworth, 1981).
McMahan, J., *The Ethics of Killing* (Oxford: Oxford University Press, 2002).
McMahan, J., '"Our Fellow Creatures"', *Journal of Ethics* 9 (2005), 353–80.
Monk, R., 'Philosophical Biography: The Very Idea', in J. Klagge (ed.), *Wittgenstein: Biography and Philosophy* (Cambridge: Cambridge University Press, 2001), 3–15.
Mulhall, S., *Inheritance and Originality* (Oxford: Oxford University Press, 2001).
Mulhall, S., 'Fearful Thoughts', *London Review of Books* 24 (22 Aug. 2002), 16.
Mulhall, S., *The Wounded Animal: J. M. Coetzee and the Difficulty of Reality in Literature and Philosophy* (Princeton: Princeton University Press, 2009).
Mulhall, S., 'Autobiography and Biography', in R. Eldridge (ed.)., *The Oxford Handbook of Philosophy and Literature* (Oxford: Oxford University Press, 2009), 180–98.
Mulhall, S., 'The Work of Saintly Love: The Religious Impulse in Gaita's Writings', in C. Cordner (ed.), *Philosophy, Ethics and Humanity: Essays in Honour of Raimond Gaita* (Oxford: Routledge, 2011), 21–36.
Mulhall, S., 'Quartet: Wallace's Wittgenstein, Moran's Amis', in *The Self and Its Shadows: A Book of Essays on Individuality as Negation in Philosophy and the Arts* (Oxford: Oxford University Press, 2013), 283–319.
Mulhall, S., 'Sharing a Dream of Scepticism', *Harvard Review of Philosophy* 19 (Spring 2013), 118–36.
Mulhall, S., *The Great Riddle* (Oxford: Oxford University Press, 2015).
Mulhall, S., 'A Nice Arrangement of Epigrams: Stanley Cavell on Soren Kierkegaard', in K. Gjesdal (ed.), *Debates in Nineteenth Century European Philosophy: Essential Readings and Contemporary Responses* (London: Routledge, 2016), 248–57.
Mulhall, S., 'Deep Relationality and the Hinge-Like Structure of History: Michael Fried's Photographs', in M. Abbott (ed.), *Michael Fried and Philosophy: Modernism, Intentionality and Theatricality* (Oxford: Routledge, 2018), 87–103.
Mulhall, S., 'The Well is Not the World: William Golding's Sense of Reality in *Darkness Visible*', in A. Falcato and A. Cardiello (eds.), *Philosophy in the Condition of Modernism* (London: Palgrave, 2018), 325–54.
Mulhall, S., 'Martin Scorsese's Screening Room: Theatricality, Psychoanalysis and Modernity in *Shutter Island*', in C. Barnett and C. Elliston (eds.), *Scorsese and Religion* (Leiden: Brill, 2019), 231–47.
Mulhall, S., 'Two Shoes and a Fountain: Ecstasis, Mimesis and Engrossment in Heidegger's *Origin of the Work of Art*', *Proceedings of the Aristotelian Society* 119/2 (2019), 201–22.
Nietzsche, F., *On the Genealogy of Morality*, trans. C. Diethe, ed. K. Ansell-Pearson (Cambridge: Cambridge University Press, 1994).
Nietzsche, F., *The Birth of Tragedy and Other Writings*, ed. and trans. Raymond Geuss and Ronald Speirs (Cambridge: Cambridge University Press, 1999).
Nolan, C., *Inception: The Shooting Script* (San Rafael, CA: Insight Editions, 2010).
Nuttall, A. D., *Shakespeare the Thinker* (New Haven: Yale University Press, 2007).
Ong, Y.-P., *The Art of Being: Poetics of the Novel and Existentialist Philosophy* (Cambridge, MA: Harvard University Press, 2018).
Parfit, D., *Reasons and Persons* (Oxford: Oxford University Press, 1984).

Pippin, R., *Henry James and Modern Moral Life* (Cambridge: Cambridge University Press, 2000).
Pippin, R., *Fatalism in American Film Noir* (Charlottesville, VA: University of Virginia Press, 2012).
Rachels, J., *Created from Animals* (Oxford: Oxford University Press, 1990).
Rhees, R., *Wittgenstein and the Possibility of Discourse*, ed. D. Z. Phillips (Cambridge: Cambridge University Press, 1998).
Ricks, C., 'Shakespeare and the Anagram', *Proceedings of the British Academy* 121 (2002), 111–46.
Sartre, J.-P., *Being and Nothingness*, trans. S. Richmond (London: Routledge, 2018).
Taylor, C., 'Explanation and Practical Reason', in his *Philosophical Arguments* (Cambridge, MA: Harvard University Press, 1995).
Taylor, C., *Sources of the Self* (Cambridge, MA: Harvard University Press, 1989).
Thorne, K., *The Science of Interstellar* (London: Norton and Company, 2014).
Tiger, V., *William Golding: The Unmoved Target* (London: Marion Boyars, 2003).
Tolstoy, L., *Childhood, Boyhood, Youth*, ed. and introd. Judson Rosengrant (London: Penguin, 2012).
Wittgenstein, L., *Remarks on Frazer's* Golden Bough, ed. R. Rhees, trans. A. C. Miles (Doncaster: Brynmill Press, 1979).
Wittgenstein, *Philosophical Investigations*, 4th ed.: ed. and trans. P. M. S. Hacker and J. Schulte (Oxford: Blackwell, 2009).

Index

For the benefit of digital users, indexed terms that span two pages (e.g., 52–53) may, on occasion, appear on only one of those pages.

Absorption and Theatricality 128–9, 273–8
acting 220–1, 293–4
Adler, A. 18–20
'Age of the World Picture' 265–70
Amis, K. 108–11, 158
analogy 291
Andersen, H.C. 74–5, 86–8, 107
Anscombe, G.E.M. 28–9
apostle 18–20, 159–60
art 29, 36–7, 159–60
Art and Objecthood 125, 290
As You Like It 84–6
ascetic ideal, the 10–13, 67–8, 96, 151–3, 160, 165, 169–70, 205–6, 217–18, 226, 231, 233, 235, 282
Attwell, D. 144–5, 180–1
authority 18–20, 57–8, 61, 69, 72–4, 87–8, 96, 117, 240
On Authority and Revelation 18–28
autobiography 99–101, 105, 113–14, 117, 144–6, 150, 153, 164

Batman Begins 227–9
Becher, B. and H. 285–8, 290
Beckett, S. 125, 170
Being and Nothingness 114–15
Being and Time 112–14
Being vs Becoming 11–12, 14, 25, 28, 40–1, 68, 97, 103, 124, 131, 188–9, 219, 224, 242–3, 248, 258, 267–8
Bennett, J. 257
Biographer's Tale, The 102, 121–2
biography 105, 113–14, 118, 120–1, 153, 172–81
Borgmann, A. 260–2
Boyhood (Coetzee) 150–5
Boyhood (Tolstoy) 150–1
Bradley, F.H. 142
Byatt, A.S. 102, 121–2

Caravaggio, M. 291–2, 294–7
Carey, J. 75–6
Caro, A. 126
Cartier-Bresson, H. 284–5

Cavell, S. 18–28, 32, 53, 71–5, 90, 125–44, 288–9, 291
centre of variation 55, 260
Childhood 150–1
Christianity 1–4, 8–9, 18–19, 21, 62–4, 80, 88, 90–1, 142–3, 160, 227–8, 265–6, 297
Claim of Reason, The 26–9
Coetzee, J.M. 44–5, 95, 123, 144–81, 215
Common Humanity, A 49–50
confession 10–11, 13, 148–51, 153–5, 164–5, 167–8, 211, 214–15, 225, 232
Conradi, P.J. 102
conversation 53–5, 70, 190, 198
Crary, A. 48–51, 57
criteria 132–3

Dark Knight, The 229–31
Dark Knight Rises, The 231–4
Darkness Visible 75–98
de la Mare, W. 36–7, 45
Demand, T. 287
Derrida, J. 270–2
Descartes, R. 114–15, 253–4, 262, 265–6
Diamond, C. 28–9, 41–7, 57, 62, 64–6
Diderot, D. 128–9, 273–5, 278, 295
difficulty of reality 43, 62, 118
Dostoevsky, F. 149–50
Doubling the Point 144–50
Dunkirk 248–51
Dusklands 170–1

Ethics of Killing, The 31–7
Eliot, T.S. 135–44, 159, 181
Emerson, R.W. 218–19
enframing 259–60

fantasy 234–6
fear 227–9
Flowers for Algernon 48–9
Following 184–215
Four Honest Outlaws 291–2
Frazer, J. 89–90
Frege, G. 8

INDEX

Freud. S. 21–4, 72, 108, 181, 201, 211, 217
Fried, M. 125–31, 134, 144, 273–97

Gaita, R. 42, 49–52, 54–68, 70, 121
Galileo 253–4
Gaslight 201
gender 189–90, 199–204
Genealogy of Morality, The 1–15, 182–6
genealogical method 6–8, 14–15, 30–1, 46, 68, 267
generic object 132–3, 138, 193–5, 286
genetic fallacy 6–8
genius 73–4
genre 189–90, 288–9
God 64–6, 116–17, 122–3, 135, 142–3, 149, 196, 266
Golding, W. 75–98, 116
Gordon, D. 291–4
grammar 132, 138, 193, 196, 205
Gursky, A. 285–6

Hacker, P.M.S. 259n 14
Hamlet 139–40
Hare, R.M. 56
Hauerwas, S. 59–61
Hegel, G.W.F. 286–7
Heidegger, M. 112–14, 144, 156–7, 176–9, 258–65, 270–3, 278–82, 286
Hyman, J. 259n 14

Inception 186–206
Insomnia 221–5
intermediality 134
Interstellar 237–48, 275

Judd, D. 125

Kannemeyer, J.C. 128–9
Kant 12, 52, 73, 133, 223, 266–7, 269–70, 280
Keyes, D. 48–9
Kierkegaard, S. 18–30, 32, 64, 72–5, 78, 90, 129–30
King Lear 129–30
Kittay, E.F. 48–9, 51–2, 57
Kubrick, S. 185, 248

language 26–8, 33–5, 81–3, 85
language-games 53–4
Lawrence, D.H. 49
Lee, H. 114n 11
Legge, J. 45
Locke, J. 254–5

das Man 156–7
Manet, E. 273–81, 295–6

Manet's Modernism 295–6
Marioni, J. 291–3
Marvell, A. 135–9
Marx, K. 21–4, 72
McCabe, H. 116–17, 122–3, 169, 172, 180
McDowell, J. 44–7
McGowan, T. 206n 10, 231n 11
MacIntyre, A. 28–9, 104–7, 111–12, 115–18
McMahan, J. 31–49, 51–2, 55–6, 70
medium 127–8, 130–1, 134, 284–9, 293–4
melodrama of the unknown woman 190–206
Memento 206–12
Mill, J.S. 27
minimalism 125–31, 134, 290, 292–3
modernism 71–5, 123–44, 273–97
Moment of Caravaggio, The 294–7
Monk, R. 121
moral individualism 31–2, 50
moral luck 222, 250–1
moral perfectionism 53, 87, 218–24, 234, 241–3
moralism 70
Morris, R. 125
Moultonboro III 126–7
Murdoch, I. 56

narrativity 104–22
Nietzsche, F. 1–15, 21–5, 28–32, 58, 61, 67–8, 72, 77–8, 97, 101–4, 106, 123–4, 131, 142, 160, 179, 182–6, 188–9, 205–6, 210, 217–19, 226, 228–30, 241, 245–6, 248, 250–3, 258–60, 265, 267–8, 280, 282
Nolan, C. 182, 186–251
Nuttall, A.D. 85–6

objecthood 125–31, 134, 278–80
Ong, Y-P. 74
'Origin of the Work of Art' 270–3
original sin 4, 62–3, 200–1, 225, 227–8

palimpsest 5–7, 77–8, 83, 88–9, 95–6, 98
Paper Men, The 116
Parfit, D. 33
Parsifal 182
perspectivism 161
photography 244–5, 282–97
Pippin, R. 182n 1, 286–7
plagiarism 196, 200–6, 208, 220, 241
presentness 130, 134, 144, 168, 181, 212, 293–4, 297
Prestige, The 215–21
Price, H.H. 134–6
private language 162–6, 256
punishment 3–5

qualitative dialectic 21–5, 296
'The Question Concerning Technology' 259–95

Rachels, J. 38–9
Ray, C. 291–3
Rhees, R. 53–4
reasoning in transitions 59–60
remarriage comedies 190–206
remorse 51, 62
representation 265–71, 275–8
revelation 18–20, 55, 69, 72, 74–5, 78, 96
Ricks, C. 140n 30
Romulus My Father 49
Rousseau, J-J. 148–9, 154–5, 167–8, 228
Ruff, T. 285–6

sado-masochism 2–3, 14, 67, 97, 151–2, 160, 209–10, 217–18, 226–7, 233
Sala, A. 291–3
Sartre, J-P. 114–21, 179
scepticism 131–4, 136–8, 140–1, 149, 162–6, 182, 186, 189, 191–2, 207–10, 244–5, 276, 294, 297
science 11–12, 251–3, 256–7, 262–5
sculpture 126–7
screen 245
secondary qualities 253–7
self-alienation 19–24, 72, 133–4, 156–7, 168, 183–5, 221–2, 279
selfhood 103–5, 153, 157–8, 168, 179–80, 185, 215–21, 241
shape (literal vs depicted) 126–7
Shakespeare, W. 84–6, 129–30, 137–40
Shepard tone 249
Singer, P. 48–9, 51–2, 70
Smith, T. 125, 128
speciesism 35–6, 40
standing reserve 259–60, 266–7
Stella, F. 126–7
Stevenson, C. 28–9
Struth, T. 285–7
Summertime 147, 172–81

tableau 128–9, 274, 277–8, 281, 294–5
Taylor, C. 59–60
technology 226, 234–6, 243–5, 248, 258–65, 273, 282
Technology and the Character of Contemporary Life 260–1
tesseract 237–40
testimony 13, 56–8, 69–70, 126, 176, 186, 241, 260, 264
That Uncertain Feeling 108–11
theatricality 125, 128–30, 140–1, 144, 226, 274, 282
Thorne, K. 246–7, 253n 13
To His Coy Mistress 135, 138–9
Tolstoy, L. 36–7, 132–4, 153, 160
truth 10–12, 80, 104, 145–6, 168, 180, 211, 273
'On Truth and Lying in an Extra-Moral Sense' 101–4

Unnameable, The 101–2

Van Gogh, V. 270–2, 280–2
Virgil 78, 88–9

Wagner, R. 182
Wall, J. 190, 284–5
Wilder, L.I. 45–6
will to power 2–3, 8–9, 14–15, 204, 259–60
will to truth 14–15, 107–8, 123–4, 205–6, 230–1, 251–2, 267
William Golding: The Man Who Wrote Lord of the Flies 75–6
Winter's Tale, The 189–90, 199–200
Wittgenstein, L. 26–8, 53–5, 89–90, 100–1, 131–4, 141, 162–5, 285, 291
world-picture 268–70
Why Photography Matters as Art as Never Before 282–97

Youth (Coetzee) 155–72
Youth (Tolstoy) 156–8